The Rise of Westindian CRICKET

FROM COLONY TO NATION

Frank Birbalsingh

HANSIB

First published in 1996 by Hansib Publishing (Caribbean) Limited

This revised edition published in 1997 by Hansib Publishing (Caribbean) Limited
PO Box 2773, St John's, Antigua, WI

Printed in the United Kingdom by Hillman Printers, Frome

British Library Cataloguing-In-Publication Data.
A catalogue record for this book is available from the British Library.

ISBN 1-870518-47-0

In memory of Kenneth H. Birbalsingh
(1928-1990)

Epigraphs

"From its beginning to this day cricket in the West Indies has expressed with astonishing fidelity the social relations of the islands."

C.L.R. James, "Cricket in West Indian Culture", *Cricket***, p. 119**

"Cricket has always been more than a game in Trinidad. In a society which demanded no skills and offered no rewards to merit, cricket was the only activity which permitted a man to grow to his full stature and to be measured against international standards... The cricketer was our only hero-figure."

V.S. Naipaul, *The Middle Passage***, p. 44**

"The most he ever play was in the street, with a bat make from a coconut branch, a dry mango seed for ball, and a pitchoil tin for wicket."

Samuel Selvon, "The Cricket Match", *Ways of Sunlight***, p. 162**

" 'You see dat shot?' the people was shoutin':
'Jesus Crise, man, wunna see dat shot?'
All over de groun' fellows shakin' hands wid each other
*as if **they** wheelin' de willow*
*as if was **them** had the power."*

Edward Brathwaite, "Rites" *The Arrivants***, p. 200**

*"It is an original pattern, not European, not African, not a part of the American main, not native in any conceivable sense of that word, but West Indian, **sui generis**, with no parallel anywhere else."*

C.L.R. James, "Appendix", *The Black Jacobins***, pp. 391-392**

Contents

CHAPTER FIVE

Ascension - Frank Worrell (1960-63)

CHAPTER SIX

Sobers is de King (1965-66)

CHAPTER SEVEN

Players

CHAPTER EIGHT

Writers

CHAPTER NINE

"Test", "Rites" and *Beyond a Boundary*

Publisher's Note

HOUSE STYLE: Readers unfamiliar with Hansib's publications may note the use of 'Westindies' (not 'West Indies'). This has been used in all Hansib publications since 1973 in a tribute to the formation of the Caribbean Community (Caricom) at Chaguaramas, Trinidad, on 4 July 1973 and as an appropriation of the name given by the "discoverers" to assert the region's united, unique and distinctive identity.

Foreword

BY IAN MCDONALD

This is a wonderful book about the greatest game in the world and how Westindians became its leading exponents at the highest level. It is important to be the best in the world - at cricket as at anything else. It is simplistic and shallow-minded to say or think that cricket is just a game and therefore to lead the way in it means little. Economic or military success is not everything in history, just as material well-being and the exercise of power are not all that matter to people. It means a great deal to be a cultural leader in the world - in the arts, in literature, music, theatre, architecture, style and fashion, scholarship - and in cricket which, as much as any game, represents an international cultural experience of abiding significance. To lead in cricket gives us stature in the world. Pride and self-confidence grow as we prevail among the best anywhere. It is an important part of growing into nationhood.

Frank Birbalsingh's book is well named. I have for long believed that cricket is central to what keeps us together as Westindians and vital to what moulds our nationhood. C.L.R. James instructed me in this many years ago when I first read *Beyond a Boundary*. So when I was asked to pay a tribute to that great West Indian cricket commentator, Tony Cozier, I tried to reflect what I had grown to feel cricket means to Westindians:

> It is very hard to explain to outsiders the importance of cricket in the West Indian psyche. As one would expect, C.L.R. James has done it best. He has pointed out, for example, that English people have a conception of themselves breathed from birth. King Alfred and the burnt cakes, Richard the Lion Heart, the Crusaders, Shakespeare, Mighty Nelson, the Iron Duke and Waterloo, the Charge of the Light Brigade, the few who did so much for so many, the success of Parliamentary democracy--these and such as these, C.L.R. points out, constitute a national tradition. But for West Indians our icons, to a remarkable extent, are cricketing icons: imperious Challenor, "Furioso" George John rolling up his sleeves as if to hurl an iron spear, the leaping Constantine, Headley in all his glorious, defiant genius, "those two pals of mine", Ramadhin and Valentine, the silken elegance of Stollmeyer, Collie Smith the genius-hero who died young, the indescribable magic of Rohan Kanhai, Sobers and his 365 and so much more, Hall with crucifix blazing in the sun and Griffith inseparable from the other end, the great Gibbs who could spin a ball on marble ground and make it bounce on feathers, the three immortal Ws, Worrell in Australia, the tied Test and little Joe Solomon caught forever in that famous picture throwing down the last Australian wicket, Roy Fredericks hooking Lillee and Thomson

again and again to the boundary at Perth, Holding of the whispering death, Greenidge of the thunder bat, Clive Lloyd and his magnificent pride of fast bowlers, Viv Richards the Master Blaster. These and a hundred others, these are our Knights of the Round Table. And in their exploits we begin to weave a nation's historical fabric, our own Bayeux Tapestry beyond any price.

A book like this distils such deeds. In the writing of W.B. Yeats there is a wonderfully eloquent phrase: he speaks of "a community bound together by imaginative possessions." Yeats used this phrase in the context of discussing the importance of a National Theatre for his beloved Ireland. When I think of cricket and the hope of Westindian nationhood the phrase strikes with me a chord that sings. So little binds us together; but cricket does. Economically, we are much divided and increasingly seem tempted to go our separate ways. Politically, we remain deeply suspicious of each other and therefore cannot summon the will to come together in the many ways we must know are necessary for practical nationhood. But cricket! There we are different and better and more confident and more together! Truly it is supremely the one imaginative possession which binds our community together. Here is a book which celebrates that most precious of Westindian possessions.

However, I must not be too solemn about Frank Birbalsingh's lovely, multi-faceted book. After all, it is not simply a treatise on the growth of Westindian nationhood. It is very much a glorious anthology of cricket at its best - exciting matches, our heroes in their hey-day, remarkable feats, extraordinary failures, unexpected turning-points, classic confrontations, stern deeds mixed with frolic in the sun. Apart from the seriousness of its history, this book can be treasured and dipped into for delight as a marvellous compendium of great cricketing events and memorable figures in the game.

Cricket is not simply the play out in the middle. It is not only the cricket itself that we enjoy with such keenness and delight. It is the long discussions, the great arguments over the selection of teams and the comparison of heroes. It is the spectacle of the ground - the crowds full of good humour, the tingle of excitement in the air, the sun blazing and the flags flying and the girls in their fashions showing off. It is the cool beer and the iced rum and the tall stories told of long ago days. It is the umpires coming out to the wicket slowly and the boys in the green trees. It is the tension growing and the hum of noise dying away as the field is set for the first ball of a new Test series. It is the batsman adjusting his cap - or is it his armed helmet these days? - and tapping his bat waiting for that first ball while a couple of million at least of us lean over our radios in every village and town from the Rupununi to Carriacou. It is all these things, and it is also what is written about this great game - books like this one. Cricket more than any other game, by far, has attracted memorable writing. And this book, in my opinion, is a splendid addition to the literature. The tales are well told. It brings back such vivid memories.

We are in considerable debt to Frank Birbalsingh for his labour of scholarship and love. His book deserves to become both a rich mine of cricketing exploits and information as well as a classic text in our Westindian history.

Introduction

In the beginning was the British empire, at the centre of which - in England - cricket was born. From England, through colonial conquest, cricket was taken overseas to British possessions like those in the Westindies. It is no use pretending that, like other colonial appendages, for example, Christianity, Western education or the English language, cricket was a purely charitable or humanitarian gift that, in a Conradian sense, was intended to instruct, uplift, improve, or amuse Westindians. While not denying the integrity or dedication of individual British (and other) missionaries, teachers or government officials, historical evidence suggests that cricket was originally intended for the amusement of English people who had gone to the Westindies to promote colonialism: we know from C.L.R. James, the finest Westindian writer on cricket, that the game was first played by English soldiers garrisoned in the Westindies in the eighteenth century. By the first half of the nineteenth century, the game had taken firm enough root to inspire in Charles Dickens's *The Pickwick Papers* (1836) the creation of the redoubtable Alfred Jingle Esq. of No Hall, Nowhere, who claimed to have played cricket "thousands of times" (p.119) in the Westindies, and to have scored 570 runs during a single wicket tournament against Sir Thomas Blazo. Even if Jingle made up this entire exploit, the novel acknowledges that Dickens and his contemporaries knew that cricket was commonly played in the Westindies during their lifetime.

With greater historical fidelity, we are told by Christopher Nicole, a Westindian author and novelist like James:

> "The first Westindian intercolonial cricket match was played in Barbados, on the Garrison Savannah, on 15th and 16th February 1865, and the opponents were British Guiana." (*West Indian Cricket*, p.19)

This means that, by the second half of the nineteenth century, a tradition of inter-territorial - intercolonial matches as they were called up to the 1950s - had become established. Trinidad was later to take part in triangular tournaments with Barbados and Guyana, but Jamaica, the most populous English-speaking territory, did not participate until later because it was separated by more than one thousand miles of sea from Barbados, Trinidad and Guyana.

The first international tour by Westindian cricketers was made in 1886 to the United States (Philadelphia) and Canada, where cricket did not become as firmly established as in other former British colonies. But in the earliest international period in the 1890s and for the next sixty years, most cricket was played overwhelmingly against England. Of thirty-five Test matches played by

13

Westindies up to 1950, twenty-five were against England: the logical outcome of long established colonial links with the so called mother country. Before 1900 three English teams had completed tours of the Caribbean. Then Westindies toured England for the first time in 1900, followed by two more tours, in 1906 and 1923, until Westindies were finally admitted to the international Test playing fraternity in 1928. At the time, this fraternity consisted only of England and Australia which began Tests in 1876/77, and South Africa which began in 1889.

The Rise of Westindian Cricket tells the story of the growth or rise of Westindian cricket from 1928 to 1966. In order to follow the story, a brief historical sketch of the Westindies is necessary. The region consists of islands in the Caribbean Sea, together with adjoining, mainland territories whose coastline, in Central and South America, forms a border with this sea. ("Westindies" is used interchangeably with "Caribbean" throughout *The Rise of Westindian Cricket*.) Some islands, like Cuba and Puerto Rico, are Spanish-speaking; Martinique and Guadeloupe are Francophone; while Curaçao and Aruba are Dutch-speaking. At once, one gets a hint of the racial diversity, linguistic variety and cultural mixing that are essential features of the word "creole" which is generally applied to anything that is characteristically Westindian. The pattern in most territories, from the fifteenth century onward, was for European conquerors, driven mainly by economic motives, to set up mainly sugar plantations. These plantations generated huge profits in the sixteenth, seventeenth, and eighteenth centuries; but in the process, aboriginal peoples of the region, for example, Caribs and Arawaks - so called Amerindians - were virtually exterminated: they had nowhere to hide from their European conquerors on most islands, although some did find refuge in the forests of mainland territories like Belize (formerly British Honduras) and Guyana. As labour for their plantations, European owners brought over slaves from Africa during three centuries until 1834, when slavery was abolished in British territories. By then, several million Africans were brought over, the descendants of whom today form the main population of the whole region, including the English-speaking Westindies.

Cricket is played mainly in the English-speaking Westindies, that is to say, in several islands and two mainland territories - Belize and Guyana - which were colonised by Britain. In the beginning, Test cricket occurred only in the largest of these territories - Jamaica, Trinidad, Guyana and Barbados; but today, there are Test matches in Antigua as well. (As a British colony, Guyana was known as "British Guiana" until it gained Independence. "Guyana" is used in *The Rise of Westindian Cricket* for the sake of consistency. Since 1888 the island of Trinidad was amalgamated with the neighbouring island of Tobago with which it today forms the nation of Trinidad and Tobago. For the sake of brevity, "Trinidad" is used for "Trinidad and Tobago".)

After 1834, although slavery was abolished, the English-speaking Westindian territories retained their sugar plantations and continued as colonies of Britain until the 1960s when, following a short-lived Federation (1958-62), most of the larger territories became independent - Jamaica and Trinidad in 1962, and Guyana and Barbados in 1966. Despite its disappearance as a formal institution, slavery and its practices continued to affect daily life in the Westindies: they also play a role in the development of Westindian cricket. The chief legacy of slavery is the model of the sugar plantation, which supplied the structure on which Westindian society was based. The model consisted of a small group of European (white) owners and administrators, a somewhat larger group of mixed (brown) African and European overseers, supervisors, and technicians, and the large majority of the population - the African (black) workers. It is a model in which race and colour coincide with economic well being and social influence to ensure that whites formed the richest, most educated, professional and powerful class of society; mixed blood people a partially educated, skilled middle class with intermediate power or influence; and blacks the poorest, least educated, least skilled, and least powerful.

The structure of Westindian society was further complicated after 1834, by the arrival of indentured labourers to fill the vacuum left by the lost labour of the freed Africans on sugar plantations. Indentured labourers were brought chiefly from India, China, and Madeira. By far the largest number came from India and settled mainly in Guyana and Trinidad. These new comers fitted into the existing feudalistic, hierarchical plantation social structure as best they could, and added more variety to the mix of racial and cultural patterns already there. By the middle of this century, this variety was reflected in the remarkable racial, ethnic and cultural diversity of the Westindies: Africans formed the overwhelming majority of the population, while other groups consisted of (white) Europeans, including Portuguese, (brown) African/European mixtures, Indians, Chinese, Jews, Syrians and various combinations of mixture among all these. One anomaly in the general pattern of Africans forming more than ninety percent of the population in most territories, is that Indians were concentrated in Guyana and Trinidad in numbers that today give them a majority in each of these two territories.

So far as cricket is concerned, certain difficulties arose from this history of diversity and complexity in the racial, social, cultural, political and territorial formation of the Westindies. Such difficulties involved team selection, leadership, and a host of structural and financial issues that restricted the rise of Westindian cricket. The mere geographical separation of mainly island territories has always been a problem, especially before air travel, because of the difficulty of communication between centres where cricket is played both within and between each territory. This is why, for instance, Jamaica joined intercolonial tournaments so late: it was too far away from Guyana, Trinidad, and Barbados. The smallness of populations and the poverty of the region as a whole have meant that, up to the 1960s, the best cricketers could find employment only in English leagues; and younger Westindian cricketers could not benefit from their skills. Caribbean history also spawned attitudes of racial inferiority/superiority, and feelings of humiliation and self-hatred coupled ambivalently with sentiments or impulses of defiance, resistance and liberation. When, in their writing, cricketers like Roy Marshall, Wesley Hall and Frank Worrell mention problems of factionalism or insularity in the Westindian team of the early 1950s, what they are talking about are conflicting loyalties, divisions, tensions, fears, rivalries and other aspects of colonial fragmentation that stem, directly or indirectly, from Westindian history.

One historically-derived aspect of Westindian cricket that is not necessarily a "difficulty" is the continuing supply of excellent fast bowlers. By the last decade of the last century, the plantation origins of Westindian society had produced a situation in which the best batsmen were generally white, and the best bowlers black and fast. Because of the feudalistic plantation social hierarchies that then existed, it was convenient for white employers to get batting practice by having their black workers bowl at them. This tended to increase the batting skills of whites and bowling skills of blacks. As recently as the 1940s, Roy Marshall reveals in his autobiography *Test Outcast*, that his status as a white Barbadian and the son of a plantation owner, allowed him to receive batting practice from one of his father's black employees; the senior Marshall laid a concrete pitch so that Roy could better develop his batting skills. If one remembers too, the astonishing batting prowess that Mr. Jingle flaunted among his English compatriots gained not a little from the fact that it was demonstrated against Quanko Samba, a black fast bowler who promptly expired following his slavish exertions.

In fact as in fiction, from Woods and Cumberbatch in the early 1900s, through George John in the 1920s, Constantine, Francis and Martindale in the 1930s, to Hall and Griffith in the 1960s, and Holding, Marshall, Ambrose later on, black Westindian fast bowlers are a direct product of what James calls "social relations", that is to say, the peculiar features of Westindian social history. Nor did the supply of black fast bowlers slacken after Independence, although the same cannot be said for white Westindian batsmen. In the first half of this century, Barbados alone had established a great tradition of white batsmen such as Harry Ince, Tim Tarilton, George Challenor, E.L.G. Hoad, John Goddard, Roy Marshall and Denis Atkinson. But after the social reversals that inevitably followed Independence in the 1960s, this great tradition had all but disappeared: the last good crop of white Westindian batsmen consisted of Jeffrey Stollmeyer, Gerry Gomez, John Goddard, Roy Marshall, Denis Atkinson and Bruce Pairaudeau, all of whom played mainly between 1947 and 1957.

What were later to become typical Westindian attitudes and expectations about cricket also were a direct outcome of Westindian history. Examples may be seen in the earliest tour of Westindies by an English team led by Slade Lucas in 1895. One of the players, Legh Barratt, kept a diary describing the hospitality that he and his English team-mates received. Their hosts, all whites, formed the local aristocracy of businessmen, administrators and officials. The following entry in Barratt's diary captures the atmosphere of their visit:

> Arrive St. Lucia 6 am. Usual deputation meet us & hand us one or two invitations. Stop at Gov. House - Governor on leave. Commence match v St. Lucia. Good wicket, pretty little ground. I made 27. The Government voted £150 for our entertainment here. We spend a quiet evening with billiards at club. (*Wisden Cricket Monthly*, May, 1994, p.48)

Similar visits were paid by Barratt's group to St. Vincent and Grenada. Then to Trinidad where they were greeted on board their ship by a deputation consisting of the Colonial Secretary, the Solicitor General, and twenty others. Barratt, Slade Lucas, and two of their friends were guests of the Governor Sir Fred and

Lady Broome. The visitors evidently received the most lavish hospitality available. True enough, they had not come to play Test cricket, but the relaxed, holiday atmosphere of their visit established a precedent for subsequent English tours. Barratt's account of relaxation over billiards and tennis, cooling doses of cocktails, egg swizzles, lime squash and iced whisky and soda is probably the kind of thing that Len Hutton had in mind when, as captain during the M.C.C. tour of 1953/54, he wanted to restrict the number of cocktail parties that were scheduled because he thought they might affect his men's cricket. Hutton sounds rueful when he writes: "The days when the Westindies were weak opponents and an M.C.C. tour there could be looked upon as a pleasure cruise had gone probably for ever." (*Just My Story*, p.69) One can see from Barratt's diary where the idea of an English tour of Westindies being a pleasure cruise came from.

Still in Trinidad, Barratt provides further observations in his entry for March 2:

> Eventful day. I start from Gov. House at 8.30 & drive a gentleman's tandem 10 miles through most beautiful scenery passing through several coolie villages & in passing cannot help noticing the scantiness of their clothing & the multitude of their jewellery, each coolie girl having as a rule 4 or 5 bangles on each wrist... Mr. Bush also had a fall & being very heavy he got a nasty bruise. One of the niggers got hold of his leg & tried to pull him off. (*Wisden Cricket Monthly*, May, 1994, p.49)

Barratt is serenely detached from the exotic Trinidadian environment, and he beholds the habits and behaviour of "coolies and niggers" - a majority of the population - with genuine wonder, totally unaware that the very words he uses to describe these people may be offensive. He has no self-doubt or second thoughts: he confidently judges Trinidadians by Eurocentric, Victorian, social Darwinist standards that define certain people as primitive or undeveloped. This definition is justified by plantation values in which white political power and economic and social control inevitably bred feelings of confidence, superiority and condescension. At the same time, no one is surprised that in their match against Trinidad, Barratt reports, with due wonder and alarm, that he and his friends had to face: "a very fast black bowler (Woods, 6 for 39) [who] bowls most of the team." (ibid.)

Barratt's diary corroborates the (racist) plantation ethics which regulated British colonial society in the Caribbean at the turn of the century, when "coolies and niggers" were subservient to local whites; but it does not as clearly show that, in the Eurocentric world order at that time, local whites, themselves felt subservient to their kith and kin in the metropolis or mother country - England. This comes out when Westindies made their first visit to England in 1900. *The Times* depicted the visiting team with greater politeness than Barratt, though with a distinct touch of condescension as consisting of "white colonists and coloured players." (Marcus Williams, ed., *Double Century*, p.123) More importantly, the Westindian captain, Aucher Warner, brother of Sir Pelham, betrayed obsequiousness when he replied to the welcome he and his men received at a luncheon at Crystal Palace in London. His reply was reported in *The Times*:

Mr. A. Warner thanked the Englishmen for their reception, and said that they had come to learn cricket and he felt sure that whatever were their match results the trip would be beneficial to Westindian cricket. Mr. W.L. Murdoch pointed out in a very good speech that the same spirit of humility existed among the Australians when they first visited England in 1878. He was sure that Westindians would as years went on develop their talent as Australia had done. (Ibid., p.123)

As a famous Australian captain, Murdoch shares Aucher Warner's sentiments of colonial humility or inferiority vis à vis the mother country. Like Australia, twenty years earlier, Westindies came as pupils to learn from England. This is why, as Tony Cozier reports, a cartoonist attributed to a member of the Westindian team in 1900, the words: "We have come to learn, sah" (*The Westindies: Fifty Years of Test Cricket*, p.3). Although colonial suppliance may have been reflected previously in other places, for example, Australia, the Westindian version expressed here by the word "sah" has a strong creole flavour redolent of historic master/slave relationships which are an essential part of Westindian social relations.

Attitudes of condescension on one side and obsequiousness on the other survived for a long time in the Westindies. In the Playfair *Official Souvenir* to the 1950 Westindian tour of England, the Foreword by Sir Pelham (Plum) Warner opens with a recollection of the author's ancestor Sir Thomas Warner, the first Governor General of the Westindies who died in 1648. Sir Pelham speaks with pride of his birth in Trinidad, of his brother being the first captain of a Westindian cricket team to visit England, and of the fact that "whatever success I may have attained at cricket was largely due to my earliest lessons at Harrison College, Barbados". (p.3) His affection for the Westindies is not in doubt; but he speaks, proprietorially, of "our Dominons and Colonies" and continues with unmasked chauvinism:

> The Westindies are amongst the oldest of our possessions and the Caribbean Sea resounds with the exploits of the British Navy. Nowhere in the world is there a greater loyalty to, love of, and admiration for England. (p.3)

As one of England's great cricket captains (1901 - 1911), a cricket correspondent for *The Times*, and probably the best player/writer the game has yet seen, Warner's chauvinism and paternalism seem unworthy of him. But he was born in 1873, and like Barratt, another Victorian, reflects outmoded paternalistic notions of an era of global imperialism that vanished, at least in form, soon after World War Two, although its substance still prevails in the poverty and underdevelopment of contemporary third world countries such as those in the Westindies.

Warner's paternalism is matched by the obsequiousness of a "Message" from R.K. Nunes, President of the West Indian Cricket Board of Control, and a former captain of Westindies, that appears in the same 1950 Playfair Official *Souvenir*:

> We received the privilege of Test match status in 1928 after three visits in 1900, 1906 and 1923. Although we have not yet won a Test match in England, we have a margin of successes against England under our own

conditions. We are proud of having received fixtures for four Test matches, each of five days, and it is our responsibility to show that this honour is deserved. I know that all English cricketers will be gratified if we do well in the coming season for it is always satisfactory to the mentor to observe the progress of the pupil. On our side, it is an understatement to say we look forward with pleasure to our tour. (p.5)

Nunes rivals the Rev. William Collins in the presence of Lady Catherine de Burgh in Jane Austen's *Pride and Prejudice*. Such fawning obsequiousness cannot be entirely justified by requirements of politeness and graciousness in an *Official Souvenir*! It sounds more like colonial mimicry which is the opposite side of the same coin as imperial paternalism.

So far, from Aucher Warner to Nunes, Westindian cricket leadership remained in white hands. There is no doubt that a society structured on the basis of white masters, brown middlemen and black slaves ("coolies and niggers") had to have cricket leadership from the top group - the whites. In pre-Test days this was certainly true. After Aucher Warner in 1900, teams to England in 1906 and 1923 were led by H.B.G Austin, a towering figure, literally and metaphorically, in early Westindian cricket. Up to the 1920s, it was also inevitable for the leading batsmen as well to be white, in the same way as the leading fast bowlers were black. The economic security and high social standing of whites meant that they could afford equipment, playing facilities, and the time to practise. In the case of foreign tours, financial strength gave them a distinct advantage. In *Beyond a Boundary*, C.L.R. James illustrates this point through an incident involving Learie Constantine's father "Cons":

In those days black men were usually bowlers. The boat with the team to England in 1900 had left and "Cons", as he was called, though chosen, had remained behind. Organization was not what it has become. He was not a rich man who could pay his own way. He was not a professional for whom everything had to be found. He had not gone because he could not afford it. People who thought he had gone saw him standing in the street. A public subscription was organized on the spot, a fast launch was chartered and caught the boat before it reached the open sea. Constantine Snr. scrambled on board to hit the first Westindies century made in England (st. Reynolds b. Grace, 113) at Lord's of all places. (p.106)

Perhaps James's narrative gifts have inspired him to add a little embroidery to the story of Cons, but there is no doubt about the story itself.

By the 1930s, the social and political structure that nourished white Westindian excellence and leadership in cricket began to be questioned. Black cricketers of distinction - Learie Constantine and George Headley - appeared, and a process of change began to reverse the black/white ratio in the Westindian team. In 1906, the touring team to England consisted of four blacks and ten whites; in 1928, in their first Test series, the Westindian team had ten black or coloured cricketers, and five whites; and in 1933 there were nine black or coloured cricketers on the team to England and four whites. But throughout all this change, the position of white captains remained sacrosanct.

There were no lengths to which the West Indian Cricket Board of Control (WICBC) would not go to preserve white captaincy. One can see why from a list of the names of former presidents of the WICBC as given by Michael Manley:

> First, Sir Harold Austin [H.B.G Austin] the godfather of Westindian cricket, and the man who founded the Board [in 1927]... He was followed by Laurie Yearwood, a white Barbadian of the very upper class. Then, Fred Grant of a distinguished Trinidadian family of commerce, who was the elder brother of G.C. and R.S. Grant... R.K. Nunes was a Jamaican lawyer and of a family that came as near to aristocracy as the colonies can produce. Then the redoubtable Sir Errol Dos Santos himself... followed by John Dare [John St. F. Dare] of British Guiana, T.N. Pierce of Barbados, R.C. Marley, again of Jamaica, and finally, Jeffrey Stollmeyer of Trinidad. (*A History of Westindian Cricket*, p. 117)

All former presidents of the WICBC were white, which makes nonsense of the old canard that politics should not be mixed with sport; for politics has always been mixed with sport in the Westindies as everywhere else, although the injustice of it is not as striking as it was in South Africa under the fascist perversion of apartheid. Politics, for example, ensured that Ranji was left out of the England side to play Australia in 1896, and it was politics that forced Ranji's nephew Duleep to withdraw from the 1929 English team when their South African opponents objected to him. South Africa was to repeat this outrage again by objecting to D'Oliveira as a member of the English team in 1968.

In one instance, in 1930, the WICBC offered the captaincy to Jack Grant, a white Trinidadian who, at the age of twenty-three, had barely completed his studies at Cambridge university. Although he played for Cambridge, Grant had never before been captain in a first class cricket match, had never played in a first class match in the Westindies, and scarcely knew the men he was to lead against an Australian team that included the likes of Bradman, Ponsford, Kippax, McCabe, and Grimmett. It was as if the mere combination of Grant's whiteness and his connection with Cambridge university somehow magically equipped him for the job. In his autobiography, Grant admits: "It could not be disputed that my white colour was a major factor in my being given this post". (*Jack Grant's Story*, p.31) In the circumstances, he coped amazingly well with the huge burden on his young, untried shoulders, which was enough justification for the Board to retain him as captain for two more Test series. Perhaps he would have continued as captain had he not retired prematurely from international cricket because of personal reasons.

Grant was succeeded by his younger brother Rolph, who was picked as captain for the 1939 tour of England with the nineteen year old Jeffrey Stollmeyer as his vice-captain. This looked like a clear example of grooming a young, inexperienced white cricketer - Stollmeyer - for the captaincy. In his autobiography, Stollmeyer claims he was as surprised as the public that he was even selected for the tour: "A crescendo of objections came from every quarter of the Caribbean. 'What has Stollmeyer done to be pitchforked into the team?' said the British Guiana Chronicle." (*Everything Under the Sun*, p.33) Not only that: as a student at the Imperial College of Tropical Agriculture at the time, Stollmeyer would have been unable to write his college examinations if he left with the team for England. Instead, a special examination was set for him so that he could leave with the team. Stollmeyer sees this as "a noble gesture by the college" (p.34); but if he was being groomed for higher things, those who were grooming him had the power to prevail on his college if it were necessary. It was not a gesture that most other students could expect, as Stollmeyer himself hints when he writes: "I have often wondered what my fellow-students thought about this unusual procedure." (p.34)

The 1939 Westindian team included black players such as Constantine who at the age of thirty-eight, had sixteen years' experience in international cricket, and Headley who was thirty years old and held an unbroken Test batting record since 1930. Rolph Grant, meanwhile, had appeared in four Test matches, and Stollmeyer in none. More importantly, in *Everything Under the Sun*, Stollmeyer is eloquent in praise of the tactical acumen of both Constantine and Headley. Of Headley, Stollmeyer writes: "he taught me so much about the finer points of the game," (p.36) and: "he [Headley] had a greater tactical sense than any cricketer with whom I have played." (p.37) Unless Constantine and Headley were unwilling to accept the responsibility of captaincy, there can be no justification on grounds of expertise or experience, for the appointment of Rolph Grant and Jeffrey Stollmeyer as captain and vice-captain respectively in 1939. Michael Manley sums up the situation well:

> Rolph Grant, himself a man of great decency and intelligence, was far more importantly the son of a wealthy and powerful Trinidadian family. Victor [brother of Jeffrey] Stollmeyer's parents owned a major plantation and were significantly active in the island's commerce. A profound connection was made between the ownership of property and fitness to lead. Understood in its context, fitness to lead is here an unconscious extension of the notion of fitness to rule. It was the families who were accustomed to ruling who were assumed to produce the sons who were capable of leading. Constantine and Headley were never even considered. (*History*, p.66)

Whether or not there was an official "whites only" policy in appointing Westindian cricket captains is a pointless semantic conundrum. In practice, until the 1950s, only whites were appointed for a full series.

Just as Jack Grant (1930) and Jeffrey Stollmeyer (1939) were appointed captain and vice-captain respectively, although both were raw and untried, so again was Denis Atkinson made vice-captain against Australia in 1954/55, although he had played in only eleven Tests with indifferent results, whereas Frank Worrell who had played in twenty-three Tests and was a batsman with an international reputation, and experience of English league cricket and Commonwealth tours, was completely passed over. Another grooming process was evidently what the WICBC had set in motion. The process they had started for Stollmeyer in 1939 had prospered, and had led to his relative success as captain in home series against India in 1952/53, and against England in 1953/54. Now, in 1954, he was appointed captain against Australia in another home series, but Worrell who had been his vice-captain one year earlier against England, had abruptly been replaced by Atkinson. The justification that Atkinson was an amateur while Worrell was not, was a smokescreen that concealed the racial implications of the replacement which must have come as a rebuke to Worrell for some breach he had committed; but the only discernible breach, in terms of Westindian social relations was that he had risen further in the Westindian cricket hierarchy than any other black man. If there was another breach, his captain - Stollmeyer - would surely have known. Here is Stollmeyer's reaction to Atkinson's appointment:

> The Board, (WICBC) in its wisdom, had replaced Worrell as vice-captain and put in his place the very much younger and inexperienced Denis Atkinson. It was a preposterous decision in any circumstances and was the cause of much dissension and bad cricket played by our team in the series. (*Everything*, p.151)

One may regard Stollmeyer's description of this decision - "preposterous" - as a tactful euphemism for racial discrimination sanctioned by time-honoured Westindian social and political precedent. In the event, Stollmeyer was injured before the first Test, and again during the third, so Atkinson acted as captain in the first, third and fourth Tests of the tour.

Another illustration of the peculiar interdependence between political or social factors and cricket is the appointment of John Goddard as captain for the Westindian tour of England in 1957. Goddard had been in virtual retirement since 1952; but after Stollmeyer's retirement in 1955, he re-emerged as vice-captain to Denis Atkinson on the Westindian tour of New Zealand in 1955/56. Then, he was made captain in 1957. Manley again analyses the issue well:

> One is obliged to criticise Goddard as a captain, but one can only admire his courage as a player. No man ever stood up more unflinchingly to fiercely struck balls at silly mid-off or short extra-cover. That his selection in 1957 was a travesty was not his fault. He was nothing more than an honourable part of an environment not yet itself completely honourable; not yet willing to give honour to where honour is due on a basis of merit and merit alone. (*History*, p.117)

Manley's approach to this whole question of an unwritten "whites only" policy of Westindian cricket captains seems correct: to indict the political and social structure and its plantation values of race, colour and class, rather than blame the individual white players who were involved. This too is what black player/writers from Constantine to Worrell have done: to comment with warm admiration on the cricketing abilities of such men as Jack Grant, Rolph Grant, or John Goddard (in 1957), although not entirely agreeing with their appointment as captain.

But the complexity of Westindian history does not permit an easy dismissal of the whole society as racist or fascist. Race is a basic factor, as is colour or class; and white Westindian conservatives and/or racists have always existed. Their longevity is illustrated by E.W. Swanton in *West Indies Revisited* (1960) where he refers to such people as "those rare planter-types... who apparently suppose themselves still to be basking in the blessed aura of Queen Victoria." (p.280) Swanton mentions one of their remarks which he says occasionally got a dusty answer from him: "Between ourselves, I hope you beat these black fellows." (p.280) In 1960, in a book, it is unlikely that Swanton would be as explicit in his vocabulary as Legh Barratt was, in 1900, in a private diary. Roy Marshall who grew up in Barbados in the 1930s and 40s, has also written in *Test Outcast*:

> Being a white Westindian myself, the son of a white planter and living a fairly sheltered life, I suppose I did grow up with slight racialist feelings. It was never anything that was said or done but just that I was brought up in a white man's world and white men, at the time, probably ruled the day-to-day life in Barbados.
>
> As a result of my fair skin I was brought up in an atmosphere which gave the impression that the white man was superior. (p.40)

But if racism and conservatism had prevailed entirely, Westindian society could not have implemented the democratic changes that led to Independence, without provoking massive turbulence, revolution or war. That democratic change was achieved through mainly constitutional methods, is due to the flexible and fluid nature of the social system itself.

This flexibility is illustrated in the appointment of Gerry Alexander as Westindian captain in the 1957/58 home series against Pakistan. Now, Alexander is not white: he is of mixed blood, but closer to white than black in both colour and features. He is also Cambridge-educated and a veterinary surgeon from an upper middle class family in urban Jamaica; so that although not white by race, he is white by class and colour and is regarded as "Jamaican white". In other words, race, class and colour operate fluidly, to allow a non-white individual to acquire the accoutrements of a white life style, through luck, exceptional ability, or other means, and to be accepted in a class traditionally reserved for pure whites. How much all this has changed since Independence is not relevant here. Suffice to say that it was the system during Alexander's cricket career, and it led to a dispute between him and Roy Gilchrist, a black fast bowler from rural Jamaica who was described by James as "an ebullient plebeian", and who was convinced that, through Alexander, he was being victimised by the historic condescension that the colonial upper classes traditionally visited upon blacks like himself. Alexander was the last Westindian captain with any claims to whiteness. When he was succeeded by Frank Worrell in 1960, a veritable revolution had been wrought in a process that began sixty years earlier with the appointment of a Westindian captain, Aucher Warner, who belonged to a family that came as close as a colonial family could to aristocracy.

It goes without saying that the tradition of appointing white captains could not have been maintained if, the administrative body appointing them - the WICBC - did not belong to what Manley calls: "an honour-roll of the upper echelons of the class structure of the region." (History, p.63) But this white hegemony was as deeply entrenched in cricket as in every other facet of Westindian history and society, and it should not be viewed in isolation, like some Caribbean perversion, although the lengths to which it was formerly taken - slavery and indenture - are indeed perverse. As already mentioned, the Westindian social structure is itself the product of an Eurocentric world order that greatly changed during this century although its influence has not completely disappeared. This influence is part of the story of the rise of Westindian cricket.

In view of this influence and the difficulties it entailed in team selection, leadership, insularity, factionalism, etcetera, it is a wonder that Westindian cricket rose at all. Yet, many commentators, both in the Westindies and abroad, have confirmed its rise. Bridgette Lawrence suggests that Westindies rose to the top, from their position as:

> "underdogs of world cricket ... to dominate the game with a spirit and poise not previously seen in the international cricket arena." (Lawrence and Goble, *Westindian Test Cricketers*, p.7).

E.W. Swanton, who has had long experience of the Westindies as a journalist and a cricket organizer, expresses astonishment over the growth of Westindian cricket:

> how extraordinary that within modern times a few scattered communities with a combined population roughly akin to the 3 million or so of Sydney or Melbourne should have produced a string of memorable batsmen at least equivalent to the combined output of England and Australia. (G. Plumptree. ed., *The Essential E.W. Swanton*, p.36)

Swanton slightly underestimates the population of the Anglophone Caribbean which was about five million in 1985 when he was writing; but his point is taken. In their first Test series - against England in 1928 - Westindies were humiliated, whereas in 1966, they steam-rollered England to become undisputed champions of the world. The story of what happened in between these two series forms the essential subject of *The Rise of Westindian Cricket*.

The first six chapters of *The Rise of Westindian Cricket* describe selected Test matches with Westindies between 1928 and 1966. Of one hundred and nine such matches sixty-two are described; they are arranged chronologically to represent stages in the development or rise of Westindian cricket. Chapter One considers the earliest stage from 1928 to 1939, when Westindies played twenty-two Test matches, seventeen against England, and five against Australia. They lost twelve matches, won four, and drew six - results which leave no doubt about their lowly status. Chapter One is entitled "The Headley Era" because George Headley dominated everything through his batting; the chapter considers at least two matches from each of the six series during the period.

Since there was no Test cricket during the Second World War, Westindies did not appear in Tests again until 1947/48 when they hosted England in four Test matches. In 1948/49, they toured India for the first time and engaged in a series of five Test matches. Chapter Two considers six of these matches, three from each tour. Of the nine matches in both tours, Westindies won three and drew six. The title of the chapter "The Post-War Years" confirms that although war had halted cricket in the Westindies, as in most places, a fresh start had been made to re-launch Westindies.

Chapter Three considers the third phase of Westindian cricket in which there were thirty-five Test matches. Sixteen of these are described, at least two from each of the seven series in which Westindies were involved, except the series against New Zealand in 1955/56 which is represented by one Test. The results in these series from 1950 to 1957 are inconsistent: eleven matches won, fourteen lost, and ten drawn. The chapter takes its name from five players who could be regarded as the main protagonists of Westindian cricket at this stage: three batsmen from Barbados whose names begin with the letter "W": Everton Weekes, Frank Worrell, and Clyde Walcott; and two spin bowlers, Sonny Ramadhin from Trinidad, and Alfred Valentine from Jamaica, who are known in the Westindies simply as Ram and Val.

Chapter Four deals with four series that were played between 1958 and 1960, one each against England and India, and two against Pakistan. Of the eighteen matches involved, Westindies won seven, lost four, and drew seven. At least two matches are presented from each tour. Gerry Alexander, captain during this period, acted as an intermediary figure who helped to consolidate Westindian resources, as the team fortified itself during a rather difficult time in the administration of the game.

Chapter Five covers the years from 1960 to 1963, when Westindies were protagonists in three series, one each with Australia, India, and England. Frank Worrell served as captain. Fifteen matches were played of which nine were won, three lost, two drawn, and one tied. These results show how far Westindies had "ascended" since the Headley era when they won four matches out of twenty-two. At least three matches are presented from each series.

Chapter Six considers the final stage consisting of six matches from two series between 1965 and 1966, when Sobers was captain, and Westindian supremacy became unchallenged in world cricket. The series involved Australia and England, and of the ten matches, Westindies won five, lost two, and drew three. The title of the chapter suggests that Sobers dominated Westindian cricket in the mid-1960s much as Headley had done in the 1930s. The difference is that Sobers led a team that established clear supremacy over the two most powerful teams in international cricket at the time - England and Australia. This is the final chapter in which descriptions of Test matches are presented in chronological sequence.

Chapter Seven consists of biographical sketches of some cricketers who represented Westindies between 1928 and 1966. Not every major Westindian player has been chosen. George Headley, the Ws, Sobers, Kanhai, Gibbs, Ramadhin and Valentine are obvious choices, as are some players of historical significance, for example, George Challenor and Learie Constantine. But a lesser known cricketer like Robert Christiani is included, out of personal preference, whereas, important names like Jackie (G.C.) Grant and Denis Atkinson (former captains), Charlie Griffith, Conrad Hunte and many others are omitted. As elsewhere in *The Rise of Westindian Cricket*, the aim is to be representative rather than comprehensive: to evoke the spirit of the game through comments on matches and performances by individuals who made significant contributions to Westindian cricket. Biographical sketches are arranged chronologically by the date each player entered Test cricket.

Chapter Eight reviews a selection of books by Westindian writers who mainly consider cricket during 1928 to 1966. Since James's *Beyond a Boundary* is included in the following chapter, it is not reviewed here. James's friend Learie Constantine has written more books than any other Westindian cricketer, and the volume and quality of his output make him the foremost player-writer produced by the Westindies. James and Constantine were the first Westindians to write about cricket for an international audience. James helped Constantine with his first work *Cricket and I* (1933). The impact of this book is recorded in *Beyond a Boundary*:

> Constantine's *Cricket and I* came first. To the general it was merely another book on cricket. To the Westindians it was the first book ever published in England by a world-famous Westindian writing as a Westindian about people and events in the Westindies. (pp.123-124)

Apart from reviews of books by Constantine and other famous player-writers, for example, Clyde Walcott, Frank Worrell and Jeffrey Stollmeyer, there are reviews of publications by professional writers or journalists such as Frank Eytle and Tony Cozier. The genre of cricket writing is not as highly developed in the Westindies as it is in England or Australia. C.L.R. James (1901-1989) is the first professional Westindian cricket journalist of quality. His position is today taken by Tony Cozier who has produced several excellent Annuals on Westindian cricket. Cozier also broadcasts on the game.

Chapter Nine comments on the cricket writing of three Westindian authors, two of whom, V.S. Naipaul and Edward Brathwaite, do not normally take cricket as their subject. Although there are occasional references to cricket in Naipaul's fiction, "Test" is his only extended piece on the game. Edward Brathwaite is an academic historian who is also a poet. His poem "Rites" gives his most extensive treatment of cricket. As already suggested, C.L.R. James is a special case in the sense that his voluminous writings cover topics that vary widely from fiction and literary essays to history, political theory and sociology as well as cricket.

Chapter Ten attempts a summary of the development of Westindian cricket, including a definition of the game which, although brought from England, had acclimatized itself to Westindian reflexes, temperaments and grounds over two centuries. During this process of acclimatization Westindian cricketers faced numerous difficulties or peculiarities of their history, region and time. Chapter Ten will elucidate the rise of Westindian cricket despite these difficulties or peculiarities.

The Rise of Westindian Cricket has been many years in the making, and benefits from help, advice, suggestions and information from many quarters. I have to thank colleagues, friends, correspondents, and others who helped in various ways: Harry Ramkhelawan, publisher of *Indo-Caribbean World*; Romeo Kaseram, editor of *Indo-Caribbean World*; Daniel Bishop; Clem Seecharan; Dick Ewen; Maurice Elliott; Ian McDonald; Robert Christiani; the late Sir Lindsay Grant; Gerry Gomez, the late Jeffrey Stollmeyer; and Stephen Green, Curator of the M.C.C. Library. Special thanks to Kissoon Lall for carrying out the burdensome task of checking facts and figures, and for help in proofreading and revision. For computer services thanks to Maureen Principe and Lisa Haberman. I am greatly indebted to Chandra Hodgson for computer services as well as revision of the manuscript. Finally, thanks to Arif Ali and Hansib Publishing Limited.

CHAPTER ONE

The Headley Era

(1928-39)

First Test vs. England
Lord's, London, England, 23, 25, 26 June, 1928

The first Test match that Westindies ever played was against England. If England regarded the Westindians as mere neophytes in Test cricket, they did not show it in their team selection: they fielded the strongest eleven they could muster. Their star opening batsman Jack Hobbs was omitted only because he was injured. Otherwise, they had Herbert Sutcliffe, Hobbs's illustrious partner, Walter Hammond, famous for previous assaults on Westindian bowling, and Douglas Jardine. In the bowling department, England were led by Harold Larwood and Maurice Tate, two of the most dangerous fast bowlers of their time, and "Tich" Freeman the best leg-break and googly merchant they then possessed.

Against this formidable line-up Westindies fielded George Challenor, the veteran Barbadian batsman and his opening partner, the Jamaican F.R. Martin, to be followed by M.P. Fernandes (Guyana), captain R.K. Nunes (Jamaica), W.H. St. Hill (Trinidad) and C.A. Roach (Trinidad). These batsmen all had substantial records. In Learie Constantine (Trinidad), G.N. Francis (Barbados), and Herman Griffith (Trinidad), Westindies also had men who could bowl at least as fast as Larwood and Tate. In addition, C.R. Browne (Guyana) and Joe Small (Trinidad) were supporting bowlers.

The English captain Percy Chapman won the toss and batted. After the openers had provided a good start, Hammond and Tyldesley rattled up 77 runs in fifty minutes, until Hammond (45) was bowled by Constantine: 174 for three. Then, in scarcely over an hour, Chapman and Tyldesley plastered another 96 runs on the board before Tyldesley (122) was caught by Constantine off Francis: 231 for four. By close of play, England had scored 382 for eight wickets. One couldn't really fault the Westindian bowlers: it was their fielding that let them down in the form of dropped catches. In the end, Westindies did rather well to dismiss England for 401 early the next morning, with Constantine claiming four wickets for 82 runs, while Francis, Griffith and Small earned two wickets each. Tyldesley's century was the first against Westindies in a Test match.

Everything now depended on the Westindian batsmen, and Challenor and Martin opened confidently, taking the score to 70 without loss by lunch. Soon after lunch, Challenor was caught by Smith off Larwood for 29. Then calamity! Tate bowled Fernandes for 0, and started a collapse that reduced Westindies from 86 for one to 96 for five. Nunes played a captain's innings to get 37 before being bowled by Jupp; and Constantine, plucky as ever, essayed a few brave blows that netted him 13; but none of this could stop Westindies from being dismissed for a mere 177. The irony was that they were not undone by those they feared most - Larwood, Tate, Freeman - but by spin bowler Wallace Jupp who took four wickets for 37 runs in 23 overs.

In the second innings, Larwood was injured and could not bowl. In such a situation, it is surprising that Chapman enforced the follow-on. The fact that Test matches lasted only three days at that time probably encouraged him to go for it. At any rate, Challenor was immediately bowled by Tate for 0 and started another tragic collapse in which Westindies sank to 44 for 6 wickets. At the end of the second day, with only four tailend wickets standing, Westindies required 169 runs to make England bat again. It was an impossible task. Small and Roach, batting at numbers 8 and 9 respectively, fought gamely back with a partnership of 56 on the final day. When Roach was caught by Chapman off Tate for 16, Small found another willing ally in Browne who helped him to add a further 47 runs. If only the earlier batsmen had shown similar pluck and imagination! In scoring 52, Small earned the distinction of being the first Westindian to get a half century in a Test match, never mind that his team lost the match by an innings and 58 runs.

Of the leading Westindian batsmen, Challenor scored 29 runs in the match, Fernandes 8, and St. Hill 13. In extenuation, one might observe that several Westindians were already forty years old, or close to that, and were probably past their best. More importantly, Westindies did not have a specialist wicket-keeper, and Nunes, in addition to his duties as captain, deputised courageously behind the stumps. The result was not only dropped chances, but a probable decline in Nunes's batting as well. But there is no need to make excuses. No one could seriously have expected Westindies, in their first Test match, to beat as seasoned a team as England. Constantine, Francis, and Griffith did all that could be expected of them, and would have had better results if the fielding was of better quality. The opening stand in the first innings was also excellent. And in the second innings, Small, Browne and Roach showed a determination lacking in their colleagues higher up. Despite their defeat, Westindies would have been entirely justified in feeling that they had enough resources to do better next time.

Second Test vs. England
Old Trafford, Manchester, England, 21, 23, 24, July, 1928

After they lost their first Test at Lord's in 1928 by an innings and 58 runs, Westindies had mixed experiences against various counties, suggesting that, for all their potential, they lacked consistency as a team. In particular, George Challenor, Learie Constantine and E.L.G. Hoad, who did not play in the first Test, produced some good county performances. The question was whether these could be repeated in the second Test at Old Trafford, for which Westindies brought in Hoad and O.C. Scott, both making their Test début, in place of M.P. Fernandes and J.A. Small. Nunes won the toss, and a determined opening pair - Challenor and Roach - put on 48 before Challenor (24) was run out. Roach and Martin proceeded to build on this good start, and had reached 94 without further loss by lunch time. It was the most favourable position that Westindies enjoyed of the three times they had batted in a Test match. But the satisfaction gained from this lunch time score quickly evaporated after the interval, when three wickets fell rapidly and only 19 runs were added. The visitors had moved, in other words, from 94 for one to 113 for four. And, as if this were not bad enough, Hoad (13) and Constantine (4) were dismissed while another 20 runs were added. At 133 for six, the position could not have been more bleak. Fortunately, there were two modest stands of 25 between Nunes and C.R. Browne, and 27 between Browne and Scott and, in the end, Westindies limped to a total of 206. A.P. "Tich" Freeman, the leg-break specialist was the chief destroyer, taking five wickets for 54 runs in 33.4 overs, while V.W.C. Jupp chipped in with 18 overs for 39 runs and two wickets.

The Westindian bowlers now had their work cut out for them. For one thing, Jack Hobbs, the English star opening batsman who had missed the first Test because of injury, had returned to the side to resume his fabled partnership with Herbert Sutcliffe. It did not take these two veterans long to register their presence: they rattled up 84 runs in merely an hour before play ended on the first day. The next day, Hobbs and Sutcliffe took the score to 119 before Hobbs was caught for 53 by St. Hill off Browne. Sutcliffe went five runs later for 54, caught off Griffith by Nunes who was both captain and wicket-keeper. Ernest Tyldesley, who had made a century in the first Test, was mercifully bowled by Browne for 3, and with the English total at 131 for three, Westindies could consider themselves back in the game with a fighting chance. As luck would have it, a stand of 120 between Walter Hammond and Douglas Jardine thrust England ahead of their opponents and threatened to push the game entirely beyond their grasp. Hammond was finally caught by Roach off Constantine for 63, while Jardine was run out for 83 by a brilliant throw from Constantine, illustrating the priceless value of this great all-rounder who could bat, bowl, or field with equal distinction. After Jardine, the remaining English batsmen did not reveal much stamina, and from 311 for six, they declined to 351 all out. The Westindian bowlers lacked penetration. Constantine could not recapture the fiery spells which he had unleashed, with such success, on some county sides. Griffith was more successful with three wickets for 69 runs in 25 overs. Scott also helped with two wickets for 28 runs, and Browne with two for 72.

Facing a substantial deficit of 145, Challenor and Roach began the Westindian second innings in poor light and were quickly out. Each made 0, although, with the help of extras, they had accumulated a grand total of 2. Yet out of such gloom and disaster, Martin and St. Hill contrived a courageous stand of 55 in which they restored a measure of Westindian self-respect. Martin made 32 and St. Hill 38. Unfortunately, Hammond caught Martin (32) off Freeman, and St. Hill (38) off White before end of play on the second day when the score stood precariously at 71 for four. Since Freeman had already been so destructive, the prospect of facing him on the last day could not have been relished by the surviving Westindian batsmen. Evidently, only a miracle could save them: they were 74 behind with six wickets in hand. In the event, of the six batsmen who remained, only Nunes and Constantine scrambled to double figures, for Freeman cut through the Westindian tail with surgical skill. The visitors were utterly humbled, skittled out for 115 and losing by an innings and 30 runs. Freeman took five wickets for 39 runs in 18 overs, and White three wickets for 41 runs in 14 overs. Having lost their first Test match by an innings and 58 runs, and their second by an innings and 30 runs, Westindies could not have made a more disastrous start in Test cricket.

First Test vs. England
Kensington Oval, Bridgetown, Barbados
11, 13, 14, 15, 16 January, 1930

After their disastrous venture into Test cricket in the summer of 1928 - they lost all three matches against England, each by an innings - Westindies did not play Test cricket for nearly eighteen months until January 1930. The English team which toured Westindies in 1929/30 under the Hon. F.S.G. Calthorpe, was not exactly equal in strength to the one that had trounced Westindies in England eighteen months earlier. The big names - Hobbs, Sutcliffe, Ernest Tyldesley, Hammond, Tate, Larwood - were all missing: these players apparently needed a well-earned rest after their arduous tour of Australia, the winter before, directly followed by an equally arduous summer series against South Africa in 1929. Yet, such was the richness of their cricketing resources in those halcyon days of empire, that with most of their best players at home, England could still send two teams overseas in 1929/30, one including Woolley and Duleepsinjhi to New Zealand, and another to the Westindies that included men of the calibre of Hendren, Ames, and Voce, as well as the more venerable George Gunn (fifty-one years old), and Wilfred Rhodes (fifty-three years old.) By contrast, Westindies presented a more youthful appearance. Although a few players had already toured England, for example, Roach, Constantine and Griffith, some were absolute beginners like the youthful George Headley, and the schoolboy J.E.D. Sealy who, at 17 years and 122 days, was the youngest Test cricketer at the time.

In their first innings in the Bridgetown Test match, the Westindian openers, Roach and his captain Hoad were off to a good start, not being parted before the score had reached 90. Another goodish partnership between Roach and Headley brought the score to 157 before Headley was bowled by O'Connor for 21. Then, 22 runs later, Roach was caught by Hendren off Astill for 122, having completed the first century made by a Westindian in Test cricket. From 179 for three, the Westindian score moved to 303 for four, thanks to a superb partnership of 124 between DeCaires (80) and Sealy (58). The remaining batsmen, including Constantine, Browne, and L.A. Walcott (Clyde's father) did not prosper, and Westindies were all out for 369 which looked slightly disappointing because the last six wickets had made only 66 runs. Still, it was the highest total Westindies had so far achieved in Test cricket. Stevens was the most successful English bowler, taking five wickets for 105 runs in 27 overs. If his figures betray somewhat rough treatment, Voce's figures suggest this more strongly: 27-1-120-2. In England's first innings, when Stevens was run out with the score at 96 for two, Westindies were poised for a breakthrough. But another wicket did not fall until England had reached 264, and that was followed by some good lower order innings particularly from Haig (47) and Calthorpe (40), which enabled England to reach a total of 467. Sandham, the opener, topscored with 152, while Hendren contributed 80. It was a superb partnership of 168 between these two that paved the way for an English lead. Evidently, the Westindian bowlers were no more successful than their English counterparts: the wickets were more or less evenly divided, at heavy cost, among Constantine (3), and Griffith, St. Hill and Browne (2 each).

English tactics now required the use of their lead to press for victory, and when Hoad was caught off Calthorpe for 0, with the Westindian second innings score at 6, these tactics were clearly working. What stopped them was the genius of George Headley. First, with Roach as his partner, Headley took the score to 162 for two, then with DeCaires, he advanced it to 304 for three, by which time Westindies were out of danger. Eventually, they were all out for 384. Roach contributed 77, giving him a match aggregate of 199, and DeCaires 70 which gave him a match aggregate of 150. Headley made the top score - 176 runs - a century in his Test début. England had the impossible task of making 287 for victory in less than three hours; they finished with 167 for three and the match was drawn.

In the Westindian second innings, Stevens was again the most successful English bowler with figures of: 26.4-1-90-5, while in England's brief second knock, Griffith took two wickets for 37 runs. Although a draw may not seem an impressive achievement, it was the best result that Westindies had achieved in the four Test matches they had so far played. In the two innings of this match alone they totalled almost as many runs as they had done in their first two Test matches in England. No doubt it helped for them to be playing at home, and it would be unfair to underestimate the contributions especially of Roach, DeCaires and Sealy. But the main difference between this Westindian team and the one that toured England eighteen months earlier was George Alphonso Headley. There is a story that Headley was all set to leave his native Jamaica to study dentistry in the US, when a delay in obtaining his visa allowed him enough time to play against Lionel Lord Tennyson's visiting English team in 1927/28.

The eighteen-year-old lad made scores of 71 and 211 against the Englishmen, and chose to remain in Jamaica and forget dentistry. Do we dare imagine what might have happened to Westindian cricket if George Headley had obtained his visa in time? Headley was not just the first black Westindian to achieve genuine greatness as a batsman: he was the first Westindian to focus positive world attention on a region, until then, known mainly for sugar and rum, products of a long and shameful history of slavery and exploitation. This is why cricket is not merely a game in the Westindies, where its historical, social, cultural and political implications give it a significance that goes far beyond the realms of sport.

Second Test vs. England
Queen's Park Oval, Port of Spain, Trinidad
1, 3, 4, 5, 6 February, 1930

Having acquitted themselves so creditably in their first Test match on home soil in January 1930, Westindies could approach the second Test of the 1929/30 English tour with some confidence. The first Test draw was their best result so far in Tests, and following it, they must have been heartened to see England beaten in the first colony game in Trinidad. Whether this victory influenced the Westindian selectors is not officially known, but the team which faced England during the second Test included no fewer than seven Trinidadians. England's captain the Hon. F.S.G. Calthorpe won the toss and elected to bat, although he may have regretted it when his batsmen created something of a sensation by losing three wickets in quick succession for 12 runs: Gunn was run out for 1; Sandham, after a century in the first Test, was bowled by Griffith for 0; and Stevens was caught by Small off Constantine for 8. Hendren stemmed this tide of destruction by adding 49 runs with O'Connor, and 81 with Ames. At 142 for five, however, England were scarcely out of the woods, and the Westindian fast bowlers, Griffith and Constantine, polished off the remaining five English wickets for 66 runs.

England's total of 208 runs was the lowest they had compiled against Westindies in a complete innings: it was an achievement largely of Griffith and Constantine who took seven wickets between them. Constantine claimed two wickets for 42 runs in 16.1 overs, while Griffith collected five wickets for 63 runs in 22 overs. Were it not for the pluck of Hendren (77) and wicket-keeper Ames (42), there is no telling what greater humiliation these two might not have inflicted on England. At any rate, 208 runs were not at all a bad total for a team to confront in its quest of their first victory in a Test match. Yet, no sooner had their innings started than Roach, who had made 199 in both innings of the first Test, was clean bowled by Voce for 0. Hunte and St. Hill held the English bowlers at bay while compiling 89 runs until the latter was lbw to Astill for 33. Then, fresh from his triumphant 176 in the first Test, George Headley (8) was hit wicket to Voce: 104 for three. As if all this was not horror enough, the normally resolute DeCaires was caught and bowled by Voce for 0, which brought the score to 104 for four and severely dented any Westindian hope of victory. In truth, England's originally fragile-seeming 208 now took on a less fragile aspect and, by the time Westindies had reached 168 for seven, looked distinctly formidable. But this match had changed direction more than once already, and it now produced another change that completely warmed Westindian hearts; for Constantine, who had not found form in any of the four Tests that he (and Westindies) had so far played, chose the occasion to reveal that penchant for hurricane hitting which had made him justly famous in county games: in barely fifty minutes, he slammed 52 desperately needed runs to catapult his team to a total of 254 and a slender lead of 46.

For England, Voce and Astill each took four wickets. Astill's wickets came in 24.2 overs and cost 58 runs, while Voce used 28 overs and yielded 79 runs; but it was the latter who did the worst damage by accounting for Roach, Headley, DeCaires and Constantine, potentially the most dangerous of the Westindian batsmen. As if to match the sensation of their first innings start, England again found themselves struggling at 52 for three in their second innings. Never before were Westindies so close to victory in a Test match: at that stage, England were only six runs ahead with seven wickets intact. Yet this much sought after victory seemed not yet to have assumed a rightful place in the constellation of Westindian stars, and the home team accordingly endured a resistance of truly grand heroism mounted once more by Hendren and Ames, who came together in a fourth-wicket stand of 237 runs that thrust England to 289 before Ames was caught by a substitute off Small for 105. For his part, Hendren was on 205, still not out, when Calthorpe declared at 425 for eight. It was a magnificent, fighting knock that pulled England out of the jaws of defeat and, simultaneously, if unexpectedly, transported them within reach of victory. Hendren's 205 was also the first double century in Tests between England and Westindies.

Again, Constantine and Griffith were the most successful Westindian bowlers, although with less impressive figures than in the first innings - Constantine: 40-4-165-4; and Griffith: 38-8-99-3. If Westindies failed to win this match, the reason, as in the first Test, was with their bowling more than anything else. The English bowlers now had their tails up, and Voce, in particular, displayed real venom in the final innings when Westindies needed 380 to win. There were credible displays of defiance especially from DeCaires (45) and Headley (39); but these were not enough to prevent the innings from falling completely apart: Westindies reached a total of 212, thereby conceding victory by 167 runs. The record, at that stage, was that Westindies had played five Test matches, all against England, and had lost four while drawing one. Most of the English bowlers contributed to their memorable second Test victory, the spearhead of which was Bill Voce who returned the extraordinary figures of: 37.2-15-70-7. His bowling proved a perfect complement to the heroic batting effort of Hendren and Ames. This match is interesting for at least two reasons. For one thing, to play seven Trinidadians belies the representative nature of the Westindian team, especially since four of these players - Betancourt,

Grell, Small and St. Hill - were never picked in a Test match again. For Grell and Nelson Betancourt who captained the side, this was their first as well as last Test match. Secondly, Headley's failure signalled the vital role he was destined to play in Westindian cricket: if anyone had the strokes, stamina, temperament, and skill to repulse England, it was him. This meant that for the foreseeable future, Westindian fortunes were intimately linked to the performance of George Headley. An interesting footnote to this match is that E.A.C. Hunte, the Westindian wicket-keeper, is recorded as R.L. Hunte, because a copy typist misheard "R.L." for "Errol". The result was that Hunte was given two separate career records.

Third Test vs. England
Bourda, Georgetown, Guyana, 21, 22, 24, 25, 26 February, 1930

Despite their unauspicious entry into Test cricket in 1928, when they lost their first three Test matches, each by an innings, Westindies were hopeful at the start of their next encounter, once more against England, but this time in the Westindies, in 1929/30. For the new series Westindies discarded older players like Challenor and Nunes, and brought in fresh blood, not only DeCaires and Sealy, but also George Alphonso Headley. A Barbadian, E.L.G. Hoad had captained Westindies in the Barbados Test, and in Trinidad, a Trinidadian Nelson Betancourt. Now Maurice Fernandes, a Guyanese, was chosen as captain for the third Test at Bourda.

Westindies began their first innings of the third Test as follows: 144 for one; 336 for two; 400 for three. One opener E.A.C. Hunte was dropped four times in making 53, but the other opener, Roach, who had made a "pair" in the Trinidad Test, contributed a brilliant 209, including three sixes and 22 fours. It was the first double century by a Westindian in a Test, and it confirmed the historical value of Roach's batting since he had already gained the distinction of scoring the first Westindian Test century in the first Test of the same series. Roach was vigorously supported by Headley who made 114, but after they left, Westindies collapsed to 471 all out. It was a solid total nevertheless, if only the Westindian bowlers could match the success of their batsmen. Happily they did so, skittling England out for 145. Francis, who snatched four wickets for 40 in 21 overs, and Constantine four for 35 in 16 overs, had given Westindies a real chance for the first Westindian victory in a Test match.

With a lead of 326, Fernandes played safe and batted again. Indeed, cautious batting cost Westindies dearly in their second innings, except for Headley who scored yet another glorious century (112). Headley received support from C.R. Browne (70 not out), while none of their colleagues could rise above 22 in a Westindian total of 290. At the time, Headley was the fifth batsman in cricket history to score a century in each innings of a Test, and the first to do so before the age of 21. At any rate, faced with the impossible task of scoring 617 to win, the English batsmen craftily tried to play out time. They were led by Hendren in yet another valiant innings, this time of 123. But Constantine bowled with unrelenting fire to take five wickets for 87 runs, and England could muster only 327 runs, their last wicket falling fifteen minutes before stumps were finally drawn. It was a close-run thing, and although Westindies won by the substantial margin of 289 runs, what a calamity it would have been if Fernandes's safety-first tactics had allowed England to play out time, and deny Westindies their first Test victory ever! It was a victory too sweet for words. But far sweeter was the performance of George Headley. It does not discredit the contributions of other Westindian players to say, not only in this match, but throughout the 1930s, that Headley carried Westindies on his shoulders.

Fourth Test vs. England
Sabina Park, Kingston, Jamaica
3, 4, 5, 7, 8, 9, 10, 11 (no play), 12 (no play), April, 1930

The fourth Test match between Westindies and England in April 1930 produced 1815 runs - the highest total of runs ever scored by two sides in a Test match, except for the 1,981 runs scored by South Africa and England in their equally extraordinary, play-to-finish match in Durban, South Africa in 1939. The fourth Test was the last in England's 1929/30 tour of Westindies. Since each side had already won one match while one was drawn, the fourth Test would decide the rubber, and to facilitate a decision it was agreed to play to finish. The two England/Jamaica matches immediately preceding the fourth Test produced high scores. In the second innings of the first match Andy Sandham, who opened for England, made 155 and shared a partnership of 322 with George Gunn (176). In the second match which produced a total of 1,236 runs, Sandham (126) again excelled, while C.C. Passailaigue made 183 for Jamaica.

These two matches probably raised expectations of high scoring in the fourth Test; but it is doubtful that anyone could have expected England, who batted first, to run up a total of 849 in their first innings. This is the highest total in·Test matches between England and Westindies. At the time, it was the highest innings total in Test matches, but it was exceeded by England's 903 for seven declared against Australia at Kennington Oval in 1938 when Len Hutton made his celebrated 364. Because of his superb form in the colony matches, it was not surprising that Sandham again figured prominently among England's batsmen. He made the top score - 325 - which was then the highest individual score by any batsman in a Test match, surpassing the existing record of 287 made by R.E. Foster for England against Australia at Sydney in 1903. George Gunn (85) joined Sandham in a first wicket partnership of 173, and with the score at 418 for three, Ames (149) joined in another partnership of 249. The pitch was evidently harmless and runs bountiful; yet it took stamina for Sandham to bat for more than ten hours. It is interesting that twenty-eight years later, his record was overtaken twice in the same Westindian home series, firstly by Hanif Mohammed (337), and secondly by Sir Garfield Sobers (365 not out).

In their defence one must admit that Westindies were without the services of probably the most dangerous members of their fast attack - George Francis and Learie Constantine. Consequently, the brunt of the bowling fell on Herman Griffith and O.C. Scott. Scott's figures were 80.2 overs for 266 runs and five wickets. If Westindies lacked two of their best strike bowlers, their batting at least was intact. Yet, except for captain R.K. Nunes who opened their first innings and scored 66 runs, no other Westindian batsman reached 50, and the side were all out for 286. At this stage, with an English lead of 563 runs, it seems incredible that England's captain the Hon. F.S.G. Calthorpe did not enforce the follow-on. Instead, he allowed England to bat again and add another 272 runs before declaring for nine wickets. Again, it was Griffith and Scott who did most of the bowling, with Scott achieving four wickets for 108 runs in 25 overs. With a match analysis of nine wickets for 374 runs, Scott holds the record for the most runs conceded in a Test match. The fact that the match was play-to-finish and the threat of imminent rain probably entered Calthorpe's calculations, and persuaded him to bat again in order to avoid any possibility of England batting last on a rain-affected wicket. At any rate, what he now offered Westindies was daunting if not preposterous - 836 runs to win, with the threat of rain at any time.

The Westindian start to their second innings was not encouraging. Roach (22) was caught by Gunn off Rhodes with the score at 44. But Nunes and Headley plastered 227 runs on the board in an exhilarating second-wicket stand that ended with Nunes being bowled by Astill for 92. Soon afterwards, the rains came when the match had reached its seventh day and the Westindian total was 408 for five. For two days it rained, preventing play, and eventually forcing a draw since the English players had to return home to meet their commitments in county cricket. This indecisive end came after nine days, at which stage Westindies still needed 428 runs for victory with five - mainly tailend - wickets intact. It is pointless to speculate whether Westindies could have won if the weather had not intervened. The crucial fact is that Headley was already out, stumped off Wyatt for 223. In the four Test matches of his first series, Headley had made 703 runs for an average of 87.87. He hit four centuries including one in his first Test, one in each innings of the third Test, and a double century in the fourth Test. As if these prodigious feats of batsmanship were not enough by themselves, Headley accomplished them when he was still 20 years old! Headley was the youngest batsman to be credited with a double century until Pakistan's Javed Miandad achieved this feat at the age of 19 years, 141 days, in the third Test against New Zealand at Karachi in 1976, but he (Headley) remains the only batsman to score four centuries before the age of twenty-one. Such feats suggest that Headley was the greatest of all Westindian batsmen; for his batting pointed his team and nation in an entirely new direction. Before him, Westindies had lost all three of the Test matches they had played. After he joined the team at the beginning of the 1929/30 English tour, they were able to draw the series by winning one match, losing another, and drawing two others. What Headley had done was to provide a spectacle that caught the attention of a wider Westindian audience than had ever before witnessed a similar enterprise of collective or national distinction. The political result, whether Westindians then realized it or not, was to stimulate latent feelings of self-awareness and nationalism, and engender more articulate forms of expression that would lead Westindies away from colonial domination, and set them more steadfastly on the road to political self-determination.

Third Test vs. Australia
Exhibition Ground, Brisbane, Australia
16,17,19,20 January, 1931

During the English tour of Westindies in 1929/30, there was a different captain for each of the four Tests, but none of them was chosen to lead the team to Australia at the end of 1930. Instead, the selectors chose G.C. (Jackie) Grant, a young Trinidadian who had averaged 44.75 for Cambridge University in 1930, and had made a century against Sussex, but had never been captain of a first class eleven. This unusual situation of four captains in their second Test series, and a complete neophyte in their third illustrates the problem of captaincy that plagued Westindies right through to 1960; for Grant's selection suggests that playing ability and leadership qualities were not the only criteria for a Westindian cricket captain, at least not in the 1930s.

From the opening matches of the tour, Westindies knew they were up against it. They lost by four wickets against New South Wales; by an innings against Victoria; and by ten wickets against South Australia; so no one was greatly surprised when they were beaten by ten wickets in the first Test at Adelaide. What was surprising was that they got Australia out for 376. Unfortunately, their batsmen did not match the achievement of the bowlers. Whatever the circumstances of his selection as captain, Grant took his responsibilities seriously in the first Test, making 53 in the first innings, and 71 (the top score) in the second; but his batting efforts alone could not protect his team from their fate. A worse fate lay in store for Westindies in the second Test: they lost by an innings and 172 runs. Again they exceeded themselves by dismissing the powerful Australian batting line-up - Ponsford, Bradman, Kippax, McCabe and all - for a mere 369; but again their batsmen failed.

With these two defeats behind them, Westindian prospects for the third Test were not exactly encouraging. Their two brightest stars - Headley and Constantine - which had blazed with such incandescence against England in the Westindies only months before - had faded out almost completely: in the four Test innings they had played, Headley had scored 27 runs, and Constantine 35; in addition Constantine had captured two wickets for 145 runs. Added to these tribulations was the ominous fact that Bradman had not yet come off: in the two Australian innings so far completed, he had made 4 and 25. Surely a Bradman blitz was imminent! No wonder that his massive presence and authority were both royally registered in the third Test with an innings of 223 out of an Australian total of 558. This gives some idea of what the Westindian bowlers had achieved in the first two Tests to restrict Australia to scores under 400. The truth is that Westindies had again started off well in the third Test when Francis bowled the Australian opener Jackson for 0 and the score was 1 for 1. But Ponsford and Bradman then seized command and blasted 229 runs before Ponsford was caught by Birkett off Francis for 109. One wonders what might have happened if Bradman had not been dropped in the slips off Constantine when he was 4. If that is speculation, there is nothing speculative about the fact that Bradman's 223 was then the highest Test score by an Australian in an home series.

Roach and Martin opened for Westindies and Roach (4) was lbw to Oxenham when the total was 5. Headley and Martin had just begun to repair the damage when Grimmett had Martin (21) lbw: 36 for two. Martin's departure signalled a regular procession of Westindian batsmen as they came in and out of one end while Headley maintained a lonely, despairing vigil at the other. For apart from Headley himself (102) only Martin and wicket-keeper Barrow (19) reached double figures. Headley's 102 was the first century scored by a Westindian against Australia, and one can imagine his feelings as he watched his colleagues so completely mesmerized by Grimmett, Ironmonger and Oxenham that Westindies managed no more than 193 runs. The bowling figures were: Grimmett: 41.3-9-95-4; Ironmonger: 26-15-43-2; Oxenham: 30-15-39-4. Headley's success itself is partly due to changes that he made in his grip and stance to reduce his vulnerability to Grimmett. He had found in the first two Tests that his preference for off-side play had made him vulnerable to Grimmett's leg-breaks.

Forced to follow on, 365 runs behind, Westindies fared worse in their second innings with Grimmett proving almost unplayable. So complete was the rout that apart from Headley (28) no one else reached 20, and the entire team was dismissed for 148, thus losing by an innings and 217 runs - their worst defeat in the ten Test matches they had so far played. Grimmett bagged five wickets for 49 runs in 14.3 overs; Oxenham two for 37 in 18 overs; and Ironmonger and McCabe one wicket each. In both innings Grimmett had acquired nine wickets for 144 runs. Not even against England, on their very first Test series three years earlier, had Westindies been so humiliated. One reason was the nugatory effect of their principal weapon - three strike bowlers, Francis, Constantine, and Griffith - who encountered pitches unhelpful to fast bowling. In picking these three, the Westindian selectors expected hard surfaces that would help speed and bounce like pitches in the Westindies. Instead, the Australian wickets helped slow bowlers, and Westindies had selected only one specialist slow bowler - O.C. Scott. Australia were therefore able to run up huge totals, and through their specialist slow men, Grimmett and Ironmonger, to make light work of the Westindian batsmen. Other mitigating factors were Grant's inexperience as captain and the time that Headley took to adjust his grip and stance.

Fifth Test vs. Australia
Sydney Cricket Ground, Sydney, Australia
27, 28 February, 2, 3, 4, March, 1931

Of the seven Test matches Westindies played between 1928 and 1930, England won four, Westindies one, and two were drawn. This was not exactly a bright Test cricket beginning for Westindies; but individual players had distinguished themselves. George Headley, for example, hit a century in each innings of the Third Test played in Guyana in February, 1929; Roach made 209 in the same Test; and Francis and Constantine often produced fast bowling that struck blind terror in the hearts of some of their English opponents. It was therefore interesting when Westindies were invited to tour Australia in 1930/31, a time when Australia had players of the calibre of Ponsford, Kippax, McCabe and Grimmett, not to mention Don Bradman, then at an early stage of establishing his reputation as the most prodigious run-getting machine the world had yet seen. The ensuing encounter is a woeful tale of brutish domination that, even from this distance in time, more than fifty years later, excites sorrow and pity. Seldom can a team have suffered such humiliation: they lost the first four Tests by the following margins - ten wickets; an innings and 172 runs; an innings and 217 runs; and an innings and 122 runs. In the first match, Australia only needed their openers in their second innings to win, while in the remaining three matches they did not need a second innings at all. Kippax had made a century, Ponsford two, and as one might expect, Bradman made 223 in the third Test, and 152 in the fourth. In the fourth Test, Ironmonger took seven Westindian wickets for 23 runs in 20 overs. How Westindies endured such slaughter and survived as a team is impossible to imagine, especially since they had equally bad luck in the intervening state matches. To their credit, they did not disintegrate, and after their defeat in the fourth Test, they actually rallied to beat New South Wales by 86 runs. This victory undoubtedly helped to revive their battered morale and restore some confidence before they faced Australia again in the fifth and final Test.

On the opening day of the fifth Test, the Westindian skipper Jack Grant won the toss and elected to bat on a perfect wicket. At last things looked as if they would work out for him and his team. Not only did George Headley fulfil his role as mainstay by making a century, but F.R. Martin, the Jamaican opener whose highest score in the previous Tests was 39, suddenly produced a brilliant innings of 123 not out. One writer has said it was the best innings of Martin's life; and it helped Westindies to declare at a total of 350 for six wickets. Grant declared because rain had fallen on the second day and made the wicket suspect. He hoped to trap the Australians on a deteriorating pitch, and succeeded completely as Australia tumbled unceremoniously to 224 all out, Francis taking four wickets for 48 runs in 19 overs, and Martin two for 67. With a lead of 126, Westindies now found themselves caught on the same wearing pitch; but they struggled on bravely, Roach making 34 and Headley 30. At the end of the third day, they were 124 for five with Grant 27 not out. The fourth day was completely lost because of rain.

When play resumed on the fifth day Grant promptly declared setting Australia 251 for victory. Since it was a play-to-finish game, Grant's decision was bold, to say the least. As usual, if he succeeded, he would be credited with splendid instincts, astuteness and fine tactical judgment; if he failed he would be accused of recklessness and a lack of proper sympathy for the men he was leading. But when, soon after play started, Griffith bowled Bradman for 0, Grant knew that he had been justified, and his men knew that God had restored justice to the world by offering them hope of redemption. At long last might they be delivered from the Australian scourge. No doubt inspired by such thoughts, Griffith and Constantine launched a fierce attack that knocked away the pride of Australia's batting and, by lunch, had the enemy reeling at 74 for five. After lunch, Fairfax and McCabe put up stiff and determined resistance; but Westindies were not to be denied. They could sniff victory, and the scent itself so unnerved them that they made mistakes in the field that could very well have let victory slip from their grasp. In the end, however, they won by the narrow margin of 30 runs. The narrowness of the margin did not matter. They had suddenly come alive and beaten Australia for the first time! What is more, they had done so after being pulverized in four previous matches and being given up for dead. It was a truly miraculous recovery, for Australia had given nothing away: they fought hard to the bitter end.

It is true that Westindies lost the series 4:1; but the importance of this match is that it was the first Test victory gained by Westindies outside of their home territory. It was also important in confirming Westindian potential both to Westindians themselves and to the cricketing world at large. It would be another twenty years before Westindies would tour Australia again. By that time George Headley would have retired, Jack Grant would be a missionary in Africa, and Constantine would be studying law in England. But such players would be replaced by others - Weekes, Worrell, Walcott, Ramadhin and Valentine - who would lay England low in 1950, and threaten to do the same to Australia in 1951/52.

First Test vs. England
Lord's, London, England, 24, 26, 27 June 1933

By the summer of 1933, Westindies had played twelve Test matches in all, seven against England, and five against Australia. Their results against both countries were equally dismal: four matches lost, and one won, except that they also drew a couple of matches against England. With such a record behind them, Westindies evidently saw their tour of England in 1933 as an opportunity to redeem themselves. There were some initial difficulties: Learie Constantine could not obtain continuous release from obligations with his club (Nelson) in league cricket, and F.R. Martin, one of the most reliable Westindian batsmen, was injured early on the tour and missed all three Tests. Nevertheless, Westindies acquitted themselves creditably in the preliminary matches up to the first Test. In a match in which O.C. DaCosta made 105 not out, they achieved their first victory of the tour, against Essex, and followed this up with a ten-wicket victory against Cambridge University. Most impressive of all, they defeated a powerful M.C.C team at Lord's by 152 runs. This was a remarkable victory in which Headley made 129 runs, and Constantine, in his own inimitable fashion, hit a whirlwind 51 out of 66 runs in merely twenty-five minutes. Westindies also beat Hampshire, and drew other county matches before the first Test. In the course of these encounters, several of their batsmen made centuries, while Headley made two double centuries, one against Somerset and the other against Derbyshire.

The English team that faced the tourists in the first Test had themselves just returned from a winter tour in which, under Douglas Jardine, they had inflicted a 4:1 walloping on Australia. It was the notorious bodyline tour in which English fast bowlers, Harold Larwood and Bill Voce in particular, were accused of intimidating bowling. For good or ill, neither Larwood nor Voce appeared in the England side facing Westindies in the first Test in 1933. The opening day of the Test was virtually washed out by rain. Only forty-five minutes of play were possible, during which time the English openers made 43 runs. The next day, England went on to a total of 296 runs in which the top scorers were C.F. Walters (51) and wicket-keeper L.E.G. Ames (83 not out). The most successful Westindian bowlers were the fast men: E.A. Martindale with four wickets for 85 runs in 24 overs, and H.C. Griffith - three wickets for 48 runs in 20 overs. Left arm spinner Ellis Achong, who has the distinction of being the only player of Chinese background to play Test cricket for the Westindies, took two for 88 in 35 overs.

One would not think 296 a match-winning score, but Westindies contrived to make it look like that when, in just over ninety minutes, they lost six wickets and scored 55 miserly runs. Eventually, they were dismissed for 97, and one shudders to think what their total might have been had not captain Grant (26) and Achong (15) hit out with some success. One can gauge the acute discomfort of the Westindian batsmen from the mere figures of the English bowlers: G.O.B. Allen sent down 13 overs for 13 runs and two wickets, while Hedley Verity contributed 16 overs for 21 runs and one wicket. But it was R.W.V. Robins who was the chief scourge, sending down 11.5 overs and acquiring six wickets for 32 runs. Westindies were 0 for one wicket when Roach was caught off Macauly for 0 to give him a "pair" in the match. (Roach had previously made a "pair" in the second Test against England in 1930.) Headley went on to 50 before he was bowled by Allen, and, as so often, his departure spelt disaster, since only Grant (28) and Hoad (36) offered much resistance. Together, Grant and Hoad added 52 for the fourth wicket, and held out some hope of saving the match. But once they were gone, wickets fell rapidly to bring the score to 146 for nine. Then the Westindian fast bowlers G.N. Francis and H.C. Griffith hoisted the third highest partnership of the innings - 26, before Griffith was bowled by Verity for 18. It was the end of the innings and the match: Westindies were all out for 172, and lost by an innings and 27 runs. This time, wickets were more evenly shared among the English bowlers, G.G. Macaulay taking four for 57, Verity four for 45, and Allen and Robins one wicket each. These bowlers still dominated the match even if the Westindian batsmen did somewhat better against them in their second innings. Like the first Test in the second Westindian tour of England, this Lord's match certainly deserves to be remembered. It was the fourth Test that Westindies had played in England, and not only had they lost all four, but they had lost each by the margin of an innings.

Second Test vs. England
Old Trafford, Manchester, England, 22, 24, 25 July, 1933

After a crushing defeat in the first Test of their tour of England in 1933, Westindies did not fare any better in the county matches that immediately followed. Yorkshire, for example, beat them decisively by 200 runs, Hedley Verity taking 14 wickets in the match for 83 runs. But amidst the gloom there were a few good Westindian performances: against Yorkshire, Learie Constantine claimed nine wickets for 94 runs, and against Nottinghamshire, Martindale had eight wickets for 66 runs. For the second Test match at Old Trafford, Westindies dropped Francis, Griffith and Merry, and brought in Constantine, Wiles and Valentine. Grant won the toss and decided to bat. With the score at 26, opener Roach was bowled by Clark for 13, and it looked as if Westindies were once more heading for disaster. But on a perfect wicket, two Jamaicans - George Headley and Ivan Barrow - called a decisive halt to such gloom by mounting a magnificent double century stand that proved to be the highest partnership Westindies had yet achieved in England. In addition, by reaching his century before Headley, Barrow gained the distinction of being the first Westindian to score a Test century in England. With the score at 226 Barrow was bowled by Wyatt for 105, while Headley went serenely on until the end of the first day's play when the score was 333 for six and he was 145 not out.

The next morning Westindies were out for 375, their highest Test score in England up to that time, and Headley was left undefeated with 169, an innings without blemish, and one that deserves primal place in any responsible history of Westindian batsmanship. During the Westindian innings, Clark employed so-called bodyline bowling, that is to say, fast, short-pitched deliveries in line of the batsman's body, with a packed leg-side field waiting to snap up snicks or deflections. Jardine, Clark's captain, had also captained England in Australia the previous winter when England were accused of bodyline tactics. At any rate, Clark finished with four wickets for 99 runs, and Robins with three for 111. Verity also returned impressive figures of 32 overs for 47 runs and two wickets. The Westindian fast bowlers Constantine and Martindale retaliated with bodyline tactics against the English batsmen, and soon had England in a vulnerable position at 134 for four. At one stage, Walter Hammond was cut on his chin by a short-pitched ball from Martindale and had to retire briefly. Nevertheless, Jardine and Ames added 83 runs for the fifth wicket until Ames was caught by Headley off Martindale for 47. When Langridge was caught by Grant off Achong for 9, and their score was 234 for six, England were very vulnerable indeed. But as if to prove to his critics that bodyline bowling could be mastered, Jardine proceeded to play a defiant innings of 127. Receiving help from Robins (55), he took his side to 374 for seven, one run behind Westindies. Then, the remaining English wickets fell without another run added and Westindies retained their slender lead. Martindale had the best figures: 23.4-4-73-5, while Constantine gave good support with 25-5-55-1, and Achong: 37-9-90-2.

Since the match was well into the final day, the Westindian second innings was likely to be mere batting practice. But Barrow was soon out for 0, and although Roach (64) and Headley (24) were engaged in a reassuring stand of 81 runs, wickets fell rapidly, and Westindies faced real danger at 132 for seven. Luckily for Westindies, this was the cue for one of Constantine's swashbuckling bashes. With Achong (10) as his partner, he slammed 59 runs in fifty minutes, and by the time he was bowled by Langridge, he had scored 64 of the 93 runs that were added since the fall of the seventh wicket. Thanks to Constantinian ebullience, Westindies reached a total of 225 runs which ensured a draw, since there was no time left for England even to start their second innings. Of the English bowlers, Langridge was by far the best, taking seven wickets for 56 runs in 17 overs. Memorable features of the match include Barrow's century, the highest total (375) for Westindies in a Test match in England up to that time, and the result itself - a draw - by which Westindies had avoided defeat for the first time in a Test match in England.

First Test vs. England
Kensington Oval, Bridgetown, Barbados, 8, 9, 10, January, 1935

In the first Test of their 1934/35 tour of the Westindies, Wyatt, the English captain won the toss and put Westindies in to bat, guessing that the uncovered pitch had been seriously affected by the persistent rain that fell in the days immediately preceding the match. He was proved right when his fastest bowler Ken Farnes returned four Westindian batsmen to the pavilion in quick march. Soon, Westindies had lost half their side for 15 runs; but the remaining Westindian batsmen soldiered on, eventually reaching a total of 102. This was due mainly to a plucky innings of 15 from Hylton and a dexterous knock of 44 runs from George Headley. Headley had the good fortune to be dropped twice, but it nevertheless took skill to survive on such a pitch for two whole hours. The

Westindians hastened to repay the Englishmen with a dose of their own medicine before night fell, and such was their success that they had reduced England to 81 runs for five wickets by the time stumps were drawn.

Because of more rain overnight, play did not resume until after tea the next day. In the very first over, the two overnight English batsmen were out without addition to the score. Then did Wyatt initiate tactics that would create for this match a reputation as one of the most memorable ever played in the Caribbean. With his team still 21 runs behind Westindies, Wyatt declared the English first innings closed. His hope was to trap some of the better Westindian batsmen, in treacherous batting conditions, in case the pitch were to improve the following day. To counter these tactics, Grant opened with his tailenders. The wisdom of this move could be questioned when, with four runs scored, three Westindian batsmen had gone. With considerable courage, Hylton and Christiani stood their ground against the English menace, preferring to be hit on the body rather than put their bat in the way of the ball. Nor were they above some gamesmanship, taking the longest time to recover from each blow, and using up just as much time to "garden" the pitch after each delivery. In this fashion, they staved off further disaster until play ended with Westindies on 33 for three wickets.

It rained again that night, and play did not start on the final day until half past three. By tea-time, Westindies had lost three more wickets while they added 18 runs. At this point, Grant demonstrated his boldest tactical move: he declared during the tea interval, giving England plenty of time to score 73 runs for victory. Whether this was a stroke of genius, or a fool's gamble would soon be revealed. Wyatt didn't treat Grant's move as foolish. As Grant had done the preceding afternoon, he took the precaution of sending in his tailend batsmen first, with instructions to attempt to knock the Westindian bowlers off their length. But his batsmen ran into a ferocious spell of fast bowling from Martindale, spearhead of the Westindian attack. In no time at all, England plunged to 49 runs for six wickets of which Martindale claimed five. Thus was the match poised in its final hour with England needing 20 runs for victory and Westindies five wickets to win. In normal circumstances, if the English batting order had not been changed, those twenty runs might have cost England dearly. Now, with Hammond and Hendren still batting, the 20 runs came easily, and as if to rub salt into Grant's wounds, Hammond made the winning stroke with a mighty hit for six off none other than Martindale.

The wonder is that Westindies came so close to winning. Did Grant really believe that his men could bowl out an English team containing Maurice Leyland, Walter Hammond, "Patsy" Hendren and L.E.G. Ames for fewer that 73 runs? Like most such decisions, if it had succeeded, Grant would have been praised for shrewdness, initiative and coolness of nerve. In the event, he was criticized for losing the match. At the same time, Grant's severest critics would not deny that he played a central role in a thrilling match of extraordinary tactical moves, brilliant improvisation and challenging generalship. In his autobiography, written almost fifty years after the match, Grant says that his decision to declare a second time was justified "if our bowlers bowled as well as they had done in the first innings".

But he admits that there was a lapse in his bowlers' form, and that Hammond and Hendren got away with some "judicious hitting". Grant's final comment sets the matter to rest: "I accept all the criticism levelled at me. It was fully deserved - I would make the same decision again." (*Jack Grant's Story*, p.38)

Fourth Test vs. England
Sabina Park, Kingston, Jamaica, 14,15,16,18 March, 1935

When the fourth Test match between Westindies and England opened at Sabina Park in March 1935, the series was evenly balanced: England had won the first Test in Barbados, Westindies the second in Trinidad, while the third in Guyana was drawn; the fourth and final Test would decide the rubber. England made one change from their third Test team, bringing in Farnes for Leyland, whereas Westindies replaced Wishart, Jones and Neblett with Barrow, Mudie and Fuller. On a good wicket, Barrow and Christiani opened for Westindies, but Barrow was quickly bowled by Farnes for 3. Headley and Christiani advanced the score to 92 before Christiani (27) was bowled by Paine. This was followed by a remarkable partnership of 202 runs between Headley and Sealy - then a record for the Westindian second wicket against England. Sealy contributed 91, the second time in the series that he had gotten out in the nineties. The next batsman, Constantine, launched into a spate of fast and furious hitting which rattled up 34 runs in double quick time. When he left, the score was 352 for four. Mudie and Fuller did not last long. Meanwhile, George Headley continued to play an anchoring role, while building another mighty score like the 223 he made on the same ground five years earlier. In Rolph Grant, younger brother of captain Jack Grant, Headley found another partner, like Sealy, who was able to stay with him. Together, they moved the score from 381 for six to 528 for seven. Grant made 77 and their partnership of 147 was then a seventh-wicket record for Westindies against England. When Westindies declared at 535 for seven it was the highest total they had ever achieved, and Headley's 270 not out was then the highest individual Test score by a Westindian; it remained so for twenty-three years until it was surpassed by Sobers's 365 not out against Pakistan in 1958. Headley had batted for over eight hours, and hit thirty fours while giving one chance. The main bowling for England was done by Hollies (46 overs) and Paine (56 overs.) Paine was more successful with five wickets for 168 runs, while Hollies took one wicket for 114 runs.

England's reply was marred by tragedy when their captain - Wyatt - opened with Townsend: Wyatt sustained a fractured jaw from a ball by Martindale which sent him to hospital and put him out of the match. This blow plus the blistering pace of the Westindian fast bowlers - Martindale, Hylton and Constantine - created such unrelenting psychological and physical pressure on the English batsmen that they all but caved in. Paine and Holmes failed to score, and three wickets fell at the same total - 26. At 26 for four, England appeared demoralized, their main tormentors

47

being Martindale and Constantine. But in the midst of such gloom, wicket-keeper Ames struck a partnership with Hendren, then forty-six years old and playing his last match for England. Hendren made 40 and helped Ames in a face-saving stand of 69 for the fifth wicket. Then Ames and Iddon added 157 together. Iddon made 54 and Ames 126, the only English Test century of the tour. Ames's effort cannot be praised enough, and in the end he succumbed to a superb catch by Constantine fielding at mid-off to Mudie's bowling. His contribution was the cornerstone of the English total of 271. Out of this total, Ames, Hendren and Iddon contributed 220 runs altogether! Hylton bowled 19 overs for 59 runs, and Rolph Grant 16 overs for 48 runs and one wicket. Mudie took two wickets for 23 runs in 17 overs. But England's chief destroyers undoubtedly were Martindale: 17-1-56-3, and Constantine: 23.2-4-55-3.

Forced to follow on 264 runs behind their opponents, and still without the services of their captain, England opened their second innings with Townsend and Iddon who was immediately lbw to Constantine for 0. When, shortly afterwards, Townsend was bowled by Martindale for 11, England were 18 for two and appeared to be losing their grip on the whole enterprise. It was to shed the light of his experience on this fading enterprise that Hendren was promoted in the batting order; but he was caught by Constantine off Mudie for 11: 45 for three. In Wyatt's absence, that meant 45 for four, and unless another knight in shining armour materialized, like Ames in the first innings, England were doomed. But, in times of old as nowadays, chivalry was rare, especially when fast bowlers like Martindale and Constantine were operating. Ames managed 17 in his second innings, and Hammond secured the top score of 34. No other batsman reached 20, and five didn't reach double figures. England collapsed to 103 and Westindies won by an innings and 161 runs soon after lunch on the fourth day. Martindale's figures in the second innings were: 16-5-28-4, and Constantine's: 9-3-13-3. Mudie and Sealy also took one wicket each, but Martindale and Constantine were clearly the match winners once Headley, Sealy and Grant had given them enough runs to bowl at. In the match as a whole Martindale had taken seven wickets for 84 runs and Constantine six for 68. After seven years of Test cricket, Westindies had established a reputation for superlative fast bowling that lasts up to today. This had proved to be a match of records: of the four Test victories Westindies had so far gained, this had the largest margin. More importantly, this match gave Westindies their first Test rubber. But perhaps most important of all, in view of the racial diversity of the Westindies and their history of colonialism, is the historic fact that this Test provided the first occasion for a black man - Constantine - to lead the Westindian team. Not that he was appointed captain: Jack Grant sprained his ankle early in the English second innings and Constantine took his place. Christopher Nicole comments as follows on Constantine's performance: "Constantine took over the leadership and proved himself even more astute than the former leader" (*Westindian Cricket*, p.38) For Nicole, himself a white Westindian, to say that about an event in 1935, and for Westindians to wait for another quarter of a century before a black captain - Worrell - was appointed for a whole series, explains why there was such a fuss about the Westindian captaincy in the 1950s.

First Test vs. England
Lord's, London, England, 24, 26, 27 June, 1939

The 1939 Test series between Westindies and England was fought under the shadow of a much more dangerous battle - the second world war. Having arrived in England in spring that year, Westindies completed their three Test matches, but were unable to finish five of their remaining scheduled matches before they were instructed to board ship for Montreal. They arrived in Montreal on 3rd September, the day that England declared war on Germany. Jeff Stollmeyer who was an eighteen-year-old lad on the Westindian team has written with alarming matter-of-factness: "It is a sobering fact that, in retrospect, had we missed the *S.S. Montrose,* the next ship of the same line doing that crossing was the *S.S. Athenia,* the first ship sunk in the war." (*Everything Under the Sun,* pp 40-41.)

The 1939 tour was Westindies's third to England - after those in 1928 and 1933 - and still Westindies were in quest of that elusive Test victory in England! In 1939, at least, they could boast probably their strongest team ever. George Headley and Learie Constantine were in high maturity, and there were promising youngsters like Stollmeyer and Gerry Gomez, while the pace attack was led by E.A. Martindale, and spin by C.B. Clarke. The new captain was Rolph Grant, brother of G.C. Grant who was captain on the 1933 tour. England, meanwhile, had just returned from South Africa where they had won one:nil. Before their South African tour, England had achieved a creditable one:all draw against a very powerful Australian side in England, in 1938. England's team was therefore tried and tested: apart from the stalwart Wally Hammond as captain, they had younger batting stars like Denis Compton and Len Hutton and two of the most artful spinners ever produced by England, Doug Wright and Hedley Verity.

In the first Test of 1939 Westindies took strike, Grant himself opening the innings, partnered by Stollmeyer who was playing in his first Test match. Stollmeyer was one of four debutantes, the others being J.H. Cameron, C.B. Clarke, and Ken Weekes. Grant (22) was caught by Compton off Copson: 29 for one; but Stollmeyer assisted the incoming George Headley to put on 118 runs before he was bowled by Bill Bowes for 59, not at all a bad start to a Test career. After Sealy and Weekes fell cheaply, Headley went on to a splendid century - 106. This helped Westindies to 245 for five, at which stage, they could consider themselves comfortably placed, if not exactly on top. But they were overtaken by a disaster in which their last five wickets were swept away for 32 runs, and they had to settle for a total of 277. By the end of the day, England had scored 11 for no wicket. The next day, Monday, led by the redoubtable Hutton, England reached 147 before their third wicket fell, all three to Cameron. Cameron had made an excellent start, bowling Gimlett (22) with his second ball in Test cricket. Then Hutton was joined by Compton, and when they had scored one run, Compton was dropped twice in successive deliveries. Hutton himself was dropped the next over, although it was a more difficult catch than the other two. At any rate, these were mistakes for which Westindies would pay dearly, as Hutton and Compton gradually took full advantage of them: after settling in, they literally pulverised the Westindian attack by scoring at the frenzied rate of 100 runs per hour. In this fashion, they constructed a magnificent partnership of 248 that brought the England total to 404 by end of play on the second day. Their scores speak louder than words: Hutton - 196, and Compton - 120.

With a lead of 127, Hammond declared overnight, and it was left for Westindies to see through the third and final day's play to reach safety; on the surface, at least, not an excessively testing proposition. But Stollmeyer (0) was caught by Verity off Copson without a single run scored, and Grant was bowled by Bowes for 23. Even then, Headley and Sealy defended stubbornly during a partnership of 63, and Weekes joined Headley to add another 49 runs. With Headley still there and Constantine going hell for leather, it seemed only a matter of time before Westindies would be home and dry. Constantine was well known for trying to blast his way out of trouble, and the longer he stayed, the more quickly would Westindies build up a second innings score large enough to put the game completely beyond England's grasp. Alas, it was not to be! Constantine's bluster was short-lived. He made 17, and once he left, Westindies collapsed again like a house of cards: from 190 for five to 225 all out. The last five wickets had managed 35 runs, 3 more than in the first innings. No wonder the 1940 *Wisden* describes the 1939 Westindian team as "strong, if unreliable." (p.58) The damage was done by Copson and Wright. Copson took four wickets for 67 runs and ended with a match analysis of nine wickets for 152 runs, while Wright took three wickets for 75 runs in 17 overs. Left just under two hours to score 100 for victory, England knocked off the runs with thirty-five minutes to spare, even if they lost two wickets in the process: the seventh Westindian attempt to gain a Test victory in England had come to an inglorious end!

Once again, if anything could lift Westindian gloom, it was the achievement of George Headley who followed up his 106 of the first innings with 107 in the second. It was the second time that Headley scored two separate hundreds in a Test match, a feat which, at that time, had been achieved only by Herbert Sutcliffe. But only Headley had scored two separate hundreds, in the same Test match, twice against England, and only Headley had scored separate hundreds in the same Test match at Lord's - both records that stand to this day! Still, Westindies lost the match. Except for Headley, the stark fact is that their batsmen failed. At 37, Constantine might have been vastly experienced; but he lacked the fire of his early years. Martindale and Hylton too proved very expensive. Excuses aside, the truth was that Westindies were outgunned by England mere months before the real guns began firing.

Third Test vs. England
Kennington Oval, London, England, 19, 21, 22 August, 1939

The third Test match between Westindies and England in 1939 is one of the most memorable played by Westindies, not only because of the imminence of war - the match opened on August 19, and England declared war on Germany on September 3 - but because it ended a whole era which began with Westindies as mere novices playing in their first Test match in 1928. During these eleven years, Westindies won three Test matches against England, and one against Australia. In these years too they produced at least two outstanding players, George Headley and Learie Constantine, who drew attention to themselves and to their homeland. Headley's batting exploits made his name interchangeable with that of Don Bradman, and Constantine was then (and still is) regarded as the greatest, most pulsatingly electric fielder in the history of cricket. Westindies lost the first Test that year, while the second Test ended in a draw because of bad weather and despite two declarations by England.

For the third Test, which opened in sunny weather at the Oval, Westindies brought in Victor Stollmeyer, brother of Jeffrey, and Tyrell Johnson, a fast bowler, for E.A.V. Williams and Les Hylton. England also made three changes from their second Test team: Bill Bowes, W.H. Copson and Hedley Verity were left out, thus weakening their bowling appreciably. Wally Hammond won the toss for the first time in the series and did not hesitate to bat. Opening the bowling for Westindies, Martindale conceded 2 runs to Len Hutton in his first over. Then, Johnson ran in from the other end, and with his first ball in Test cricket, clean bowled the other English opener Keeton for 0. Imagine the excitement, especially when we realize that earlier in the season, Johnson had taken a wicket with his very first ball in first class cricket! But Johnson's uncanny luck presaged no further disasters for England as Hutton (73) and Oldfield (80) put on 131 for the second wicket. Hammond made a useful 43, and with Joe Hardstaff producing some fireworks in a vigorous innings of 94, England were able to run up a total of 352 well before end of play. The most spectacular feature of the England innings came not from the batsmen but from Constantine when he bowled a delivery to M.S. Nichols, and with almost superhuman speed, agility and dexterity, fielded the ball at cover point and, in one fell swoop, threw down the wicket before Nichols could get home at the bowler's end. No wonder spectators used to attend cricket matches just to see Constantine field!

By the end of the first day, Westindies had scored 27 runs for the loss of their captain Rolph Grant; but the next morning, in brilliant sunshine, Headley and Stollmeyer added 113 glorious runs before the latter was caught at mid-on for 59 off Hutton. Such was the brilliance of the sunshine that it was as if the Oval itself was magically transformed into a Westindian ground. It was in this atmosphere of excitement and expectation that the incoming batsman, Victor

Stollmeyer, committed one of the most grievous errors in Westindian cricket: with Headley well set on 65, and another century from his bat as certain as the rising of the sun on a new day, Stollmeyer ran out the veritable prince of Westindian batting. Not even Brutus's crafty, oratorical line: "O! what a fall was there, my countrymen;" lamenting the death of Caesar, can fully convey Westindian grief over this incident; for, because of the Second World War, it would be nine years before the prince would play Test cricket again, and by then his princely gifts would have left him, never more to be witnessed by human eye. One may guess what Headley might have done from the fact that Stollmeyer and Ken Weekes, though not of royal blood, were able to blast 163 runs off England in merely 100 minutes. As if to atone for his guilt, Stollmeyer made 96, while Weekes contributed a dashing 137. An unexpected spell of bad weather stopped play briefly after tea, but Westindies finished the second day in the strong position of 395 for six.

On the third and final day, the last four Westindian wickets added 109 runs of which Constantine contributed 79. It was his final Test innings, played in vintage style, with immense power, daring innovation and insatiable zest. One stroke that would forever remain in the minds of those who saw it was a full blooded drive off fast bowler R.T.D. Perks straight back over his head for 6. And even if it got him out, Constantine was aiming for another 6 over the wicket-keeper's head when he was caught by the wicket-keeper. Perks was the most successful English bowler, although his five wickets cost 156 runs in 30.5 overs. Nichols, the second most successful bowler, took two wickets for 161 runs in 34 overs. In the remaining time, there really was no hope of Westindies forcing victory. Their lead of 146 was quickly overtaken by Hutton (165 not out) and Hammond (138); by the end of the day England had reached a total of 366 for three, and the match ended in an inevitable draw. Hutton had scored 238 runs in the match for only once out, and in his last three innings at the Oval had amassed 602 runs for the astonishing average of 301!

Their win in the first Test at Lord's followed by two drawn matches meant that the rubber went to England. But Westindies had come a long way from 1928 when they lost all three Test matches on their first tour. For one thing, the third Test of 1939 provided a final view of Constantine whose electrifying batting, uncommonly aggressive fast bowling and sheer zestfulness on the field made an indelible mark on the minds of those who saw him. But there is no denying that this third Test match is to be remembered, most of all for providing the last example of George Headley in his prime, for although he did play in two Test matches in 1948, and one in 1954, he had long passed his best by that time when he was forty years and over. What a pity that Headley's last "genuine" Test innings had to be cut off at 65 through no fault of his own! Yet how futile to question the inscrutable ways of the Almighty! Instead, let us be grateful for the opportunity now to forever dream of what George Alphonso Headley might have accomplished that day at Kennington Oval in 1939, when his genius was in full flower, barely two weeks before the dogs of war were unleashed on an expectant and fearful world.

CHAPTER TWO

The Post-War Years

(1947-49)

First Test vs. England
Kensington Oval, Bridgetown, Barbados
21, 22, 23, 24, 26 January, 1948

The first Test match between Westindies and England in January 1948 was the first to be played on Westindian soil since England had toured under Wyatt in 1935. This Test also provided the first occasion in which a black man, George Headley, was appointed as Westindian captain in a Test match. Headley was named as captain for the Test matches in Barbados and Jamaica, while Stollmeyer was named for the one in Trinidad, and Goddard in Guyana. As it turned out, though, Headley was injured in the Barbados Test match and did not play again in the series. Several Westindians made their Test début in this match - Christiani, Ferguson, Gaskin, Goddard, Jones, Walcott and Weekes. The tourists did not represent the full potential of English strength at the time: top class players such as Hutton, Compton, Edrich, Bedser and Wright had not come. Perhaps the English selectors did not believe that a full-strength English team was warranted in the Westindies. At any rate, against less well-known bowlers such as Tremlett, Cranston, Ikin, Howorth, and the young Jim Laker, Westindies did not have much trouble in scoring 244 for three on the first day of play.

As a result of rain on the first night, batting became difficult on the second day when seven Westindian wickets fell for 52 runs. If the Westindian first innings total of 296 still looked respectable, it was mainly because of the previous day's batting. Jim Laker was the most successful English bowler with seven wickets for 103 runs in 37 overs. For Westindies, Stollmeyer (78) and Gomez (86) made the highest scores. England gave Westindies a run for their money by reaching 150 for three by the end of the second day. On the third day, however, seven English wickets fell for 103 runs, and the English first innings closed at 253 runs, 43 behind Westindies. The only English batsmen to resist with any success were J.D. Robertson, the opener,

53

who made 80, and Joe Hardstaff who was unlucky to be bowled off his pads for 98. The wickets were divided mainly between Prior Jones and E.A.V. Williams.

Because of injury, Headley did not bat at his usual position at No. 5 in the Westindian second innings. Whether this caused trouble or not, Westindies found themselves struggling against excellent spin bowling by Howorth. At 144 for five, they had lost some of their best batsmen - Stollmeyer (31), Weekes (25), Walcott (16), and Gomez (0). Since Headley was injured, only Christiani remained as an accredited batsman. It looked as if a miracle would be needed if Westindies were going to save the match, and as sometimes happens when enough people pray hard enough, it came in the form of a magnificent partnership of 96 runs between Christiani and Williams. Williams's opening scoring strokes should convince those who may not believe in miracles, or in the effectiveness of prayer in achieving them: he hit his first four deliveries from Laker for 6,6,4,4, respectively; then he took two fours off the next two deliveries he received, this time, from Ikin. After this opening burst of 28 runs in six deliveries, Williams went on to make 72 runs altogether, while leg-spinner Ferguson slogged another 56 hefty runs into the bargain. Williams's fifty took thirty minutes, and remains the third fastest fifty in Test cricket. But by far the most brilliant performance came from the charmed blade of Robert Julian Christiani who combined wristy elegance with fleet-footed athleticism to concoct an innings that left Westindies in relative safety if not in total command. It will forever remain a tragedy in Westindian cricket that Christiani was lbw to Cranston when he was one run away from a century in his first Test match.

Because of their vigorous rearguard action, Westindies were able to declare at 351 for nine and set England 395 to win. England limped to 60 for two by the end of the fourth day, completely mesmerised by the off-spin of Goddard, who used the rain-affected pitch to return figures of 14 overs for 18 runs and two wickets. These were figures sufficient to frighten the bravest Englishman, for England's star, Joe Hardstaff, had already been extinguished, and although the sturdy opener Robertson was still there with 51 not out, only reliance on extreme optimism or blind luck could have led one to expect that England would survive the final day. In the event, it was luck that did it when the most of the last day's play was lost to rain and the match was drawn. England had reached 86 for four when rain stopped play: they had escaped, but Westindies had proved that they were a force to be reckoned with. Although earlier Westindian teams had superb players like Constantine and Headley (in his prime), there was an impression that these teams lacked confidence, reliability, and consistency. It was probably due to this impression that England had not sent their strongest side to the Westindies in 1948. If for no other reason, this first Test in 1948 should be remembered as a proclamation to the world that Westindies had entered a new, modern, and more promising era of Test cricket, when no nation could feel safe in confronting them without fielding their strongest side possible.

Third Test vs. England
Bourda, Georgetown, Guyana, 3, 4, 5, 6 March, 1948

There can be few joys more satisfying than the memory of one's first Test match, especially if one was still in primary school, as I was, in 1948, when England arrived in Guyana. At a time when, through no fault of my own, my mind was inevitably indoctrinated by the dominant values of a British Caribbean colony, the prospect of witnessing our English overlords performing against us, on local soil, invoked feelings of awe and majesty such as one might expect from a divine visitation. That the match would prove to be a contest of high tension and drama was further confirmed by the presence of two local players in the Westindian team - sprightly, athletic Robert Christiani, and big, burly John Trim. This Bourda Test was the third match in the first post-war cricket series played by Westindians. England had not sent their best team and it was only after they had been hit by injury, and had fared badly in the first two Tests (although they managed to draw them both) that Hutton was hastily summoned on a rescue mission that brought him, by air, to Guyana. He promptly showed his mettle by scoring 138 in the first match against Guyana. It was an accomplishment that made my boyish imagination run riot with excitement associating Hutton's innings with other deeds of British gallantry that my colonial education had instilled in me, for example, the deeds of the "noble six hundred", as recounted by Tennyson, in "The Charge of the Light Brigade", the "relief" of Lucknow, and Kitchener's "glorious" victory at Omdurman to punish the Sudanese for Gordon's death at Khartoum.

Until that Guyana match I did not really believe that I would ever see Hutton in the flesh. I had read of his 364 against Australia in 1938, and I felt that no one capable of such a superhuman feat would deign to set foot in a remote, insignificant, colonial outpost like Guyana. But having seen him against Guyana, I felt certain he was destined for another hundred in the third Test match that was shortly to follow. These were the circumstances in which was conceived a dark and guilty secret in which I yearned for Hutton to make a hundred in the third Test, while wanting Westindies to win. To salve pangs of guilt, treachery and dubious patriotism, I had concocted a scorecard in which Hutton would be clean bowled by John Trim for exactly one hundred, and I generously allowed the remaining ten English batsmen to make 50 runs between them. Such a score would allow Westindies to face a total of 150 which, I felt, they would handle with ease.

The actual match was slightly different. Westindies batted first and lost three wickets for 48 runs, when Christiani and Worrell came together in a partnership in which the former's gaiety and flamboyance vied with the latter's languid grace to produce an exhibition of batting that has seldom been matched for beauty and style in other innings played at Bourda. These were two of the most naturally gifted stylists who ever shouldered a bat in the Westindian cause, and why their partnership did not go on forever, I will never know. Horrible to relate, when the partnership had realized 79 magical runs, Christiani hooked a short ball from Tremlett for a certain six only to see Joe Hardstaff pull off an improbable one handed catch on the deep square leg boundary. If I were an umpire in the match, far from putting Christiani out, I would have disciplined Hardstaff for unlawful interference. Gomez and Worrell added a further 97 runs, and Worrell went on to make a glorious 131 not out, before Goddard declared the innings closed at 297 for eight. This was half way through the second day after rain had interrupted play both days. With the wicket helpful to the bowlers, England were dismissed for a paltry 111, Goddard taking five for 31 in 14 overs. For me it was a revelation to watch Hutton's trappings of divinity fall away from him as he succumbed caught Williams, bowled Goddard for 31 - England's top score.

The English first innings closed early on the third day and Goddard enforced the follow-on. Wrist-spinner Ferguson who had extracted three wickets from the English first innings, now struck deadlier form, and claimed another three wickets in the second innings, including that of Hutton who was trapped by a top-spinner that hurried straight on to his stumps without deviation. Joe Hardstaff batted with energy and excitement for 63 runs before divine retribution asserted itself by ensuring that Christiani repaid him the compliment of catching him when he was going for a big hit. To their great credit, the English tailenders defended gamely, and carried the match into the final day before leaving Westindies 78 to get for victory. Westindies scored the required runs for three wickets, and went one up in the series with only one match to go. But for me, despite many good performances from Goddard, Ferguson, Hardstaff and Worrell, what I remember most about my first Test match is the scintillating batting of Christiani who, as so often, was flying like an angel, when his wings suddenly dropped off and he fell once more to the sordid earth. I also remember Hutton's reduction to more human proportions, although the guilt I felt over wanting him to make a hundred dogged me for another twenty years until I read that Neville Cardus similarly longed for Victor Trumper to make a hundred against England, then get out to facilitate an English victory.

Fourth Test vs. England
Sabina Park, Kingston, Jamaica
27, 29, 30, 31 March, 1 April, 1948

Not only did England not bring a full strength team to the Westindies in 1947/48: those players who came themselves suffered to an unusual degree from injuries. Before they arrived, their captain Gubby Allen had pulled a muscle while skipping on board the ship from England. Fast bowler Butler also pulled a muscle and later contracted malaria; Laker had strained stomach muscles;

Ikin was hospitalised with a carbuncle; Tremlett strained his ribs; Brookes chipped a finger-bone, and Hardstaff had a torn muscle. If all this reads like a casualty list after an air raid, it also explains why Hutton was flown out from England to join the team in Guyana, half way through the tour. The Hutton rescue act was only partially successful: he made a century in the Guyana match, but could not prevent an English defeat by seven wickets in the Guyana Test match. That defeat meant that Westindies were leading the four-match series 1:0 with the fourth Test left.

Since Headley was unfit for the fourth Test in Jamaica, Goddard substituted as captain, and Headley's place was filled by Weekes who had been dropped because of unimpressive scores in the previous Tests: 35, 25; 36, 20; 36. Thereby hangs a tale, as we shall hear later. Meanwhile, Westindies had also replaced George Carew, E.A.V. Williams, John Trim and Lance Pierre with Jeff Stollmeyer, Ken Rickards, Hines Johnson and Esmond Kentish. Allen won the toss and his openers Hutton and Robertson laid an excellent foundation of 129 runs. Hutton was bowled by Johnson for 56, and three runs later, Robertson was lbw also to Johnson for 64. Their team mates then made heavy weather of the Westindian bowling, as they stumbled from 132 for two when Robertson was out, to 183 for 5 by the end of the first day. This pattern of unresisting decline was repeated the following day when England were shot out for 227. Apart from Hutton and Robertson, only Allen (23) had reached 20. The rout was caused chiefly by Hines Johnson with figures of: 34.5-13-41-5. He and Ferguson (38-14-53-2) did the most damage, although Kentish took two wickets, and Goddard, Worrell and Stollmeyer bowled as well.

Opening for Westindies, Goddard (17) and Stollmeyer (30) both fell to Howorth who, in the previous year, had taken a wicket (Dyer's) with his first ball in Test cricket (in the fifth Test against South Africa at the Oval). From 62 for two, Weekes and Worrell advanced Westindies to 144 before Worrell (38) was lbw to Allen. At the end of the second day, Westindies were 168 for three, and Weekes was 68 not out. The next morning, Weekes lost his overnight partner Gomez (23) and was joined by Ken Rickards. Together they built a grand partnership that produced strokeplay of dazzling virtuosity and magically transformed the score from 204 to 320. Weekes himself played literally the innings of his life - 141 runs - which was to form the basis of his whole future in cricket. It was the top score in a Westindian total of 490 to which Rickards (67) and Walcott (45) also made useful contributions. Yet it was pure chance - Headley's illness - that Weekes played in this Test at all , and chance again that he was dropped by wicket-keeper Evans soon after he had started his innings. Weekes's very inclusion in the team was so hasty that he arrived from Barbados halfway through the first day when his team mates were already fielding, and was booed by the Jamaican crowd (because he was replacing the local hero - Headley) as he walked out to join them. Needless to say, the crowd thought differently after his 141. Weekes's 141 is also the first in his record run of five hundreds in consecutive Test innings. Bowling for England, Howorth and Laker returned the best figures. Howorth's were: 40-10-106-3 and Laker's: 36.4-5-

103-3; Tremlett collected two for 98 and Allen and Ikin one wicket each.

Undeterred by massive arrears (263), Hutton and Robertson once again showed imagination and enterprise by putting on 69 before Robertson (28) was bowled by Johnson. Hutton and Place added 32 more runs before Hutton (60) was caught by substitute fielder J.K. Holt off Goddard. But Hardstaff and Place summoned enough courage and defiance for a face-saving partnership of 113 runs before Hardstaff (64) was bowled by Johnson: 214 for three. Place distinguished himself by achieving his maiden Test century, indeed the only century of his three-match Test career which began and ended on this tour. With the score at 291 for four, England had recovered splendidly, playing themselves right back into the match, and raising plausible expectations of an exciting climax. Unfortunately, the remaining English batsmen were disappointing. The last six totalled 45 runs, and none of the last five reached double figures. This astonishing collapse was due largely to Johnson who took five wickets for 55 runs in 31 overs. In the match as a whole, Johnson, who was making his Test début, picked up altogether ten wickets for 96 (five in each innings), while Stollmeyer, in his unusual role as a bowler, collected three wickets for 32 runs, and Goddard one. But the most remarkable thing was that Johnson had achieved his impressive Test début at the ripe age of 37.

With 74 runs needed for victory, Westindies coasted home and won by ten wickets. Goddard hit 46 not out, including a six and eight fours, while Stollmeyer was 25 not out. The victory meant that Westindies had won the series by 2:0 with two matches drawn. There was no question that England had been outplayed, although they were severely hampered by injuries. In the fourth Test alone, Cranston could not bowl because of injury, while Howorth could not function at full speed. For Westindies, the series had served its main purpose of providing an opportunity for international competition. Through the war years, and immediately afterwards, the domestic, inter-territorial matches had produced huge scores, prodigious batting feats and skilful bowling performances. The England tour tested these local exploits by subjecting their practitioners to tougher, more rigorous international standards. The result was that Westindies had a clearer idea of which players to pick for their tour of India later the same year.

Second Test vs. India
Brabourne Stadium, Bombay, India
9, 10, 11, 12, 13 December, 1948

After World War Two many young players had emerged to give the Westindies a surge of new cricketing blood. These players had distinguished themselves in domestic, intercolonial competition, and needed to test their skills against more rigorous standards of international competition. The first opportunity for this was provided by the English tourists in 1947/48, a rubber won by Westindies

2:0. Westindies then had a second opportunity of international competition when they made their first tour of India at the end of 1948. In the first Test of this tour, at Delhi, they scored 631 runs in their only innings. Weekes, Walcott, Gomez and Christiani all registered centuries, and only desperate, dogged defiance by India's batsmen saved them from defeat: on the last day, a seventh-wicket stand of 58 between Adhikari and Sarwate left India 43 runs ahead with four wickets intact when time ran out and the match ended in a draw.

For the second Test, Westindies dropped Headley for Ferguson, and India replaced Tarapore and Sarwate with Shinde and Umrigar, a new player who had made 115 not out for Combined Universities in the first tour match. As in the first Test, Goddard the Westindian captain won the toss. This was taken as a signal for Westindies to run up another huge total. On the first day, on a good batting wicket, they amassed 255 for two. Rae registered 104, Stollmeyer 66, and the not out batsmen were Weekes and Walcott. The next day, Walcott was run out early for 68, but Weekes and Christiani had a field day before Christiani was lbw Mankad for 74. Weekes, meanwhile, continued to plunder and pillage until stumps were drawn on the second day and Westindies had reached 557 for five. Goddard extended the innings into the third day evidently instructing his batsmen to go for quick runs. Perhaps surfeited by his gargantuan feast, Weekes was eventually caught by wicket-keeper Sen off Hazare for 194. He had given a few chances, but his innings was still a magnificent effort full of brilliant strokes all around the wicket. Cameron and Atkinson slogged 72 runs in 45 minutes before Goddard declared at 629 for six, with another hour and a quarter to go for lunch. Mankad, Hazare and Rangachari were the main Indian bowlers. Mankad delivered 75 overs for 202 runs and three wickets, while Rangachari sent down 34 overs for 148 runs and no wicket. Compared with them Hazare was relatively inexpensive with 42 overs for 74 runs and one wicket.

No sooner had India begun their innings than the pattern of the first Test repeated itself, that is to say, with the Indian batsmen struggling against Jones, Gomez and Ferguson. Ibrahim (9) was run out when India were 27, and Mankad was also run out when they were 32 for three. Hazare (26) joined in a defiant stand of 50 with Adhikari (34) who had made a century in the first Test; but by the end of the third day, India were in despair at 150 for six. The next morning Phadkar and Umrigar fought back splendidly at least until lunch-time, but soon after lunch, Umrigar (30) was caught by Goddard off Ferguson: 229 for seven. Phadkar achieved the top score - 74 - a truly gallant effort, and when he was caught by Jones off Gomez, the tailenders contributed 40 more runs to enable India to reach a total of 273, a massive 356 behind Westindies. India had scored at less than two runs per over, confirming the dominance of ball over bat. Ferguson bowled 57 overs (twice as many as anyone else) for 126 runs and four wickets. Goddard and Atkinson each took one wicket while Gomez claimed two. Forced to follow on, India started off badly when Ibrahim was caught by Goddard off Jones for 0. Mankad (16) was caught by Ferguson off Gomez: 33 for two, but Modi and Hazare saw things through to the end of the day when the score was 95 for two.

On the fifth and final day, the proposition facing India was stark: they needed another 261 runs to clear off their deficit and avoid an innings defeat. It was a monumental task, and it says much for the citizens of Bombay and for faith in their cricketers that they apparently anticipated an heroic struggle and turned up in numbers to pack the stadium. Perhaps they knew their batsmen better than the Westindians did. At any rate, demonstrating contrasting styles, Modi played his shots while Hazare was prudent and watchful. By lunch Modi had reached his first and only Test century, and soon afterwards, he was caught off Ferguson for 112. The score was then 189 for three and the Modi-Hazare partnership had realized 156 runs, then an Indian record for the third wicket against Westindies. But with over three hours of play left, the odds were heavily on a Westindian victory. Yet, courageously, defiantly, Hazare and his captain Amarnath stood their ground throughout the afternoon. When he was 88, Hazare gave a very difficult chance to gully, but apart from that both batsmen remained steadfast and ever vigilant until end of play when India were 333 for three, still 23 runs away from clearing off their deficit. Time had run out again, and the match was drawn. Ferguson did most of the bowling taking one wicket for 105 runs in 39 overs, although Gomez and Cameron contributed 28 and 27 overs respectively. Considering the dourness of their struggle, the Indian batsmen had done well to score at the rate of two and half runs per over in their second innings. From an Indian point of view the draw had been achieved through sheer heroism, firstly from Modi, secondly from Hazare who was left with 134 not out, and also from Amarnath - 58 not out. Certainly, these batsmen deserve credit. At the same time, on a pitch that was unhelpful to them, the Westindian bowlers revealed a conspicuous lack of penetration in being unable to dismiss India twice. Goddard used as many as eight bowlers. So far as Westindies were concerned, then, their first two Tests in India had revealed a troubling disparity between tremendous batting firepower and undistinguished, or at any rate, unpenetrating, bowling resources.

Fourth Test vs. India
Chepauk, Madras, India, 27,28,29, 31 January, 1949

The first three Test matches played by Westindies in India in 1948/49 were all drawn. The pattern in each match was for Westindies to pile up a huge total in their first innings (631 in the first Test; and 629 for 6 wickets declared in the second), while India tended to collapse in their first innings and make an improbable recovery in the second. This happened so regularly that Vallabhai Patel, India's Deputy Prime Minister ventured the opinion that India should play their second innings first. The fourth Test was played on a wicket known to favour pace, for in the match immediately preceding the fourth Test, the Westindian medium-fast bowler Gerry Gomez took nine wickets for 24 runs at Chepauk. For the fourth Test India made two changes: they brought in Rege (opening batsman) and Chowdhury (fast bowler) for Ibrahim and Bannerjee, while Westindies strengthened their pace attack of Gomez and Prior Jones by bringing in John Trim to play in his first Test in India.

Rae and Stollmeyer opened for Westindies, and although they gave a couple of chances, batted with confidence and aggression almost up to tea, when Rae (109) was caught on the fine leg boundary by Rege off Phadkar. His partnership with Stollmeyer had realized 239 runs - then a record for Westindian opening partnerships in Tests, and Rae's three sixes gave some idea of his aggressive style. He was followed by Walcott who continued just as aggressively, punching the bowlers around until stumps were drawn at 315 for one. Stollmeyer who had batted all day was 157 not out. Within minutes the next morning, Stollmeyer (160) and Walcott (43) were back in the pavilion, the former caught by wicket-keeper Sen off Chowdhury, and Walcott being lbw to Phadkar. It was Stollmeyer's first century in Tests, and it remains his highest Test score. Christiani (18) was caught by Modi off Phadkar, and his departure brought Weekes and captain Goddard together. As lunch approached, India's captain Lala Amarnath asked Phadkar to try fast, short-pitched bowling supported by a packed leg-side field. Considering that Westindies possessed superior resources of fast bowling, this seemed an unwise tactic, although it paid some early dividends in so far as India were able to collect nine Westindian wickets for 267 runs on the second day, seven of them going to Phadkar. This second day was certainly more eventful than the first. Apart from some fielding lapses, there was the controversial run out of Weekes for 90 which killed his chance of a sixth successive Test century. Gomez made 50 and Cameron 48, and Westindies were all out for 582. The Indian bowling was shared mainly between Phadkar (45 overs); Chowdhury (37 overs); Mankad (33 overs); and Ghulam Ahmed (32 overs). Chowdhury and Mankad collected one wicket each in addition to Phadkar's seven.

Mushtaq Ali and Rege gave India a spirited start, putting on 41 runs before Mushtaq was lbw to Trim for 32. Eleven runs later, Rege was bowled by Jones for 15. Hazare then was brilliantly caught by Goddard off Ferguson for 27. Meanwhile, Modi (56) had batted patiently before he chopped a ball from Ferguson on to his wicket: 136 for four. Amarnath (13) was unlucky to tread on his wicket while facing Trim: 158 for five. But Adhikari and Phadkar carried the score to 220 before Adhikari fell to Jones for 32, and at close of play India were 225 for six, with Mankad and Phadkar not out. India's situation was nothing less than perilous. It did not help them either that the next day (Sunday) was an unscheduled rest day (to mark the first anniversary of Gandhi's death). Whether the unexpected rest helped them or not, on the following Monday, Westindies shot out the remaining Indian wickets for a mere 20 runs to bring the Indian total to 245. Only Phadkar (48) showed any resistance as India followed on 337 runs behind. Trim was the most successful bowler: 27-7-48-4; but he was helped by Gomez: 28-10-60-1; Jones: 16-5-28-2; Ferguson: 20-2-72-2; and Goddard: 8-1-26-1. The question was whether India could repeat their improbable second innings rescue act once again. When Rege was caught off Jones without a run being scored, and Modi bowled by Gomez with only 7 runs on the board, the signs were not propitious, and India was in grave danger of sinking into the abyss. Before lunch, Mushtaq also, centurion of the third Test, was caught by Walcott off Jones: 29 for three. At this rate, far from staging a rescue, India looked unlikely to carry on to the next day.

After lunch, Hazare and Amarnath (16) tried to initiate the overdue rescue, but luck was against the Indian captain, and just as he had trod on his wicket in the first innings, he was now hit on the chest by a ball from Jones which fell on his stumps. India were then 42 for four, and two runs later Adhikari, who had made 114 not out in the first Test, was caught by wicket-keeper Walcott off Jones for 1. At 44 for five what India needed was not a rescue but a miracle. Only Hazare seemed to have the technique to cope with the variable bounce that the pitch was now producing. But he could find no one to stay with him. There were modest contributions, to be sure, from Mankad (21), and Sen (19), but they were scarcely what was needed, and India were all out for 144. While Hazare made 52, five of his countrymen failed to reach double figures, and only Mankad exceeded 20. The Westindian fast bowlers made a clean sweep, Jones taking four wickets for 30 runs, Gomez three for 35, and Trim three for 28. Since Amarnath was the first to introduce leg theory into the match, he could hardly complain if the Westindian bowlers administered some of the same medicine to his batsmen. This decisive victory - by an innings and 193 runs - reflected a glaring disparity in the relative strength of the two teams. In the previous three matches, India had somehow always summoned enough resources to conceal the disparity, but on a wicket that suited neither their bowlers nor batsmen, it finally caught up with them. It also confirmed the prodigious batting potential of the post-war Westindies team.

Fifth Test vs. India
Brabourne Stadium, Bombay, India, 4, 5, 6, 7, 8 February, 1949

The intercolonial cricket matches played in the Westindies during and immediately following World War Two threw up important names - Rae, Stollmeyer, Worrell, Weekes, Walcott, Christiani. Then came the English tour of Westindies in 1947/48, followed by the Westindian tour of India in 1948/49. These tours allowed the newly emerging Westindian players to prove themselves in the Test arena, after which, the stage was set for their historic conquest of England in 1950. This chronology explains why the Westindian tour of India in 1948/49 is sometimes regarded as no more than a convenient opportunity for blooding promising Westindian players, by providing them with opposition of mediocre or moderate strength. Weekes, for example, seized the opportunity by scoring four of five successive Test centuries, and missing the sixth only by being run out for 90 in the fifth Test against India. But the Indian tour was interesting in other ways as well: it was not only the first visit by Westindies to

India, but the first series that India was playing as an independent country, having ceased to be a British colony in 1947. In any case, while the impression of India's mediocrity might be suggested by such formidable Westindian totals as 631 (First Test), 629 for six (Second Test), and 582 (Fourth Test), it is surprising that the margin of final victory was one: nil. Despite huge Westindian scores, India held on to draw the first three Tests. In the process, several Indian batsmen scored centuries - Adhikari, Modi, Hazare, and Mushtaq Ali. It was only in the fourth Test that India's resistance gave way as they succumbed to defeat by an innings and 193 runs. This would be enough to crush the spirit of the most stout-hearted team. That it did not crush India is evident from the way the Indians played in the fifth Test, as if they still harboured hopes, however faint, of winning the match and squaring the series.

The Westindian captain, Goddard, won the toss for the fifth time in the series, and Westindies batted first to reach a total of 286. This was small by Westindian standards; but it might have been smaller were it not for several lapses by Indian fielders. Their fielding apart, it was clear that India were prepared to make Westindies fight to win the series. But India's batsmen failed to capitalize on the breakthrough that her bowlers had made, and at the end of the second day, the Indian score stood at 132 for five. Perhaps, with captain Amarnath and all-rounder Phadkar still in possession, and Mankad yet to come, the situation was not as perilous as it looked. In fact, on the morning of the third day, India collapsed for 193, and were in deep peril of losing the match and series. But again, although facing a deficit of 93, and with inadequate cooperation from their fielders, India's bowlers - mainly Bannerjee, Phadkar and Mankad - stuck manfully to their task, and restricted Westindies to a second innings total of 267, their lowest for the tour.

India were now left to make 361 runs for victory in 395 minutes. It was not at all a bad proposition assuming the weather did not interfere. Unfortunately, India's openers made a disastrous start, and by tea on the fourth day, India were 21 for two. After tea, Amarnath and Modi strove courageously to restore the situation, and had some success until Amarnath (39) was bowled by Atkinson, leaving India at close of play on 90 for three. When play resumed on the final day, India needed 271 runs to win with seven wickets intact. Since interference was not likely from the weather, the outcome of the match was entirely left to the determination and skill of the Indian batsmen. As we know, four of them had already made centuries against this Westindian team. Would their nerves now hold? Modi and Hazare appeared to answer this question with a magnificent stand of 139 before Modi was caught by Walcott off Goddard for 86. As so often after a long stand, Hazare was also out soon afterwards, clean bowled by Prior Jones for a truly heroic 122. At tea, India were 289 for six - 91 short of victory, and with three wickets left (since wicket-keeper Sen was injured and would not bat).

If India's chances of winning were still flickering, the glow became very faint indeed when, Adhikari (8) was caught by Trim off Jones, and Bannerjee (8) was bowled by Jones. This left the last Indian pair - Phadkar and Ghulam Ahmed - to do or die. Phadkar evidently did not feel suicidal. With courage and astuteness, he farmed the bowling, shielding his less skilled partner, as he gradually pushed the score along. Run by run they went until their partnership had realized 34 and the Indian score was 355, six short of victory. With one and a half minutes of play left - plenty of time to start the final over - the Indian team and crowd were both confident of victory. The tension was riveting as Phadkar and Ghulam Ahmed contemplated that final over, and assessed their strategy for making the required runs - six runs in six deliveries. Then, to the consternation of players and crowd alike, umpire Joshi suddenly lifted the bails, pulled up stumps, and ended the match as officially drawn, without allowing Prior Jones even to complete the last delivery of the over he was bowling.

It is claimed that umpire Joshi was motivated by a magnanimous sense of traditional Indian hospitality toward guests and visitors. Such an explanation no doubt mollifies the Indian sense of disappointment in having struggled so hard and come so close to victory, only to have it snatched away, not by the opposing team, but by a "deus ex machina". It must have been intolerable. But who is to say that umpire Joshi did not act out of a very practical sense of patriotism rather than of hospitality? Since either Phadkar or Ghulam Ahmed could have been out in the final over, before making the required runs, it is perfectly possible that umpire Joshi saved India from defeat. At all events, the match came to an abrupt end, with the gallant Phadkar undefeated on 37, and Indian pride somewhat restored. We shall never know whether Indian pride would have been fully restored by winning the final match and squaring the series, or whether India would have lost the series by two games instead of one: nil. If nothing else, this Fifth Test match proved that the Indian side of 1948 was not a bunch of mediocre rabbits. This is supported by Jeffrey Stollmeyer who played in the match and in his book *Everything Under the Sun* calls it: "the most dramatic Test match in which I have ever taken part." (p.72)

CHAPTER THREE

The Ws, Ram and Val

(1950-57)

Second Test vs. England
Lord's, London, England, 24, 26, 27, 28, 29 June, 1950

If their second Test match against England in 1950 is not the most memorable ever played by Westindies, it is undoubtedly the most historic, for it proved to be the first Test victory gained by Westindies over England in England. As an assault on the imperial power that had enslaved Westindians for three centuries and ruled them for longer, this victory had the special sweetness of retribution justly meted out on perpetrators of such heinous crimes as slavery and indenture and all their attendant evils. No wonder it was a victory that brought more joy to descendants of former slaves and indentured labourers than any other in the whole history of cricket. That George VI, king of England and ruler of the British empire should have attended the event was wholly fitting, as was the fact that the match was played at Lord's, cricket's holiest shrine, and imperial citadel of the cricketing world.

Legend tends to suggest that the entire 1950 tour was one triumphant march from start to finish, with the mighty Ws swatting English bowlers like flies, and Ramadhin and Valentine scattering English batsmen like frightened rabbits. Like most legends, this is only partly true, alas! When the second Test started, although Westindies already had some success in county matches, they had lost the two most important matches at that stage of the tour - the one against M.C.C., and the first Test match at Old Trafford; and although Valentine had collected eleven wickets in the first Test, he and Ramadhin were sadly lacking in experience as Test bowlers. For all that, Westindies made a good start when they batted first on the opening day of the second Test. Rae made a century and at 233 for three, his side clearly had the advantage. But Bedser bowled both Weekes (63) and Worrell (52) in a fiery new ball spell, and Westindies ended the first day on 320 for seven. Whatever promise one could see in this score vanished quickly the next morning when, after fifteen minutes, Westindies were all out for 326. The England team boasted not only the genius of Len Hutton, but the skill of trusted warriors like Washbrook and Edrich. There was also wicket-keeper Godfrey Evans who had made a century in the Old Trafford Test, not to mention younger batsmen like Doggart and Parkhouse, and captain Norman Yardley, himself no novice with the bat. After Hutton and Washbrook had put on 50 without loss, their team appeared set for a big score. Then the Westindian captain John Goddard took off his pace men, Jones and Worrell, and Ramadhin and Valentine lined up for their baptism at cricket's scared shrine. This bowling change signalled the most critical reversal in the history of Westindian cricket.

One might have expected Ramadhin and Valentine to approach the English guardians of their shrine in awe and reverence. Instead it was the English batsmen who seemed awestruck and bewildered. They kept pushing and prodding at Ramadhin in particular with a tentativeness and a crease-bound caution that hinted at inward fear and trembling. Once Ramadhin's arm came over to bowl, they couldn't tell whether the ball would turn left or right, go straight, keep low, lift, or disappear altogether into thin air. Like blind men with only a thin white stick to guide them, they negotiated the perilous traffic of Westindian bowling, groping and hoping to survive. In the event they were shot out for 151, Ramadhin taking five for 66, and Valentine four for 48. As Denys Rowbotham put it in *The Guardian* the next day "Her (England's) batsmen were beaten partly by a young bowler (Ramadhin) who has discovered a new trick - that of bowling an off-break and a leg break with an almost identical action without resort to the googly, but even more by persistent accuracy." (Matthew Engel, ed. *The Guardian Book of Cricket*, p.38) Such was Ramadhin's "mystery" that it was believed that whenever he touched his cap it was a signal to the wicket-keeper that a leg-break was coming. With a lead of 175, the game had swung Westindies's way. But when they had reached 199 for five in their second innings, they were in danger of losing the initiative. Then came the second crucial turning point of the game - a magnificent sixth wicket partnership of 211 between wicket-keeper Clyde Walcott and that most resilient of all-rounders, Gerry Gomez. Their partnership enabled Westindies to declare at 425 for six, leaving England to make 601 to win in two days on a wicket that was still good.

It was a daunting proposition which became quite impossible when Len Hutton, England's batting mainstay, was out for 10. But England did not surrender that easily. If one considers that Washbrook accumulated 114 runs when he could make neither head nor tail of Ramadhin, his innings must be accounted one of the bravest ever played. In the end, Ramadhin pinned him down for sixty-six continuous, scoreless minutes until, like a triumphant matador slaying a brave but exhausted bull, he put him out of misery by bowling him.

Apart from Washbrook, only Parkhouse resisted with a valiant 48, before England were all out for 274 and Westindies won by 326 runs. Ramadhin had match figures of: 115-70-152-11, and Valentine: 116-75-127-7. Together, they bowled 231 overs in the match while Jones, Worrell, Gomez, and Goddard totalled 66.4 overs between them. More importantly, 145 of the overs of Ramadhin and Valentine, well over half, were maidens. These figures reveal what the English batsmen were up against, and tell virtually the whole story of the match: it is a story of two Davids, armed only with sling shots, with which they successfully stormed an ancient, fortified, English citadel and opened its gates for calypsonians to enter and celebrate the first Test victory of their countrymen on English soil. Nothing - not even the universal mastery of Westindian fast bowlers in 1980s - can equal the unique achievement of Ramadhin and Valentine in this match: their uniqueness is that, at Lord's, in the month of June, in the year of 1950, two colonial innocents, one descended from African slaves and the other from Indian indentured labourers, dared to confront the imperial British lion in his den, and with nothing but sheer skill and natural courage to rely on, tamed the royal beast into docile submission.

Fourth Test vs. England
Kennington Oval, London, England, 12, 14, 15, 16 August, 1950

The Westindian triumph at Lord's in 1950 brought their four-match series with England to level pegging at 1:1, but their ten-wicket victory at Trent Bridge in the third Test put them ahead 2:1. All eyes were then turned on the fourth Test where an English victory would mean an inconclusive rubber, and a Westindian win would give them the rubber, their first ever in England. Whereas Westindies made one change from their third Test team, bringing in Prior Jones for Hines Johnson, England effected a complete overhaul. Norman Yardley, captain in the three previous Tests, declared himself unavailable for the winter tour to Australia, and Freddie Brown was appointed both for Australia and the Oval Test against Westindies. In addition, England left out Washbrook, Parkhouse and Insole, and brought in Hutton, Compton and Sheppard. Wicket-keeper McIntyre replaced Godfrey Evans who had a broken thumb, and in the bowling department, Bailey, Hilton and Wright came in for Shackleton, Jenkins and Hollies. There is no question that these changes vastly strengthened England; for next to Hutton, Compton was England's premier post-war batsman, and it was a great blow to England that he had missed all three of the previous Tests that summer because of a knee injury.

Goddard won the toss and immediately enlisted the trusted firm of Rae and Stollmeyer to open the innings; they put on 72 runs before Stollmeyer (36) was lbw to Bailey. Rae went on to his second century of the series, as he and Worrell added 172 runs; eventually, he was bowled by Bedser for 109. Weekes obliged with a breezy knock for 30 before he was caught by Hutton off a long hop from Wright, and when stumps were drawn early because of rain, Westindies were 295 for three: Worrell 110 not out. The next day, illness intervened and Worrell retired temporarily. Neither Walcott (17) who was bowled by Wright, nor Christiani (11) who was caught by McIntyre off Bedser, lasted long; and Gomez (74) was caught by McIntyre off Brown: 446 for six. Worrell returned and was soon lbw to Wright for a magnificent 138, composed with his usual style and grace to register his second three-figure innings of the Test series: 480 for seven. The tailenders were quickly disposed of leaving Goddard 58 not out and the total at 503. Wright had the best figures: 53-16-141-5, while Bailey took two wickets for 84 runs and Bedser two for 75.

Hutton and Simpson opened for England with little over an hour of play left on the second day, and at the end they had made 29 without loss. The next morning, first Simpson (30) was caught by Jones off Valentine, then Sheppard (11) was bowled by Ramadhin, and England were 120 for two with Hutton remaining solid as a rock. Compton joined Hutton and in exactly the invigorating type of stand that England had been expecting from them all summer, they added 109 runs and showed every sign of adding many more when there was a tragic misunderstanding: Hutton played a stroke and began to run, but changed his mind and stood his ground while Compton (44) who had charged down the pitch was run out. This was a grievous blow for England. At stumps on the third day, mainly due to Hutton's stalwart 160 not out, England finished on a promising note of 282 for four. After heavy rain that night, Hutton and Bailey found the going tough when play resumed the next day. They had reached 310 when Bailey (18) was caught by Weekes off Goddard. Then, from 310 for five England plunged to 326 for nine and finally 344 all out: the last five batsmen totalled 11 runs. England was saved from disaster mainly by Hutton's 202 not out, surely one of the highest peaks in the career of this great batsman. How often has a batsman come in first, carried his bat, and scored over sixty percent of his team's total! Of the 179 overs bowled by Westindies, Ramadhin and Valentine accounted for 109. Ramadhin's figures were: 45-23-63-1, and Valentine's: 64-21-121-4. Goddard had unusual success as a bowler taking four wickets for 25 runs in 17.4 overs.

Needing 160 runs to avoid an innings defeat, England followed on. After his marathon knock lasting 470 minutes, Hutton was brave if unwise to open the English second innings. His was the wicket that Westindies most dearly cherished and when, having scored 2, he was caught by Christiani at short leg off Goddard, all Westindians knew they had won the match and the rubber: it was only a matter of time; for the loss of Hutton had deprived the English ship of its rudder. Although Simpson (16) and Sheppard (29) offered some resistance, their colleagues seemed completely dazed by Ramadhin and Valentine, more by the latter. From 50 for three wickets the score plunged to 85 for nine; then it was all over at 105. A lamentable, funereal English procession preceded a joyous celebration of Westindian victory by an innings and 56 runs. Valentine's figures were: 26.3-10-39-6, and Ramadhin's: 26-11-38-3. In the match as a whole,

Valentine had harvested 10 wickets for 160 runs and Ramadhin four for 101. Between them they accounted for 14 of the 20 English wickets in the match. It is out of deeds like these that the romantic legend was born in England, in 1950, of "two little pals of mine, Ramadhin and Valentine". It is a legend of two young men, with scarcely any experience of first class cricket, who spearheaded an attack that brought Westindies not only their first Test victory in England (the second Test), but also their first rubber: they had won by the handsome margin of 3:1. What a difference from the first tour of England in 1928 when Westindies lost all three Tests, each by an innings!

One needs the authority of *Wisden* to sum up the extraordinary impact of the Westindian team on England in 1950:

> In the summer of 1950 Westindian cricket firmly established itself. Actually it was the twenty-second year since they were given Test status in 1928, but whereas some cricket bodies take a long time to grow up, there was no question that the representatives of the Caribbean reached maturity on their seventh visit to the cradle of cricket. [It was the fourth visit of Westindies to England, although the seventh series the two teams had played.] Those of us who saw them overwhelm G.O. Allen's M.C.C. team on their own fields in the early months of 1948 were prepared for surprises, but I do not think that any of us expected they would go from one triumph to another and outplay England in three out of four Tests. (*Wisden*, 1951, p. 207)

First Test vs. Australia
Woolloongabba, Brisbane, Australia
9, 10, 12, 13 November, 1951

The Westindian tour of Australia in 1951/52 was billed as the "championship" of the world, for both Australia and Westindies had already beaten England; and it was left to the two victors to settle the matter of world supremacy between themselves. For their first Test against Australia, while it was true that Westindies were up against a team from which Bradman had just retired, that team still contained batsmen like Arthur Morris, Lindsay Hassett, Neil Harvey and Keith Miller. Even more threatening was the fact that Australia possessed the most deadly pair of fast bowlers in the world at that time - Miller and Lindwall. By contrast, Westindies were richly blessed in batting, but they had only all-rounders Worrell and Gomez to use the new ball, which meant that they would have to rely, as they had done in England, on the mesmerizing powers of legendary spin twins, Ramadhin and Valentine.

From the opening over of the match, it seemed that Lindwall sent shivers through Rae who was unfortunate enough to be facing him, while Stollmeyer watched from a position of relative safety at the other end. Rae could not have seen the first two balls as they whizzed past him before he could move. The third he saw so late that by the time he brought his bat down, the ball hit his bat away and careered on to his wicket: Westindies 0 for one wicket. If this was a contest in which two teams were vying for championship of the cricketing world, it was an ominous indication of who might be the champions. Worrell and Stollmeyer played some surprisingly wristy shots before getting out, and at lunch Westindies were 89 for three with Weekes and Christiani batting. Not a whit deterred by their shaky situation, Weekes and Christiani also played their shots, but the Australian attack was relentless, and despite some brilliant moments, the Westindian innings fell apart for 216. It was a disappointing result on a good wicket, for a team in which Roy Marshall, Gerry Gomez and John Goddard were batting at numbers 7, 8, 9 respectively. It seemed that formidable talents were being prodigally squandered. Either that, or the Australians were just too good. At any rate, by end of play Australia were 16 without loss, and the advantage was all theirs. What happened overnight is not known, but the team that had batted without sufficient resolution the day before, now bowled with fire and menace. In no time at all Ramadhin and Valentine, erstwhile destroyers of England, had reduced Australia to 85 for four. Keith Miller staged a brief rally, but Valentine was particularly menacing, and only poor Westindian fielding and a swashbuckling innings of 61 by Ray Lindwall, who was dropped before he had even scored, took Australia to a total of 226. Valentine had sent down 25 overs and been rewarded with five wickets for 99 runs.

At the start of their second innings, Westindies could thank their bowlers for putting them back in the game, even though they had been profligate with their resources, both in batting and fielding. But although Stollmeyer and Rae did rather better in the second innings, they soon went, and it was up to Weekes and Worrell to restore some hope as they brought the score to 88 for two at the last over of the second day. Suddenly, unaccountably, except in the mind of the Almighty, Worrell walked down the pitch to swing mightily at Doug Ring's leg-break pitched on the off stump. Langley had all the time in the world to stump him. What possible explanation could there be for such bizarre lunacy on the second to last ball of the day from a man whose subsequent career proved that he possessed one of the finest cricketing brains ever produced in the Westindies! Nor was the Almighty, in His infinite wisdom, to let us off that lightly. To confound the calamity we had already endured, Goddard who came in as night watchman, drove the only ball he received - a full toss - straight back into the bowler's hands. So, in that fateful last over, Westindies descended from cautious optimism at 88 for two, to danger and desperation at 88 for four.

On the third day, Ring narrowly missed his hat trick when Christiani slashed at his first ball and was lucky not to get out. This second innings seemed destined to mix glory and gall in equal proportion. Weekes's 70 was a most glorious display of forceful aggression and inventive strokeplay, but after Marshall and Gomez had put on 45 runs in a courageous eighth-wicket stand, Marshall committed a suicidal, skied drive that could have come from the bat of a rank amateur. Brave Gomez soldiered on to the second highest score of 55, and

Westindies were all out for 245, leaving Australia 236 for victory. Australia reached 108 for two by end of play and needed 128 on the last day. It is an indication of Westindian strength in all departments of the game, that when play started on the final day, Australia were by no means home and dry. Such was the Westindian bowling potential that once Ramadhin and Valentine had swung into action again, they made Australia struggle hard to get those 128 runs. They got them, but not before losing seven wickets. At 225 for seven, for example, with Lindwall and Ring batting, and Ramadhin threatening devastation, anything might have happened. But Lindwall and Ring hung on for the eleven runs needed for victory, and Ramadhin finished the innings with five wickets for 90 runs in 40 overs.

For Westindies to have dropped so many catches and committed so many batting blunders, yet only lose by three wickets is eloquent proof of their immense potential. Why that potential was not more effectively harnessed and directed to achieve success is a continuing question of controversy in Westindian cricket. Hindsight shows us what that potential could achieve once it was harnessed, later on, by men like Worrell and Lloyd. But in the early 1950s the Westindian team consisted largely of talented individuals. Circumstances were also against them in Australia. They came from different parts of the world, and by different routes, to meet up in Australia, and more or less instantly perform as a team. Much too has been written of Goddard's tactical blunders, including his almost superstitious reliance on the prowess of Ramadhin and Valentine. He prematurely curtailed the opening spell of Gomez and Worrell, and rubbed the ball into the ground in order to make it more suitable for Ramadhin and Valentine to grip and bowl. In the Australian second innings of this match, Gomez and Worrell bowled five overs between them for 14 runs and one wicket, while Ramadhin and Valentine bowled 80.7 overs for 207 runs and six wickets. Gomez was taken off after he had bowled three overs for 12 runs and one wicket. The gap between Westindian potential and performance, in the 1950s must be related, to some extent to the question of captaincy. That Westindies lost the first Test of the Australian tour in 1951/52 is a matter of historical record. That they did so despite numerous blunders and mistakes is the stuff of legend.

Third Test vs. Australia
Adelaide Oval, Adelaide, Australia, 22, 24, 25 December, 1951

When Shakespeare wrote in almost the very last lines of *King John*: "This England never did, nor never shall/Lie at the proud foot of a conqueror" the game of cricket had not been invented. We may therefore excuse the bard who, despite his gifts, insight, perception and flawless language, failed utterly to predict the conquest of England by the Westindian cricket team in 1950. (See Appendix iii) Perhaps, in 1950, the English team was in a somewhat depleted state, due partly to the loss of players like Hedley Verity in war, and partly to the disappearance of those like Walter Hammond, through retirement. For all that, Westindies were cock-a-hoop in 1950; virtual champions of the cricketing world: if only they could beat Australia! Thus when the Westindian tour of Australia began in 1951/52, passions in the Westindies were as never before; for never before had they dared aspire to such dizzying heights of international exposure and achievement.

Since there were few short wave radio sets available in the Westindies at the time, hasty arrangements were made to congregate in the middle of night, in homes or shops, wherever a set was available, in order to catch, against the incessant crackling and infernal sputtering of trans-Pacific static, any figures or a familiar name that would count as precious news, albeit in Australian tones, of the fortunes of the boys down under. The Westindian team's opening encounters in Australia did not augur well. In their first scheduled game against the state of Queensland, they were trounced by ten wickets. They then lost the first Test match at Brisbane by a narrow margin, and the second Test match at Sydney by seven wickets. More importantly, at Sydney, Miller and Hassett collared Ramadhin and neutralized his mystery - potentially the deadliest weapon in the Westindian bowling armoury.

The state matches between the second and third Tests deepened the gloom over Westindian fortunes. At Adelaide, set 321 to win by South Australia, one of the weaker state sides, they could only muster 93 pitiful runs; and at Perth where they set Western Australia 247 to win, and where John Trim was bowling at his very best, they allowed the home team to recover from a dismal 149 for seven and win the match by one wicket. At home Westindians felt an uncertain mixture of nervous foreboding and dwindling hope when they sat down bleary-eyed to listen to a static-disfigured commentary on the third Test match at Adelaide. How could they believe that this was a contest of potential champions when, in two Tests and twelve innings, the three supposedly mighty Ws had not produced a single century between them! The highest Westindian Test score had come from the inimitable artistry of Robert Christiani with a wonderfully poetic 76 in the first innings of the Sydney Test. Yet such is the splendour of cricket that when we least expect it, the game produces events to lift our spirits again and revive even the slenderest shred of hope that we may still harbour.

There are many learned opinions delivered on the subject of what happened on the opening day of the third Test at Adelaide Oval on December 22, 1951; but none of them fully explains how Westindies dismissed Australia for 82 runs (Worrell: six for 38); how they went on themselves to compile 105; and how they later neutralized two Australian second innings wickets for a mere 20 runs! There was nothing wrong with the wicket or the weather. Yet 22 wickets fell that day for 207 runs! Perhaps the spirit of Christmas had something to do with it, or it may have been the absence of the Australian captain Lindsay Hassett due to injury. Sunday, December 23 was a rest day. On Christmas Eve Ring and Langley, the not out Australian batsmen, took their score to 145 for three. Then, within the space of half an hour, Ring, Morris and Harvey were out, and the score was transformed to 172 for six. Miller struck some brave blows to steady things at 227 for seven, but the Lord had chosen irrevocably to speak through the noble instrument of Valentine's left arm, as Australia slipped to a total of 255, and Valentine returned glorious figures of six wickets for 102 runs. Now, on the evening of Christmas Eve, the time had truly come for the word of the Lord to be fulfilled, and prayers went up for Westindies as they set about their task of getting 233 runs for victory.

Stollmeyer and Marshall, no doubt pious men both, played with gravity and reverence wholly befitting the occasion. Anyone who has witnessed the flashing blade of Roy Marshall will know what it meant for him to take one full hour to make five runs. That he did so under pain from a pulled muscle confirms his heroism. Firmly did the stalwart opening pair stand their ground until, at close of play, they had brought the score to 54 without loss. The next day was Christmas. All that was needed was 179 runs for victory. The fact of the matter was that if they lost this match, Westindies would lose the whole five match series and relinquish their bid for "championship" of the cricketing world. When the score was 72, Marshall was caught by Langley off Ring for 29, and when it was 85 Stollmeyer was caught by Miller off Ring for 47. But these two had done their duty nobly in laying a solid groundwork for the others to build on; and Weekes and Worrell continued building until the score reached 139 for two at lunch: 94 more runs to get.

What was served for Christmas lunch is not known, but immediately after lunch the Westindian score declined sharply to 141 for four. Crisis loomed. But it was Christmas after all, a time of peace and goodwill, when the Lord was disposed to be merciful as, through Christiani and Gomez, two of His most steadfast and stout-hearted warriors, he granted Westindians the most precious of Christmas gifts. Westindies reached 233 for four and won the match by six wickets, with Gomez 46 not out, and Christiani 42 not out. The series now stood at 2:1 in Australia's favour; but Westindies had at least earned the breathing space to live and fight again another day.

Fourth Test vs. Australia
Melbourne Cricket Ground, Melbourne, Australia
31 December 1951, 1, 2, 3 January, 1952

After losing the first two matches in the five-Test series, against Australia in 1951/52, Westindies feared that the "championship" was going to be decided far too early. This was undoubtedly one reason why they fought so hard in the third Test and won it. When, less than a week later, on New Year's Eve 1951, Westindies faced Australia in the fourth Test match at Melbourne, the options for each team were different: Australia could lose this match and wait for the fifth Test to secure the rubber, whereas Westindies had to win this fourth Test to have any chance at all at the rubber.

Goddard won the toss and Jeff Stollmeyer and Ken Rickards opened the Westindian innings. Both openers fell cheaply, as did Weekes but Gomez and Worrell added 72 invaluable runs before Gomez (37) was caught by Langley off Miller: 102 for four. Christiani and Worrell blended grace with invention to advance the score to 194. But in gliding Miller to deep fine leg Christiani chose to ignore Worrell's restraining upraised hand, and charged back for a suicidal second run, only to be run out for 37. Worrell went on to make an heroic 108, despite an injured hand that made batting excruciatingly painful. In reply to a Westindian total of 272, Australia had reached 64 for three by lunch-time on the second day. Neil Harvey composed a magnificent innings of 83 to give Australia the advantage at 176 for five, after which John Trim worked up terrific pace with the new ball, and blasted the Australian tail with a devastating spell of four wickets for 10 runs that gained Westindies a small but useful lead of 56. During the thirty-five minutes of play that were left on the second day, there was a bizarre display of tactical manoeuvres that produced ironic results. Goddard held back Ken Rickards, and asked wicket-keeper Simpson Guillen to open the Westindian second innings with Stollmeyer. Guillen (0) was immediately caught by Johnston off Lindwall, and Goddard himself came in only to fall lbw to Lindwall for 0. Finally, Rickards entered to restore the original opening partnership, after the Westindies had lost two wickets for 0! On the third day, Westindies were 60 for four when Christiani and Stollmeyer came together in a brief blaze of glory that produced 37 elegant and stylish runs. Stollmeyer (54) was lbw to Miller, and made way for Gomez to partner Christiani in a brave struggle that an Australian eye witness describes thus: "Gomez is dauntless from courage, and Christiani from pride." At any rate, despite the courage or pride of Gomez (52) and Christiani (33), Westindies could manage no more than 203 in their second innings.

Needing 260 for victory, Australia were 68 for one when stumps were drawn on the third day. On the fourth day, Ramadhin and Valentine struck something like the form with which they had devastated England eighteen months before, and pinned the Australian batsmen down for maiden after maiden. At lunch, the score was 128 for four with Graeme Hole and Lindsay Hassett batting, and 132 needed for victory. When Hole (13) was caught by Gomez off Worrell: 147 for five, the match began to swing toward Westindies, but for the obduracy of Hassett. Lindwall threatened mayhem when he lashed 29 quick runs before he was caught by Guillen off Ramadhin: 192 for six. With Australia needing 68 runs and Westindies four wickets to win, the odds were still slightly on Westindies. Finally, Hassett - the stumbling block - was lbw to Valentine for 102, an innings of extraordinary grit and gallantry. Then, Langley was also lbw to Valentine, and the score stood at 222 for nine: 38 runs left, and Doug Ring and Bill Johnston - two bowlers - to get them. Surely only a miracle could stop a Westindian victory at this stage!

Whatever it was, it was stopped. Ring and Johnston got the needed runs and won the match and the rubber for Australia. It is easy to blame Goddard: when Ramadhin and Valentine had pinned down the top order Australian batsmen, he used one slip for Ramadhin and two for Valentine instead of additional close fieldsmen to induce the batsmen into possible error; also, with different field placing, Lindwall might not have gotten away with slogging 29 runs so quickly at a crucial stage in the psychological development of the game; finally, three opportunities were missed in running out Ring and Johnston, due mainly to nerves and over-excitement. But it is no use crying over spilt milk. One needs to remember that merely ten years later, a Westindian team playing in Australia, in different circumstances, not only controlled their nerves, but did it with such accomplished professionalism that they achieved the first tied result in the history of Test cricket.

First Test vs. India
Queen's Park Oval, Port of Spain, Trinidad
21, 22, 23, 24, 27, 28 January, 1953

After their triumph in England in 1950 and humiliation in Australia in the winter of 1951, Westindies must have considered India's first tour of their homeland in 1952/53 with sobriety as well as relish: for while, at the time, India could not be considered equal in strength to either England or Australia, they possessed several players of repute: batsmen of the calibre of Hazare, Umrigar and Manjrekar, outstanding all-rounders like Mankad and Phadkar, Ramchand the best available Indian fast bowler, and a number of younger players with promise. For their part, Westindies boasted the three Ws, the most formidable combination of run-getters they had yet produced, Ramadhin and Valentine, still at the peak of their spinning prowess, and a lively pair of fast or medium-fast bowlers in Frank King and Gerry Gomez. It looked as if the main question would be whether the Indian bowlers could contain the Westindian batsmen, Weekes in particular, who had virtually run amok in India in 1948/49 scoring a total of 779 runs in seven Test innings. If that happened again, India would be relegated to a largely defensive role in the series.

In the first Test, Hazare won the toss, and Mankad and Apte opened for India. Mankad (2) was lbw to King early, and Apte and Ramchand put on 94 useful runs before Apte (64) was out: 110 for two. Soon after, Ramchand (61) and Hazare (29) were gone: 158 for four. Umrigar and Phadkar then took the score to 208 for four by end of play. The next day belonged entirely to Umrigar. Mixing defence with aggression, and receiving valuable support from Gaekwad, he advanced the Indian score from 210 for five to 328 for six before he was caught by wicket-keeper Binns off Valentine for 130. It was a timely, tempered knock that included two sixes, one off Ramadhin to take Umrigar to his century, and the other off Gomez, hit clean out of the ground. All this, shortly before the end of the second day's play, helped India to reach a respectable total of 417 runs. India's cautious scoring at just over two runs per over indicated a safety first policy that was no doubt mindful of the opposition's mighty batting potential.

India must also have been mindful that Test matches had been extended to six days instead of five. At any rate, Gomez was the most successful bowler with 42 overs for 84 runs and three wickets; but Valentine carried most of the Westindian attack - 56 overs for a paltry 92 runs, and accounted for the crucial wickets of Umrigar and Hazare.

Westindies started their first innings badly with Ramchand bowling Rae for 1. Captain Stollmeyer and Worrell put on 33 runs before another disaster struck, and Worrell (18) was bowled by Gupte, the ball trickling off the batsman's pads on to his wicket. By the time Stollmeyer (33) was next out with the total at 89, India had, improbably, seized the initiative. Weekes and Walcott asserted their customary confidence and power to advance the total by 101 runs before Walcott was caught in the slips off Mankad for 47. Meanwhile, Weekes remained, and helped by Bruce Pairaudeau, plundered no fewer than 219 runs in a partnership that wrested the initiative in the match decisively back from India. Pairaudeau went on to get 115 runs, a century in his maiden Test, while Weekes, true to his reputation for savaging Indian bowlers, opened his account on the tour with 207 runs, the highest Test score made at Queen's Park Oval up to that time. The remaining Westindian batsmen did not last long, and from a total of 409 for five, Westindies finished on 438. In the circumstances, India could consider themselves lucky to face a deficit of only 21 runs. For such luck they owed much to Subash Gupte, their right arm leg-spin and googly bowler, who bagged seven wickets for 162 runs in 66 overs. Gupte and his fellow spinner Mankad contributed 129 overs, more than two-thirds of the total overs bowled by their team. This illustrates the Indian reliance on spin which remains one of the most memorable features of their 1952/53 Westindian tour.

In their second innings, India ran into trouble by losing four wickets for 106 runs. Strangely enough, it was Walcott in his unaccustomed role as a bowler who was responsible for having Ramchand caught by the wicket-keeper for 17 and, more importantly, for getting Hazare caught and bowled for 0. India might have been in worse trouble, had Umrigar and Phadkar not contrived a fifth-wicket stand of 131 runs that took their score to 237 runs for five wickets, and relative safety from defeat. In the end, India were all out for 294 runs in their second innings, and set Westindies the well-nigh impossible task of scoring 274 runs to win in 160 minutes. Predictably, Rae and Stollmeyer played out the time. In the process, they compiled 142 runs, Rae being 63 not out, and Stollmeyer 76 not out when the match ended in a draw.

This first Test match had set the tone for the series: wonderful Westindian strokeplay against slow bowling of great resourcefulness, particularly from Mankad and Gupte. If Mankad's experience made him a force to be reckoned with, Gupte proved more dangerous, turning the ball at extraordinary angles, and achieving spectacular bounce on hard Westindian wickets. Even more spectacular was the ground fielding of the Indians without which neither Mankad nor Gupte might have passed muster. The Guyanese journalist Ernest Eytle describes India's fielding as follows: "India's greatest asset was her brilliance in the field. I have never seen any fielding in any part of the world equal theirs of the first Test in Trinidad." Eytle singles out Gadkari, Gaekwad and Umrigar for their "superb returning to the wicket, and general hostility", but the whole Indian team should take credit for contributing to one of the most exciting forms of entertainment that the game of cricket can offer: a contest between inspired, brilliant, stroke-making batsmen and artful, skilful spin bowlers who are backed up by strategic field placings, fast, clean, often-running pick-ups, and accurate, over-the-wicket throw-ins. Other aspects of cricket have their own appeal, but on a sunny afternoon, under blue, Westindian skies, with a faithful bottle of rum by one's side, the contest of high class strokeplay against high class spin bowling and high class fielding will take cricket lovers closer to the portals of heaven than most of us could ever hope to get.

Second Test vs. India
Kensington Oval, Bridgetown, Barbados
7, 9, 10, 11, 12 February, 1953

By achieving a draw in the first Test of their tour of Westindies in 1953, India proved that they were not completely at the mercy of a dominant Westindian batting line-up. Mankad and Gupte had shown that, supported by excellent fielding, they could contain Westindian batting excesses. For the second Test, Westindies dropped Rae and wicket-keeper Binns, and brought in Christiani and wicket-keeper Legall. India likewise made two changes from their first Test team: they dropped Shodhan and Gadkari for Roy and Manjrekar. In the Barbados match that preceded the second Test, sixteen-year-old Garfield Sobers made his début in international cricket: he scored 7 not out, took four wickets for 50 runs in the Indian first innings, and three for 92 in the second. Before the start of the second Test, there was a heavy downpour which later proved fateful to the extent that it gave Stollmeyer an advantage in winning the toss. At first, it didn't look like that; for by lunch, both Stollmeyer (32) and Worrell (24) were out, and Westindies were 81 for two. Before tea, Pairaudeau (43) and Weekes (47) were caught by wicket-keeper Joshi off Hazare: 168 for four; and after Gupte had accounted for Christiani (4) and Gomez (0), the home team finished the first day on 262 for eight, not a particularly auspicious start. The next day Westindies were dismissed for 296. Even this, for them, modest total would not have been possible were it not for a feisty ninth-wicket stand of 58 between Walcott and Ramadhin. Walcott topscored with 98, and must have had mixed feelings to be given out, lbw to Phadkar, by his uncle, Harold Walcott when he was so close to a century. As in the first Test, India relied mainly on Mankad and Gupte who bowled 87 overs out of a total of 116, and took three wickets each. They had set the Indian batsmen a target well within their capacity, and given a fillip to Indian hopes.

These hopes dipped when Roy (1) was caught by Worrell off King with the

Indian score at 6. Then Manjrekar, who a few days earlier, had made 154 in the Barbados match on the same ground, was lbw to Ramadhin for 25, and India were 44 for two. Apte and Hazare came together in a splendid stand that took India to 155 for two by the end of the second day, at least an evenly balanced position, if not exactly one favourable to India. But cricket would not have its reputation for mixing delight with disaster, if it did not also mix expectation with uncertainty. With eight wickets in hand, and 141 runs behind Westindies, who would not have expected India to get a first innings lead? Yet, within fifteen minutes on the third day, Apte (64) had been caught by Worrell off Valentine, and Hazare (63) had been caught by Weekes off King, and taken India's resurgent hopes with them. The ever reliable Umrigar, helped by Ramchand, advanced the total from 164 for four to 204 for five before Ramchand was bowled by Ramadhin. Thereafter, apart from a contribution of 17 by Phadkar who helped Umrigar put on 37 for the sixth wicket, India's remaining batsmen surrendered for 253. Valentine, the most successful Westindian bowler, collected four wickets for 58 runs in 41 overs, while Ramadhin sent down 30 overs for 59 runs and two wickets. Since India had to bat last in the match, it was an ominous sign that the overs of Ramadhin and Valentine cost them less than two runs each.

Spirited bowling by Phadkar in the Westindian second innings had Pairaudeau lbw before a run had been scored. Phadkar followed this up by bowling Worrell to make the total 25 for two. Mankad bowled Weekes for 15, and Stollmeyer and Walcott carried the total to 91 for three before end of play. At that stage, even considering their first innings deficit of 43, India had miraculously bounced back to once more get within sight of victory. On the fourth day, India bowled as if victory was more clearly in view: three more Westindian wickets fell while 84 runs were made to bring the score to 175 for six. From there on, little Westindian resistance was evident, and their second innings closed at 228. The middle order batsmen made modest contributions - Walcott (34); Christiani (33); and Gomez (35). No one really got going, except Stollmeyer, who achieved the top score of 54. Phadkar had turned in a stunning performance of five wickets for 64 runs in 29.3 overs, and India now had 273 runs to get for victory, and more than two days to do it.

Time was not a factor, nor, apparently, the weather: it was entirely up to India's batsmen. Batsmen of the calibre of Umrigar, Hazare and Manjrekar certainly had the potential for the task. But before play ended on the fourth day, Apte (9) was bowled by King, and Mankad (3) was bowled by Gomez while only 17 runs were on the board. The fifth day was decisive. The pitch finally showed its (un)true quality, confirming that India's fate had been more or less sealed when Stollmeyer won the toss. Although Valentine had carried the brunt of the Westindian bowling in the series so far, Ramadhin now became literally unplayable, mysteriously mixing off-breaks and leg-breaks, turning the ball hugely, and causing intense bafflement, confusion and alarm in the ranks of India's batsmen. Hazare (0), Umrigar (6) and Ramchand (34) were all clean bowled by Ramadhin. The highest partnership India could muster was a third-wicket stand of 57 runs between Roy (22) and Manjrekar who carried his bat defiantly for 32. It gives some idea of the Indian débacle to note that apart from

Roy, Manjrekar and Ramchand, no other Indian batsman reached double figures. Such was Ramadhin's devilry that India abjectly crumbled to a wretched total of 129, and ceded victory by 142 runs.

In India's second innings, Westindies bowled a total of 79.5 overs of which Ramadhin and Valentine contributed 59.5. Ramadhin's figures tell almost the whole story: 24.5-11-26-5. One had to feel sorry for the Indians who had fought gamely right up to the fifth day. Nor must Valentine's sterling support be forgotten in this Indian second innings: 35-16-53-2. For all that, the palm goes undoubtedly to Ramadhin. His was an extraordinary performance that seemed to drain him so completely that, over the next two Test matches, he took only two wickets. This is why, believe it or not, he was dropped from the fifth and final Test in the series.

Fifth Test vs. India
Sabina Park, Kingston, Jamaica
28, 30, 31 March, 1, 2, 4 April, 1953

The 1952/53 series between Westindies and India was dominated by the glorious batting of the three Ws on one side, and the magnificent spin bowling of Vinoo Mankad and Subash Gupte on the other. The Ws scored 1,571 (60 percent) of the total (2,643) runs of their entire team in the five match series, and Mankad and Gupte took 42 (nearly 70 percent) of the total (61) wickets taken by their entire side. Victory in the second Test gave Westindies an early advantage which they maintained through two drawn matches in the third and fourth Tests, so that by the time the two teams faced each other for the fifth and final Test at Sabina Park, all Westindies needed was a draw to win the rubber. India, meanwhile, faced an uphill task of winning the match if they were to draw the series. The betting, in other words, was clearly on Westindies. For the fifth Test, India were without their renowned all-rounder, Dattu Phadkar, who was replaced, because of injury, by J.M. Ghorpade. Westindies too had to call in replacements, Gerry Gomez, Robert Christiani and A.P.H. Scott being brought in for Leslie Wight, Roy Miller and Sonny Ramadhin.

Hazare won the toss, and his openers Roy and Apte started cautiously on an easy paced wicket with a fast outfield. With the score at 30, after ninety minutes play, Apte was run out for 15. The incoming Ramchand (22) stepped up the tempo briefly, but fell lbw to Valentine when the total was 57. Soon afterward, Hazare (16) was caught by Valentine off Frank King and India were 80 for three. Roy and Umrigar restored some enterprise to the innings and took their score to 216 for three by close of play. On the second day, Roy's splendid effort ended when he was caught off King for 85: 230 for four. He and Umrigar had put on 150 runs, then a record for India/Westindies matches. But after Umrigar was bowled by Valentine for a fighting 117, his second Test century on the tour,

India suffered a collapse from 277 for five to 312 all out. For Westindies, Valentine returned the most impressive figures: 27.5-9-64-5. One can gauge the respect paid to the Westindian bowlers generally from the fact that King, Gomez and Worrell all bowled at a rate of less than two runs per over.

By the end of the second day, Westindies had a total of 103 for the loss of Stollmeyer (13), their captain. Stollmeyer's departure proved to be the cue for vintage batting on the third day, particularly after Pairaudeau was bowled by Gupte for 58: 133 for two; for it brought Weekes and Worrell together in a partnership that smashed 197 runs in 170 minutes off unflagging Indian bowlers until Weekes was caught off Gupte for 109: 330 for three. Worrell and Walcott then hastened the score to 400 for three before close of play. On the fourth day, Worrell and Walcott continued the onslaught by amassing 213 runs in an incomparable display of inspired strokeplay, until Walcott was caught off Mankad for 118: 543 for four. After two long partnerships that spread over three days, Worrell was finally out, also caught off Mankad, for a glorious innings of 237 runs: 554 for five. Whether the remaining Westindian batsmen were too mesmerised by such glory, or had simply lost touch by being kept waiting so long, it is impossible to say, but once Worrell had gone, they were all out for 576 as their last five wickets fell for a mere 22 runs. The Ws accounted for no fewer than 464 of this total: it was the first time that they had all scored centuries in the same innings of a Test match. Mankad and Gupte bowled 147.1 overs between them, while the remaining three Indian bowlers contributed 59 overs. Considering the devastation wrought by the Ws, the Indian spinners showed amazing stamina. Nor were their figures dishonourable: Gupte: 65.1-14-180-5, and Mankad: 82-17-228-5.

Faced with a deficit of 264, all hope of victory had vanished from Indian minds, and survival became paramount. From this point of view, India's openers did well to reach the end of the fourth day having scored 63 runs. The next day Apte was lbw to Valentine for 33. Manjrekar came in instead of Ramchand in what turned out to be an astute change of the batting order; for Roy and Manjrekar proceeded to construct a defence that yielded 237 runs before it finally cracked at 317 after Manjrekar had compiled 118 golden runs. Ten runs later Roy's tough-minded resolution also cracked when he was lbw to Valentine for 150, and India were left on 327 for three when stumps were drawn. Despite the heroic feats of Roy and Manjrekar, India were only 63 runs to the good at the start of play on the final day - hardly a position of safety. And when Umrigar (13), Hazare (12) and Gadkari (0) all fell cheaply, bringing India to 368 for seven, it really seemed that the heroism of Roy and Manjrekar had been completely undone. But Ramchand and Ghorpade came to the rescue with timely, if modest innings of 33 and 24 respectively, and Shodhan even deserted his sick bed to contribute a priceless 15 not out to help his side to a total of 444, which left Westindies 181 runs to get for victory in 145 minutes.

Since Pairaudeau and Stollmeyer were out for 15 runs, the Westindian batsmen played out time and the match ended in a draw that belied its excitement right up to the last couple of hours when it was clear that Westindian pursuit of victory was not worth the risk of compromising the 1-0 lead they already had.

India's first visit to the Westindies ended with a 1-0 Westindian victory just as Westindies's first visit to India, three years before, had produced the same result. This result owed much to the resplendent prowess of the Ws who were then at the height of their powers. But despite this Westindian advantage, India were not humiliated. While they often came close to losing, they had an uncanny capacity for extricating themselves from trouble. Stollmeyer summed it up best at the very end, when he said that they were a hard team to beat. It was a gracious compliment from the captain of the stronger team.

First Test vs. England
Sabina Park, Kingston, Jamaica
15, 16, 18, 19, 20, 21 January, 1954

In the first Test of England's second post-war tour of Westindies, the Westindian team was substantially unchanged from the one in 1950: Ramadhin and Valentine were still there, as were the three Ws, Stollmeyer and Gomez. (Worrell did not play in the Jamaica Test because of injury). Newcomers included Clifford McWatt as wicket-keeper, Esmond Kentish as fast bowler, and J.K. Holt as batsman. McWatt and Holt were making their Test début. England, meanwhile, had been completely revitalized, and unlike 1947/48, had sent a full complement of their best players. The stalwarts - Hutton (the current captain), Compton, Bailey, Evans, Lock - remained; but there were talented, new batsmen like May and Graveney, and young fast bowlers like Trueman, Statham and Moss. What is more, just six months earlier, in the summer of 1953, this team had beaten Australia and regained the Ashes for the first time in almost twenty years.

In the first Test in 1954, Stollmeyer won the toss and elected to bat. Merely 6 runs were on the board when his partner, another newcomer, Michael Frederick (0) was caught by Graveney in the slips off Statham. Stollmeyer and Holt stayed together until well after tea, when Stollmeyer (60) was lbw to Statham: 140 for two. Weekes (21 not out) and Holt (76 not out) carried the total to 168 by the end of the day: not quick scoring, but understandable considering that England's four fast bowlers tended to reduce the over rate. On the second day, Holt who had played an indispensable role, was unlucky to be given out lbw to Statham when only 6 runs short of his century. Still, at 216 for three, Westindies were strongly placed. By tea, the score was 316 for six with the best batsmen out. Then, in one of those unexpected rallies that depend just as much on luck as pluck, Gomez and McWatt contrived 88 runs before McWatt, who had been dropped four times, was bowled by Lock in the last over of the day when Westindies were 408 for seven.

The next morning, Westindies were dismissed for 417, Gomez being left not out on 47. Statham had sent down 36 overs for 90 runs and four wickets, while Lock had been rewarded with three wickets for 76 runs in 41 overs! By lunch, England were 29 for one, and soon afterwards, when Valentine bowled Hutton

(24), the unbounded delight of the crowd confirmed that England had been struck a mortal blow. As if to confirm the crowd's delight in his demise, Hutton's departure did spell a collapse as England slid from 49 for two to 94 for five, and by end of play, to 168 for nine. The damage was done entirely by Ramadhin and Valentine. It would not be at all surprising if some Englishmen did not regard Ram and Val as nemesis figures sent by God to punish them for sins they had incurred as British colonists all over the world. Their bowling figures in this innings were: Ramadhin 35-14-65-4; and Valentine 31-10-50-3.

The fourth day opened with England adding two runs to their overnight total, and Stollmeyer deciding not to enforce the follow-on despite a lead of 247. Although Westindian crowds are not famous for restraint, Stollmeyer could not have expected the vehemence of this crowd's disapproval of his decision: they booed him, both when he came in to open the Westindian second innings, and shortly afterwards, when he was caught by Evans off Bailey for 8: 28 for one. Yet again, the crowd's reaction proved to be prescient when Westindies suddenly plunged from 28 for one to 94 for five, and by close of play, had barely managed to limp to 203 for six, mainly because of a face-saving partnership between Weekes and McWatt. Early the next morning Westindies declared at 209 for six (Weekes 90 not out), leaving England to get 457 runs to win in nine and a half hours. The wicket was as good as gold. If, at the beginning of the fifth day, an English victory was not impossible, by the end of the day, having already compiled 227 for two, such a victory was very possible indeed. For such good fortune, England were chiefly indebted to their opening batsman Watson who made 116. A few minutes before lunch on the final day, May was caught by McWatt off Kentish for 69, which left England needing 180 runs for victory with three and a half hours and seven wickets left.

At that stage, Stollmeyer was in an unenviable position: if England won, press and public would be baying for his blood, for, it would be said, and not entirely without justification, that he had let England off by not enforcing the follow-on. But Stollmeyer responded with tactical resourcefulness. Kentish was instructed to bowl wide of the leg stump, while the field, from fine leg to mid-on was ringed with fieldsmen sufficiently set back to allow singles but to cut off boundaries. At the other end, Ramadhin was called upon to bowl as tidily as possible. It was a perfect strategy: England were too close to victory to resist going after runs despite risk. Consequently, they suffered a deadly reversal. Compton (2), Graveney (34), Evans (0) and Lock (0) were all out on the same score - 282 - and England plummeted from 277 for three to 285 for nine. At one point, seven wickets fell for 6 runs! The result was an English total of 316, and Westindian victory by 140 runs. Kentish surprised everyone, not least himself, with figures of: 29-11-49-5. Best of all, Stollmeyer could feel vindicated: he had taken a gamble which almost became a close run thing; but, in the end, he had won. Still, such was the vehemence of the crowd's hostility toward Stollmeyer that he vowed never again to play in Jamaica, a vow he happily abandoned when he appeared again at Sabina Park in the fifth Test of the same series. The behaviour of the crowd may also be relevant in this match since the wife and son of umpire Burke were physically attacked presumably in protest against Burke's decision giving Holt lbw when only six runs short of his century.

Second Test vs. England
Kensington Oval, Bridgetown, Barbados
6, 8, 9, 10, 11, 12 February, 1954

The second Test match in England's 1953/54 tour of Westindies was played two weeks after Westindies had won the first Test in Jamaica. At the start of their tour, England had the enviable record of going through thirteen consecutive Tests without being defeated. Their failure in Jamaica was therefore surprising, but probably no more than a temporary lapse, considering the somewhat narrow margin by which they lost - 140 runs. For the second Test, England replaced Fred Trueman and Alan Moss with Jim Laker and C.H. Palmer who was also the team manager. Westindies, meanwhile, dropped George Headley, Michael Frederick and Esmond Kentish, while Everton Weekes could not play because of illness. These vacancies were filled by Frank Worrell, Frank King, Denis Atkinson and Bruce Pairaudeau.

Hutton lost the toss for the seventh successive time in Test matches, and Stollmeyer's men batted in what looked like perfect conditions. The score was 11 when Westindies suffered their first blow: a misunderstanding between Stollmeyer and Holt which led to Stollmeyer being run out for 0. Another blow quickly followed with Worrell being bowled by Statham, also for 0. And when, soon afterwards, Holt was caught cheaply in the slips off Bailey, Westindies were in a crisis at 25 for three. Attempting a rescue, Walcott and Pairaudeau advanced the total to 58 without further loss by lunch-time. On this fragile foundation, after lunch, Walcott built a fabulous citadel, giving him mastery of all he surveyed, while Pairaudeau enacted an efficient, supporting role. Together, they pushed the total to 190 before Pairaudeau was caught by Hutton off Laker for 71. Walcott's century came and went, and by end of play, the score was 258 for five with Walcott 147 not out and Atkinson 18 not out. Walcott and Atkinson added another 61 runs the next day before Atkinson was caught by Evans off Laker for 53: 319 for six. But nothing could stop Walcott. He went on and on, past his double century, so that when the Westindian first innings ended at 383, he had scored 220 runs, his only double century in Tests, and at the time, one of only six double centuries made by Westindians. Despite Walcott's overpowering assault on them, at least two English bowlers returned respectable figures - Laker: four wickets for 81 runs in 30.1 overs; and Statham: three wickets for 90 runs in 27 overs.

Opening for England, Hutton and Watson negotiated the pace attack of King and Gomez with ease. It was when Ramadhin and Valentine came on that they began to flounder. Watson was stumped off Ramadhin for 6, while May (7) was caught by King also off Ramadhin to make the score 45 for two. The mesmerizing power exercised by Ram and Val might be gauged from their figures at lunch on the third day: Ramadhin had bowled 27 overs for 25 runs and taken two wickets, and Valentine 27 overs for 17 runs and one wicket. Hutton, the most successful English batsman made 72 before he was caught by Ramadhin off Valentine, and by the end of the third day, England had lost nine wickets. All the English batsmen could manage was 181 runs off 150 overs! It took them four hours to accumulate 97 runs. Batting at a rate of a little over one run per over it was no wonder that they were barracked by the crowd. When the last English wicket fell without addition the next day, Ramadhin had delivered 53 overs for 50 runs and taken four wickets, while Valentine had sent down 51.5 overs for 61 runs and three wickets.

As in the first Test, Stollmeyer did not enforce the follow-on, and the Westindian second innings opened with a bizarre repetition of misunderstanding between Holt and his captain, causing the latter to be again run out, this time for 28 runs: 51 for one. Thereafter, Holt conjured up a batting display that dominated this innings as magisterially as Walcott's had done the preceding one. His array of strokes was nothing less than brilliant, and by the end of the fourth day, he had taken his personal score to 166 not out, while Westindies had reached 272 for one, with Worrell 74 not out. Lock and Laker had done most of the bowling for England with no reward at all, although Laker's 30 overs for 62 runs prove that he commanded respect.

Stollmeyer waited until the fifth morning to declare, after Holt was out at his overnight score and Westindies had added 20 more runs. He offered England a target of 495 runs and nearly ten hours to get them on a wicket which had some cracks but was still in good condition. This proposition was not dissimilar to the one offered at the same stage of the first Test. The two main differences were that now England needed 50 more runs, and they had already lost the crucial wicket of Peter May. By the end of the fifth day, England had responded much as they had done in the first Test: they had scored 214 for three and needed 281 more runs to win with seven wickets standing. As it turned out, of the seven remaining English batsmen, only Graveney and Compton offered any real resistance by putting on 77 runs for the fourth wicket. Once Compton was out, Graveney could find none of his compatriots to stay with him. His was a lonely vigil of grit and defiance that left him 64 not out, while England collapsed for 313, and yielded victory to Westindies by a convincing margin of 181 runs. To appreciate Graveney's defiance one must realize that while he courageously held up one end, six wickets fell for 55 runs at the other. Wickets were shared more or less equally between the Westindian bowlers - King, Gomez, and Stollmeyer - who claimed two each. But there was no doubt about the real match winners: Ramadhin turned in 37 overs for 71 runs and three wickets, and Valentine 39 overs for 87 runs. They did not win the match by themselves, but Ram and Val confirmed that they had not completely lost the potency that won them the astonishment of the world in 1950.

Third Test vs. England
Bourda, Georgetown, Guyana
24, 25, 26, 27 February, 1, 2, March, 1954

Nowadays, the third Test match between England and Westindies in 1954, is recalled chiefly for its notoriety in providing the occasion for angry spectators to throw bottles and missiles onto the field, and by their alleged threats, to make it necessary for police to guard umpire Menzies's house during the match. At the start of their tour, England had to redeem two defeats: one incurred on their tour of Westindies in 1947/48, and the other sustained in 1950, when Westindies toured England and levelled everything in sight. Soon after 1950 England began to rebuild their team, and by 1954, could already be said to have completed the task; for they had won the Ashes back from Australia in the summer of 1953. By arriving in the Westindies later the same year, one of their aims must have been to test the genuineness of their rebuilding. But they had lost the first Test in Jamaica by 140 runs, and the second in Barbados by 181 runs. Since it was a five match series, the fate of the entire rubber depended on the outcome of the third Test at Bourda.

With grim resolve, Hutton played his usual anchoring role and batted the whole of the first day for 84 runs. At close of play, England had reached 153 for two, Hutton and Compton being the not out batsmen. Ramadhin's figures for the day were 31 overs for 39 runs and one wicket, and Denis Atkinson's 28 overs for 24 runs and one wicket. If these figures suggest somewhat unenterprizing cricket, it should be acknowledged that after he reached his century on the second day, Hutton offered the crowd more entertainment. But when he was finally out for 169, he had still made only sparing use of the vast repertoire of strokes he was known to possess. In the end, although other batsmen made useful contributions, for example, Compton (64), Wardle (38), and Bailey (49), England's first innings total of 435 rested squarely on the firm foundation patiently constructed by Hutton. Ramadhin did the main damage with figures of: 67-34-113-6, followed by Atkinson with: 58-27-78-3. Although Valentine collected only one wicket for 109 runs, it was a notable event since it was his hundredth wicket in Tests.

J.K. Holt had pulled a muscle and Worrell opened the Westindian innings with captain Stollmeyer. The crowd had scarcely settled down for play to re-start when Worrell hung his bat out to Statham's second ball, and was caught by wicket-keeper Evans for 0. Two overs later, Stollmeyer was bowled by Statham, and Westindies were two wickets down for 12 runs in perfect batting conditions! If there was any uncertainty before, the English plan to win this match at all costs now became abundantly clear. With Weekes and Walcott at the crease, Hutton placed himself at silly mid-off, and called up Bailey to stand near to him, not more than six yards from Walcott's bat. Walcott's response was a powerful back drive off Statham that went between Hutton and Bailey for four. Attempting again to disperse these two fieldsmen standing in such intimidating positions, Walcott went for the drive once more and edged the ball on to his wicket. In slightly less than one hour, Statham had taken three wickets for 12 runs, and Westindies were 31 for three. At this crucial juncture, with Statham threatening rampant devastation, rain intervened and washed out play for the rest of the day.

Resuming on the fourth day, Christiani and Weekes staged a brief rally that produced 62 runs before Christiani (25) was caught at mid-wicket off Laker. The catch was taken low down and aroused some suspicion in a partisan crowd already growing restive from the dismal turn of events. When Weekes who was heroically leading the Westindian resistance, was bowled by Lock for 94: 132 for five, the restiveness of the crowd increased. There was doubt in some spectators' minds about whether the ball had hit Weekes's wicket without interference from the wicket-keeper, and this caused tempers to become even more frayed. The subsequent fall of Denis Atkinson's wicket bringing Westindies to 139 for seven wickets did nothing to relieve spectators' discontent. Thus it was not altogether surprising that when McWatt and the injured Holt fought a brilliant defensive action to realize 99 salving runs, and when McWatt - a local boy - went for a desperate run to achieve the hundred partnership only to be run out, that tempers suddenly snapped; for umpire Menzies, who had already earned the crowd's displeasure in giving Christiani and Weekes out, was involved again in giving McWatt out, and although his decision was correct, to many in the crowd, it was the last straw. Bottles and other missiles then descended. Ever intent on victory, Hutton refused to take his team off the field, and play resumed after a brief interruption. Eventually, the Westindian innings finished on 251, and Hutton enforced the follow-on. This time, not Statham alone, but all the main English bowlers engaged in a spirited attack that swept away the top Westindian batsmen, who by the end of the fifth day, had limped to 205 runs for six wickets in their second innings. It is impossible to deny that the behaviour of the crowd was disgraceful. Although their anger was not directed at the English players, it is regrettable that it was directed against umpire Menzies who had to scamper to the safety of the pavilion at the end of play.

The sixth day was a mere formality. Westindies fell for 256, and England scored the needed 75 for the loss only of Peter May, thus winning by nine wickets. It was a good, hard fought engagement between two fine teams, one of which had a distinct edge in determination and the will to win. England deserved to win. It is a pity that such a keenly fought contest should be remembered mainly for sensational reasons. What should be remembered is the valiant 99 run partnership between McWatt and Holt which remains the eighth wicket record for Westindies against England. For their part, Westindies were unlucky that Holt was injured. He was in great form, as his scores in the previous two matches would show: 94; 90 not out; 11; and 166. Hutton too played a crucial role as captain and batsman. But the decisive blow was struck on the morning of the third day, when Statham ripped through Westindian defences with as magnificent a spell of aggressive, penetrating, controlled fast bowling as was ever seen on the hard, true surface of Bourda Green.

Fifth Test vs. England
Sabina Park, Kingston, Jamaica
30, 31 March, 1, 2, 3 April, 1954

It is largely due to Hutton's resolve during England's 1953/54 tour of Westindies that his team won a convincing nine-wicket victory in the third Test at Bourda. The fourth Test at Queen's Park Oval, Port-of-Spain was played on matting which produced a harvest of runs and an inevitable draw. Batting first, Westindies hoisted a colossal 681 for eight declared (Weekes, 206, Worrell, 167, Walcott, 124). England replied with 537: May, 135, Compton, 133. This was followed by a Westindian second innings total of 212 for four declared, and England's 98 for three. Since England were already down 2:1 in the series, this inconclusive fourth -Test result meant that they could not win the rubber even if they won the remaining Test - the fifth.

In the fifth Test, Hutton lost the toss for the ninth time in ten Test matches and Westindies batted first. J.K. Holt was the first Westindian batsman to go - caught Lock, bowled Bailey for 0: 0 for one. When Weekes got an inside edge and was bowled by Bailey for 0, the score became 2 runs for two wickets, and when Stollmeyer (9) snicked a catch off Bailey to Evans behind the stumps, it was 13 runs for three wickets. At this stage, Bailey's figures were: 5-4-3-3, and soon afterwards Worrell (4) was caught by Wardle off Trueman, and the Westindian score stood at 13 for four. There is no rational explanation of these disasters. Miracles defy explanation: that is why they are miracles. All that can be said is that Bailey moved the ball in the air and off the seam with great skill. It was the ball's movement rather than its pace that undid the batsmen. Only Walcott, of the top order Westindian batsmen negotiated Bailey's crafty movement with any confidence. Walcott scored 50, and while he and McWatt (22) were engaged in a seventh-wicket stand of 35, there was a flicker of modest hope, but once Walcott fell, this flicker was quickly extinguished and Westindies were all out for 139. From a Westindian point of view, the chief consolation was that Walcott was replaced by a seventeen year old lad, Garfield Sobers, who was playing in his first Test and was left with 14 not out while his senior colleagues - McWatt, King and Ramadhin - all succumbed at the other end. No doubt, Sobers's performance augured well for the future, but in their present situation Westindies had to face the discomforting fact that, in 16 miraculous overs, Bailey had taken 7 of their wickets for 34 runs, and had routed them completely.

Starting to bat shortly before the end of the first day, England reached 194 for five by the end of the second day, with Hutton himself 93 not out. Slow, cautious batting confirmed an English strategy, eloquently embodied in Hutton's own innings, to dig in and lay a firm foundation for victory. England batted well into the third day when they reached a total of 414, of which Hutton's contribution - 205 - was the first double century made by an English captain in an overseas Test; it was a monument to dogged concentration and iron discipline. Without detracting from these qualities in Hutton's batsmanship, it must be noted that Frank King, the fastest and most dangerous Westindian bowler, was injured on the second day and did not play for the rest of England's innings. Nevertheless, were it not for Hutton, the Westindian bowlers could be said to have performed creditably. Sobers's first Test performance spoke volumes: 28.5-9-75-4. His first wicket was that of Trevor Bailey who later became his biographer. Faced with a deficit of 275 runs Stollmeyer and Holt had acquired 20 without loss by the end of the third day. Since the wicket was still good, Westindian fortunes were not necessarily as grim as they looked. If the Ws could show anything like the form they did in the fourth Test, the match could be easily saved. But early on the fourth day Holt (8) was caught by Lock off Trueman with the score at 26, and at 38, Weekes (3) was bowled by Wardle. Worrell and Stollmeyer forged cautiously ahead until, at 102, Worrell was caught off Trueman for 29. Then, after a gallant captain's innings, Stollmeyer was lbw to Trueman for 64. This brought Westindies to 123 for four, which Walcott and Gomez extended to 184 without further loss by end of play.

At the start of the fifth day, with six wickets intact, Westindies needed 91 runs to make England bat again. Play had scarcely begun, before Gomez (22), who had added 1 to his overnight score, was lbw to Laker: 191 for five. Atkinson faced a desperate situation, and helped Walcott to produce a vital sixth wicket partnership worth 82 runs. But Walcott, on whom all now depended, received a painful blow on the wrist which made things even more desperate. Somehow, despite his discomfort, Walcott continued his match-saving innings until, overcome by pain and fatigue, he finally surrendered. His heroic innings of 116 runs is one of the bravest and best in Westindian cricket. The rest was anti-climax as Westindies struggled to 346. This left 72 for victory, which England achieved for the loss of one wicket. It was the first Westindian defeat at Sabina Park. The most decisive elements of the match were Bailey's seven for 34 and Hutton's 205 which formed essential parts of a magnificent, defensive action in which England drew the rubber after being down nil: two. Nor is the magnificence of this feat diminished by suggesting that injuries to King and Walcott, at crucial stages of the match, may have contributed to England's victory in the fifth Test. Fortune favours the brave, and if fortune favoured England, it also favoured Westindies by giving them their first reliable view of one of their players destined to become the greatest all-rounder to ever play cricket.

First Test vs. Australia
Sabina Park, Kingston, Jamaica, 26, 28, 29, 30, 31 March, 1955

Australia first played Test matches against Westindies in 1930/31, then in 1951/52, both times in Australia; and both times they administered a severe thrashing on the tourists. So in 1955, when Australia paid their first visit to the Westindies, their hosts had much to avenge. There was much in favour of such a prospect as well. Westindian strength lay in the form of the three Ws and Ram and Val, and the fact of playing on home territory for the first time, with partisan vocal support to bolster their spirits. Besides, Australia were smarting from a sharp 3:1 defeat inflicted on them by England's speedsters, Frank Tyson and Brian Statham, on a tour that had ended mere weeks before the start of the first Test between Westindies and Australia at Sabina Park.

Batting first, Australia's opening pair of Morris and McDonald were not separated until the score had reached 102, when McDonald was stumped by Binns off Valentine for 50. Morris (63) followed soon after, lbw to Valentine: 137 for 2. Harvey and Miller batted calmly for the rest of the day and advanced the score to 266, with Harvey on 84 and Miller on 64. On the second day, since Worrell (Frank King's partner as opening bowler) was injured, and Valentine's bowling finger bandaged, Harvey and Miller proved extra hard to dislodge, and went on to claim centuries. Not until the score reached 361 did Harvey fall, bowled by Walcott for a grand 133. Lindwall entered briefly and left before Miller's equally grand innings of 147 was abrogated by Walcott: 417 for 5. By the end of the second day, Australia were safely ensconced on a total of 515 for 9 with Johnson and Johnston in possession. Since captain Ian Johnson had pulled a ligament and could not play on the third day, Australia declared overnight. Ramadhin and Valentine had done most of the Westindian bowling, exactly 100 overs between them, Valentine being more successful with three wickets for 113 runs, whereas Ramadhin had to be satisfied with one for 112. Strange to say, it was Walcott who proved the best bowler with his off-cutters that claimed three wickets for 50 runs in 26 overs. Sadly, Frank King toiled in vain for 28 overs and 122 runs.

The Westindian opening pair of J.K. Holt and Glendon Gibbs were separated when Gibbs (12) was lbw to Ron Archer at 27. Wicket-keeper Binns, who had made a century in the Jamaica match that immediately preceded the first Test, came in instead of the injured Worrell, but lasted only four balls, caught at leg slip off Archer for 0, with the score 27 for 2. At 56, Weekes was run out for 19, and after a patient 31, Holt was caught in the gully off Lindwall, and Westindies were 75 for 4. Despite injury to his right foot, Worrell bravely entered the fray using Binns as a runner; but he was in evident discomfort and was bowled by Johnston for 9. At 101 for 5, Westindies were in complete disarray. Their main batsmen were all out, except for Walcott, and the Jamaican debutante, Collie Smith, who at the age of 20, had the precocious distinction of having scored 169 against the tourists in the Jamaica match. Intent on proving that this achievement was no flash in the pan, Smith stayed with Walcott until the total had reached 239 when he was lbw to Lindwall for a spirited 44. One run later, Walcott himself fell to Miller for a valiant 108, and soon afterwards the Westindian team itself surrendered for a total of 259. As might be expected, it was the heroes of legend, Lindwall and Miller, who destroyed Westindies. Lindwall devoured four wickets for 61 runs, and Miller two for 36. Archer collected another two wickets and Johnston one.

Forced to follow on 256 behind, Westindies made a spirited start through Holt; but when he had scored 20, his partner Gibbs, another debutante, was bowled by Johnston for 0. Only desperation could then have prompted vice-captain Denis Atkinson, who had assumed the captaincy because Stollmeyer was injured, to launch the inexperienced Smith at number three in place of the injured Worrell. Yet, as sometimes happens, desperation breeds wisdom, and although Holt was 20 when Smith entered, he was 48 by the time Smith had reached 50. Eventually, at 122, just after their century partnership, Holt followed a Benaud leg-break and was caught behind for a solid 60. Weekes (1) was then caught and bowled by Benaud: 132 for 3. This again brought Smith and Walcott together as in the first innings, and they ended the fourth day not out 92 and 28 respectively. On the fifth day, once the new ball was taken, Lindwall had Walcott (39) caught by Archer, while Walcott's brilliant young partner who had achieved 104 runs and the distinction of a maiden Test century, was caught by Harvey off Miller: 213 for five. Smith, still twenty years old, was 100 days older than George Headley when he became the youngest Westindian century maker in a Test - against England in Barbados in January, 1930. After the departure of Walcott and Smith, the team collapsed to 275 all out, and with a whole day to spare, Australia gained the required 20 runs for the loss of Morris's wicket. Miller and Lindwall this time accounted for five wickets, while Archer and Benaud claimed two each, and Johnston had the remaining wicket.

Humiliating as the outcome was for Westindies, how much worse would it have been if they had been without Walcott and Smith! Out of the eleven Test matches they had played against Australia they had lost nine. Such failure cannot be easily explained. Apart from Walcott, Smith and Holt, Atkinson was the only Westindian batsman to reach 30 in either innings. If Worrell's injury excuses him, what can be said of Weekes, who in twelve innings so far against Australia, had passed 50 only twice? Weekes's "failure" against Australia was far from singular. Although Valentine had some success in this match, neither he nor Ramadhin were half as effective against Australia as they were against England. Nor could all this misfortune be completely unrelated to the public protest against Atkinson's appointment as vice-captain instead of Worrell. Such protest had the potential of creating much disunity in the team, and since it was provoked by an appointment whose implicit purpose appears to have been maintenance of a white Westindian captain, it seems rather dated and insignificant today after four decades of successful, and in some cases, distinguished black, Westindian cricket captains.

Third Test vs. Australia
Bourda, Georgetown, Guyana, 26, 27, 28, 29 April, 1955

After being trounced by nine wickets in the first Test against Australia in 1955, it must have come as a distinct relief for Westindies to secure an honourable draw in the second Test at Queen's Park Oval, Port-of-Spain. It was not that

Australia had lost their appetite for runs, for they had piled up another huge total of 600 for nine wickets, with centuries from McDonald, Morris, and Harvey: it was more the fact that Westindian batsmen showed greater resolution against Lindwall and Miller. Walcott distinguished himself by making a century in each innings of the match, and Weekes, whose reputation for dazzling pyrotechnics had sagged against Australia, handsomely redeemed himself with scores of 139 and 87 not out.

For the third Test, Westindies dropped young Collie Smith, who after a maiden century in the first Test, had the misfortune of scoring zero in both innings of the second Test. That his second zero was the result of a dubious umpiring decision did not cut any ice with selectors, who wielded their shears with alacrity to cut out not only Smith, but wicket-keeper McWatt, fast bowler Butler, and even the revered spin twins Ramadhin and Valentine. No doubt it was felt that Bourda would not respond much to spin; but when an Australian spinner called Hill took ten wickets in the Guyana match immediately preceding the third Test, the selectors quickly restored Ramadhin to the team. This meant, finally, that Denis Atkinson, Clairmonte Depeiza and Norman Marshall had replaced Smith, McWatt and Valentine.

Whether such extensive chopping and changing had anything to do with the dismal Westindian performance in their first innings must be left to the reader's imagination. Suffice to say that on a wicket generally deemed to be perfect, Westindies, including two of the mighty Ws (Worrell was injured and was omitted) were shot out in just over three hours for 182. Except for Weekes who made a glorious 81, no other batsman exceeded 16. Nor could the pace of Lindwall and Miller be entirely blamed for the débacle: while the openers, Holt and Stollmeyer, fell to Miller, it was Benaud with his slow leg-breaks who polished off the lower order batsmen and returned resounding figures of: 3.5-1-15-4. Walcott, fresh from two heroic centuries at Queen's Park Oval, was caught and bowled by Archer for 8. It was Archer's slower ball, which seemed to fool Walcott as he played too soon, to give the surprised bowler a dolly catch merely a few feet away from the batting crease. This was a crucial blow, as was the dismissal of Sobers who was caught from a ball that might have come off his boot or off the ground. At any rate, by the end of the first day, Australia had reached 83 for one and were clearly in the driver's seat.

On the second day, Harvey was the second Australian to go, caught by Holt off Ramadhin for 38 with the score at 135 for two. McDonald was next bowled by Atkinson for a solid 61 and Australia were 147 for three. When Miller (33) was caught behind off Sobers, it seemed that the pitch was responding to the left-hander's spin. This was confirmed when Sobers disposed of Archer and Johnson in quick succession. Benaud sought to defend by attacking, and hit out lustily for 68, before Australia were eventually dismissed for 257. This was a triumph for Westindies considering that Australia had made 500 plus in the first Test, 600 in the second, and at 147 for three in the third, were evidently heading toward a similar total. After their feckless first innings batting, Westindies had bowled and fielded themselves back into the game, and faced a deficit of only

75. Marshall was one of the architects of Westindian success: he had bowled very steadily indeed, delivering 33 overs for 40 runs and one wicket. But the chief wicket takers were Atkinson with three for 85 and Sobers with three for 20 in 16 overs. By the end of the second day, Holt and Stollmeyer had reduced their deficit by 17, so that Westindies were not at all badly placed when play began on the third day. If trouble was expected, it could come from the pitch which Sobers had used so effectively the day before.

Trouble came, but not from the pitch. When their score had reached 25, for some reason not yet ascertained, three Westindian batsmen - Holt, Stollmeyer and Weekes - all lost their wickets. Holt (6) hung his bat out to Miller and was caught by wicket-keeper Langley: 25 for one. Stollmeyer (17) hit a full toss straight back to the bowler Johnson: 25 for two; and Weekes was caught behind off Johnson before he had scored: 25 for three. With Australia threatening to run through their side, Walcott and Worrell held the fort until lunch when the score was 92, and they had at least wiped off the deficit. They constituted the last real line of Westindian defence and battled as if they knew it. After lunch they kept Archer, Lindwall, Johnson and Benaud at bay, as they gradually advanced to 150. At 73 Walcott was well on his way to his fifth century in five consecutive Tests and Westindian spirits revived. Then tragedy. Going back in an attempt to glance Lindwall, Walcott trod on his wicket and was out hit wicket. It was a sorry end to a magnificent innings. Walcott and Worrell had contributed 125 desperately needed runs which had all but steered Westindies to safety. Now danger. Danger intensified 12 runs later, when, by a remarkable coincidence, Worrell was also out hit wicket: he tried to deflect Benaud into the slips and hit the wicket with his bat. He had made 56, and proved indeed to be the last link in the chain of Westindian resistance, for the five remaining wickets fell for 45 runs, as Westindies declined from 162 for five to 207 all out. The Australian bowling had been steady on the whole, and might not have achieved such success except for captain Ian Johnson whose off-spin earned him seven wickets for 44 runs in 22 overs. His was truly a captain's spell of bowling. Australia was left to get 133 for victory. On the third day itself they scored 40, and on the fourth they lost two wickets before claiming their second Test victory of the tour.

Fourth Test vs. Australia
Kensington Oval, Bridgetown, Barbados
14, 16, 17, 18, 19, 20 May, 1955

Anyone who grew up in the Caribbean would know that youthful cricketing experiences engendered in an atmosphere of shared, communal excitement, and eager, public participation, do not quickly leave the mind. Thus it was, that although I saw only the Guyana Test of the five matches that Australia played against Westindies in 1955, I feel that I saw all five. For, as a schoolboy then, I did not miss a single detail of the tour, whether a particular match was played in my territory or not. Even during our school lessons, one of us would steal out, at the end of each period, to get the current score from the nearest "cakeshop" where, throughout most of the day, a radio would blare out continuous, ball-by-ball cricket commentary that could be heard on the open street and well beyond.

The Australian tour of the Westindies in 1955 was unlike any similar visit that Australia might make of the Caribbean nowadays. This is not simply because it was the first time that Australia was touring the Westindies: it was because the Australian team of that era was universally considered to be invincible. In 1953, England had regained the Ashes from Australia; but they did so in a less than convincing way, squeaking through to a narrow victory in the last match. In 1954/55 they beat Australia more convincingly by three games to one; but again they were narrow victories due partly to the exceptional performance of one man - 'Typhoon' Tyson - the Northamptonshire fast bowler who battered Australia with such fiery pace that none but Neil Harvey could withstand him. If these two English triumphs suggested that Australia was beginning to decline, we in the Westindies did not believe it. As schoolboys, we trembled when we thought of the awesome passage of Bradman's Australians through England in 1948. We felt even greater terror when we remembered how the most powerful Westindian team we then knew - the one that had savaged England in 1950 - was humbled by Australia in 1951/52. When the 1955 tour started therefore, we looked ahead with both expectation and awe, to the moment when such figures of legend as Ray Lindwall, Keith Miller, Arthur Morris and Neil Harvey would materialize on the field before our very eyes.

As it turned out, our worst fears were all too quickly realized in the first three Tests, two of which were won by Australia and the other drawn. Australia did not just win: they won by nine wickets in the first Test, and by eight wickets in the third. Their totals also fully lived up to their reputation for brutal domination - 515 for nine in the first Test, and 600 for nine in the second. McDonald, Miller and Morris had each scored a century, while Harvey had already scored two centuries. So no one was really surprised when Australia batted first in the Barbados Test match, and casually ran up a total of 668, courtesy of yet another hundred from Miller, and a less expected century from Lindwall. With one Test left to play, and two victories under their belt, this impregnable first innings total meant that the Australians had won the rubber; because it was impossible for them to lose the current Test, and in the unlikely event of them losing the fifth and last, they would come out of the series at least one up.

As they began their reply to Australia's dismaying first innings total, the most that Westindies could hope for was to avoid further humiliation by resisting as stoutly as possible. Alas, we felt in our bones that this was not to be, and true enough, the Australian bowlers were again able to smash through Westindian defences early as the team sank rapidly to 147 for six with the mighty Ws, and the young, promising Collie Smith, all swept contemptuously away. Another massive innings defeat seemed inevitable, since the batsmen at the crease for the seventh wicket were Denis Atkinson the Barbadian all-rounder who was also captain, and Clairmonte Depeiza, another Barbadian, who was the wicket-keeper. After them, there were the bowlers Ramadhin, Valentine, and Dewdney. Atkinson was capable perhaps of about 50 Test runs in the best of times, while Depeiza was completely untried, playing in only his second Test match. In the fragile grasp of these two did Westindian fortunes lie! At 147 for six, facing a total of 668, they were exactly 521 runs behind. It was a task from which most brave men could have run away and surrendered without disgrace or dishonour. No one would have blamed Atkinson and Depeiza if, as non-specialist batsmen, they demurred in facing up to dreaded speed merchants like Lindwall and Miller. After all, their specialist batting colleagues had already been summarily executed by the same attack.

But wonder of wonders, Atkinson and Depeiza showed no sign of flinching. To this day it is impossible to say what went on in their minds. All we know is that they showed no fear, and began improbably, against all odds, to mount one of the longest sustained, most valiant, and finest enterprises of resistance ever recorded in the history of Westindian cricket. From 147 for six they went steadily forward with Depeiza defending dourly while Atkinson scored. Unbelievably, the score began to climb in such a way that all we could see in our Latin and French school books was a Westindian total moving from 150 to 200 to 250, then 300 and 350. By that stage, we knew that something was going on that had nothing to do with logic or reason: a veritable miracle was in the making. As the score approached 400 the thing began to seem real, and even the Australian total of 668 no longer looked unassailable. Atkinson had long passed his century, and was going on to a second. He stood nervously on 199 for quite a while, before he grabbed a single. Meanwhile, the equally gallant Depeiza had brought his own score close to his coveted maiden century when Keith Miller, as uncompromising an enemy as ever, let loose three successive bouncers at him. Any one of these missiles might have felled a less determined foe. But Depeiza, hardened by his long and dedicated struggle, was not disposed to surrender now: he reached his century. He and Atkinson had spent an entire day at the crease, compiling 307 runs in the process. Their partnership of 347 is still a world record for the seventh wicket. Atkinson (219) had batted for nearly six hours and Depeiza (122) about twenty minutes less.

It does not matter how or when they got out. In a sense, they were never out. But in reality, Westindies made 510 and Australia had a first innings lead of 158. It could so easily have been more like 458, had it not been for the miracle wrought on 18th May, 1955, in Bridgetown, Barbados by Denis St. E. Atkinson and Clairmonte Depeiza. In their second innings, Australia made 249, which left Westindies 408 to win. Except for Walcott, most of the top batsmen failed again; but a draw was achieved with the Westindian score at 234 for six, and, believe it or not, with Atkinson and Depeiza once again together at the crease on scores of 20 and 11 not out respectively. In the end, what remains is the memory of Atkinson and Depeiza, brave, defiant, tireless, going on and on and on. Their partnership record will forever celebrate their courage. Another record is that Atkinson became the first to score a double century and take five wickets in the same innings of a Test match.

Fourth Test vs. New Zealand
Eden Park, Auckland, New Zealand, 9, 10, 12, 13 March, 1956

Before 1950, Westindies, India, Pakistan, and New Zealand were unofficially classified as lesser powers within the world of international cricket, secondary in strength and importance to England and Australia, and to some extent South Africa. This unstated classification persisted throughout the 1950s, except in the case of Westindies, who were regarded as having come of age during their tour of England in 1950. In 1952 when Westindies first played against New Zealand, they carried themselves as a major cricketing power by winning the first Test by five wickets; they were foiled by rain from almost certainly inflicting an innings defeat on New Zealand in the second Test. Despite changes in both teams, this basic relationship had not changed substantially when Westindies again toured New Zealand for a full series of four Test matches in 1955/56. New Zealand still relied on Bert Sutcliffe and John Reid for their batting, while Westindies retained Goddard, Weekes, Ramadhin and Valentine from 1952, but had introduced younger players like Sobers and Collie Smith. New Zealand, meanwhile, had just visited India and played five Tests, the last of which was completed in January 1956, merely one month before the start of their first Test against Westindies. They had fared badly in India, failing to win a single Test and losing two by an innings. In their series against Westindies they seemed doomed to a similar fate when, as it turned out, they lost the first three Tests. They were defeated partly by Weekes who dominated the Westindian batting with good support from older players such as Goddard and captain Denis Atkinson, but more importantly by Ramadhin and Valentine, to whose legendary spinning prowess the New Zealand batsmen simply had no answer.

In the fourth Test which began at Eden Park, in 1956, New Zealand had little to play for but their self-respect. Even this seemed in doubt when they batted first and lost four wickets for 87 runs. Captain John Reid, however, found a partner in Beck, and the pair put on 104 runs which enabled their team to reach 255. Reid made 84 and Beck 38. Tom Dewdney was the most successful Westindian bowler, taking five wickets for 21 runs in 19.5 overs, of which 11 were maidens. Although his colleagues were less successful, their figures vividly reflect the torture they inflicted on the New Zealand batsmen: Atkinson, for instance, bowled 32 overs for 45 runs, and Valentine 41 overs for 46 runs and two wickets. Contrary to expectation, the Westindian batsmen fared even worse against the New Zealand pace bowlers MacGibbon and Cave, who had removed five of them by the time the Westindian score reached 94. Were it not for a sixth-wicket stand of 45 between Atkinson and A.T. Roberts of St. Vincent, who was making his Test début, it is unlikely that Westindies would have reached 145, their lowest total in all four Tests. It was a refreshing change for New Zealand to be in the driving seat with a lead of 110. Although they lost wickets cheaply in their second innings, they were able to push the score along and reach 157 for nine before Reid declared. Their top score of 41 came from Simpson Guillen of Trinidad who was a member of the Westindian team that toured Australia and New Zealand in 1951/52. Guillen played against New Zealand in 1952 and had since settled there. His example was later followed by Bruce Pairaudeau, who served as an opening batsman for Westindies against New Zealand in 1955/56, and also settled there. But Guillen is probably unique as the only Test cricketer who has represented two countries, and played for each one against the other. (The Nawab of Pataudi (snr.) represented both England and India but never played for England against India.) The wickets in New Zealand's second innings were taken chiefly by Atkinson who returned the following impressive figures: 40-21-53-7.

Reid's declaration had left Westindies four hours either to get 268 runs for victory, or bat out and draw the match. The first prospect was surely not implausible for a team which had just decisively won three consecutive victories against New Zealand. But cricket, like death, is a great leveller; and although it seems hard to believe, six Westindian wickets fell for 22 runs, including that of the mighty Weekes, who had made a century in each of the preceding three Tests, but was now caught by McGregor off Alabaster for 31, the top score. Such was the scale of the disaster that Westindies managed only 77 runs, at that time their lowest Test score. Three batsmen reached double figures - Weekes, Atkinson and Binns. After twenty-six years of Test cricket, New Zealand had at last achieved a victory. While the whole team deserved credit for this signal achievement, chief credit goes to their pace bowlers, of whom Cave took four wickets for 21 runs in the second innings, and Beard three for 22 runs. Westindies duly won the series 3:1, but their loss in the fourth Test drove home the lesson that they still had some way to go before they completed the process of replacing their older players from the early 1950s with new blood, in their effort to rebuild a team that would perform more consistently.

First Test vs. England
Edgbaston, Birmingham, England, 30, 31 May, 1, 3, 4 June, 1957

In *A History of Westindies Cricket*, Michael Manley links patterns of rise and fall in Westindian cricket with developments in Westindian history. Part of his proposition is that the prosperity enjoyed by the Westindian team soon after World War II was inwardly flawed because of the rotten colonial structure out of which it emanated. The Westindian tour of England in 1957, the first since 1950, tests this proposition. The 1950 Westindian cricket team possessed two match-winning combinations, the batting of the three Ws, and the bowling of Ramadhin and Valentine. After 1950, these combinations continued to flourish, except against Australia. Now, in 1957, they faced an English team that had revitalized itself by acquiring talented young batsmen like Peter May and Colin Cowdrey, and dynamic fast bowlers like Fred Trueman and Brian Statham.

As captain in the first Test at Edgbaston, May won the toss and decided to bat. By lunch England were 61 for two. More significantly, Ramadhin had bowled 12 overs for 11 runs and one wicket! After lunch, evidently sensing the threat implied by Ramadhin's figures, May attempted to hit him off his length only to loft a catch to mid-wicket - 116 for five. Such was Ramadhin's domination, that at a later stage in the innings he had figures of seven wickets for 22 runs and England seemed unlikely to reach 150; but big hitting by Trueman (29 not out), and his last-wicket stand of 36 with Statham helped England to a total of 186. Ramadhin's final figures were: 31-16-49-7. By the end of the second day, Westindies had reached 316 for five, thanks largely to an innings of 90 from Clyde Walcott. The third day was dominated by Collie Smith and Frank Worrell in a stand of 190 to which Worrell contributed 81 and Smith, playing in his first Test in England, 161. Smith's innings was one of tremendous vim and vigour, and soon after he left, Westindies were all out for 474. England had reached 102 for two by the end of the third day.

The events that unfolded on the fourth day of this match are astonishing. The bare facts are that after the third English wicket fell at 113, May and Cowdrey came together in an extraordinary partnership that took the score to 378 when stumps were drawn, May being 193 not out and Cowdrey 78 not out. On the fifth day the extraordinariness of this English batting success increased with every run. Eventually, May who scored 285 not out and Cowdrey 154, enabled England to declare at 583 for four, thus setting Westindies 296 for victory. Ironically, it was not victory that Westindies sought but survival; for they found themselves barely able to draw the match by making 72 for seven. Had brave Collie Smith not spent 64 minutes in making 5 runs, and had not captain Goddard astutely utilized all of 40 minutes to score 0 not out, Westindies may well have lost. What had happened was bad enough from a Westindian point of view, but losing the match would have added insult to injury.

May's 285 was then the highest score by an English captain. His 411 with Cowdrey was (and still is) the highest for any English partnership in a Test match. Ramadhin achieved two less enviable records: he bowled 774 balls - the most in a Test match; and in the second innings, his 588 balls were the most bowled in a single innings of a Test match. But without detracting from the grandeur, courage and application of May and Cowdrey, how were they able to 'master' Ramadhin? Their second innings batting was in complete contrast to their performance in the first, and it is impossible to believe that Ramadhin's form deteriorated so completely, so quickly. Ramadhin's figures on the fourth day alone were 48 overs for 74 runs and no wicket, and in the English second innings as a whole, his figures were: 98-35-179-2. These figures do not suggest deterioration. Neither do they suggest that Ramadhin was mastered. When considered together with numerous unsuccessful appeals that he made for lbw, Ramadhin's figures confirm that May and Cowdrey did not 'master' him in the sense of scoring heavily off him: what they did was to devise a successful strategy of defending their wickets.

Under the prevailing interpretation of the lbw rule, it was safe to pad out deliveries, without playing a stroke, so long as it was done well forward of the wicket. This rule was changed in 1970 so that a batsman could still be given out well forward of the wicket, if instead of playing a stroke he padded a ball which the umpire believed would have hit the stumps. In his account of this match in *A History of West Indies Cricket* Michael Manley does not accuse anyone of unfair practice. There is no question that May, Cowdrey and the umpires acted strictly within the law. Still, it is interesting that to this day, Ramadhin feels aggrieved that it was legally possible for batsmen simply, as he puts it, "to kick the ball away" with impunity. Whether his feeling is justified or not, Ramadhin's "failure" in this match reflects a general decline in Westindies cricket which had set in before 1957, and which tends to support the observation of brittleness or inconsistency in the Westindian team during the 1950s. Whether inconsistency is a direct product of the prevailing social and political conditions, as Michael Manley argues, may seem debatable, but there is no doubt that these conditions did affect Westindian cricket. One effect of these conditions is the continuing appointments of white Westindian captains and vice-captains, for example, Atkinson against Australia in 1955 and Goddard against England in 1957.

Fourth Test vs. England
Headingley, Leeds, England, 25,26,27 July, 1957

The first Test of the Westindian tour of England in 1957 proved emblematic to the extent that it changed the psychological balance which was at least equally weighted between the two teams before their first encounter. More than anything else it was May and Cowdrey's monumental stand of 411 in the first Test which changed the balance toward England; for it was this stand that transformed the opening match from one in which Westindian batsmen had flaunted their gifts to score 474 runs in their first innings, to one in which they cowered and scrambled like frightened mice in the second. In the end, grateful to survive the combined wiles of Laker and Lock, Westindies escaped defeat by playing out time for 72 miserly runs, gathered at the cost of their best seven wickets. England's psychological advantage was again illustrated in the second Test when they crushed Westindies by an innings and 36 runs. And by the third Test, although Westindies earned a draw, England's first innings total of 619 for six declared left little doubt as to who held the upper hand. This is why England's one:nil lead in the rubber, at the beginning of the fourth Test, seemed like a discrepancy: psychologically, England were much farther ahead than that.

In the fourth Test, Goddard won the toss and opened the batting with Worrell and Sobers. One of the many Westindian deficiencies on the tour was the absence of a stable pair of opening batsmen: neither Worrell nor Sobers was a specialist in that position. Perhaps that is why Sobers did not last long: when the score was 16 he was caught by Lock at leg slip off Loader for 4. Kanhai and Worrell were beginning to establish some authority when Worrell (29) was bowled by Loader: 42 for two. This disaster was compounded by Weekes (0) being bowled also by Loader at the same score. At lunch, the total had inched to 47 for three with Kanhai on 10 and Walcott 4. These two, master and pupil, stood their ground until tea when the score had reached 112, with Kanhai on 40, and Walcott 38. Immediately after tea, Walcott (38) was caught in the slips trying to drive Laker: 112 for four; and after a brief stoppage for poor light, Kanhai (47) was lbw to Laker: 125 for five. The new ball was taken, and Pairaudeau (6) was immediately bowled by Trueman. With the next ball, the first in a new over, Loader yorked Goddard (1), and off his second ball, he had Ramadhin caught at square leg. Eager for a hat trick, Loader surrounded Gilchrist, the last Westindian batsman, and bowled him. It was the first hat trick in Tests since 1938 when Tom Goddard had achieved it for England against South Africa in Johannesburg. Alexander, meanwhile, had replaced Pairaudeau who had been dismissed off the last ball of Trueman's over. It was Alexander's début in Test cricket, and his bizarre experience was to stand at his end, without facing a ball, quietly observing Loader's historic hat trick at the other. He was left 0 not out, after the last four Westindian batsmen had been out with consecutive balls and Westindies had finished with a total of 142. It was an ignominious rout, engineered chiefly by Loader whose figures were: 20.3-9-36-6. He was assisted by Trueman and Laker with two wickets each. In the twenty minutes remaining on the first day, England scored 11 runs for the loss of Don Smith.

The next day, the weather was again cold and cloudy with rain always possible. Richardson was caught by wicket-keeper Alexander off Worrell from the third ball of the day: 12 for two. Captain Peter May and Tom Graveney added 30 runs before Graveney (22) who had made (258) in the preceding Test, had his middle stump removed by Gilchrist. At lunch, England were 91 for three, with May on 38 and Cowdrey 19. These two carried the score as far as 136 when May (69) gave a catch to Alexander in trying to cut Sobers. Sheppard and Cowdrey took the score to 196 for four at tea with Cowdrey on 59 and Sheppard 31, and once the new ball was taken, Cowdrey (68) was caught by Weekes at short leg off Worrell. It was a slow innings lasting 220 minutes, but it provided substance and body to the English cause, mainly through two Cowdrey partnerships, 94 with May, and 91 with Sheppard. When Cowdrey was out at 227 for five, the remaining five wickets fell for 52 runs, and the English total of 279 represented a lead of 137. Worrell was chiefly responsible for restricting England to this modest lead: he gathered seven wickets for 70 runs in 38.2 overs, while Gilchrist was left with two wickets and Sobers one.

A deficit of 137 was not insurmountable, and with three full days to go, there was every prospect of a fighting finish to the match. The following morning, Sobers and Worrell started off in sprightly fashion, adding 22 runs in fifteen minutes. But at 40, Worrell (7) was caught by Cowdrey in the slips off Trueman. Without further addition, Sobers (29) drove a ball into the covers and took off as Lock gathered left handed and ran him out: 40 for two. This was a most grievous error, for Sobers was in fine form and had outscored Worrell by more than four to one. Westindian grief was compounded when, only 9 runs later, Kanhai (0) was lbw to Loader. After that, the Westindian batsmen might as well have put on solemn robes of mourning and chanted lugubrious lamentations of dying and death as they proceeded to and from the wicket in a funereal march. Weekes (14) was caught by Cowdrey in the slips off Trueman, and Smith who had made 168 in the previous Test, was caught by Evans to give the English wicket-keeper his 200th victim in Test cricket, while the bowler Don Smith gained his first Test wicket. At that stage, Westindies were 71 for five. Walcott and Pairaudeau produced 21 runs, but once Pairaudeau (6) was caught by Trueman off Loader, the remaining Westindians capitulated obediently, and the entire team was dismissed for 132. They had lost by an innings and 5 runs with about two and a half days to spare. England had now taken an impregnable 2:0 lead in the rubber with one Test remaining. It was not only that Westindies had lost, they had done so with an abject sense of surrender and submission that contrasted sharply with their exuberance and exhilaration seven years earlier.

CHAPTER FOUR

Consolidation
- Gerry Alexander

(1958-60)

First Test vs. Pakistan
Kensington Oval, Bridgetown, Barbados
17, 18, 20, 21, 22, 23 January, 1958

Gerry Alexander's captaincy of Westindies for four series between 1958 and 1960 should be regarded as a transition period when, in politics, the Westindies changed from colonial to independent status, and in cricket, from captains such as the Grants, Goddard and Stollmeyer who represented the old, white colonial order, to Frank Worrell and Garfield Sobers who represented the new, non-white post-colonial order. Alexander, fresh from studies at Cambridge University, was initiated into Test cricket as a wicket-keeper in the last two Test matches of the 1957 Westindian tour of England. Less than six months later, in January 1958, he was leading Westindies against Pakistan! Michael Manley hints that it was racial prejudice that prevented Worrell from being selected as captain against Pakistan, whereas Tony Cozier and Jeff Stollmeyer say it was because Worrell was still at university in England. Truth in these matters is always elusive. At any rate, Worrell did not play in the series, and Alexander was selected as Westindian captain. The Barbados Test match in 1958 was not only Alexander's first Test as captain, but the first Test between Westindies and Pakistan. Since both Westindies and Pakistan had better batsmen than bowlers, the 1958 series was expected to be high scoring. Pakistan's main batting hope was the diminutive Hanif Mohammed, while their bowling was spearheaded by the artful Fazal Mahmood. Not only the Westindian captaincy, but the team itself was in a process of transition, with younger players like Garfield Sobers, Rohan Kanhai, Collie Smith, Conrad Hunte, Roy Gilchrist and Lance Gibbs being poised to replace the great names of the early 1950s -

Weekes, Worrell, Walcott, Ramadhin and Valentine.

Westindies batted first and ran up a total of 579 for nine declared. The innings lasted most of two days and was dominated by Everton Weekes (197) and Conrad Hunte (142), the significant pairing of an ageing master (Weekes) and a rising new star (Hunte). Hunte's century was made in his Test début. The main Pakistan bowlers who endured this hammering were Fazal Mahmood, Mahmood Hussain, and captain Abdul Hafeez Kardar. Fazal served up 62 overs for 145 runs and three wickets, Mahmood Hussain 41.2 overs for 153 runs and four wickets, and Kardar 32 overs for 107 runs and one wicket. Nasim-ul-Ghani who also bowled was, at that time, the youngest bowler in Tests: 16 years and 248 days old. In reply, Pakistan were shot unceremoniously out for an abysmal 106. The main damage was done by Gilchrist who appropriated four wickets for 32 runs in 15 overs, and Collie Smith whose off-spin claimed three wickets for 23 runs in 13 overs. Gilchrist's pace was bewildering, and he left the Pakistanis in no doubt about what to expect in subsequent matches.

Alexander did not hesitate to enforce the follow-on, eagerly marshalling his troops for what was expected to be an easy kill. When Hanif and Imtiaz opened the Pakistan second innings with a stand of 152, it seemed that Alexander may have under-rated his opponents, and the match might prove to be one of those not infrequent occasions when cricket confounds perfectly reasonable expectation. Not that Alexander should have acted differently. With a deficit of 473, and Gilchrist rearing to go, no one would have given Pakistan a ghost of a chance in saving this match. In the event, Imtiaz missed his century by only nine runs, and despite the thunderbolts of Gilchrist, the tripartite guile of Sobers, Smith and Valentine, and no fewer and than 111 overs bowled jointly by the Atkinson brothers (Dennis and Eric), little Hanif stood as solid as the rock of Gibraltar, not for one day and one century, not even for two days and two centuries, but for three whole days and 337 utterly unbelievable runs! Hanif's innings was the most remarkable ever played in the Westindies up to that time. Only Andy Sandham's 325 made in Jamaica in the fourth Test in 1930 comes really close. But Sandham had batted for ten hours, whereas Hanif's innings went beyond sixteen hours, and became the longest innings in first class cricket. It was also then the second highest score in Test cricket. Indeed, Hanif had come within a mere 27 runs of Hutton's 364, a record that was to be eclipsed two matches later when Sobers compiled 365 runs in the Jamaica match of the same series.

Undoubtedly this was Hanif's match, although he received magnificent support from several of his countrymen - Imtiaz (91), Saeed Ahmed (65), Alimuddin (37), and Hanif's older brother Wazir (35). Such support helped Pakistan to achieve an honourable draw. They even had the satisfaction of declaring at 657 for eight, and sending Westindies in for a token second innings effort of 28 for no wicket. It is said that Hanif's extraordinary performance, especially in facing up to Gilchrist, took so much out of him, that it affected his confidence, and forced him to bat lower down the order in later matches of the tour in order to avoid facing Gilchrist when he was most fresh. Even if this is true, Hanif scored 291 runs in the remaining four matches of the tour, including innings of 81 and 79. On the Westindian side, Hunte proved to be one of the opening batsmen Westindies were seeking since the disappearance of Rae and Stollmeyer. Alexander too had passed his test as captain, while his role as wicket-keeper freed Kanhai from that extra burden, and allowed him to concentrate on his batting. With the Ws soon to go, and Hall and Gibbs soon to come, a team had already begun to emerge that could take Westindies further along on the winding and treacherous road to cricketing supremacy.

Fifth Test vs. Pakistan
Queen's Park Oval, Port of Spain, Trinidad
26, 27, 28, 29, 31 March, 1958

Pakistan began their 1957/58 tour of Westindies with a magnificent show of heroic resistance that earned them a draw in the first Test of the series at Kensington Oval, Barbados. Their performance in the second Test at Queen's Park Oval was less heroic in so far as their batsmen, with one or two exceptions, had no answer to the place of Gilchrist. For all that, Pakistan's defeat in the second Test was by the fairly narrow margin of 120 runs. In the third Test at Sabina Park, they were utterly crushed by an innings and 174 runs, which deprived them of any chance of winning the rubber, since they were already two down in the series with two games remaining. It was in the third Test that Sobers produced his record innings of 365 not out. One reason why Pakistan performed so poorly in this match is that some of their principal bowlers were injured: Mahmood Hussain had pulled a hamstring muscle, and both Nasim and Kardar had injured fingers that prevented them from bowling. While none of this undervalues Sobers's astounding exhibition of concentration, stamina, and strokeplay at Sabina Park, the fact is that it was achieved against a depleted attack. Nor did Sobers's success damage the self-confidence of the Pakistanis who kept up their morale, even through a third consecutive defeat by eight wickets in the fourth Test at Bourda. By that stage, the rubber was safely in Westindian hands, with Westindies leading 3:0 and one Test remaining.

Evidence of Pakistan's unshaken morale was seen in the fifth Test at Queen's Park Oval, where they opened the match by removing four top order Westindian wickets in the first innings for 78 runs. Both Westindian opening batsmen, Hunte and Kanhai were dismissed for 0, and although Smith (86), Weekes (51), Walcott (47) and Alexander (38) achieved respectable scores, no other batsman rose above 14. The Westindian first innings total of 268 was their lowest of the series, and much of the credit for muzzling the Westindian batsmen must go to the Pakistani medium pacer Fazal who turned in a superlative performance: 32-10-83-6. He was fully supported by Khan Mohammad: 25-8-79-2, and Nasim: 22.1-6-53-2. Not to be outdone by their bowling colleagues, the Pakistani batsmen recovered after losing their opening batsmen for the relatively low score of 69. The recovery came in the form of two century stands in which, Wazir, older brother of Hanif, played a major role. In the first stand, Wazir and Saeed compiled 169 runs, and were separated at 238 for three when Saeed (97) was caught by Alexander off Jaswick Taylor, a Trinidadian fast bowler making his Test début. The second partnership, between Wazir and Hanif, realized 154 runs before Hanif (54) was bowled by Taylor: 392 for four. Eventually, Wazir was bowled by Gibbs for 189 a magnificent innings that helped Pakistan to attain a first innings total of 496 and a lead of 228. Never had Pakistan enjoyed such dominance over Westindies in the preceding matches. No doubt, Pakistan benefited from the fact that Gilchrist sprained an ankle and bowled no more than 7 overs. This meant that the main Westindian bowling was done by Gibbs, Sobers, Smith, Atkinson, and Taylor, and of these Taylor had the best results: 36.5-6-109-5, followed by Gibbs: 41-9-108-4, and Atkinson: 31-3-66-1.

Perhaps it was such a surprise being underdogs that Westindies could come up only with token resistance. They began confidently enough, and up to the fall of the second wicket when the total was 115 - thanks largely to Hunte (45) and Kanhai (43) - Westindies seemed very well placed to wipe off the deficit. But none of the remaining batsmen, except Walcott (62) showed any desire to fight back, and a collapse ensued in which only Sobers (27) and Atkinson (19) reached double figures. Westindies were dismissed for 227 runs, losing the match by an innings and 1 runs. It was the first time Pakistan had beaten Westindies, and it revealed the true potential of the Pakistanis which, for one reason or another, had not been fully expressed in earlier matches. Nor was Fazal responsible for the Westindian collapse, although he did claim two wickets for 35 runs. It was the spinners who were responsible. For one so young (sixteen years), Nasim did exceedingly well with figures of: 30.5-9-67-6. He was assisted by Haseeb who claimed two wickets for 89 runs in 24 overs. It had been an exciting series the results of which - a 3:1 victory in favour of Westindies - did not do full justice to the Pakistanis who suffered unduly from injuries, as most touring teams are liable to do. Still, Westindian crowds had seen some brilliant performances from Hanif, Fazal, Wazir, and Nasim, and many good performances from their colleagues.

Second Test vs. India
Green Park, Kanpur, India, 12, 13, 14, 16, 17, December, 1958

In his first series as captain - against Pakistan in 1957/58 - Gerry Alexander led Westindies to a convincing 3:1 victory. The series signalled the end of an era, since 1947, when Westindies depended on three principal batsmen, the three Ws, and two principal bowlers, Ramadhin and Valentine. But in November 1958, when Westindies met India in Bombay for the first Test of their 1958/59 tour, none of the Ws was on their team for the first time since the Second

World War; and Ramadhin no longer foreshadowed menace as he once did. It is true that Worrell later returned to the team, although more as captain than leading batsman; Walcott's return was temporary; and though Ramadhin and Valentine also played in later Test series, they were already in process of being replaced by Gibbs, Sobers and Smith. As part of this Westindian process of change and renewal, two new players had made their first appearance in the Bombay Test - Basil Butcher and Wes Hall. For their second Test at Kanpur, another new player - Joe Solomon - made his first appearance. In the basic structure of the new Westindian team that was taking shape, Hunte filled the role of a reliable opening batsman, to be followed by the main batting stalwarts, Sobers, Kanhai, and Smith who replaced the three Ws; the middle order would be supported by Butcher and Solomon, while Hall would lead the fast attack and Gibbs the spinners.

Ghulam Ahmed the Indian captain who had missed the Bombay Test through illness, returned to his team at Kanpur; but he lost the toss and Westindies batted first. Hunte and Holt put on 55 comfortable runs on the harmless jute matting wicket before Hunte (29) was caught at mid-on by Borde off Gupte. Eight runs later Sobers, who had made 142 not out in the second innings of the first Test, was caught for 4 by Hardikar at long leg, again off Gupte. Within minutes the wily, Indian leg-spinner struck again bowling both Kanhai and Butcher for 0 and 2 respectively: 74 for four. Like a beast of prey, which had tasted blood, Gupte's appetite for wickets seemed to grow on what it fed. He caught and bowled Smith (20): 76 for five; then won an lbw decision against Holt, who had patiently accumulated 31 runs: 88 for six. This was disaster indeed, and it seemed the more dismaying because it followed magnificent feats that Westindies had achieved against Pakistan merely months before, for example, innings of 365 not out by Sobers, and 260 by Hunte. But, in strode captain Alexander, who along with debutante Solomon stopped the rot completely. Together they added 100 runs before Solomon (45) was lbw to Gupte: 188 for seven. Then, sheltering Gibbs, Alexander added another 32 runs before Gibbs (16) was bowled by Ranjane: 220 for eight. By now, with two bowlers - Hall and Jaswick Taylor - left, Alexander (70) began to hit out and was caught in the deep off Gupte. It was one of the most gallant rescues ever accomplished by a Westindian batsman, and it was the main reason that Westindies reached a total of 222. Alexander demonstrated his invaluable role as a middle order batsman, one which he would fulfil with distinction many times in the future. Gupte's marvellous figures of: 34.3-11-102-9 proved that he was probably the leading leg-spinner in international cricket during the 1950s. In this match, he became the first Indian bowler to take nine wickets in one innings of a Test match, and by the end of the day, India had started their first innings and were 24 without loss.

Roy and Contractor continued the next morning and were in possession until almost lunch when Contractor (41) fell lbw to Sobers and India were 93 for one. Soon afterwards Roy (46) also succumbed lbw Sobers: 118 for two. Umrigar and Manjrekar then pushed the score briskly along, and at tea India were 182 for two - 40 runs behind with eight wickets left. It was a position of great strength. But after tea, Hall ripped into the Indian batsmen with the force of a gale that tore India's strength into shreds. He removed Umrigar (57), Borde (0), and Ramchand (4) in one fell swoop, Umrigar being caught by Holt, and the other two by wicket-keeper Alexander. Suddenly, India had dwindled from 182 for two to 191 for five, and although by the end of the second day, they had reached 209 for five and still held the initiative, the wind had been knocked out of their sails. This was confirmed on the third day when only one run was added before fast bowler Jaswick Taylor had Manjrekar (30) lbw, and Hall wrapped up the tail by battering down three more wickets for a handful of runs. In the end, India limped to 222 the identical total as Westindies, and it was as if the match was starting all over again when Westindies began their second innings. What a start! Both openers - Hunte and Holt - were removed before any runs appeared on the board. Hunte was caught and bowled by Umrigar, and Holt was caught by Borde off Ramchand. Sobers and Kanhai contributed 73 runs before Kanhai (41) was caught by wicket-keeper Tamhane off Gupte. Smith was run out for 7, then Sobers and Butcher took command and carried Westindies to 160 for four by tea. When they reached 197, Butcher (60) was caught by the wicket-keeper off Ramchand. Sobers, meanwhile, had chalked up his second Test century in as many matches on the tour, and at stumps on the third day, Westindies were 261 for five, Sobers on 136 and Solomon 13.

Forcing the pace on the fourth day, Westindies suffered two reversals: Sobers was unlucky to be run out two runs short of a magnificent double century, while Solomon suffered a similar fate missing his début Test century by 14 runs. Alexander was 45 not out when he declared at 443 for seven, giving India 444 runs to win in 480 minutes. India's immediate response was for Roy and Contractor to spend the rest of the day - 250 minutes - in accumulating 76 runs. Strangely, it seems, India never contemplated a win. Yet the prospect of spending all of the last day in dour defence can hardly have been salutary for either the Indian batsmen or spectators. In the event, Contractor (50) was bowled by Taylor: 99 for one. With the total at 107, Roy (45) was run out by Kanhai, and when they had reached 173, Manjrekar (31) was also run out by Kanhai in a repeat exhibition of brilliant, accurate and athletic fielding. At this point, Alexander called for the new ball. It was an inspired decision that gave Hall and Taylor an opportunity of tempestuous fast bowling that rattled the remaining seven Indian batsmen and swept them away for a paltry 67 runs. After Hall had disposed of Umrigar (34) who was caught by Smith at short leg, the other batsmen capitulated willingly and the Indian innings folded at 240, which meant India had conceded by 203 runs. Hall claimed five wickets for 76 runs in 32 overs, and Taylor three for 68 in 30.1 overs. After faltering against Gupte in the first innings, Westindies seemed to have mastered the leg-spinner in their second innings when he bowled 23 overs for 121 runs and one wicket. As far as one could tell, the new Westindies team had kicked itself into gear, and there was no better indication of that than Hall's match analysis of eleven wickets for 126 runs.

Fourth Test vs. India
Corporation Stadium, Madras, India
21, 22, 24, 25, 26 January 1959

Having drawn the first Test on their tour of India in 1958/59, Westindies beat India in the second Test by 203 runs and in the third by an innings and 336 runs. The third Test was notable not only for its huge margin of victory, but because Kanhai made 256, his highest Test score, which was also the highest score in a Test in India, and Sobers achieved 106 not out, his third consecutive century in the three Tests of the tour. As one might expect, such overwhelming Westindian success had left India in considerable disarray. This was evident when Ghulam Ahmed the Indian captain withdrew before the fourth Test, prematurely ending his Test career despite his excellent record as an off spin bowler, including a haul of ten wickets for 130 runs in the Calcutta Test match against Australia in 1956/57. The extent of Indian disarray was further revealed when Umrigar, who was selected to replace Ghulam Ahmed as captain, also withdrew on the eve of the fourth Test, because he disagreed with his fellow selectors about the composition of the team. In the end, India made six changes, with Ghorpade, Kenny, Manjrekar, Phadkar, Tamhane (wicket-keeper), and Ghulam Ahmed (captain) being replaced by Ramchand, Kripal Singh, Joshi (wicket-keeper), Borde, Vinoo Mankad (captain), and Sengupta who was making his Test début following his century for the Indian Services against Westindies in the opening match of the tour.

Westindies batted first and Hunte and Holt had put on 63 before Mankad bowled Hunte (32). Going at a brisk rate, Kanhai and Holt moved the score to 123 by lunch. Afterwards, Holt (63) was lbw Gupte: 152 for two. Sobers joined Kanhai and they advanced to 206 when Sobers (29) was caught in the slips off Mankad, and Smith was bowled for 0, also by Mankad. Butcher and Kanhai moved further to 230 at tea, after which Kanhai was unlucky to be run out for 99. He executed a drive wide of mid-off and went for a run but Butcher sent him back too late for him to make it and by the end of the day Westindies were 283 for five. The next morning Solomon (43) was lbw Borde: 349 for six. Butcher attempted to get a fourth run and found himself in Alexander's crease while Alexander was still in it. Had Alexander (11) stayed put, Butcher, who was only a few runs short of his century, would have been run out. It was typical of Alexander's team spirit that he ran himself out to allow Butcher to reach his century. Eventually, Butcher was bowled by Ramchand for 142, and Westindies were dismissed for 500. Mankad was the most successful bowler: 38-6-95 4, while Borde was rewarded with two wickets and Ramchand with one; but Gupte, who had done the bulk of the bowling, sending down 58 overs, had to be satisfied with one wicket for 166 runs. At stumps on the second day, India were 27 for one, Sengupta (1) having been caught at second slip off Hall.

After the rest day, play resumed with Roy and night watchman Joshi who was soon caught by Alexander off Gilchrist for 17. Roy (49) was bowled by Sobers, and at lunch India were 111 for three. Shortly after lunch, Umrigar snicked a catch to Alexander off Hall, and Ramchand sustained a blow on the head from a delivery by Hall which caused him to retire. Next, Contractor (22) was run out by a throw from Kanhai: 131 for five. At this point, when half their side were out and they were already two down in the series, with one match left, India were in an unenviable position. It got worse as Mankad (4) was bowled by Gilchrist: 135 for 6, and Borde (0) was caught by Smith off Sobers: 147 for 7. A measure of relief came when Ramchand bravely re-entered and put on 74 runs with Kripal Singh who played brilliantly to reach India's top score of 53 before he was caught in the slips by Hall off Sobers: 221 for eight. One run later, Ramchand (30) was caught by Gilchrist off Eric Atkinson and the Indian innings was over. With a lead of 278 and fifteen minutes left, Alexander did not enforce the follow-on, and Hunte and Holt were able to add 8 runs for the Westindian second innings before close of play.

On the fourth day, Mankad was unable to bowl which might have helped Westindies to force the pace in order to achieve an early declaration. Hunte (30) was caught off Gupte, while the same bowler had Kanhai (14) lbw: 108 for two. Sobers (9), Smith (5), and Butcher (16) brought the score to 150 for five. Forty minutes before tea, when the Westindian total stood at 168 for five and Holt was 81 not out, Alexander declared. He offered India a proposition of making 447 runs to win in 450 minutes. By close of play, India had lost three wickets for 48 runs and the writing was already on the wall. India's best hope on the last day was the possibility of rain. Play started on time, however, and the two overnight batsmen - Umrigar and Borde - kept Westindies at bay until half an hour before lunch when Umrigar (29) was bowled by Sobers: 97 for four. After Umrigar, the deluge. Mankad was absent ill, and the remaining batsmen surrendered meekly except for Borde who resisted stoutly and had acquired 56 defiant runs before he was caught by Butcher at mid-wicket off Sobers: 149 for eight. At 151 it was all over: Westindies had won by 295 runs. Hall and Gilchrist had wrought greatest destruction claiming three wickets each, although Sobers won the prize wickets of Umrigar and Borde. Perhaps, if Alexander had enforced the follow-on, India could have been beaten by an innings; but the new Westindian captain was taking no chances. He would have remembered that both in 1948/49, and in 1952/53, India had shown remarkable resilience by recovering regularly in their second innings. But in 1958/59, the Indian team seemed to have lost the will to fight, and had already lost the series 0:3 with one match left. Meanwhile, success had enabled Westindies to continue their process of rebuilding. More than half way through their tour, Hunte and all the main batsmen, except Smith, had proved themselves, while Hall and Gilchrist had turned out as a most menacing pair of opening bowlers. The internal problem which led to Gilchrist being sent home eventually had not affected the team effort in any noticeable way.

Second Test vs. Pakistan
Dacca Stadium, Dacca, Pakistan, 6, 7, 8 March, 1959

Westindies first encountered Pakistani cricket during their tour of India in 1948/49. India had just been partitioned into two nations, one of which - the new nation of Pakistan - had not yet gained Test status in cricket. Consequently, the match between Westindies and Pakistan, at that time, was classified as an "unofficial" Test. For the record, it ended in a draw. Official Tests between the two "countries" were first played in 1957/58 when Pakistan toured Westindies. It was a five-Test series which Westindies won 3:1. Then Westindies visited Pakistan for three Tests at the end of their 1958/59 tour of India. The first Test was in Karachi where Westindies received the shock of their life in being defeated by ten wickets. The defeat was a shock because it came on the heels of a tour in which Westindies had ridden roughshod over India in a one-sided contest that they won three:nil. One of the main causes of this shocking reversal of fortune was the Pakistani medium pace bowler Fazal Mahmood who accounted for seven wickets in the Karachi Test, and who had played a leading role in bringing Pakistan an historic victory over England when he took six wickets in each innings of the fourth Test at the Oval in 1954. If the Oval Test confirmed Fazal's menace on turf, it also suggested how much more menacing he could be on the jute matting wickets of his homeland; for it was Fazal's dexterity in moving the ball both into and away from the batsman on these wickets which partly accounted for the fact that Pakistan had not lost any of the nine Tests they had played up to that time.

For their second Test in 1959, Westindies had to travel across northern India to Dacca in what was then East Pakistan (today Bangladesh). Since there was a matting wicket in Dacca, Westindies feared the worst. But their chances were slightly better since Pakistan's batting was weakened by the absence of Hanif Mohammed who had made a century in the first innings of the first Test, but had injured his knee in the second innings. Pakistan had made two changes to their first Test team: Hanif had been replaced by Alimuddin, and the spinner A. D'Souza by Haseeb Ahsan. Westindies strengthened their bowling by omitting Hunte and Jaswick Taylor and bringing in Ramadhin and Eric Atkinson. The Westindian emphasis on bowling was evident when Alexander won the toss and put Pakistan in to bat. Immediately, Hall went on a rampage that removed both openers forthwith: Ijaz Butt (2) was bowled, and Alimuddin (6) caught and bowled: 15 for two. Hall also had Saeed (6) caught by Alexander, and bowled Wazir (1), while Ramadhin bowled Imtiaz for 3. At the end of this fiasco, Pakistan were 22 for five and in danger of abysmal humiliation. But Wallis Mathias and Shujauddin summoned up heroic resources that lifted their team out of the abyss. They added 86 runs before Shujauddin (26) was bowled by Atkinson. Matthias (64) and Fazal (12) continued the rescue effort by the addition of 18 more runs for the seventh wicket. These efforts enabled Pakistan to struggle to a total of 145, which, although not exactly prosperity, was riches itself compared with what it might have been if the innings had proceeded in the same vein from 22 for five. Hall's share of the spoils was: 13-5-28-4 and Ramadhin's: 23.3-6-45-3. Gibbs and Atkinson had to be contented with one wicket each, and Sobers bowled 8 overs for 7 runs.

When it was the turn of Westindies to bat, Fazal was only too willing to return Hall's compliment. He had Kanhai (4) caught by Wazir, while Holt (4) was bowled by Mahmood: 19 for two. Sobers and Alexander defended dourly, carrying the total to 56 when the Westindian captain (14) was stumped off Nasim the seventeen year old Pakistani left arm spinner. Fazal removed Sobers (29) and Butcher (11) which brought Westindies to 68 for five. At that stage, having accounted for the main Westindian batsmen, and still intent on repaying Hall's compliment, Fazal turned his tender attentions to the tailend Westindian batsmen whom, with the help of his young accomplice Nasim, he decimated. At the conclusion of this deadly work by Fazal and Nasim, Westindies had been transformed from 71 for six to a final total of 76 which yielded Pakistan a lead of 69. The last five Westindian batsmen - Smith, Solomon, Atkinson, Gibbs, Hall - each made 0, and their sorry procession is vividly represented in Fazal's statistics: 18.3-9-34-6, although Nasim was not far behind: 7-5-4-3.

In Pakistan's second innings, Hall's fellow Barbadian Eric Atkinson made the initial breakthrough by disposing of Alimuddin for 0. Thereafter, he and Ramadhin ravaged the topmost batting order of Pakistan by removing their five best batsmen: Ramadhin accounted for Butt (21) and Saeed (22), the first clean bowled and the second lbw, while Atkinson had Imtiaz (4) and Wazir (4) caught by Smith and Alexander respectively. Wallis Matthias and Shujauddin effected another face-saving, rescue partnership, this time of 59 runs, which enabled their team to move from 71 for five to 130 for six. Eventually, Matthias (45) was bowled by Atkinson, and Shujauddin (17) was bowled by Hall. At their departure, Pakistan suffered a collapse that was as shattering as the Westindian death march at the end of their first innings. Hall bowled the last four batsmen and Pakistan finished with a total of 144, which required Westindies to get 214 runs for victory. Hall's share of the spoils this time was: 16.5-2-49-4, and Atkinson's: 22-9-42-4. Ramadhin also collected two wickets for 10 runs.

As leader of his troops, Alexander himself opened the Westindian second innings with Holt. Holt (5) became the first of Fazal's victims when he was caught by Imtiaz: 12 for one. From there on wickets fell with regularity, as four Westindian batsmen scrambled to double figures: Alexander (18), Sobers (45), Smith (39) and Atkinson (20). The rest were simply mowed down by Fazal with some help from Mahmood Hussain; and the Westindian innings folded abruptly at 172, yielding victory to Pakistan by 41 runs. This time, although he was assisted by Mahmood: 19.5-1-48-4, Fazal's statistics again proved decisive: 27-10-66-6, and his match analysis of 12 wickets for 100 runs remains the best for any Test at Dacca. Apart from the combination of Fazal and Pakistani matting wickets, there seems no other plausible explanation of the two defeats which Westindies suffered at the hands of Pakistan immediately following their overwhelming triumphs in India. It is true that Gilchrist had been sent home for disciplinary reasons at the end of the Indian tour, but it had not affected the morale of the team, and Hall, Taylor and Atkinson were not exactly slow compared to Gilchrist. Perhaps it is another example of the fickle nature of Westindian cricket in the 1950s.

Second Test vs. England
Queen's Park Oval, Port of Spain, Trinidad
28, 29, 30 January, 1, 2, 3 February, 1960

The second Test between England and Westindies in January/February 1960 provoked a reaction from the crowd, rather like the one at Georgetown during England's 1953/54 tour, when angry spectators interrupted the game by hurling bottles, cans and other missiles onto the field. The Trinidad Test opened in controversy because Gerry Alexander had been picked as Westindian captain. Alexander had successfully led Westindies in a home series against Pakistan in 1957/58, and on a tour of India and Pakistan in 1958/59. During this time, Frank Worrell was at university in England. But Worrell had now returned to the team and many people felt that he should be captain. The first Test match of the tour at Bridgetown, Barbados, ended in a tame draw, with Sobers making a double century and Worrell 197 not out. On the first day of the second Test, England were subjected to a fierce onslaught from Hall and Watson, the new pair of Westindian fast bowlers. Questions were raised about the proportion of bouncers bowled. The English batsmen resisted stoically, although Cowdrey, Pullar and captain Peter May fell cheaply, and England were 57 for three at one stage. By mid-afternoon, Dexter mounted a ferocious counter attack, scoring 77 brilliant runs, and enabling England to reach 220 for four by end of play, with the stout-hearted Barrington on 93 not out. On the second day, after Barrington fell for 121, M.J.K. Smith made 108 and helped England to a total of 382. Westindies then made 22 without loss before end of play.

On the third day, a Saturday, all Trinidad turned up at the Queen's Park Oval, eager to watch their stars -Sobers, Kanhai, Hunte, Worrell and Butcher - in action against the most remarkable pair of fast bowlers England had produced since World War Two - Trueman and Statham. If it can be believed now, more than thirty-five years later, what happened that Saturday was that on a perfect pitch, in superb batting conditions, and supported by spectators brimming with loyalty, this vaunted Westindian batting machine ground to a complete halt. Hunte was first to go caught Trueman bowled Statham for 8; Kanhai (5) was leg before wicket to a full toss from Trueman; and Sobers, double centurion of Bridgetown, was caught third ball by Barrington off Trueman for 0, a mistake induced more by pride or over-confidence than by technical ineptitude. Worrell and Solomon attempted a brief salvage operation until Solomon (23) was run out. Then Worrell (9) was caught by wicket-keeper Swetman off Trueman and Westindies were 45 for five.

Spectators stared dumbfounded: their world was collapsing around them; for if they could not believe in their cricketers, what else was left for them, as

Westindians, to believe in! One must never forget that cricket is not mere sport in the Westindies. Captain Alexander top scored with 28; but could not prevent his team from descending to 98 for eight, the damage having been done by Trueman: 21-11-35-5; and Statham who bowled 19.3 overs for 42 runs and three wickets. The critical moment came while Ramadhin and newcomer C.K. Singh were batting, and when Ramadhin tried to steal a single off the last ball of an over in order to shield his young partner. A quick throw from Dexter ran Singh out. There was no doubt about the run out itself. Yet the deluge of bottles and cans came and hell broke loose. As at Georgetown, six years before, the crowd's anger was directed not at the English players but at the umpires, in this case, Lloyd and Lee Kow. But Singh was clearly out, just as McWatt was out in 1954 at Bourda. While there is no excuse for the crowd's behaviour, it is obvious that they felt hurt by the dismal Westindian batting performance. Secondly, there was widespread suspicion about umpire Lloyd's earlier decision giving Hunte out caught from a ball that had bounced off his pad, although it might have nicked his bat first, as the umpire clearly believed. Then, lingering resentment over the issue of captaincy probably entered as well. Not that any of this justifies bad manners, lack of sportsmanship, or sheer hooliganism!

When the match resumed on the Monday morning, Westindies were dismissed for 112, and May decided to bat again despite his huge lead. Now the penitent spectators were treated to a valiant Westindian fight back in which England were summarily reduced to 133 for seven. Eventually, May declared at 230 for nine, inviting Westindies to get 500 runs in just over ten hours for victory.

Runs were less important than the Westindian ability to last out the time. By the end of the fifth day, they were 134 for two in their second innings, with Kanhai 55 not out and Sobers 19 not out. At that stage, prospects of saving the match seemed sanguine enough. On the final day, however, no sooner was Sobers out, lbw to Trueman for 31, than Worrell was lbw to Statham for 0, and Westindies were 159 for four. Butcher came in, injured and with a runner. These were the circumstances of dwindling resources and fading hope in which Providence ordained that Rohan Kanhai should play the crowning innings of his life. At lunch Westindies were 184 for four; then Butcher was lbw to Statham for 9, and Kanhai had only Alexander for real support. Perhaps, half way between lunch and tea, Kanhai thought the match could be saved; but he seemed to change his mind, and when he was in his nineties, contrived a flurry of such spell-binding strokes that Trueman found himself battered for 15 runs in one over. It was an outrageously glorious battery, fuelled by distress and defeat, to reveal Westindian batsmanship at its most glorious and best - proud, stylish, inventive, free, fearless and fun-loving. But such glory does not wholly belong to this world: it vanished as quickly as it came when Kanhai chose to hit a full pitch from Dexter straight into the hands of Smith at mid-wicket. He had made 110 miraculous, face-saving runs, plundering many of them with the boundless zest of a marauding buccaneer. Whether it was the right strategy is debatable; but he had lifted the hearts of the crowd and made them feel that the sorrows of the previous Saturday had been fully atoned for. The match effectively ended with Kanhai's final strokes, and England won by the unambiguous margin of 256 runs, after Westindies had stumbled to 244 in their second innings.

Fourth Test vs. England
Bourda, Georgetown, Guyana, 9, 10, 11, 12, 14, 15 March, 1960

Following their victory in the second Test at Port of Spain, England drew the third Test of their 1959/60 Westindian tour. They then engaged in a high-scoring, if inconclusive match against Guyana before facing Westindies once more in the fourth Test. May was ill and Cowdrey deputised as captain while Raman Subba Row was brought into the English team to replace May. For Westindies, Nurse and Solomon were replaced by Walcott (recalled from retirement) and Worrell who had been ill during the third Test. In addition, C. K. Singh replaced Ramadhin who was not fit. England won the toss for the fourth successive time and Cowdrey opened with Pullar. They made a late start because of rain, facing three overs before lunch and scoring 11 runs without loss. It was a placid wicket that offered little encouragement to the Westindian pace men Hall and Watson; Cowdrey and Pullar remained together until close to tea when Pullar (33) glanced Hall into Alexander's gloves: 73 for one. Subba Row and Cowdrey stepped up the tempo slightly, but Subba Row (27) succumbed to Sobers via the wicket-keeper. Cowdrey and Barrington who was not fully fit, carried the score to 152 for two when stumps were drawn.

The next day, Cowdrey was caught by Alexander off Hall without adding to his overnight tally of 65. Dexter came in, but his partner Barrington who had been in discomfort from the after effects of a blow he had sustained from Hall on the previous day, retired temporarily. The incoming batsman M.J.K. Smith was instantly executed, bowled for 0 second ball by Hall: 161 for four. When Illingworth (4) was similarly dismissed by a long hop from Sobers, and wicket-keeper Swetman (4) lbw to Watson, England had declined rapidly to 175 for six. In sharp contrast to their first day's performance, they had already lost four wickets for 23 runs during the second morning. Dexter, however, was batting well and was not out with Allen at lunch: 206 for six. But after lunch, Alexander called for the new ball, and Dexter (39) mishooked Hall to give Hunte at backward short-leg a difficult catch that he did well to hold: 219 for six. Barrington re-entered, despite continuing discomfort, and helped the English tail to wag effectively, so that Allen reached 55 (his first fifty in a Test) and England advanced to a total of 295, while Barrington himself got 27. Westindies had had much the better of the day's play, gathering eight English wickets for 143 runs, thanks largely to Hall who returned figures of: 30.2-8-90-6. Hall was helped by Sobers (three wickets) and Watson (one). Batting briefly toward the end of the second day, Westindies reached a total of 32 without loss.

The next morning, steady English bowling and brisk out-cricket made scoring difficult. It took the Westindian openers, Hunte and McMorris, two hours to achieve 67 runs, after which Hunte (39) gave a slip catch to Trueman off Allen. Ten runs later McMorris (35) was caught by Swetman off Statham. Kanhai and

Sobers came together, but their progress was impeded by two stoppages for rain, and at stumps the Westindian total was 139, with Kanhai 31 not out, and Sobers 33 not out. That the match might begin to stagnate was suggested by the fact that England's 64 overs during the day had produced no more than 107 runs. English tactics of tight bowling and defensive field placing were having their effect. The next day was slow going as well, and all Westindies could manage was 192 more runs. Still, Sobers produced another magnificent century (142 not out), his third in the series, and Westindies finished the day on a total of 332 for four, having lost Kanhai (caught Dexter bowled Trueman) for 55, and Walcott (bowled Trueman for 9). It was a favourable though not a commanding situation for Westindies, considering that they were only 37 runs ahead and two more days were left.

The challenge on the fifth day was for Westindies to overcome the English policy of containment and clock up enough runs quickly enough to declare. Since the overnight batsmen were Sobers and Worrell, Westindies were well equipped for such a challenge. But Worrell was beaten by Allen's third ball of the morning and bowled for his overnight score of 38. Five runs later, Sobers (145) was also beaten by Allen's turn and stumped: 338 for six. Alexander and Scarlett added 55 runs before Alexander (33) was run out. Soon afterwards, Westindies declared at 402 for eight wickets. The English bowling had been shared between Trueman, Statham, Illingworth and Allen, of whom Trueman and Allen were the most successful with three wickets each, while Statham got one. Facing a modest deficit of 107, Cowdrey and Pullar proceeded cautiously. Westindies were handicapped by the fact that Watson was injured and could not bowl. Yet, with the English total at 40, Cowdrey (27) was stumped off Singh. Dexter came in instead of Subba Row or Barrington, and he and Pullar advanced the total to 110 before stumps for the additional loss of Pullar (47) who was lbw to Worrell.

Everything now pointed to stalemate since England was starting the final day with virtually a clean slate and with eight wickets in hand. In the event, Dexter and Subba Row both got centuries, following a superb third-wicket partnership of 148 in which they carried England to impregnable safety and scotched any Westindian pretension of a victory bid. Dexter got 110 before he was caught by Worrell off Walcott, and Subba Row was lbw Worrell for 100 exactly. The other batsmen made negligible contributions in actual figures although they served England well in lasting through to the end when the English total stood at 334 for eight and the match had drifted to a perfunctory draw. Worrell collected four wickets, Singh two, and Sobers and Walcott one each. Since their victory in the second Test, England had foiled two victory bids by Westindies. One was in the third Test when Kanhai and Alexander had eighty minutes to make 90 runs for victory on the last day. Kanhai, who was the main Westindian hope, was hampered by cramp and was refused a runner by May the English captain: hence the draw. The second victory bid was in this fourth Test in which rain, injury and highly disciplined English out-cricket combined to facilitate a draw. As E.W. Swanton has pointed out in his book *West Indies Revisited*, from World War Two to the Bourda Test in 1954, Westindies and England had played ten Test matches of which Westindies had won seven and England one, and even that solitary English victory was achieved at Old Trafford in 1950 on what Swanton calls "a travesty of a pitch." (p.205) Since that Bourda Test to this one in 1960 there had been eleven more matches between the two teams, but the results had been completely turned around with England winning six and Westindies none. Nothing describes more eloquently the course of Westindian cricket during the 1950s, from a period of relative prosperity in the early years to one of decline half way through the decade.

Fifth Test vs. England
Queen's Park Oval, Port of Spain, Trinidad
25, 26, 28, 29, 30, 31 March, 1960

At the start of the fifth and final Test of England's Westindian tour in 1959/ 60, England were leading one:nil, and it would require nothing less than a straight Westindian victory to prevent England from winning their first rubber in the Westindies after five visits spread over thirty years. So far, after they had lost the second Test match, Westindian victory attempts in the third and fourth Tests were foiled by a combination of factors such as injuries, interruptions by bad weather, and defensive English tactics. So prospects for the fifth Test were not exactly sanguine. Besides, England had replaced Statham with Moss, and Swetman (their wicket-keeper) with Parks. Statham had to return home because of illness in the family, and even if Moss lacked his experience, Parks would strengthen England's batting and was familiar with local conditions in Trinidad where he was on a coaching engagement. Meanwhile, Ramadhin who was unfit for the fourth Test, had returned to the Westindian team, and a new fast bowler, Charlie Griffith, was brought in for the all-rounder Scarlett.

On the opening day of the match, England made excellent progress compiling 256 for three, more than either side had managed in a single day throughout the series. They owed their success chiefly to a magnificent stand of 191 between Cowdrey and Dexter who carried the total from 19 for one to 210 for two when Dexter (76) misread Sobers's googly and was caught and bowled. The next over, Sobers had Cowdrey (119) caught by Alexander: 215 for three. Cowdrey's innings reflected a special sense of responsibility after assuming the captaincy in place of May who had returned to England because of a previous operation wound that had not healed sufficiently. The start of play was delayed slightly on the second day because of rain, and Smith came in instead of Barrington who was batting the night before when he was hit on the hand by the second to last ball of the last over. Since play had ended without the over being completed, the umpires ruled that Barrington (18 not out) had retired, and must be replaced by another batsman - hence Smith. Subba Row (22) was the first to go on the second day, caught by Hunte off Hall: 268 for four. Barrington re-entered, and lunch was taken early because of another interruption by rain. After lunch, England's strong position (308 for four) came under severe attack from Ramadhin who, in a spell lasting for most of the lunch/tea session, obliterated four enemy wickets for 25 runs in 15 overs. It was like old times, in 1950, when his "mystery" completely baffled batsmen. Barrington (69) was caught behind: 317 for five; Smith (20) clean bowled: 350 for six; Illingworth (0) was caught by Sobers; and Allen (7) caught by a substitute fielder: 374 for eight. In the end, thanks principally to Ramadhin, England's first innings total which had threatened to run out of bounds had been restricted to 393.

Westindies were off to an inauspicious start when their turn at the wicket came: in trying to hook a bouncer from Trueman, Hunte was hit on the head and had to receive stitches; Kanhai, who had not fielded all day because of a bruised hand, could not bat, and was replaced by Alexander; and McMorris (13) suffered a tragic run out when a straight drive by Alexander was accidentally deflected from the bowler on to McMorris's stumps. The result of these misfortunes was that, at the close, Westindies were 49 for one: Alexander 15 not out, and Sobers 9 not out. The jinx continued against Westindies on the third day as they lost more than two hours of play because of rain; but they managed to add another 101 runs in the course of the day for the loss of Alexander (26). When stumps were drawn, Walcott was 34 not out and Sobers 61 not out.

On the fourth day, Westindies added 65 runs before lunch and lost Walcott (53) who was stumped by Parks off Allen: 190 for three. Up to lunch-time when they were 215 for four, they could entertain plans of securing a first innings lead that might prove too much for England on the last day on a turning wicket. Soon after lunch, however, Worrell (15) was bowled by Trueman: 216 for four; Kanhai (6) chopped a ball from Moss on to his stumps: 227 for five; and at 230, Sobers was bowled by Moss when 8 runs short of his fourth consecutive hundred in the series. Far from establishing a first innings lead, Westindies were now in danger of not drawing level with England. But Hunte returned with plaster on his head wound, and proceeded to add 65 for the eighth wicket with Hall. As time was running out, Alexander's victory plans were becoming less realistic. In a bold move, he declared at 338 for eight (55 behind England), with Hunte 72 not out and Griffith 5 not out. He gambled, no doubt, on capturing one or two wickets before the close, and his gamble paid off, to some extent, when Cowdrey (0) was immediately caught by Worrell off Hall, and England were 18 for one when stumps were drawn.

The next day, the overnight batsmen, Allen and Pullar forged ahead until Allen (25) was run out: 69 for two. Pullar (54) lasted until about lunch, when he was caught and bowled by Sobers: 102 for three. After lunch, Dexter had two "lives", one of which was a simple return catch to Worrell. It was a grave error, but Westindian hopes flared up when Subba Row (13) was lbw to Ramadhin: 136 for four, and Barrington (6) was caught at shortleg off Sobers: 145 for five. England were 200 ahead at this stage, and the scenario of Westindies having to make less than 300 for victory on the final day looked increasingly possible. This possibility grew stronger when, half an hour before tea, Dexter (47) was brilliantly run out by Hunte: 148 for six. At tea, with Smith and Parks in possession, England were 168 for six - 223 ahead. But Providence intervened once more by sending showers that stopped play for about half an hour and further frustrated Westindian hopes of victory.

In a last, calculated gamble, Alexander consulted with Worrell before calling for the new ball and entrusting the fate of Westindies into the hands of his fast bowlers. A successful blitzkrieg from them might be just what was needed to provide Westindies with the outside chance of getting about 250 runs for victory in the fourth innings. But it was not to be. Smith and Parks proved as solid as rock and as immovable as stone. They carried England to a total of 238 for six at the close, and their solidity put paid to all Westindian optimism when, on the final day, they extended their partnership to 197 runs and completely crushed any lingering Westindian hopes of victory. Cowdrey did not declare until half an hour after lunch when English safety was utterly beyond dispute. He declared at 350 for seven setting Westindies 406 to win in scarcely enough time to make half that. Inevitably, time ran out: Westindies were left on 209 for five, and the match ground to an inevitable draw. England had won the first rubber in the Westindies since their first visit in 1929/30.

CHAPTER FIVE

Ascension - Frank Worrell

(1960-63)

First Test vs. Australia
Woolloongabba, Brisbane, Australia
9, 10, 12, 13, 14 December, 1960.

The first Test between Westindies and Australia in 1960 is one of the most memorable games in the history of Westindian cricket. The teams were led by Frank Worrell and Richie Benaud. Westindies batted first, and Davidson accounted for Hunte (24), Cammie Smith (7), and Kanhai (15) with the score at 65. Crisis was averted with the timely return to form of Sobers who joined Worrell in a sublime partnership of 174 runs that combined the dynamic fireworks of an inspired young genius with the finely tuned artistry of an ageing master. Sobers made 132 before he was caught by Kline off Meckiff. It was his tenth Test century and a scintillating innings the like of which, critics said, had not been seen in Australia since the days of Bradman and McCabe. Then Worrell was caught by Grout off Davidson for 65 which took him 159 minutes: time that was worth as much as the runs themselves. At 243 for five, Westindies had recovered somewhat. Solomon put on 40 runs with Lashley (19), followed by another partnership of 64 with Alexander before he was out hit wicket to Simpson for an invaluable 65. In this fashion, by the end of the day, Alexander and Ramadhin were left not out with the score at 359 for seven.

The next morning, a Saturday, after Ramadhin (12) was quickly dispatched, Hall hit with tremendous power to amass 50 runs out of a partnership of 86 with Alexander. It was great stuff, and it helped Westindies to a first innings total of 453 to which Alexander's contribution of 60 was indispensable. Davidson was the outstanding Australian bowler, claiming five wickets for 135 in 30 overs. Kline also picked up three tailend wickets, but Benaud had no luck in 24 overs which cost him 93 runs. In their first innings, although the Australian opening batsman Colin McDonald took a physical battering from Hall, he bore his pain manfully, and contributed 57 brave runs; but after he was caught by Hunte off Sobers, Harvey (15) was bowled by Valentine and Australia were 138 for two. Bobby Simpson, meanwhile, was batting steadily and was unlucky to be bowled by Ramadhin when he was 8 runs short of his century. This happened shortly before play ended on the Saturday with Australia 196 for three, the not out batsmen being O'Neill and Favell.

On Monday, O'Neill was dropped twice and made good use of his luck by proceeding to build a mammoth personal score of 181 runs that formed the cornerstone to an Australian first innings total of 505. Notable contributions also came from Favell (45), Mackay (35), and Davidson (44), but it was O'Neill who was chiefly responsible for Australia's prosperity. Hall was the most successful Westindian bowler with four wickets for 140 runs in 29.3 overs, while Sobers bowled 32 overs for 115 runs and two wickets. The next day, Smith (6) was caught by O'Neill off Davidson soon after the Westindian second innings began. Kanhai and Hunte then blasted 50 runs in twenty-eight minutes before Hunte (39) was caught by Simpson off Mackay. Sobers (14) was yorked by Davidson: 114 for three. Crisis threatened as Kanhai was caught by Grout off Davidson for 54 with the score at 127. But Worrell and Solomon established calm as they had done in the first innings, this time with a partnership of 83 runs, until Worrell (65) was also caught by Grout off Davidson: 210 for five. When Lashley was bowled by Davidson for 0 and the score became 210 for six - actually 158 for six, if one considered the deficit - the match reached its climax; for a Westindian collapse at this point would have meant certain defeat. Solomon and Alexander devoted themselves to sheer survival, and at one stage took 12 overs to score 12 runs. Eventually, Alexander was bowled by Benaud for 5, but Solomon utilised all of 222 minutes before he was lbw to Simpson for 47 runs shortly before end of play on the fourth day.

On the historic fifth and final day, a Wednesday, the overnight batsmen Hall and Valentine needed thirty-eight long and precious minutes to make 25 runs. When Hall (18) was finally bowled by Davidson, Australia was left to make 233 to win in about five and a half hours. It was an inviting challenge, and Benaud and his men did not flinch from it. But Hall contrived a spell of fast bowling such as he had never before given any sign of achieving. Doubts that may have existed about his wayward direction simply vanished as he kept his aim unerringly on target, and in a torrid spell, removed Simpson (0), Harvey (5) and O'Neill (26), and reduced Australia in no time at all to 49 for three. Worrell bowled McDonald (16) which meant that four wickets were down for 49, and when Hall had Favell caught by Solomon for 7, Australia were 57 for five and the match as good as in Westindian hands. Mackay's resistance was short-lived: he was bowled by Ramadhin for 28. Then the real drama began as Davidson and Benaud, through a combination of brave aggression and stolid defence gradually swung the match back to Australia by carving 134 runs, until Davidson (80) was run out by Solomon aiming at the wicket from sideways: 226 for seven. Davidson had accomplished a rare feat by completing the match double of 100 runs and ten wickets in a Test - the only player in the history of the game to do so.

One over was left, and Australia needed six runs to win with three wickets intact. Tension was such that nonplussed Westindian fielders allowed Grout and Benaud to steal a single from under their very noses as Hall's first delivery hit Grout and fell only a couple of feet in front of him. The next ball was a bouncer and Benaud (52) went for the hook that could bring four runs and virtual victory; but he was caught by Alexander for an heroic captain's knock: 228 for eight. The third delivery produced no score, while the fourth yielded another stolen single. Four runs to get and four deliveries left! Grout hit Hall's fifth delivery toward square leg where Kanhai was comfortably placed to take the catch; but the tension was too much for Hall as he dashed madly after the catch himself and dropped it! This gave the batsmen another single. Now, going all out for victory, Meckiff struck the sixth delivery heftily toward the square leg boundary where Hunte miraculously gathered the ball inches from the fence, and threw a spectacular return that enabled Alexander to run out Grout. Since the batsmen had run 2, the scores were tied at 232 for nine. Kline, the last batsman, entered the fray and hit Hall's seventh delivery for what looked to be the winning run. But Solomon again threw down the wicket from sideways, and Meckiff (2) was run out to leave the Australian total dead level at 232 and produce the first tie in the history of Test cricket. Many elements went into the making of this match, including the batting of Sobers, O'Neill, Worrell, and Davidson, the bowling of Hall and Davidson, and the fielding of Solomon; but the decisive element was the leadership of two captains who knew, or acted as if they knew that cricket, well and truly played, can reflect the best and noblest possibilities in humankind.

Fourth Test vs. Australia
Adelaide Oval, Adelaide, Australia
27, 28, 30, 31 January, 1 February, 1961

If the Westindian cricket tour of Australia in 1960/61 was dramatic and entertaining, it wasn't just that the quality of play was superb: it was the sportsmanship that was rigorously testing, yet mutually admiring. No wonder the tour produced the (then) unique result of a tied Test in the first match at Brisbane, and also contrived to evoke a spontaneous outpouring of people on to the streets of Melbourne to bid goodbye to the tourists as they were about to depart from Australia at the end of their tour. The second and third Test matches were almost as absorbing as the first. So was the fourth, although it is nowadays almost forgotten, except for a crucial incident in the final session of play on the final day. When the fourth Test opened at Adelaide Oval, both teams had won one match each, and it was evident that whichever side won the fourth Test would have the advantage of setting the tactical agenda for the fifth and final Test: the fourth Test could therefore be decisive in the rubber. Immediately before this Test, the Westindian players showed excellent form in annihilating a weak South Australian Country Eleven by an innings and 215 runs: Sobers and Solomon, for instance, scored a century partnership in only thirty-nine minutes. The Australians, on the other hand, seemed less buoyant: because of illness and injury, they had to leave out three of their most reliable players - Davidson, Meckiff and Harvey.

The match opened on a scorching, hot day, and Hunte (6) was soon lbw to Hoare: 12 for one. Kanhai and Cammie Smith scored quickly until Smith (28) was caught and bowled by Benaud only to be followed by Sobers (1) being bowled by Benaud: 91 for three. Captain Worrell and Kanhai scored at break-neck speed, adding 107 runs before Kanhai (117) was caught at slip off Benaud: 198 for four. It was a vintage innings, all power, daring and speedy reflexes, and it was thanks mainly to Kanhai that Westindies ended the day on 348 for seven, and finished the second day 393 all out. Worrell contributed 71, Nurse 49, and Alexander 63 not out. Benaud took five wickets for 96 runs in 27 overs, and Kline no wicket for 109 runs in 21 overs. It gives some idea of how fast Westindies scored, to realize that the two main Australian bowlers conceded nearly four runs per over.

In their reply, Australia lost Favell (1) at 9 and O'Neill (11) at 45. McDonald and Simpson steadied things with a stand of 74 before McDonald (71) was caught by Hunte off Gibbs: 119 for three. Then Simpson and Burge took the score to 213 when Burge (45) was bowled by Sobers. At end of play, Australia had reached 221 for four, with Simpson on 85 and Benaud on 1. Simpson fell for his overnight score early on the third day; but captain Benaud rallied his troops by scoring a gallant 77, and seeing them through to a total of 366, only 27 behind Westindies. It was a splendid recovery, considering that Australia were 221 for five when Simpson was out. Sobers took three for 64 in 24 overs, and Gibbs five for 97 in 35.6 overs. Gibbs achieved the rare feat of a hat trick in Test cricket when he had Mackay lbw, Grout caught by Sobers, and Misson clean bowled in consecutive deliveries. It is the only hat-trick in an Adelaide Test.

Cammie Smith roared ahead like an out-of-control fire engine when the Westindian second innings started. In just about one hour he scored 46, including ten fours. When he was caught by Hoare off Mackay with the score at 66, he had set a tone of dash and derring-do for the innings. The tone perfectly suited Kanhai who went even faster than Smith, so that when stumps were drawn on the fourth day, Westindies were 150 for one wicket with Kanhai 59 not out, and Hunte 44 not out, although Hunte had started batting almost one hour before his more dashing partner. Kanhai continued his fierce onslaught on the fifth day, calling his partner for such sharp singles that Hunte had to caution him. It was in vain, however. Perhaps the fire blood which Edgar Mittelholzer observes in the Guyana plantations of his Kaywana novels courses through Kanhai's veins! For when he was 99, on the verge of a separate hundred in each innings of the same Test match, he called for another impossible single and caused poor Hunte to be run out for 79 after a dazzling partnership that had realized 163 breath-taking runs. Kanhai showed remorse by staying for nearly an hour on 103. He seemed to recover; but briefly; for he was soon lbw to Benaud for 115 - the bowler's 200th Test wicket. Kanhai is the first Westindian to score a separate hundred in each innings of a Test in Australia.

His first hundred lasted for 126 minutes, and his second for 150 minutes. By tea on the fifth day Westindies had reached 360 with Alexander on 45 and Worrell 40. Worrell held back until about 5.30pm when Westindies were 432 for six, before declaring and giving Australia 35 minutes to bat before stumps. He had left his opponents 460 runs to make in 395 minutes, an astute gamble that he was well on the way to winning that very day when McDonald (2), Favell (4) and Simpson (3) were all back in the pavilion and the Australian score only 31.

On the final day, since the wicket was lifeless and of no use to Hall, it was Sobers, Gibbs and Valentine who carried the attack to the Australians of whom O'Neill and Burge fought back most stoutly with a brave stand of 82. Runs were no matter. Survival was all, and the air itself became heavy with concentration, tension and desperation as, bit by bit, wicket by wicket, the battle swung inexorably toward Westindies. After O'Neill was caught and bowled by Sobers for 65 and Benaud dismissed in an identical manner for 17, the score was 144 for six. At tea, following an invaluable 42 from Grout, the total had moved to 203 for seven. At this stage, mere bowlers - Hoare, Misson and Kline - remained. Of these, Misson (1) was caught by Solomon off Worrell, and Hoare (0) was bowled by Worrell: 207 for nine. Now Mackay and Kline, Australia's last pair, stood between Westindies and victory. Surely they could not survive for long! This thought was evidently in the minds of the Westindian players, when, with almost an hour's play remaining, Mackay pushed forward to Worrell and Sobers caught the ball. Sobers and other Westindian players, certain that Mackay was out, began to walk off the field. But Mackay stood his ground; and umpire Egar's finger did not budge.

This was the crucial incident mentioned earlier: it changed the course of the match, and as it turned out, the fate of the entire rubber. Try as they might, the Westindian bowlers could not dislodge Mackay and Kline, who blocked, pushed, padded and defended for one hundred minutes until the game was drawn, with the Australian score at 273 for nine: Mackay 62 not out, and Kline 15 not out. From an Australian point of view, Mackay and Kline were heroes. Today, it scarcely seems possible that so much could have happened in one match: a hundred in each innings by Kanhai, Gibbs's hat trick, Benaud's 200th Test wicket (not to mention his heroic 77 not out in the first innings), Alexander's 63 and 87 unbeaten in both innings, and Mackay's defiant 62 not out. For Australians the last ditch heroism of Mackay and Kline must stand out. But what probably stands out for most Westindians is the catch that the record books tell us Sobers never took.

Fifth Test vs. Australia
Melbourne Cricket Ground, Melbourne Australia
10, 11, 13, 14, 15 February, 1961

If the enthralling tied Test at Brisbane served as a fitting prologue to the Westindian tour of Australia in 1960/61, the final Test match of the series at

Melbourne proved to be a superb finale to the tour's five-act drama. According to Bill Frindall in *The Wisden Book of Test Cricket - 1876/77 to 1977/78*, this match concluded: "the most enterprising and exciting rubber of recent times." (p.518) The state of the rubber at the end of the fourth Test was 1:1, with one match drawn and one tied. The scene was therefore set in Melbourne for a decisive contest that would bring down the curtain on what seemed certain to be a thrilling dénouement. Benaud won the toss and put Westindies in to bat. Neither the weather nor the pitch seemed to offer a full explanation of the Australian captain's decision. Could it have been that he did not wish to expose his men to Hall - spearhead of the Westindian fast attack - when he was fresh? Cammie Smith (11) opened the innings with his usual bravado but was caught, somewhat unluckily, off a full toss from Misson: 18 for one. Kanhai and Hunte batted more soberly until Kanhai (38) was caught by Harvey off Benaud, shortly before lunch: 75 for two. Hunte (31) and Worrell (10) were next out; but Sobers and Lashley lifted the score from 107 for four to 200 for five, before Lashley was also caught off Benaud for 41. Thereafter, the Westindian innings slid irrevocably downward, especially after Sobers (64) was caught by Grout off Simpson: 204 for six. Play closed that day with Westindies 252 for eight. The next morning, in an unanticipated show of sturdy resistance, Solomon and Hall managed to consolidate an invaluable partnership of 65 runs before Hall was bowled by Misson for 21. Then, in trying to shield Valentine, Solomon was run out for 45, and the innings folded at 292. Sobers had made the top score, while the most successful Australian bowler was Frank Misson who claimed four wickets for 58 runs. Davidson delivered 27 overs for 89 runs and one wicket, and Benaud 21.7 overs for 55 runs and two wickets.

The Australian openers, Simpson and McDonald, carried the score as far as 146 before McDonald was lbw to Sobers for 91. Simpson was caught by Gibbs off Sobers for 75, and O'Neill (10) was bowled by Gibbs: 181 for three; but Westindies could not capitalize on this breakthrough; and Burge and Mackay played out the time to leave Australia 236 for three when stumps were drawn. Westindies fought back valiantly when play resumed the following Monday. In quick time, they removed Mackay (19) and Harvey (5): 260 for five; and by lunch-time they had taken a further two wickets, so that Australia were finally out for 356, a lead of only 64. Australia had scored 128 runs while losing seven wickets that Monday. For this grand achievement Westindies principally had to thank Sobers: 44-7-120-5, and Gibbs: 38.4-18-74-4. Sobers had bowled unchanged for 41 eight-ball overs.

In their second innings, in almost even time, Hunte and Smith added 54 runs before Smith (37) was lbw Davidson. Smith was again going great guns before he was stopped, and Kanhai (31) followed suit until he hit a Benaud long hop into the hands of mid-wicket. Worrell then wisely sent in Solomon as night watchman, and he and Hunte took the score to 126 for two before play ended. Early on the Tuesday morning, Hunte was caught by wicket-keeper Grout for 52. Sobers, next in, did not bat like himself, and was caught by the wicket-keeper off Simpson for 21. At lunch, Alexander and Solomon were at the wicket, and the score was 201 for four. After lunch, Solomon (36) made a bad call and was run out for the second time in the match. Worrell and Lashley failed, and with the score at 262 for seven,

Westindian fortunes looked like failing too. Alexander made a valiant 73, helping Westindies to reach a total of 321, by no means a formidable score, but one that set Australia 258 to get for victory. For Australia, Davidson had shown great courage in taking five wickets for 84 runs although he was injured.

The Australians began their second innings with Simpson hitting Hall for four fours and a two in the first over. They soon lost McDonald for 11, but had reached a total of 57 for one by the end of fourth day. By lunch on the final day, the match seemed all but over when Australia had scored 153 for one, with Simpson 92 not out and O'Neill 37 not out. After lunch, Simpson was bowled by Gibbs without adding to his score. O'Neill also came close to getting out shortly after lunch. Bowler Worrell and wicket-keeper Alexander made a very confident appeal for lbw against O'Neill, but it was turned down by umpire Egar. Between lunch and tea Worrell and Gibbs bowled unchanged and made the Australian batsmen fight, tooth and claw, for every solitary run.

But gradually, perhaps inevitably, Australia drew closer and closer to the target. By tea, they were 53 runs short with five wickets and more than enough time left. After tea, when Australia were only four runs short of victory, umpire Egar was involved in another controversial decision. Grout cut a ball from Valentine and started to run. Alexander pointed to one bail from Grout's wicket which had fallen to the ground. Square leg umpire Hoy confirmed both that Alexander had not dislodged the bail, and that Grout's bat had not hit the wicket. But Grout remained. Even if Grout had been given out it is by no means certain that Westindies would have won the fifth Test. As it turned out, they lost by two wickets. But they remained moral victors as we can tell from the spontaneous gesture of crowds in thronging the Westindian players to thank and congratulate them on the streets of Melbourne, as they were about to leave Australia.

First Test vs. India
Queen's Park Oval, Port of Spain, Trinidad
16, 17, 19, 20 February, 1962

Westindies first visited India under John Goddard in 1948/49, and India, under Hazare, paid their first visit to the Westindies in 1952/53. Then Gerry Alexander took Westindies again to India in 1958/59, and India, under Nari Contractor, came for a repeat Westindian visit in 1961/62. This history of Indian/ Westindian encounters suggests that, up to 1962, Westindies seemed to grow stronger and India weaker. Westindies won in India in 1948/49, and at home in 1952/53, but in each case only by the narrow margin of one:nil, with four games drawn. Under Alexander, however, Westindies won three:nil, so that when India arrived in 1962, they felt that they had a score to settle. Meanwhile, Alexander had been replaced by Worrell as Westindian captain, a change that resulted in a hugely successful Westindian tour of Australia in 1960/61, even though Westindies narrowly lost the Test series itself: one:two.

Contractor and his men had little time to become acclimatized after their arrival in 1962. They had only one match, against Trinidad, which ended in a draw, before the first Test at Queen's Park Oval in February. In the first Test India batted first on a good wicket; but they had no answer to the pace of Hall and Stayers. This was to prove a recurring theme throughout the series. In this case, Hall quickly disposed of openers Contractor and Mehra, and Stayers accounted for Manjrekar and Sardesai. Since none of their batsmen could stop the tide of disaster, India soon found themselves in the abject state of 89 for six wickets. Then Surti and Durani, bowlers rather than batsmen, held on for dear life till stumps, by which time they had pushed the score to 114. The next day, against all expectation, the overnight bowler/batsmen continued to survive and push forward despite everything that Worrell could throw at them. Improbably, they added 57 more runs which brought their partnership altogether to 81 and helped their team to reach a total of 203. While this represented a creditable Indian recovery, considering their desperation in mid-innings, it could hardly be regarded as a credible challenge to the likes of Hunte, Kanhai, Sobers and Worrell. Durani made 56 and Surti 57. The Indian dislike for pace meant that Hall and Stayers had a field day during the Indian first innings. Hall bowled 20 overs for 38 runs and two wickets, while the less experienced Stayers contributed 18 overs for 65 runs and three wickets.

Cammie Smith and Hunte opened for Westindies, and Smith (12) was soon caught by Umrigar off Desai: 13 for one. After some aggressive flourishes, Kanhai was caught and bowled by Borde for 24 when the score was 67. Sobers and Hunte then stabilized the situation somewhat before the former (40) was bowled by Umrigar: 136 for three. Worrell's 0 and Stayers's 4 made the score 140 for five. Then Hunte (58) who had batted patiently, and had virtually carried the innings so far, was caught and bowled by Durani: 148 for six. At this point, after the second day, India's 203, which had earlier seemed flimsy and fragile, began to take on a more sturdy appearance. This was reinforced by the fact that the Westindian wicket-keeper, Jackie Hendriks, had fractured a finger and might not bat, for it meant that Solomon, the last recognized batsman, was to be followed by Gibbs, Hall and Watson who were not exactly famous for feats of batsmanship. But on the third day, Hendriks decided to ignore doctor's orders and go out to bat. It proved a fateful decision: he set about the Indian bowlers with such exhilaration that he made the performance of his top order colleagues looked quite inept by comparison. When Solomon was eventually caught by wicket-keeper Engineer off Desai for 43, he and Hendriks had added 64 runs to take the total to 212. Gibbs (0) came in briefly and was caught by Durani off Umrigar. Hendriks found another willing partner in Hall, with whom he forged a partnership of 70 before he was caught by Durani off Borde for 64. The innings closed at 289 with Hall 37 not out. It was a peculiar team effort to the extent that the last five batsmen had scored 149 runs, 9 more that the first five. Of the Indian bowlers, Durani was the most successful with 35.2 overs for 82 runs and four wickets. Along with scoring 56 runs and salvaging some self-respect for his team, this was a terrific effort by Durani; he was helped by Umrigar, Borde and Desai who took two wickets each.

If, when India began their second innings after tea on the third day, they felt some relief facing a deficit of only 86, it was short-lived: their main batsmen again shrivelled under the heat of pace generated by Hall and Stayers. Contractor (6) went first bowled by Hall: 6 for one. Manjrekar (0) was next out hit wicket to Hall. Then Hall had Sardesai (2) caught behind by Smith: 8 for three. Smith had been keeping wicket since the first day when Hendriks fractured his finger, and Hall's three wickets had fallen in the space of four balls. Mehra and Umrigar essayed a rescue which took the score to 35 before the former was bowled by Stayers for 8, and at stumps on the third day, India found themselves at 49 runs for four wickets. On the fourth day, Umrigar and Borde added 11 runs to their overnight total before Sobers disposed of Umrigar for 23. Borde advanced to 27 before he too was bowled by Sobers: 70 for six. This meant that 16 more runs were needed to make Westindies bat again. Since all their main batsmen had gone, India deserves credit for avoiding the humiliation of an innings defeat by struggling to a total of 98. Hunte and Smith had no trouble at all scoring the 15 runs required for victory by ten wickets. The Indian batsmen could not blame pace entirely for their undoing in the second half of their second innings. While it is true that by demolishing three wickets for 11 runs, Hall had crippled them, it was the spinners who finished them off. Sobers claimed four wickets for 22 runs in 15 overs, and Gibbs two wickets for 16 runs in 7.5 overs. India were completely outclassed by a superb fighting force led by an astute general.

Fifth Test vs. India
Sabina Park, Kingston, Jamaica, 13, 14, 16, 17, 18 April, 1962

It is a matter of historical record that India's tour of Westindies in 1961/62 was a sorry compound of unmitigated disaster and woe. Before the team left India, as we are told by Tony Cozier in *The West Indies: Fifty Years of Test Cricket*, that astrologers had detected unauspicious signs in the heavens. Subsequent events proved this prediction correct not only because India sank lower in ignominy with virtually every match they played, but also in the way they suffered from injury and illness, the worst of which was the misfortune suffered by captain Nari Contractor when he was hit in the head by Charlie Griffith in the Barbados match immediately preceding the third Test: he almost lost his life but for a series of operations that he underwent. India's new captain for the third Test was the Nawab of Pataudi who, at the age of twenty-one, was the youngest Test captain ever. Pataudi possessed excellent pedigree as a batsman, his father having scored 102 in his Test début for England against Australia at Sydney in 1932. There might also have been something in the fact that, following the vagaries of historical change, the older Pataudi captained India on their third tour of England in 1946. Despite all his inherited advantages, however, it was surely a tall order to pit the young Nawab against an astute and experienced general like Worrell leading seasoned troops like Hunte, Kanhai, Sobers, Hall and Gibbs.

Under Contractor, having already lost the first Test by ten wickets, and the second by an innings and 18 runs, India now, under Pataudi, lost the third Test by an innings and 30 runs, and the fourth by seven wickets. In the midst of such disaster and tribulation, the best that could be said is that in the second innings of the fourth Test India contrived a magnificent, if unavailing rally that produced 422 runs mainly through the efforts of Umrigar (172 not out) and Durani (104). India's disasters were matched by political disturbances and riots in Guyana causing the fifth Test match, which was scheduled for Bourda in April 1962, to be changed to Sabina Park, Jamaica. At any rate, their fight back in the fourth Test seemed to engender more resolution in India, and for the fifth and final Test they dropped Sardesai who was in poor form, and replaced him with Ranjane, a bowler. In this final encounter Westindies won the toss and batted, and Ranjane justified his choice by dismissing Hunte for 1 in his first over. McMorris and Kanhai took the score to 64 before the former was lbw to Durani for 37. Durani followed this up by bowling the new batsman, Solomon, for 0, and when Kanhai was caught and bowled by Ranjane for 44 the Westindian total stood at 93 for four. It was the most successful start that India had achieved in the series. But Sobers and Worrell reversed some of this success by taking the score to 140 before Worrell (26) was lbw to Ranjane. Thirty-four more runs were added by Hall and the magisterial Sobers who clocked up another century - 104 runs - top score in a modest Westindian total of 253. The main bowlers responsible for putting India in such a good position were the new-comer Ranjane with four wickets for 72 runs, Nadkarni with three for 50, and Durani two for 56.

But, as so often on the tour, the good work of their bowlers was undone by India's batsmen. Jaisimha (6) was caught by Sobers off King: 11 for one; and both Mehra (8) and Manjrekar (0) were caught by Allan off King when the total was 22. Whereas, in their previous matches, it was the pace of Hall that terrorized Indian resolve, terror now emerged from the Jamaican medium-fast bowler Lester King who was making his Test début and who, in addition to Jaisimha, Mehra, and Manjrekar, had also disposed of Durani and Borde by the end of the day when India were limping at 33 for five wickets. On the second day, Hall had the overnight Pataudi (14) caught by Kanhai, and with six of their main batsmen gone, it was left to Nadkarni and Surti, both left handed all-rounders, to salvage what they could of Indian self-respect. This they did with great courage, adding another 72 runs before the more adventurous Surti was bowled by Gibbs for 41. With even greater courage, the injured Umrigar (32) helped Nadkarni (61) to add another 59 runs and India were able to reach a modestly respectable total of 178. Although King was the chief destroyer with five wickets for 46 runs, it was Gibbs who finished off the innings with three for 38. In the Westindian second innings the irrepressible Surti dismissed Hunte and Solomon each for 0, (Solomon's second 0 in the match). Sobers (50) was in an aggressive mood and added 74 runs with McMorris (42). Then, following changes in the batting order, Allan and Gibbs were both lbw to Durani, and Westindies found themselves at end of play on 138 for six. The next day, Worrell and the injured Kanhai (41) put on 78 runs, but after Kanhai was bowled by Ranjane, Worrell ran out of partners, and sadly, had to be content with 98 not out when the innings ended at 283.

Set to make 359 for victory in two full days, India lost Jaisimha (6) and Durani (4) both lbw to King; but Mehra and Borde moved the score safely to 37 by end of play. On the fourth day these two added 40 more runs before Mehra (39) was caught by Allan off Sobers, and Borde (26) was bowled by Hall: 80 for four. Sobers bowled Pataudi for 4 and nudged the total to 86 for five. A quick despatch seemed imminent except that Manjrekar and Umrigar held on doggedly for the rest of the day. Further gestures of dogged defiance on the final day, especially from Manjrekar (40), Umrigar (60) and Surti (42) were unavailing, and India capitulated for 235. Their defeat by 123 runs was the narrowest of the series, and showed that they did not entirely lack material and spiritual resources. In this instance, however, they simply had no answer to Sobers (five wickets for 63 runs) on a wearing pitch. The real cause of their undoing on this ill-fated tour was an inadequate psychological approach to Westindian pace rather than mysterious predictions of celestial or other origin.

First Test vs. England
Old Trafford, Manchester, England, 6, 7, 8, 10 June, 1963

Following their arduous tour of Australia in 1960/61, Westindies enjoyed relatively easy passage in a home series in 1961/62 when they crushed India 5:0. To become "world champions" they had to beat England and Australia, and they took one step nearer this goal during their tour of England in 1963. Captain Frank Worrell won the toss in the first Test match of the tour, and as the Westindian openers Hunte and Carew faced up to Trueman and Statham, it was clear that there was little "life" in the pitch. Nevertheless Trueman soon had Carew (16) caught behind: 37 for one. It was Carew's Test début. By lunch, Kanhai and Hunte had moved the score briskly to 82 without further loss. After lunch, these two superb strokeplayers flourished against the English bowlers, including the spinners, Titmus and Allen. Hunte's role was that of anchor man, while Kanhai fenced and flashed in the process of creating what one commentator calls: "fanciful inventions of new ways to hit a cricket ball." (J.S. Barker, *Summer Spectacular*, p.24) Deploying an impressive array of orthodox and unorthodox strokes, including his unique falling hook, Kanhai scored confidently until he had reached 90 and his century was just for the asking. Then he drove the English captain Dexter wide of mid-on and charged down the pitch for what was a certain run; but, for some reason, Hunte did not leave his crease and Kanhai was run out. As the light began to fade, Hunte reached a well made century. It was probably due to the fading light that Butcher fell lbw for 22 in trying to hook Trueman. At any rate, Sobers and Hunte advanced the score safely to 244 for three before play stopped for the day.

The next day, after a slow start, Hunte and Sobers gradually consolidated their total by adding 120 runs before Sobers (64) was caught by Edrich off Allen: 359 for four. Sobers had batted brilliantly, hitting sixes off both Statham and Allen. Hunte, meanwhile, playing the innings of his life, went on to score 182 before he was caught by Titmus off Allen: 398 for five. It was an innings that mixed patience with aggression and it then represented the highest individual score against England at Manchester; it was also probably designed to accord with a plan of securing a large enough total that might make a Westindian second innings unnecessary. Worrell and Solomon put on 81 runs before Solomon (35) was lbw to Titmus: 479 for six. Worrell went on to play a beautiful innings, executing the latest of late cuts with maximum delicacy and elegance. It was a virtuoso performance by an old maestro who had remembered everything and had nothing more to learn. At 501 for six Worrell declared. He was 74 not out, and young Derek Murray, playing in his first Test match, 7 not out. In the late afternoon, Hall and Griffith had a go at the English openers Edrich and Stewart, although they did so with more speed than direction, and the English pair survived, having scored 31 by the time stumps were drawn.

Early the next morning, Hall struck three heavy blows against England. He had Edrich (20) and Barrington (16) caught behind by Murray, and bowled Cowdrey (4) while he shuffled across his wicket leaving his leg stump entirely unprotected. In the process England sank rapidly from their overnight 31 for none to 67 for three. But Dexter was undeterred by such gloom and disaster, and with character and courage, demonstrated that lordly disdain for which he is now famous. Several times he thought nothing of driving Hall, hard and high, straight back over his head for four. And as if this did not fully demonstrate his complete control, he lashed Gibbs for two sixes in one over. It was a wonderful spectacle that made partisan Westindian spectators sorry to see Dexter go for 73 when he was caught by Worrell off Sobers: 108 for four. When Close (30) was later caught by Hunte off Gibbs, the English innings crumbled from 181 for five to 205 all out. Hall captured three wickets for 51 runs in 17 overs and Gibbs five for 59 in 29.3 overs. Following on, Edrich and Stewart demonstrated true English grit in piling up 93 professional-looking runs until Edrich (38) was caught at backward square leg off Worrell. Wicket-keeper Andrew played the role of night watchman in helping Stewart to take the English score to 97 for one by close of play.

At the start of the fourth day, England were 199 runs behind. If their chances of saving the match partly depended on the state of the pitch, they found little comfort in the fact that Sobers and Gibbs had been able to get the odd ball to jump on the third afternoon. Predictably, Hall and Griffith made little impression on Andrew and Stewart; but no sooner had Worrell given the ball to Sobers than Andrew (15) was caught by Murray: 131 for two. Gibbs bowled Barrington (8) with his quicker ball: 160 for three; and five runs later Stewart (87), who had played with stalwart caution and courage, was caught, again by Murray, off Gibbs. Cowdrey and Dexter came together, the last English pair from whom England might seriously expect salvation. But Westindian fortunes were riding high and Gibbs and Sobers were bowling with real sting. Cowdrey (12) was caught off Gibbs at silly mid-off, and all English hopes rested with Dexter and Close. After lunch, the batsmen decided that attack was their best means of defence, and forced Worrell to remove both silly mid-off and silly mid-on. Their aggression was short-lived, and when Dexter (35) provided Murray with his sixth catch of the match off Sobers, the end was clearly in sight. Except for some lusty hits by Trueman (29), the remaining English batsmen surrendered and managed to reach a total of 296, just enough to make Westindies bat again and score one run for victory by ten wickets. In England's second innings, Gibbs returned the following figures: 46-16-98-6, while Sobers signalled support with: 37-4-122-2. Gibbs's match analysis of eleven wickets for 157 runs is the best of his career. England had neither bowled nor fielded badly: they were let down by their batsmen, with the exception of Dexter, Close and Stewart. Under Worrell's leadership, Westindies had showed themselves capable of almost any challenge. It was the first victory achieved by Westindies at Old Trafford, and since it came directly after five victories over India, it was the first time that Westindies had won six Tests in a row.

Second Test vs. England
Lord's London, England, 20, 21, 22, 24, 25 June, 1963

The 1963 Test series between England and Westindies produced several good matches, one of which - the Second Test - is probably the most thrilling Test match ever played. The 1963 Westindian Test team under Frank Worrell consisted of many players who had toured Australia in 1960/61, and taken part in the remarkable tied Test at Brisbane. England were under Dexter, with Barrington and Cowdrey as his leading batsmen, while Trueman provided pace and Titmus and Allen spin. The grey, damp and chilly setting at Lord's on the opening day of the match suited the absorbing drama that was about to be enacted over the next five days. Westindies won the toss, elected to bat, and faced accurate bowling, especially from Trueman and Shackleton, who swung the ball menacingly in the air as well as off the pitch. In the heavy atmosphere, against such bowling, backed up by good fielding, batsmen had to struggle to survive. To their credit, most Westindian batsmen succeeded in curbing their naturally flamboyant strokeplay. Hunte made 44, Sobers 42, and Kanhai 73, all in a subdued manner, mixing restraint with flashes of aggression. At the end of the day, Westindies could not feel greatly disappointed in their score of 245 runs for six wickets. In such inhospitable conditions, their position could have been much worse. The next morning, the overnight batsmen, Solomon and Murray were quickly parted. Their partnership had realized 44 runs. There was further resistance from Solomon (56) and Hall (25) before the innings came to an end with the score at 301. The excellence of Trueman's effort may be judged from his figures: 44-16-100-6. The testing character of this Westindian first innings told us what to expect during the rest of the match. Little or nothing was given away; each run had to be earned, and each wicket closely guarded. Dexter had not used Titmus at all. If he was right in thinking that the wicket favoured fast bowling, his batsmen would know what to expect when they ventured out to face Hall and Griffith.

Edrich was out to Griffith's first ball. Shortly afterwards, Stewart was caught, again off Griffith, when the score was 20. Awe must have descended on the English players; but not on their captain. In his own majestic style - body erect and head straight - Dexter proceeded to play one of the truly great short innings of modern cricket. It was a rare spectacle to watch Hall running in almost from the boundary to bowl to Dexter, and have the ball driven like a rocket back past him to the long-off or mid-off boundary. The faster Hall bowled the more powerfully did Dexter drive. Nor could it be said that the bowling was loose or the fielding slack. Even Westindian supporters expressed unashamed rapture, and loudly confessed their mixed feelings when Dexter was suddenly out with the score at 102. Dexter had received 75 balls and scored 70 runs in 80 minutes. Solid innings from Barrington (80) and Parks (35) helped England to end the day at 244 for 7 when it could be said that battle honours were even. Up to this point in the match, whenever one side appeared to gain an advantage it was quickly cut off and shifted to the other side.

In this fashion, by the end of the second day, the match had developed into a contest of such quick-shifting fortunes and unpredictable twists, enough to make almost any result seem possible. On the third day, (a Saturday) the gates were closed early and thousands failed to get in. Erratic bowling by Hall and Griffith helped England to reach a total of 297 of which Titmus contributed 52. The Westindian batting proved equally erratic at the start of their second innings and sustained blows that no Westindian spectator that day could quickly forget. In no time at all two wickets had fallen for 15 runs and Butcher and Kanhai were struggling. But Trueman and Shackleton would not relax their pressure, and first Kanhai (21), then Sobers (8) went as Westindies sank to 84 for 4. When Solomon was caught by Stewart off Allen for 5 soon after tea, the score was 104 for 5 and there was little doubt that Westindies were sinking inexorably. If anyone could bring salvation, it was Butcher; for at the other end was Worrell, well past his prime as a batsman, and he was to be followed by Murray, Hall, Griffith and Gibbs, not exactly famous for their batting prowess. With the scent of victory in his nostrils, it is not hard to imagine Trueman scything quickly through this fragile Westindian tail.

This was the moment in the match, with Westindian fortunes at their lowest ebb, that Butcher and Worrell contrived a partnership of heart-stopping resistance rare in the annals of Westindian cricket. As Worrell offered a steadying hand to this gallant, regenerative enterprise, Butcher settled himself in to one of the best innings ever achieved by a Westindian. To form an impression of Butcher's achievement, consider the resolution it took, with his side in mortal danger, to drive Allen straight over the bowler's head for six! If that were not enough, consider again what qualities of hand and eye were required, in such threatening conditions, to repeat the stroke! Never before had Butcher played better, deploying with confidence, a wide array of brilliant, punching drives, and those sweetly-timed, flicking leg side strokes that were his speciality. Gradually, unbelievably, under the combination of Butcher's wondrously growing confidence and Worrell's practised, if unscoring watchfulness, Westindian fortunes began to revive, and as if to celebrate the revival, when he was on 96, Butcher despatched Shackleton to the boundary and reached his century. At stumps on the third day, Butcher was 129 not out and Worrell 33 not out, while the Westindian total stood at 214 for 5.

With the weather still darkly threatening on the morning of the fourth day, Westindies had the advantage when play began: they were 218 runs ahead with five wickets intact. Yet after less than half an hour's play, they lost their last five wickets for only 15 runs. This left England with 234 runs to get in nearly two days. But the devilish uncertainty which had thus far haunted this match would not be so easily exorcised. The English second innings never found its bearings, and was soon floundering at 27 for two. Dexter was still there. How English hearts must have longed for him to reproduce the majestic grandeur he displayed in the first innings! But alas the king had lost all semblance of majesty, and Dexter was clean bowled by Gibbs for 2 making England 31 for three. As England's fortunes declined, Hall grew more deadly with each delivery. Bowling fast and short, with close-in fieldsmen on either side of the pitch, he threatened both the batsmen's physical safety and their wickets. With desperate and dogged application, Barrington and Cowdrey dourly defended themselves and their wickets. Ironically, this provoked a painful climax to the tragic drama that the weather had so far consistently foreshadowed: Cowdrey was struck on his left fore arm by a rising ball from Hall, and sustained a fracture which put him out of cricket for the season. As if to confirm their connivance in the tragic event, bad light and rain soon stopped play prematurely for the day. England had reached 116 for three, and Barrington was 55 not out. With Close, Parks, and Titmus still among the remaining batsmen and 118 runs required, an English victory was not as distant a prospect as it seemed when Dexter was out.

True to form, the weather heavily influenced events on the final day. It held up the start until 2:20pm and play was scheduled to end at 6:00pm Time had become a factor in England's calculations. Westindies struck the first blow when Barrington (60) was caught by wicket-keeper Murray: 130 for four. It was then up to Close and Parks to face the tireless Hall who bowled unchanged from 2:20pm to 6:00pm with only a break for tea in between. This must surely be one of the most spectacular exhibitions of sustained, top class fast bowling in the history of cricket. It was matched by an equally spectacular exhibition of courage from Brian Close who was hit numerous times all over his body, but stood his ground without flinching. While the mounting score brought England steadily closer to victory, first Parks, then Titmus supported Close as he soldiered fearlessly on against the thunderbolts of Hall and Griffith. Eventually, when Trueman was caught by Murray off Hall for 0, the score was at 203 for seven and Close realized that merely 45 minutes remained to get 31 runs. With only Allen, Shackleton, and the injured Cowdrey as possible partners, he decided that England's best hope was to attack. At one stage, he walked defiantly down the pitch to meet Hall as he ran up to a bowl. To his credit, Hall withheld the delivery at the very last moment, fearing he might inflict another injury. No doubt, there will be continuing debate about the wisdom of Close's attack at this critical stage of the game. It almost succeeded. When he was caught by Murray swinging at Griffith, he had brought England within 15 runs of victory. He himself had made 70 invaluable runs and shown exceptional fighting qualities.

It was now up to Allen and Shackleton who, through dabs, pushes and prods, advanced the score to 227. At this stage in the last over of the match, Hall had three deliveries to go, and England needed six runs to win with two wickets in hand. Allen went for suicidal run and Shackleton was run out. Cowdrey, arm in plaster, came out and stood at the non-striker's end. Allen realized that whatever he did, he must not expose the wounded Cowdrey to the fury of Hall. Any result was now possible as Allen prepared to receive the final two balls. If he got out, England would lose. If he scored six runs, England would win. If he blocked both balls without scoring, the match would be drawn. As it happens, he fended off both balls successfully and the match was drawn.

Up to the 1960s, there was one other Test match which was generally regarded as producing similar nerve-wracking excitement in its final moments: the tied Test in Brisbane in 1960. It is no coincidence that virtually the same Westindian team, under one captain, took part in both matches. One feature of both matches is that Frank Worrell was able to elicit from his players performances of a special Westindian character. This is evident in several examples of the Lord's match in 1963. There was, for example, the resilient and plucky batting of Hunte, Sobers, Kanhai and Solomon in the first innings, and Hall's magnificent bowling on the final day. But the finest example undoubtedly was Butcher's 133 in the second innings. It is not just the physical fact of the number of runs which he scored; nor yet his wonderful psychological mastery of a tight and demanding situation. After all, Barrington and Close showed as much pluck and resilience, and Dexter similar mastery. Yet none of these English batsmen quite matched the bold, adventurous, risk-taking spirit of Westindian cricket which Butcher demonstrated when he stood scarcely a foot out of his crease and without any backlift to speak of, twice, almost casually, lifted David Allen over the long-on boundary. The strokes seemed completely effortless, as if the ball was made to feel uncomfortable by the bowler's spin on the pitch, and entreated to be rescued and taken far away to the more free and spacious regions of the sight screen. When strokes achieve such spontaneous naturalness, cricket ceases to be sport and becomes art. And art is timeless, unforgettable.

Third Test vs. England
Edgbaston, Birmingham, England, 4, 5, 6, 8, 9 July, 1963

Frank Worrell's appointment as Westindian captain in 1960 was an historic departure from the precedent of white or near-white captains in Westindian cricket, and its first impact was a hugely successful tour in 1960/61 which was more evenly balanced than the 2:1 margin of victory for Australia might suggest. Under Worrell's generalship this success was followed by a home series in which Westindies crushed India 5:0 in 1962. In their quest to be world champions, Westindies needed another success on their tour to England in 1963. This was the context in which, after a splendid victory in the first Test and a drawn contest of high drama in the second Test at Lord's, the two teams met once more for the third Test at Edgbaston. It rained for almost a full week before the match started, and England's captain, Dexter, who had won the toss and decided to bat came in for some criticism in exposing his team to poor batting conditions. Hall quickly bowled Richardson for 2, after which Stewart and Dexter took the score cautiously to 50. The pitch was soft and wet; runs were hard to come by, and wickets began to fall. Sobers bowled Dexter for 29 and Barrington for 9, and finally had Stewart lbw for 39 after he had put up a stout defence. All this brought England to 89 for four. Sharpe and his Yorkshire captain Brian Close gathered 40 gritty runs before Sharpe (23) was caught by Kanhai off Gibbs: 129 for five. Soon afterwards, the light deteriorated to a point that play had to be stopped early, leaving England on 157 for five. No doubt Dexter's critics felt that this low score justified them.

Poor weather caused another interruption the next morning at about 12.40 when England were 194 for eight. A heavy shower was followed by sunshine, but the match did not resume until after tea, and by evening England were all out for 216, thanks largely to a resolute innings of 55 by Close. Hall and Griffith had collected two wickets each, but it was Sobers who crippled England with five wickets for 60 runs in 31 overs. An overnight storm delayed start of play until 12.50 on the third day. By this time the ground was thoroughly soaked. The pitch itself remained as slow for Trueman and Shackleton as it had been for Hall and Griffith, and it was not surprising that Trueman decided to shorten his run and concentrate on swing rather than pace. By lunch Westindies were 23 for none. Soon afterwards, Trueman bowled Hunte, and when the score had reached 70 for one, Kanhai's appeal against the light was turned down. It was a fateful decision; for half an hour later Westindies were 110 for four. And again the rain came down and stopped play early. The next morning Westindian misfortunes multiplied. In no time at all Butcher (15) was lbw to Dexter, Worrell (1) was bowled by Dexter, and Sobers (19) was bowled by Trueman. Hall and Murray, a most unlikely pair, slogged 48 improbable runs which made their total of 186 look rather less disgraceful. The most successful English bowlers were Trueman with five wickets for 75 runs in 26 overs, and Dexter: four for 38 in 20 overs. With their slender lead of 30 the English openers attempted consolidation, and put on 30 before Richardson (14) was caught by Murray off Griffith: 30 for one; but the next three wickets fell cheaply and brought the score to 69 for four. At that stage, the game could be considered evenly balanced, always depending on the weather. Dexter and Sharpe, in a crucial stand of 101, tilted the balance significantly toward England before Dexter (57) was stumped by Murray off Gibbs: 170 for five. No sooner had Dexter left than a minor procession brought England to 189 for eight. Then Sobers, who had bowled so superbly in this match, seemed to lose control, and allowed Sharpe and Lock to plunder 37 runs in the final twenty-five minutes of the fourth day, so that England were able to finish on 226 for eight, 256 runs on.

The question on the final morning was when Dexter should declare. Sharpe and Lock were allowed to put on 52 more runs, and realize a partnership of 89, at that time, a ninth-wicket record for England/Westindies Tests, before a declaration came. By that time, England had reached 278 for nine. This left Westindies 280 minutes to make 309 runs for victory; it also gave Trueman and company just over five hours to bowl out Westindies. It looked an evenly balanced contest. Whatever each team may have expected, no one could have predicted the bewildering events of the Westindian second innings: Carew was first lbw to Shackleton for 1; Hunte was caught at second slip off Trueman for 5; and after a brief flurry from Kanhai and Butcher, Westindies found themselves 78 for five. To cut a short story shorter, Westindies were dismissed for 91 runs, while Trueman finished with figures of: 14.3-2-44-7. His match analysis of 12 wickets for 119 runs is the best by any bowler at Edgbaston. Only Kanhai, Butcher and Solomon reached double figures. The remaining eight batsmen achieved a grand total of 25 runs between them! Perhaps Trueman was too devastating, or Westindian inexperience of treacherous English batting conditions may have proved fatal. Or could it have been the fabled mercurial Westindian temperament, so common during the 1950s: up one minute down the next? Whatever the explanation, Westindians could take comfort in the fact that the series was not yet over. At the end of the third Test, the tally was one match each, with one draw and two to play. Worrell himself took the defeat philosophically. As the general in command he knew, more than any one else, that losing one battle didn't necessarily mean the entire war was lost.

Fourth Test vs. England
Headingley, Leeds, England, 25, 26, 27, 29 July, 1963

In their 1963 tour of England, having won the first Test, drawn the second, and lost the third, Westindies entered for the fourth Test with what might be considered a clean slate. Since a fifth Test remained, they had either to win the fourth or at least draw it if they were to retain a chance of winning the series. Worrell won the toss and Hunte and McMorris made a moderately good start in dull weather against the English fast bowlers Trueman and Shackleton: they put on 28 runs before McMorris was caught at slip off Shackleton for 11. Kanhai started aggressively despite Trueman's menace which had soon disposed of Hunte: 42 for two. With Butcher's subsequent dismissal for 23 the score became 71 for three, and at lunch Kanhai and Sobers were the not out batsmen: 91 for three. As the wicket dried out, batting became more comfortable, and Kanhai and Sobers looked like putting together the grand partnership that many of their admirers felt was long overdue from two of the most gifted Westindian batsmen of their generation. When their partnership had realized 100 runs in just over 100 minutes they seemed about to satisfy their admirers. Such was their command that one commentator spoke of Kanhai's "polish and belligerence," and of Sobers's "imperial majesty" as they brought the score first to 150, then to 200. Shortly after tea, however, when the partnership had realized 143 runs, nowhere near what might be expected from two batsmen of such rare, if contrasting genius, Kanhai (92) was bowled by Lock: 214 for four. He beat his forehead in frustration and disappointment: it was the second time in the series that he was out in the nineties, yet another sign of the startling impetuosity of his genius. Sobers meanwhile was joined by Solomon and continued onward and upward to his century. When he had reached 102, he on-drove Lock very firmly, deliberately placing the ball immediately to the left of the bowler's wicket, only to watch Lock launch himself into an acrobatic leap and bring off a miraculous one-handed catch inches away from the ground. A subsequent picture of this dismissal carried the caption: "Sic transit gloria mundi" a fitting comment not only on the surpassing excellence of Sobers's achievement, nor on the tragedy of his downfall, but on the inescapable transience of all human endeavour. At all events, thanks mainly to Sobers and Kanhai, Westindies finished the first day of the match on 294 for five.

On the second day, Murray and Solomon acquitted themselves creditably with a partnership of 61 that helped Westindies reach 397. Trueman was England's most successful bowler with four wickets for 117 runs in 46 overs, while Lock collected three for 54 in 28.4 overs. In England's first innings, Stewart fell to Griffith for 2 runs, Bolus to Hall for 14, and Dexter was bowled by Griffith for 8. At that stage the score was 32 for three. As if this was not calamity enough, Close was bowled by Griffith for 0, and two runs later Sharpe was caught by Kanhai off Griffith also for 0. At 34 for five England's humiliation cannot have been more complete. It was not the fault of the pitch, nor should subsequent murmurings about Griffith's "suspect" action be attributed to anything more than English frustration. The fact of the matter was that England's batsmen could not easily cope with the sheer pace of Hall and Griffith, and were soon in disarray at 93 for eight. The innings had disintegrated completely when, in one of those reversals that defy reason, logic and expectation, Titmus and Lock, renowned spin bowlers, defied the deadliest missiles from Hall and Griffith, as well as the wiles of Sobers and Gibbs, to put on 75 runs by the end of the second day. The next morning, Titmus and Lock quickly succumbed and England were all out for 174, almost double what they were at 93 for eight. Lock (53) and Titmus (33) had effected a dramatic rescue. On the Westindian side, Griffith was the chief architect of England's misfortune. His figures: 21-5-36-6 constitute a sterling performance that could prove match-winning. He received strong support from Gibbs with 14 overs for 50 runs and three wickets, and Hall: 13 overs for 61 runs and one wicket.

With a lead of 223 Worrell did not enforce the follow-on. At first, his decision seemed disastrous since both Hunte and McMorris had returned to the pavilion, courtesy of Trueman, with the score at 20. This was the tactical turning point of the match, for Worrell might have ordered his men to dig in and the consequences could have been fatal. Instead, Kanhai and Butcher cheerfully hoisted 65 runs in less than half as many minutes. As so often with Kanhai, though, his blitzkrieg was short-lived, and he was lbw for 44 to Shackleton: 85 for three. Butcher and Sobers continued in the same exhilarating fashion, and when they were four runs short of their hundred partnership, Butcher went high and hard for another four only to see Dexter take a brilliant running catch. Butcher had made 78 and the score was 186 for five. Two runs later, Sobers was caught by Sharpe off Titmus for 52 and the rest was a formality: Westindies were all out for 229 runs, and England had to get 453 for victory.

In his wisdom, Worrell gave the ball to Sobers instead of to Hall or Griffith, and Sobers promptly bowled Stewart for 0 with the last ball of his first over. Dexter (10) had an anxious time before he was lbw to Griffith: 23 for two, and England were staring blankly at defeat. Bolus and Barrington resisted until about six o'clock when the total was 80, and England looked like weathering the storm. But within minutes, both batsmen fell to Sobers, Bolus being caught by Gibbs for 43 and Barrington lbw for 32. The score was then 95 for four and the prospect of defeat had again become stark reality. The next day Sharpe (13) was caught at short-leg off Gibbs: 130 for five. Close and Parks fought an uphill task with courage and spirit, and had reached 199 when Close was caught by Solomon off Griffith for 56. Parks ran out of partners and finished with 57, the top score in a total of 231. Gibbs garnered four wickets for 76 runs, Sobers three for 90, and Griffith three for 45. Griffith's match analysis - nine wickets for 81 runs - is the best of his career. It played a major role in helping Westindies to claim a handsome victory by 221 runs and ensure that they could not lose the series.

Fifth Test vs. England
Kennington Oval, London, England, 22, 23, 24, 26 August, 1963

The fifth and final Test in the series between England and Westindies in 1963 is remembered mostly as the occasion when Rohan Kanhai gave one of the finest displays of attacking batsmanship seen in Test cricket since World

War Two. Westindies had won the first and fourth Test matches and England the third. The second was drawn. So that when the fifth Test began, England were obviously hoping for a win that would square the series. But it was equally obvious that Westindies wanted a win that would give them victory by three matches to one, and avenge the humiliating 3:0 defeat they had suffered during their tour of England in 1957. The Westindies team of 1963 bore little comparison to the one that had toured England in 1957. For one thing, players like Sobers and Kanhai who were fledgling beginners in 1957, had accomplished mighty deeds on cricket grounds from Kingston to Adelaide in the intervening period. More importantly, the traditional, white captaincy of John Goddard had been replaced by the revolutionary, black leadership of Frank Worrell. In 1963, so far as Kanhai himself was concerned, despite recurring knee trouble, he performed well in the first four Tests, including 90 in the first Test and 92 in the fourth. Because of his knee, it was doubtful whether he would play in the fifth Test, and Seymour Nurse stood by to replace him. But after several injections, Kanhai declared himself fit on the opening day of the match.

England made 275 in their first innings largely due to a century stand for the fifth wicket between Close (46) and Sharpe (63). Charlie Griffith took six wickets for 71 runs. Westindies began well in their first innings, being at one stage 179 for three. But two run outs - of Sobers (26) and Butcher (53) - caused them to decline sharply to a total of 246. England were 69 for four in their second innings, when another good stand of 52 between Sharpe (83) and Parks (23) helped them to reach a total of 223. This left Westindies with 253 to get for victory, and although they had made 5 runs for no wicket at the end of the third day, they had to consider the fact that, since 1902, no one had won a Test match at the Oval by making more than 200 in the fourth innings. When play resumed on the fourth and final day, Trueman found that he could not continue because of a bruised heel. This was a blow to England, since Trueman had already taken 34 wickets in the series, more than any bowler on either side. But England still had the services of Lock, one of the finest spinners at the time, and Statham and Shackleton who could bowl with unnerving accuracy. There was also support from Dexter and Close as change bowlers. It was against this background that Hunte and Rodriguez, the Westindian openers took guard on the fourth day. At lunch they were still together, and the score was 78.

Soon after lunch Rodriguez (28) was caught by Lock off Dexter: 78 for one. Then Kanhai came in. While Hunte and Rodriguez had spent two and a half hours compiling 78 runs, Hunte and Kanhai needed one hour to produce almost twice as many. This gives some idea of Kanhai's domination of the bowling. The Westindian strategy was for Hunte to stand secure at one end, while Kanhai attacked from the other. This he did with a vengeance. With daring hooks, fierce cuts and powerful drives, Kanhai plundered runs from all bowlers on all sides of the wicket. In vain did Dexter, the English captain erect a semicircular wall of fielders on the off-side, for somehow Kanhai found holes or drove with such power and speed that, as happened once with Dexter himself, the ball passed through his legs before he could bend to reach it. There was scarcely a stroke that Kanhai did not play that day, some orthodox, many not. But the stroke that delighted the crowd the most was his flamboyant falling hook which left him lying flat on his back across the crease, while the ball careered to the boundary. The scoring rate was about five runs per over. Close's first eighteen balls yielded 24 runs. Lock was moved from the leg trap and sent to reinforce the covers. Kanhai studied the move briefly, then drove three fours through extra cover. At the rate he was going, Dexter realized that Kanhai had to be stopped if England was to have a chance. He tried containment. He spread the field. He tried bowling changes. Nothing seemed to help. Once, Kanhai unleashed a stroke of such daring unorthodoxy that Close the bowler himself cheered in spontaneous, disbelieving admiration. Kanhai caught up Hunte who had a two-and-a-half hour start on him; then he swept ahead; and the game began to slip irrevocably from England. By the time the partnership had realized 100, Kanhai's share was 66. With his score at 71 he hooked Lock for six. Then, as happens so often when Kanhai is in full spate, he overreached himself. He attempted to repeat the stroke and was caught by Bolus running in from the deep between square leg and mid-wicket. Kanhai walked off laughing, and the crowd which had cheered, shouted, waved and gesticulated for ninety delirious minutes, summoned what energy remained to yell and scream as their hero made his way into the pavilion. He had scored 77 runs off 103 balls, and he hit ten fours and a six.

Some might think that the outcome of the match would have been different if Trueman was fit on the final day. But the combination of Hunte's steadiness and Kanhai's devastation suggests that Trueman would not have changed much. As it was, Hunte and Butcher saw Westindies through to victory, Hunte making 108 not out, and Butcher 31 not out. Obviously, Kanhai had not won the match single-handedly. Apart from Hunte, Westindies were greatly helped by Griffith's hostile bowling, not to mention Worrell's inspired leadership and the feat of young wicket-keeper Murray who, playing in his first series, had taken six catches in this Test and made 24 dismissals in the series as a whole. But Kanhai's contribution was not merely the runs he accumulated. When he was out the score was 191 for two. He and Hunte had conjured 113 runs of which Hunte's share was 36. By scoring more than twice as fast as his partner, Kanhai demoralized the bowlers and forced them to accept the inevitability of a Westindian victory. While the match is memorable for many reasons, including fighting innings from Close and Sharpe, solid batting by Hunte, and consistently hostile bowling by Griffith, it is remembered most of all for Kanhai's ruggedly audacious collaring of the bowlers during ninety deliriously joyous minutes, in which he knocked English hopes literally, metaphorically and decisively for six. It was a fitting epitaph for Frank Worrell's last match as Westindian captain.

CHAPTER SIX

Sobers is de King

(1965-66)

First Test v Australia
Sabina Park, Kingston, Jamaica, 3, 4, 5, 6, 8 March, 1965

After their 3:1 victory over England in 1963, Westindies had to defeat Australia in 1965 in order to claim the "world championship" of cricket, an albeit unofficial title, but one for which they had laboured mightily since 1928. The two teams had last met in 1961, and older Australian stalwarts like McDonald, Harvey, Davidson, Benaud and Mackay had since given way to new stars such as Lawry, Cowper and Hawke. More to the point, Peter Burge, one of the new batting stars and Bob Veivers one of the best Australian off spinners were both unavailable for the tour of Westindies in 1965. Westindies, on the other hand, had retained their chief 1961 stars - Hunte, Kanhai, Sobers, Butcher, Hall, Griffith and Gibbs - who were now in the prime of their cricketing strength and manhood. If they had a problem it was the absence of a specialist opening batsman to partner Hunte, a minor flaw really, if one considered the panoply of batting luminaries who followed the openers. More problematic was the fact that Frank Worrell had retired after his English victory in 1963, and Westindies were now led by the untried Sobers. Could the sublime genius of the world's greatest batsman/ bowler/ fieldsman also extend to his performance as captain? This was the question that most weighed on Westindian minds at the start of the Australian tour, although the weight was somewhat relieved by knowledge that Worrell's guidance was not totally lost since he had a new role as manager of Westindies.

So it happened that in March 1965, at Sabina Park, Jamaica, Sobers made his début as captain, just as eleven years before, almost to the very date, he had made his Test début against England on the same ground. Auspiciously, he won the toss. Hunte and Nurse put on 48 runs for the opening partnership before Nurse was caught by wicket-keeper Grout off Hawke for 15, and at lunch Westindies were 70 for one with Hunte and Kanhai not out. Soon after lunch, Hunte was caught by Grout off leg spinner Philpott for a solid 41; then Kanhai (17) was caught by Philpott off McKenzie: 82 for three. Sobers and Butcher made a brief rally that produced 67 runs before Butcher (39) was yorked by Mayne: 149 for four. When, at the same score, captain Bobby Simpson bowled a perfect leg-break that had captain Sobers lbw for 30, Westindies realized they faced a major crisis. Nor could they blame the pitch which, so far, remained true and fair. Yet sorrows come ever in battalions, and Solomon - the ideal man for a crisis - was caught for 0 by Grout off Mayne: 149 for six. Wicket-keeper Hendriks and all-rounder Tony White rose gallantly to the crisis by adding 32. White alone plundered 57 runs including eight fours and a six and Westindies were dismissed for 239 which constituted something of a recovery; except that 239 was scarcely the sort of total to put before mighty Australia. Mayne was the chief destroyer sending down 17.2 overs and gathering four wickets for 43 runs. Philpott and Hawke were rewarded with two each and McKenzie and Simpson with one each. It did little to help the Westindian cause that Australia's openers, Lawry and Simpson, had scored 32 without loss before the first day's play was over.

At the start of the second day when Australia needed 208 runs to lead on first innings, Westindies faced a grim prospect. But the men in green did not reckon on the resourcefulness of the team that Worrell had so patiently moulded since 1960. In particular, they did not reckon on the rampant magnificence of Hall, the giant Barbadian, who breathed fire out of both nostrils as he ran up each time, flexing mighty muscles, and tearing away Lawry (19) and Simpson (11) in a most furious battery of fast bowling. With sustained fury he hit O'Neill on his right middle finger and sent him off to be x-rayed, then blasted Cowper (26) out to reduce Australia to 42 for three. Hall's speed, accuracy and hostility were altogether breath-taking. His partner Griffith, not to be outdone, bowled Booth for 2, before yorking Graeme Thomas on his Test début for 23. Mortally wounded, Australia stumbled to 96 for five. Recovery seemed impossible, as even the Westindian spinners administered their own relentless blows while Hall summoned enough fire for yet one more wicket. There was modest resistance, to be sure, especially from Philpott and Hawke, but when stumps were drawn on the second day Australia were 211 for nine, and when the last wicket fell early next morning, Australia had capitulated at 217 and Hawke was gloriously not out on 45. Hall finished with five for 60 in 24 overs, while Griffith and White each claimed two wickets and Sobers one.

In their second innings, Hunte and Nurse added 50 runs before Nurse (17) was run out. Kanhai (16) was caught and bowled by Philpott, but Butcher and Hunte had accumulated 116 more runs until, just before stumps, Butcher (71) was caught by Booth off Philpott: 194 for three. On the fourth day, Hunte was caught by Simpson off Mayne after a responsible contribution of 81. Sobers was caught by Simpson off Philpott for 27, and an eighth-wicket stand between Solomon (76) and Hendriks (30) produced 64 runs which helped Westindies to a total of 373 and set Australia 396 to win. Mayne and Philpott were the most successful Australian bowlers with four wickets each, although McKenzie did well to bowl 33 overs for 56 runs and Hawke 18 overs for 25 runs. At any rate, when Lawry (17) was bowled by Griffith, and Simpson (16) was caught by Hendriks off Hall before the end of the fourth day, Australian hopes of victory had dipped sharply.

On the final day, Cowper (2) was lbw to Hall and O'Neill (22) was caught by Nurse off Gibbs: 75 for four. All seemed lost for Australia. Still, Hawke and Booth managed 69 runs together; but once Hawke (33) was bowled by Solomon: 144 for five, it was downhill to a total of 216 and defeat by a margin of 179 runs. Hall was again the rampaging hero battering four wickets down for 45 runs in 19 overs, while Griffith claimed two wickets, and Sobers, White, Gibbs and Solomon one each. The decisive features of the match were Hall's stupendous bowling, excellent Westindian ground fielding, and Sobers's comprehensive success as player and captain. It would not be at all surprising if some of his opponents thought of Sobers as a one-man team. In this match, he became the first player to complete 4000 runs and one hundred wickets in Tests. Yet this was by no means a one-sided match in which a strong team overpowered a weaker one; for both sides were fairly evenly balanced, and up to the fourth day, either could have won. It was the hardest and best of victories, one aptly described by Vergil in *The Aeneid*: "hic labor, hoc opus est". What a pity the greatest of Latin poets didn't know cricket! Or he might have added: "hic etiam gloria est".

Third Test vs. Australia
Bourda, Georgetown, 14, 15, 17, 19, 20 April, 1965

The Westindian victory over Australia at Sabina Park, Jamaica, in March, 1965 was their first against Australia in the Westindies. It was also the first time Westindies had led Australia in any rubber. Until then, the two teams had played fifteen Tests (five of them in the Westindies), of which Australia had won eleven, and Westindies two, while two were drawn. So this victory at Sabina Park, by a margin of 179 runs, both dented the myth of Australian invincibility and increased Westindian belief in themselves; it also confirmed Sobers's success in his first Test as captain. Heavy scoring by both teams in the second Test at Queen's Park Oval, Trinidad, precluded a decisive result, and the third Test at Bourda, Guyana became crucial if Westindies were to retain a chance of winning the series. The third Test itself was preceded by a squabble about the selection of umpires that illustrated the insularity that prevailed in Westindian society at the time. The two umpires originally appointed for the match were Cecil Kippins (Guyana) and Cortez Jordan (Barbados), but the Guyana Umpires Association objected to Jordan as a Barbadian, and influenced Kippins to resign on the eve of the match. After much unseemly chopping and changing, Jordan, and Gerry Gomez the former Westindian Test player and current Test selector were finally selected. Although Gomez was a certified umpire, he had not previously umpired in a first class match.

Batting first, Westindies soon lost their openers Davis (28) bowled by Hawke: 56 for one, and Hunte (31) caught by McKenzie off Philpott: 68 for two. Enter

Kanhai and Butcher, local boys from Port Mourant (as was Joe Solomon) to provide a ravishing exhibition of magical strokeplay. If their concentration had not been broken by an eighty minute interruption through rain, there is no telling what records they might have broken that day. As it was, by the end of the day, they had advanced the score to 201 with Kanhai, the dominant partner, 88 not out. The next day, mysteriously, the magic vanished. Kanhai (89) never got started: he was bowled by Hawke: 203 for three. Seven runs later Butcher was run out for 49, before Sobers and Nurse restored stability at least up to lunch-time. Soon after lunch, Nurse (42) was caught and bowled by Hawke: 290 for five. With his very next ball, Hawke had the incoming Solomon (0) caught by wicket-keeper Grout. In just over two hours, four top order wickets had fallen for 89 runs, and it needed an improbable eighth-wicket partnership of 44 between Hendriks and Griffith to enable Westindies to reach 355. By itself, this was not a bad score; but hardly what one would expect from batsmen who went hell for leather in scoring 201 for two on the previous day. Although the Australian bowling was consistently good on both days, it was not devilish enough to explain Westindian batting losses on the second day. Hawke had the lion's share of six wickets for 72 runs in 32 overs, while Philpott had to be satisfied with one for 75 in 26 overs, and O'Neill was lucky to get two tailend wickets for 26 runs.

Wisely deciding to open the bowling himself (instead of Griffith), Sobers bowled Simpson for 7. At 68, Cowper was caught by Hendriks off Gibbs for a well made 41. Then, three runs later, O'Neill played into the covers and called for a quick single, only to watch Kanhai score a direct hit with a spectacular throw that ran out Lawry (20). Ringing quick, astute bowling changes, Sobers brought himself back on shortly before the close and had Philpott (5) caught by Butcher at mid-on: 85 for four. It was a day of packed, exciting events in which twelve wickets had fallen for 246 runs. The next day, a Saturday, Booth and O'Neill strove manfully to swing the balance their way; but after they added 31 runs, O'Neill (27) was yorked by Griffith: 116 for five. Worse still, Thomas (8) was bowled by Hall, and Hawke (0) was caught by Sobers off Hall, as Australia sank to 130 for seven. An understandable air of desperation infiltrated the Australian camp when Booth (37) was brilliantly caught by Sobers off Gibbs, and Grout (19) was run out following a misunderstanding with Mackay: 171 for nine. Finally, when Gibbs bowled Mayne, Australia's desperation was complete: they had collapsed for 179 runs. The damage was done chiefly by Gibbs seizing three wickets for 51 in 25.5 overs, while Hall and Sobers settled for two wickets each. The Westindian lead of 176 runs did not persuade Sobers to enforce the follow-on, and by stumps, after 45 overs into their second innings, Westindies had reached 69 for the loss of Davis (17), Kanhai (0), and Butcher (18).

On the Monday, this good position - 245 runs ahead with seven wickets intact - quickly dissolved as all the remaining wickets disappeared for 111 runs. Only an eighth-wicket partnership of 30 between Sobers (42) and Hall (20 not out) enabled Westindies to reach 180. It was as sensational a collapse as Australia's in their first innings! Australia had bowled themselves back into the game. Nor could Westindies blame the pitch which was beginning to take some turn, although the ball still came through at even height. Leg-spinner Philpott acquired four for 49 in 16 overs, while fast bowler Hawke chimed in with four wickets for 43 runs in 20.4 overs. Hawke's match figures of ten wickets for 115 runs in 52.4 overs remains a record for any Test at Bourda.

Needing 357 to win, Australia got to 80 for the loss only of Simpson (23) by tea-time on the fourth day. At that stage, with Lawry and Cowper batting, an Australian victory was not impossible. But, after tea, Gibbs complained about bowling his off-breaks into the wind, and Sobers switched him to the other end where the ball would drift with the wind. Suddenly, Gibbs became unplayable. Bowling on his home turf, with the vociferous backing of his home crowd, he dealt Australia such deadly blows that they were left prostrate. He first bowled Lawry (22) round his legs, then had Cowper (30) stumped, while he removed O'Neill (16) and Philpott (6) via Sobers in the trap at short leg. At one stage, he had inveigled four wickets for 5 runs, and by the time he had finished, his full tally was six wickets for 29 runs in 22.2 overs. Utterly shattered by these blows, Australia stumbled to a total of 144 runs and lost the match by 212 runs. Sobers contributed two wickets, and Griffith and Solomon one each; but it was Gibbs's magnificent match figures of nine wickets for 80 runs that put Westindies in an impregnable position of 2:0 for the first time in a series against Australia with two matches left to play. In the process, Gibbs also took his 100th Test wicket when he bowled Lawry for 22.

Fourth Test vs. Australia
Kensington Oval, Bridgetown, Barbados
5, 6, 7, 8, 10, 11 May 1965

In their "world championship" series against Australia in 1965, Westindies were leading 2:0 after the third Test with two matches left, and while they could no longer lose the series, they knew that Australia would not easily acquiesce to their winning it. This tough, fighting spirit manifested itself when captain Bobby Simpson and his partner Bill Lawry opened their batting in the fourth Test, and at stumps on the first day were still together with a score of 263 on the board. Hostile Westindian bowling and athletic fielding did not make for easy runs, but the Australians knew they had to win this Test to deprive Westindies of the "world championship". Their target was a big enough total that would allow them to bowl Westindies out twice. Since the first day confirmed that they were playing on a perfect batting strip that would make bowlers struggle for wickets, the scene was set for what might be called an "epic" contest between two highly motivated, expertly-led teams, neither willing to give an inch. The Westindian aim was to clinch a title they believed should rightly have been theirs as long ago as 1952 when John Goddard's team squandered their chances of beating

Australia. Perhaps Sobers's team was no more talented than Goddard's, but with Sobers as captain and Worrell as manager, the tone of their leadership and morale had changed completely and Westindies were less likely to squander their talents.

The pattern on the first day repeated itself on the second, with the bowlers labouring hard and being unable to dislodge the two stubborn Australians, Simpson and Lawry, who added another 119 runs to their overnight total before the ever faithful Hall finally got Simpson to play on. By that time, the score was 382 and Simpson's contribution an invaluable 201. Cowper's entry increased the tempo of scoring. The Australians realized that a large score by itself was not enough: they would also need time to bowl out Westindies. Meanwhile, Lawry's long vigil ended when he drove Solomon high and wide of mid-wicket only to watch Sobers bring off a superb catch. Like Simpson, Lawry had done yeoman service: he had made 210. He and Simpson were the first pair of opening batsmen to score double centuries in a Test match. At the end of the second day, Australia were 583 for two and Gibbs's figures: 64-15-154-0 eloquently expressed both the unrelenting effort and lucklessness of the Westindian bowlers.

The next day the Australians went for quick runs even if it meant sacrificing a few wickets, and twenty-two minutes before lunch Simpson declared at 650 for six. The Westindian bowling figures tell the whole story: Hall 27-3-117-2; Griffith: 35-3-131-0; Sobers: 37-7-143-1; and Gibbs: 73-17-168-2. The Westindian openers fared badly as Davis (8) was bowled by McKenzie: 13 for one, and Hunte was hit on the face by Hawke and forced to retire. Butcher (9) was caught by Simpson off O'Neill, and Westindies were 99 for two when Nurse joined Kanhai. These two were still together at stumps when the score had reached 165. The next day a quick breakthrough was what Australia needed, but they were foiled by Nurse and Kanhai who remained until their total had reached 299. Kanhai was then caught off McKenzie for 129 runs made with all his usual style and flourish. Hunte re-entered at this point and stayed with Nurse until close of play when Westindies were 424 for three.

On the fourth day, it looked as if Australia's plans were foiled, although Westindies had still not saved the follow-on. Nurse who had never scored a Test century, had now made 201 when he was caught by Simpson off Hawke. It was a timely innings - just what Westindies needed, and Hunte was caught by Simpson off McKenzie for a solid 75 that confirmed his courage and resilience despite injury. At 448 for five Australian hopes still flickered although Sobers was batting. Surprisingly, it was not Sobers who destroyed these hopes: it was Griffith, in an unaccustomed role with the bat: he hit out for 54 runs including two sixes and a last wicket partnership of 34 with Gibbs. There was a tragic element in the final stages of the innings, when wicket-keeper Hendriks was hit by a ball from McKenzie and had to be taken to hospital. The incident threw a pall over the proceedings, although Griffith's antics enabled Westindies to reach a total of 573, only 77 behind Australia. By close of play Australia were 139 for two, 216 on with 8 wickets intact. Lawry was 58 not out, and O'Neill 56 not out.

On the final day, since both wicket and weather were perfect, Simpson's best option was an early declaration. This meant quick runs in order to set Westindies a tempting target that might cause them to lose wickets in going for it. His declaration came at 11.40am when Australia were 175 for four. His proposition was a target of 253 runs at a rate of about 56 runs per hour. Hawke and McKenzie threw themselves into the attack knowing that time was short. But Hunte and Davis would not budge. On the contrary, they appear not to have ruled out the possibility of a victory of their own when they put on 145 runs before Davis (68) was caught off Philpott. Australian pulses must have quickened when Kanhai was out immediately - lbw to McKenzie for 1. Butcher's brief partnership with Hunte suggested that the latter's role was to stand guard while his colleagues tested the water at the other end for the possibility of victory. When Butcher (27) was caught by Booth off Philpott, Westindies were 183 for three and tension building to an unexpected climax.

As if to reassure himself, his team and the world of his responsibilities, Sobers now came in instead of Nurse. His antagonist Simpson gave the new ball to McKenzie for one last do or die offensive. Westindies needed 39 runs with 35 minutes remaining, and Sobers and Hunte gradually advanced the score to 216 when Hunte was caught by wicket-keeper Grout off McKenzie for another superb contribution - 81. Then Nurse (0) had scarcely taken guard before he was lbw to Hawke: 217 for five. Westindies had become vulnerable, for Simpson and his troops knew that if they could dislodge either Sobers or Solomon, only Hall, Griffith and Gibbs would stand between them and victory, because Hendriks was injured and would not bat. Simpson gave Sobers easy singles to concentrate the attack on Solomon, but the boy from Port Mourant was not to be moved. He survived as did Sobers, and Westindies were 242 for five when time ran out and the match was drawn, perhaps the best of all conclusions for a contest between such valiant antagonists. The draw meant, however, that Westindies had won the rubber and, for the first time in their history, the "championship" of world cricket.

Second Test vs. England
Lord's, London, England, 16, 17, 18, 20 June, 1966

The 1966 Westindian cricket tour of England is remembered as Sobers's tour. Seldom before had one player so utterly dominated an entire series; for Sobers did not just excel as bowler, batsman or fielder: he was all these things, as well as captain. It was a unique performance, probably incapable of being repeated. In five Tests, Sobers topped the Westindian batting aggregate and averages with 722 runs for an average of 103.14; he also collected twenty wickets (second only to Gibbs's twenty-one) at an average of 27.25. In the first Test at Old Trafford England could only come up with 167 in reply to a Westindian first innings total of 494; they duly succumbed after doing somewhat better - 277 - in their second innings. The match that followed at Lord's was less predictable. At best, the Westindian first innings total of 269 might be considered modest on a goodish wicket. The moisture that had helped the swing of the English bowlers had dried out by the time England went in to bat, and this probably helped the English bowlers so that England achieved a first innings lead of 86.

There were two notable features in England's first innings. One was a graceful innings of 96 by Tom Graveney. Graveney's technique was perfection itself, all silken elegance and velvet stroking, coordinated by exquisite timing. It was an innings of rain-water purity, completely untarnished by sudden, jerky, or hasty movements, or anything as remotely crude as force. Graveney's gentlest touch of the bat sent the ball speeding to the boundary as if propelled by an electric shock. On the evidence of this innings, England has never boasted a purer batting stylist than Tom Graveney. The other notable feature was the run out of Basil D'Oliveira for 27 when he and wicket-keeper Jim Parks were going great guns for the English sixth wicket. Hall bowled to Parks who drove the ball powerfully back, making a direct hit of the stumps at the bowler's end. As the ball lost pace and bounced away, Hall scooped it up while, simultaneously, plucking all three stumps out of the ground and clutching them to his chest. It all happened in a blinding flash, and it completely confused D'Oliveira who had instinctively moved out of his crease backing up in readiness for what looked like runs. It was not D'Oliveira's fault that Hall had run him out, although it was a particularly sad end to his maiden Test innings. Hall was amazingly quick.

The climax to the match came on the morning of the fourth day when Westindies started their second innings. Although the English bowlers did not look menacing, perhaps there was pre-lunch moisture in the wicket, for Lord's has some notoriety in the respect. At any rate, Carew (0) was caught by Knight off Higgs: 2 for one; Butcher (3) was lbw Higgs: 22 for two; and Hunte (13) was caught by Milburn off Knight: 25 for three. Kanhai and Nurse resisted briefly; but Kanhai (40) was caught by Parks off Knight, and Nurse (35) was caught by Parks off D'Oliveira; and at ten minutes before lunch, Westindies were 95 for five, barely nine runs on, with five tailend wickets left. The damage was done chiefly by the pace men, Higgs and Knight, with two wickets each. Sobers was still there in the middle, partnered by his cousin Holford, a newcomer to Test cricket, picked more for his leg-spin than anything else. After them, it was wicket-keeper Allan, and the bowlers Griffith, Hall, and Gibbs who were left to bat. The obvious strategy was for England to leave Sobers alone while they ran through the five non-batsmen at the other end. Consequently, Cowdrey, the English captain gave Sobers easy runs to lure him away from the batting end, while his bowlers concentrated on Holford. It was a strategy that seemed certain of success.

If cricket can sometimes rise from the level of sport to higher realms of art and philosophy, one reason is its capacity to reflect contradictions which we encounter in daily life and which confirm our final incomprehension of the real forces that influence human destiny. As it turned out, this was a game that would either validate human free will or confirm our hapless domination by wayward circumstance. Sobers certainly did not bat like a man who could be dominated by anything or anyone. Fully aware of the perilous fate of his team, he seemed equally confident of the immense cricketing talents with which God had chosen to bless him. Without any hint of panic or fear, he exhibited the calm courage and splendour of someone not wholly created out of flesh and blood. His command was total of all he surveyed, and in addition to his own batting, he gave counsel to his cousin, who imbibed such inspiration that he too began driving fluent fours, shunning any further attempts of shielding him.

The records show that Sobers and Holford carried the Westindian total from 95 to 369 before Sobers declared. But mere numbers cannot capture the drama of that encounter between inspired Caribbean genius and calculating English professionalism. England did not commit glaring mistakes. It is true some commentators felt that Cowdrey should have attacked Sobers instead of Holford. But it is doubtful that any strategy could have contained Sobers that day. The fact is that the English bowlers did surprisingly well. Higgs sent down 34 overs at less than three runs per over, and Titmus 19 overs for less than two runs each. Yet the restrained batting suggested by these figures was not evident in the way that Sobers cut, pulled, drove and hooked with complete freedom. He reached his century with a majestic cover drive off Jones, whereupon one Westindian supporter ran to the pitch to congratulate him, while others threw their hats gleefully in the air unmindful of whether they would descend to earth again. One group of Westindian spectators who had been flying a Jamaican flag, pulled it down and replaced it with a Union Jack at half mast. By the time Holford reached his own century (in his second Test match), Westindies were safe, human free will had been validated, and cricket transformed into philosophic discourse. Holford was 105 not out, and Sobers was 163 not out. England could not make 284 runs in the few hours left, although Milburn scored 126 not out (also in his second Test match). Nor could Westindies bowl England out, and the inevitable draw ensued. But that gallant sixth wicket partnership of 274 between two cousins remains the centrepiece of the match, and one of the most memorable episodes in the history of Westindian cricket. It also remains the highest partnership for Westindies's sixth wicket in Tests against England.

Third Test vs. England
Trent Bridge, Nottingham, England
30 June, 1, 2, 4, 5 July, 1966

In 1966 Westindies won their first Test against England at Old Trafford by an innings and 40 runs. Then came the second Test at Lord's in the second innings of which Sobers and Holford staged one of the most stirring of all dramas in Westindian cricket - a partnership of 274 runs that magically extricated a draw out of certain defeat, and gave Westindies a 1:0 lead in the five match series. For the third Test at Trent Bridge, both teams made changes: Lashley and Hendriks replaced Carew and Allan for Westindies, while England brought in Russell, Illingworth, Snow and Underwood (in his Test début) for Barrington, Titmus, Jones and Knight. Hunte and Lashley opened for Westindies, and from the start, despite a wicket that held no visible terrors, things began to go wrong. At 19, Hunte (9) was lbw to Higgs. Kanhai struggled to regain form by playing a few shots, but he soon hit Higgs straight to Underwood at mid-on and was caught for 32. Butcher got an inside edge and was bowled by Snow for 5 before Lashley (49) was caught by wicket-keeper Parks, again off Snow: 140 for four. Sobers gave every impression of imposing himself with another magisterial innings, but the impression was fleeting as Snow found his outside edge and Parks caught him for 3.

At 144 for five, Westindies were not much better off than they were in the second innings of the previous Test at Lord's when they were 95 for five. Sobers and Holford were batting then; now it was Nurse and Holford. Now Holford was lbw to D'Oliveira for 11. Nurse remained in splendid isolation at one end, and as he began to run out of partners, mistimed a drive off Snow, and was caught by Illingworth at mid-on for 93. With admirable application he had made virtually half the total which was then 190 for seven, and once he had gone, the remaining wickets tumbled quickly leaving Westindies with a final total of 235. In good batting conditions, this total represented an impressive success for England's bowlers. Snow: 25-7-82-4, and Higgs: 25.4-3-71-4 were the chief architects of success, although D'Oliveira: 30-14-51-2 made a major contribution.

Supremely confident in his unique gifts as the greatest all-rounder in the history of cricket, Sobers displaced the redoubtable Hall to open the bowling himself. And as if to confirm his gifts or his own belief in them, he had Boycott lbw for 0 with his second ball. Ten runs later, Milburn (7) the heavy weight centurion of Lord's, slashed at Hall and was caught by Sobers in the slips: 10 for 2. Then Russell (4) was bowled by Hall: 13 for three. But with steady nerves and commendable caution, Graveney and Cowdrey warded off further casualties till close of play while adding 20 runs. It took more than steady nerves for Graveney and Cowdrey to remain in possession for most of the next day. They had advanced the score to 182 before Graveney (109) was caught in the slips by Holford off Sobers. Composed in Graveney's high maturity, it was an innings marked by effortlessness, grace and serenity; it was Graveney's third hundred in consecutive Test appearances at Nottingham. Cowdrey successfully resisted a fresh new ball attack from Hall and Griffith, and was four runs short of his century when he was caught by wicket-keeper Hendriks off Griffith: 221 for five. Then Parks (11) was caught by Butcher off Sobers, and Illingworth (0) was caught by Lashley off Griffith before close of play when England were 254 for seven.

On the third day, England's last three wickets added 71 more runs to push their total to 325 and their lead to 90. Such prosperity was largely due to D'Oliveira who confirmed his reliability with 76 solid runs. Sobers had taken four wickets for 90 runs in 49 overs, Hall four for 105 in 34.3 overs, and Griffith two for 62 in 20 overs. Hunte (12) fell cheaply again in the Westindian second innings, as did Lashley (23), both to D'Oliveira. At 65 for two, Westindies were 25 runs behind with eight wickets intact. This is when, apparently following instructions, Butcher and Kanhai went into hibernation, playing maiden after maiden, until the end of the day when Westindies were 138 for two. At that stage, Westindies were 48 ahead, with Kanhai 50 not out and Butcher 47 not out. Both batsmen (and Westindies) were severely criticised for negative tactics in the Sunday papers that followed the next day, but Sobers felt the tactics were justified, as did Learie Constantine. Monday would tell.

Kanhai (63) went early on Monday morning, caught Cowdrey bowled Higgs, and Nurse (53) a little later lbw Higgs: 282 for four. Then, in complete contrast to the stone walling tactics of Saturday, Butcher and Sobers put on 173 runs in 127 minutes of high adventure and swashbuckling extravagance. Saturday's slow train had become Monday's express. But after tea, the untiring Higgs accepted the second new ball and put an end to these high jinks by having Sobers (94) caught by Underwood: 455 for five. Meanwhile, with the aid of several chances, Butcher had roared into his second hundred, and when a declaration came at 482 for five, he was 209 not out; his innings lasted 461 minutes, and he had shared in century partnerships for three successive wickets. Higgs was the most successful English bowler with three wickets for 109 runs, and D'Oliveira two for 77.

Needing 393 for victory, Boycott and Milburn opened for England and survived for about half an hour until close of play on Monday when they had scored 30 runs. On Tuesday the final day, Milburn (12), who had hooked Hall for 6 the day before, tried it again and was caught at mid-on: 32 for one. Russell (11) was caught by Sobers off Gibbs: 71 for two, and Graveney and Boycott put on 54 before Boycott (71) was caught by Sobers in the slips off Griffith. Graveney (32) also succumbed to Griffith when he was caught by Hendriks. By lunch, Parks (7) was caught by Lashley off Hall and with the score at 142 for five, England's hours were numbered. Nor could the pitch be blamed for this dismal showing. Even if the pitch responded slightly to spin, most of the wickets so far had fallen to the fast bowlers. Cowdrey (32) and D'Oliveira (54) offered some resistance; but England were all out for 253 conceding victory by 139 runs. Sobers claimed one for 71, Hall two for 52, Griffith four for 34, and Gibbs three for 83. (In this match Hall had overtaken Ramadhin's 158 wickets in Tests to become the leading Westindian wicket-taker.) As Cowdrey said afterwards: "The better team won". England were simply outplayed. Westindies could not now lose the series since they were leading 2:0 with two matches left.

Fourth Test vs. England
Headingley, Leeds, England, 4, 5, 6, 8 August, 1966

In the third Test at Trent Bridge in 1966, Westindies beat England to take a 2:0 lead in the five match series. This made the fourth Test at Headingley all the more vital since a Westindian win would confirm both their victory in the series and their "title" as world champions which they won by beating Australia in 1965. For the fourth Test, England brought in Barber and Titmus for Russell and Illingworth, while the Westindian team remained unchanged. Sobers's luck was also unchanged as he won the toss yet again and chose to bat. Lashley (9) was bowled by Higgs when Westindies reached 37. Hunte and Kanhai added another 50 runs by lunch when Hunte was 38 not out and Kanhai 39 not out. Soon afterwards, Kanhai (45) drove Underwood low to mid-off where Graveney did well to hold the catch. It was Underwood's first Test wicket and the score was 102 for two. At 122 Hunte (48) was lbw to a full toss by Snow, and Westindies were 137 for three as rain stopped play for the day, Butcher and Nurse being the not out batsmen.

The next day, Butcher (38) was caught by Parks off Higgs: 154 for four. If Cowdrey and his men felt pleased with holding the powerful Westindian batting line-up in check, their pleasure did not last, for Nurse and Sobers took the score firstly to 247 by lunch, and then to 390 by tea: Nurse was on 85 and Sobers on 152. Sobers had to be seen to be believed. Seldom do mere figures bespeak a batsman's glory, but between lunch and tea when Nurse managed 37 runs, Sobers blasted 103 - nearly three times as many. It seemed that he could take whatever liberties he liked, and after tea he did just that, evidently going for quick runs so as to declare and unleash Hall and Griffith on an exhausted enemy for at least a short period that very afternoon.

One criticism levelled at Cowdrey was that he did not use Barber's right arm leg-spin enough. There is probably some truth in this, for when Barber eventually came on he did cause discomfort, noticeably to Nurse. More to the point, he bowled Sobers (174) with his googly, although, by that time, the great man had plundered and pillaged enough runs to achieve his highest Test score in England, and with Nurse had established a new Westindies fifth-wicket record in all Tests - 265. This innings and his 163 not out at Lord's in the second Test were the high spots in what we have later come to regard as Sobers's golden summer of '66. It was his third century of the rubber and it took him past 5000 runs in Tests. His exit must have revitalized the English bowlers who then quickly disposed of the remaining Westindian batsmen. Higgs bowled Holford (24) and Griffith (0), while Snow accounted for Nurse (137) via Titmus at mid-off. Although he was overshadowed by the transcendent brilliance of his illustrious partner, it was Nurse who had kept the innings together by providing steady application as he had done in the first innings of the third Test at Trent Bridge. When the declaration came at 500 for 9, the most successful English bowlers were Higgs: 43-11-94-4 and Snow: 42-6-146-3. Underwood and Barber also took one wicket each.

In the fading minutes of the second day, Hall and Griffith made a vigorous assault on Boycott and Barber who bravely parried their thunderbolts and were lucky to survive. The next day they were less lucky. Barber (6) slashed at Griffith and was caught by wicket-keeper Hendriks. More unluckily, Milburn attempted to hook Hall and sustained a blow to his left arm that forced him to go off. Then a controversy over Griffith's bowling action boiled up; it had been simmering since the Australian tour of Westindies the year before when Griffith was suspected of throwing. Now, he was advised by umpire Charlie Elliott to be careful about "illegal" deliveries. As the match proceeded, Boycott (12) was dismissed by Hall, via Holford in the gully: 18 for two, and Cowdrey ignored a delivery from Hall that knocked out his leg stump: 42 for three. This misfortune bore a curious resemblance to Cowdrey's fate in the first innings of the Old Trafford Test in 1963, and there was further misfortune when Graveney (8) dragged a ball on to his wicket: 49 for four.

Solid as ever, D'Oliveira impassively surveyed the wreckage as England was engulfed by gloom and both Parks (2) and Titmus (6) disappeared into darkness shepherded by Sobers. At last, D'Oliveira found an unlikely partner in the burly figure of Ken Higgs who was willing to defend stoutly while he (D'Oliveira) struck four spectacular sixes, one each off Gibbs, Holford, Sobers, and Hall. A six off a slow bowler is one thing, but to straight drive Hall for six called for a rare blend of daring, strength and skill. D'Oliveira accumulated 88 runs before he was caught by Hall off Griffith: 179 for 7. With the help of pain-killing injections, Milburn now re-entered, as he and Higgs added 59 more runs to prop up the total until, at 238, Higgs (49) was finally caught off Sobers. Running out of partners, Milburn was left on 29 not out when the innings closed at 240. Although Sobers had mopped up the English tail to emerge with figures of five for 41, it was Hall (three for 47) who did the main damage helped by Griffith (two for 37.)

Enforcing the follow-on, Sobers opened the bowling himself. In poor light, Boycott and Barber put on 28 before Boycott (14) was caught by Hendriks off Lashley's medium pace. D'Oliveira came in instead of Milburn and remained with Barber until close of play when the score was 40 for one. On the final day, England still needed 221 runs to make Westindies bat again. At 70 D'Oliveira (7) was caught at short-leg off Sobers, and at 84, Barber (55) who had done most of the scoring, was bowled by Sobers: 84 for three. By now, since Gibbs was effectively using variations of flight and pace on a wearing pitch, England seemed doomed. At 109 he had Cowdrey (12) playing for non-existent turn and being out lbw. He also bowled Graveney (19), and at lunch England were 128 for five and slipping irrevocably. After lunch, Parks (16) was caught at square leg off Gibbs: 133 for six. Then, with the convulsive abandon of a team in its death throes, Milburn and Titmus slogged 51 glorious runs. But after Milburn (42) was bowled by Gibbs, the road to victory was clear. England made 205 and lost by an innings and 55 runs. Sobers appropriated three wickets for 39 runs, but Gibbs was the main destroyer with figures of: 19-6-39-6. Having won the series by chalking up three victories with one match left to play, Westindies had at last confirmed their rise to the top of the world of cricket.

CHAPTER SEVEN

Players

George Challenor

Challenor was a batsman and medium pace bowler who was born in Barbados in 1888. He played in the Barbados cricket team very early, and embarked on his first tour of England in 1906. As a youth on this tour, he showed outstanding promise: he made 90 against Scotland, and 63 against Leicestershire, and his aggregate of 1,017 runs was one of two four-figure aggregates achieved by members of his team. Christopher Nicole writes: "It is safe to say that had he [Challenor] this year [1906] been a schoolboy at Eton or Harrow he would have been hailed as the wonder of the age." (*West Indian Cricket*, p.38) In the winter of 1912, a fairly strong English side toured Westindies under A.F. Somerset, and in their first match against Barbados, Challenor totalled 118, while in the return match he made another century. After a delay in cricket tours caused by the first World War, Challenor went on the Westindian tour of England in 1923, his "annus mirabilis", when he performed such deeds as would make him, beyond doubt, the first notable Westindian batsman. He contributed 87 to the first Westindian victory of the tour, against Sussex, and at Lord's, although they were narrowly defeated by Middlesex, he made 94 out of the Westindian first innings total of 264. Against Oxford University, his not out century again ensured victory. Then, his 101 against Essex laid the foundation for yet another victory. At Trent Bridge, versus Nottinghamshire, Challenor (102) and his Barbados opening partner Tim Tarilton (109) rattled up 209 runs in two and a half hours to win the match. There was another century against Gloucestershire, and 155 not out in the Surrey match. Although Westindies were beaten by Glamorgan, Challenor batted superbly for 110. On the tour, he made 1,895 runs for an average of 52.62, including eight centuries. At the time, no other Westindian batsman had achieved such statistics abroad.

Although he made some runs against an M.C.C. team which toured Westindies under the Hon. F.S.G. Calthorpe in the winter of 1925, Challenor never regained his 1923 form. This decline became all too clear in 1928, when Westindies toured England for the fourth time and first played Test matches. It was ironic that no batsman had done more than Challenor to prove that Westindies deserved Test status, yet he did not enjoy the reward, ending up with 101 runs in three Test matches for an average of 16.83. He retired after the 1928 tour, and worked as a school teacher before his death in 1947. His Test figures are a mockery of the batting of his prime years. This is evident from his figures in first class cricket - 5,822 runs for an average of 38.55, including fifteen centuries. He also took 54 wickets for an average of 23.97 runs. His achievement is threefold: he and players like Learie Constantine provided a credible basis for Westindies to achieve Test status in 1928; his influence on younger players, for example, Walcott and Worrell, has probably contributed more to Westindian cricket than may be ever realized; and Challenor was the first Westindian batsman to become internationally recognized. At his height, C.L.R. James claims:

> "Challenor symbolized batting, in every hovel and palace in the Caribbean." (*Cricket*, p. 283)

Learie Constantine

If George Challenor was the first Westindian batsman to gain attention abroad, Learie Constantine was the first Westindian all-rounder to make an impact on international cricket. Whether in batting, bowling or fielding, Constantine exhibited such zest and vigour that he projected a unique style of play which came to be acknowledged as an authentic archetype of Westindian cricket. Born in Trinidad in 1902, Constantine inherited an impeccable cricketing pedigree: his father played for Westindies (in pre-Test cricket days), and his mother's brother, Victor Pascall, was a member of the Trinidad cricket team at the same time.

On his first tour of England with the Westindian team in 1923, Constantine scored 425 runs in first class matches for an average of 15.74; he took 37 wickets for an average of 21.86. These results suggest greater success with the ball than the bat, a pattern that was to remain true for most of Constantine's career. On his next tour of England in 1928, he amassed 1381 runs in first class matches for an average of 34.50. Again his bowling was distinctly better - 107 wickets at 22.95 apiece. In the 1928 Test matches, Constantine did less well, managing a total of 89 runs in 6 innings for an average of 14.83. His bowling suffered too - 5 wickets for an average of 52.40. These 1928 Test figures confirm that Constantine's most memorable performances are in first class matches rather than in Tests. As C.L.R. James says:

> "Constantine is not a Test cricketer who played in the leagues. He is a league cricketer who played Test cricket. It is not enough to do justice to league cricket. Justice must be seen to be done. League cricket today is what he made it." (in John Arlott. ed. *Cricket: The Great All-Rounders*, p.77)

Constantine played first class cricket from 1922 to 1945, while his Test career lasted from 1928 to 1939. His first class batting aggregate is 4,451 runs for an average of 24.32, and his bowling figures 424 wickets at 20.61 each. His Test career figures are 33 innings for a total of 635 runs and an average of 19.24. He took 58 Test wickets at 30.10 apiece. But Constantine is remembered less for these figures than for his exuberant style in batting, bowling and fielding. In the Georgetown Test, in 1930, for example, when England were intent on playing out time to force a draw, they were foiled mainly by Constantine who bowled 40 overs and took five wickets for 87 runs in the second innings. If these figures are combined with his four for 35 in the first innings, it is clear that Constantine's contribution to the first victory by Westindies in Tests is inestimable. In the second Test against England at Port-of-Spain in 1935, he made 90, his highest Test score, out of a Westindian first innings total of 302. He followed this up with a shattering spell of bowling in which he claimed three second innings English wickets for 11 runs in 14.5 overs! Victory again.

These performances illustrate an uncanny penchant for unpredictable reversals, either through a sudden burst of lethal fast bowling or a brief, swashbuckling innings of equally murderous intent. Nowhere is this more evident than in the 1928 Westindies match against Middlesex when Constantine blasted 86 runs in his team's first innings, battered down seven wickets in the Middlesex second innings, and stormed through to a second innings score of 103 to earn Westindies an unpredictable and utterly amazing victory (see Appendix ii). In this match Constantine topscored in both innings, and at one stage, had swept six wickets away for 11 runs in 39 balls. The match illustrates the sort of devastation he could cause with both bat and ball through an approach that combined zest, combativeness, ebullience and pluck in about equal proportions.

These qualities are seen at their spectacular best in Constantine's fielding. Seldom can it be truly said of a cricketer, as it often has been of Constantine, that spectators attended a match mainly to see him field! In his career he took 133 catches in 117 first class matches, and 28 catches in 18 Test matches. Sir Pelham Warner comments as follows:

> " He: (Constantine) is the finest fieldsman the world has ever seen.
> This may sound extravagant praise, but men like Hammond and Hendren,
> who know all there is to know about fielding, are emphatic that
> Constantine stands alone. (*The Book of Cricket*, p.38)

The 1940 *Wisden* also praises Constantine for: "lissomeness of limb, the rapidity of vision and the elasticity of muscle which the climate of those [Westindian] islands engenders." (p.34) Christopher Nicole calls Constantine: "the most remarkable cricketer ever produced by these islands [the Westindies]", and continues:

"Constantine's name is not found in many places in the record books,

he was not a record hunter, and the type of cricket he played was not
conducive to breaking records. But he played the type of cricket that
the original inventors of the greatest game on earth had in mind when
they first picked up a bat, and as long as there is left one Test cricketer
who will play the game in this spirit the future of big cricket is secure."
(in *West Indian Cricket*, p.38)

But perhaps it is the 1940 *Wisden* that best sums up Constantine's performance
when it describes him as:

"a cricketer who will never be forgotten, who took great heed that
all nature's gifts should be, as it were, expanded by usage, a deep thinker
and an athlete whose every movement was a joy to behold." (p.36)

Constantine wrote seven books, six of which are on cricket. From 1957 to
1961 he was a member of Dr. Eric Williams's government in Trinidad and
Tobago. From 1961 to 1964 he served as High Commissioner for Trinidad and
Tobago in London. After 1928, except for his four years as a politician in
Trinidad, Constantine lived continuously in England where he played league
cricket for Nelson from 1929 to 1937. It was in England too that he died in
1971. He was given a full state funeral in Trinidad and a memorial service in
Westminster Abbey. Constantine was knighted in 1962, and awarded a life
peerage in 1969, when he took the title of Baron Constantine of Maraval in
Trinidad and of Nelson in the county Palatine of Lancaster. He was also
posthumously awarded the Trinity Cross, his country's highest honour. His was
probably the most varied career of any Westindian cricketer: not only politics,
diplomacy, writing, law, and broadcasting, but the twin causes of racial justice and
Westindian Independence, which he cherished most of all. If all this sounds too
grand for a man to achieve in one lifetime, consider its grandeur as the achievement
of the grandson of a slave!

George Headley

George Headley's father was Barbadian, and his mother Jamaican, while he
was born in Panama in 1909. His first ten years were spent in Cuba, where he
developed a liking for baseball. But in 1919, to the great good fortune of cricket,
he was taken to Jamaica where he eventually played for St. Catherine Cricket
Club. He first gained recognition in 1928 when he represented Jamaica and
made scores of 71, 211, and 71 against an M.C.C. team led by Lionel Lord
Tennyson. This batting success is what dissuaded the young man from going to
the US to study dentistry; for he was all set to go, and would already have left,
but for a delay in his visa. When we consider what this delay meant for the
future of Westindian cricket, we must surely see the hand of God in it. True
lovers of cricket cannot be atheists.

Headley did not get his chance in Test cricket until England came to the Westindies in 1930, and again, only infidels will fail to discern divine foretelling in the scores that he made in his first Test match - 21 and 176 - in Barbados, in January 1930. He did nothing notable in the second Test, but in the third, in Georgetown, he made a separate hundred in each innings and helped Westindies to their first victory in a Test match. His scores in the final Test were 10 and 223. Thus, in his first Test series, he made a century on début, two separate hundreds in one match, and a double century, all before he was twenty-one years old. His aggregate was 703 runs in eight innings for an average of 87.87. His début century and separate hundreds in the same Test are Westindian "firsts"; so also would have been his double century, except that Roach had made 209 in the preceding Test at Bourda.

On their tour of Australia in 1930/31 Westindies lost 1:4. For his part, Headley found that his customary off side play made him vulnerable to leg spinner Clarrie Grimmett who dismissed him for 0 and 11 in the first Test. A lesser man might have withdrawn into himself or lost confidence, but by the third Test, so successfully had Headley adapted himself to off side play that he scored 102 not out. Another century followed in the fifth Test, and his Test aggregate of 336 for an average of 37.30 represented a splendid recovery from his first four innings which yielded 27 runs. In 1933 Headley toured England for the first time with Westindies. He made 13 and 50 in the first Test at Lord's, hit 169 not out in the second Test, and finished with a total of 277 runs in three Tests for an average of 55.40. His final tally in first class matches for the tour was 2,320 runs - almost twice as many as the next highest scoring Westindian batsman.

In the four Tests that England played in Westindies during 1934/35, Headley amassed 485 runs for an average of 97.00, including 270 in the fourth Test which helped Westindies to win the rubber - their first - by 2:1. Now, as the Second World War approached, Headley made what was to be his final tour of England with the Westindies team. In the first Test at Lord's he made 106 and 107, and became the first batsman to score separate hundreds in a Test at Lord's, and the second batsman (after Herbert Sutcliffe) to twice score separate hundreds in a Test match. In three Tests, Headley totalled 334 runs for an average of 66.80. His Test career effectively ended with the English tour of 1939, although he did play three more Test matches after the war. In 1948, for instance, when he was picked to play against England, he also became the first black Westindian Test captain. (Constantine had briefly substituted as captain when Jack Grant was injured in the fourth Test at Sabina Park in March 1935, but he was not appointed.) And in 1954, when money was raised to bring Headley back from English league cricket to play in the Westindies against England, it was largely a symbolic gesture of reverence to a batsman whose playing days, at the age of 45, were long over. He died in 1983.

In his Test career, Headley compiled 2,190 runs for an average of 60.83 - the highest by a Westindian. Not only that, these figures were all from matches against England and Australia, the most powerful teams in the 1930s. He also produced eight centuries and two double centuries. In his first class career he totalled 9,921 runs for an average of 69.86, and claimed 51 wickets at 36.11

apiece. One could expect him in his prime to make a century every other match. So consistent was he that people wondered whether he should be regarded as a black Bradman or whether Bradman should be regarded as a white Headley. While Bradman scored consistently and heavily, he was not the only consistent or heavy scorer among his Australian team-mates. By contrast, it fell to Headley alone, more times than we can remember, to carry the entire Westindies batting on his shoulders. On the 1939 Westindian tour of England, Headley scored 1745 runs in first class matches for an average of 72.70. The next highest aggregate was 948 runs, and the next best average 30.83. Not for nothing did English journalists christen Headley "Charles Atlas".

By any standard, Headley was a batsman of rare genius. He could deploy a wide variety of strokes with equal facility and power all around the wicket. His back foot play, exceptional quickness of eye, and penchant for instinctive timing combined to allow him to see the ball extremely late and hit it with maximum power. Headley is named by Len Hutton [*Just My Story*, p.38) as one of the six greatest batsmen of the author's time, the other five being Hammond, Bradman, Compton, Herbert Sutcliffe and Maurice Leyland. Hutton writes:

> "he [Headley] scored nearly all his runs by the square cuts, pulls, and
> deflections of which he was such a master. He had an open-chested,
> two-eyed or rather two-shouldered stance, and anything short of a length
> he 'murdered'" (*Just My Story*, p.38)

According to Hutton, Headley could play in any conditions and was best off short balls. More praise for Headley comes from the 1940 *Wisden* which notes that he had "no living superior in the square and late cut." (p.58) The same source also alludes to Headley's wonderful execution of the hook and the late flick from thigh or hips to long-leg. (p.58)

Headley's significance to the rise of Westindian cricket and nationhood is best illustrated by personal anecdote. I first learnt of Headley in Guyana, in the 1940s, when I saw a photograph of the great man waiting in a line of cricketers to shake the hand of George the Sixth, king of England and ruler of the British empire. Although I was too young then to understand the full effect of this photograph, I later realised the inchoate possibilities it aroused in most of us who lived in an environment without electricity, radio or running water, where a bicycle represented the height of technology: that one of us - a black man - could shake the hand of a king, introduced possibilities formerly undreamt of in our colonial backwater of racial inferiority, psychological subordination and political powerlessness. Others had their Hobbs and Hammond, Trumper and Bradman, but for all their glory and lustre, none of these heroes performed the service to his countrymen that Headley performed for us: giving Westindians of all races and ranks, their first glimmering of recovery from a legacy of political subjection, and general dehumanisation.

PLATES

Photographs supplied by the Allsport Historical Collection

WESTINDIAN CRICKETERS ARRIVE IN LONDON, MAY 1923.
The team of cricketers from Barbados, Trinidad, Demerara and Jamaica, photographed on their arrival at the West India Dock. Their captain, Mr H G B Austin, is wearing a light coat. They are to play the first class counties during the coming season.

"Historical evidence suggests that cricket was originally intended for the amusement of English people who had gone to the Westindies to promote colonialism: we know from C L R James, the finest Westindian writer on cricket, that the game was first played by English soldiers garrisoned in the Westindies in the eighteenth century."

GEORGE CHALLENOR, 1928. No batsman had done more than Challenor to prove that the Westindies deserved Test status. His achievement is threefold: he and players like Learie Constantine provided a credible basis for Westindies to achieve Test status in 1928; his influence on younger players, for example, Walcott and Worrell, has probably contributed more to Westindian cricket than may be ever realized; and Challenor was the first Westindian batsman to become internationally recognized. At his height, C L R James claims: "Challenor symbolized batting, in every hovel and palace in the Caribbean." (Cricket, p.283)

THE WESTINDIES TEAM OF 1928. Three players are missing from this group, G N Francis, C A Powell and J M Neblett. Standing, Left to Right: J Scheult (Assistant Manager), W H St Hill, E A Rae, E L G Hoad, J A Small, F R Martin, L N Constantine, H C Griffith, O C Scott.
Seated Left to Right: E L Bartlett, M P Fernands, C V Wight, (Vice- Captain), R K Nunes (Captain), G Challenor, C R Browne.
"The first Test Match that Westindies ever played was against England."

West Indies v A P Freeman`s X1 at Gravesend, Kent, 1933.

WEST INDIES CRICKET TEAM, MAY 1939. Standing: Gomez, Clark, Stollmeyer, Johnson, Bayley, Weekes, Williams, Hilton and Cameron. Sitting: Martindale, Headley, Kidney, Grant, Constantine, Barrow and Sealey.

LEARIE CONSTANTINE was the first Westindian all-rounder to make an impact on international cricket. Whether in batting, bowling or fielding, Constantine exhibited such zest and vigour that he projected a unique style of play which came to be acknowledged as an authentic archetype of Westindian cricket.

GEORGE HEADLEY (right) with E A MARTINDALE,
Westindies tour of England 1939. Headley was not just the first
black Westindian to achieve genuine greatness as a batsman: he

was the first Westindian to focus positive world attention on a region, until then, known mainly for sugar and rum, products of a long and shameful history of slavery and exploitation.

WEST INDIES TOURING TEAM, 1950. Left to Right, Back Row: C B Williams, R E Marshall, A L Valentine, L R Pierre, C L Walcott, H H Johnson, A F Rae, K Testrail and Mr Ferguson the baggage manager. Front Row: S Ramadhin, P

Jones, F M Worrell, Mr Palmer Barnes the Assistant Manager; J D Goddard (Captain), G E Gomez, J B Stollmeyer, R J Christiani and E Weekes

JEFFREY STOLLMEYER (left) with **ROBERT CHRISTIANI, Westindies Tour
in England, 1950.** Stollmeyer's batsmanship was distinguished by its strength on
the leg side. His leg glide, in particular, was a thing of beauty that, combined
precision timing with supple wristness and rhythmic grace. Christiani was an
artist-cricketer. He combined instinctive improvisation and acrobatic skill with
the precision and the delicacy of a ballet dancer.

JOHN GODDARD captained the great 1950 Westindies team to England. In the summer of 1950 Westindian cricket firmly established itself. Actually it was the twenty-second year since they were given Test status in 1928, but whereas some cricket bodies take a long time to grow up, there was no question that the representatives of the Caribbean reached maturity on their seventh visit to the cradle of cricket. [It was the fourth visit of Westindies to England, although the seventh series the two teams had played.] Those of us who saw them overwhelm G.O. Allen's M.C.C. team on their own fields in the early months of 1948 were prepared for surprises, but I do not think that any of us expected they would go from one triumph to another and outplay England in three out of four Tests. (Wisden, 1951, p.207)

CLYDE WALCOTT, 1957. Walcott's reputation now became established as one of the mightiest hitters of the ball.

EVERTON WEEKES, 1950. "I admired Frank Worrell immensely, but Everton Weekes was the most explosive cricketer of all. He had incredible speed of footwork and strokemaking. He was like Bradman but more extravagant." (Henry Blofield, 'The Voice of Cricket')

FRANK WORRELL was destined to make a unique contribution to his native island, to the whole region of the Anglophone Caribbean and to the world of international cricket.

Worrell's achievement may be summed up in his own words: "to see Westindies moulded from a rabble of brilliant individualists into a real team," Quoted in Cozier, Fifty Years, p.45. This modestly understated assessment of the most valuable individual service ever rendered to Westindian cricket is typical of the calm, unassuming dignity of the man. If only someone had done for Westindian politics what Sir Frank Mortimore Maglinne Worrell did for Westindian cricket!

SONNY RAMADHIN and ALFRED VALENTINE, England, 1950. The role of Ramadhin and his comrade-in-arms Valentine in helping Westindies to win the 1950 rubber 3:1 will be relished for generations to come, as will the story of the second Test match at Lord's which constituted the Unilateral Declaration of Independence by Westindies from half a century of English colonial rule over them in cricket.

There are many well known pairs of cricketers - Hobbs/Sutcliffe, Lindwall/Miller, Compton/Edrich - but none more touched by romance than Ramadhin and Valentine, whose appearance in England, in 1950, as if out of nowhere gave them an aura of mystery or magic all through that enchanted summer.

ALFRED VALENTINE, England tour, 1950. 'The Cricketer's' description of Valentine in the early part of his career: "This left arm spinner, with his left thumb cocked like a pistol-hammer at the moment of delivery, showed on the unresponsive jute matting in Trinidad that, in addition to being able to bowl a length, he could really spin the ball and get it to turn more than the average left-hander's."

SONNY RAMADHIN in action. Ramadhin`s secret had less to do with mystery than with his single-minded concentration on attacking the stumps.

JEFFREY STOLLMEYER (batting) with Allan Rae, formed what may still be regarded as the best opening pair in Westindian cricket; in twenty-one such partnerships in the late 1940s and early 50s, these two averaged 71 runs per innings. This partnership laid the foundation for Westindian success in England in 1950.

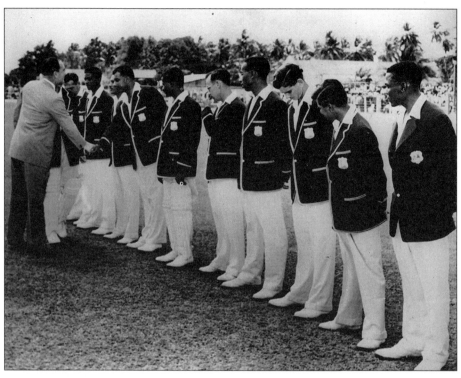

The Governor, Sir Robert Arundell shakes hands with members of the West Indies team before the start of the second Test against England at Bridgetown, Barbados, 1954.

GERRY ALEXANDER, Australia, 1961. His magnificent accomplishments in Australia suggest that the cares of captaincy restricted his performance in preceding series, which implies a noble neglect of self for the sake of his team.

"GARFIELD ST AUBRUN SOBERS, thirty years old in July, 1966 - the most renowned name of any cricketer since Bradman's high noon. He is, in fact, even more famous than Bradman ever was; for he was accomplished in every department of the game, and has exhibited his genius in all climes and conditions... We can safely agree that no player has proven versatility of skill as convincingly as Sobers has done, effortlessly, and after the manner born." (Wisden, 1967, p.38)

ROHAN KANHAI, 1957. "This 77, an innings of outrageous dare-devilry, is a perfect illustration of Kanhai's style of knife-edge riskiness, mercurial daring, and fertile inventiveness."

JOE SOLOMON, 1958, when his quiet reliability became almost legendary, and when he performed feats that are likely to live longer than those of many cricketers more flamboyant and prolific than himself.

THE INCIDENT WHICH MADE TEST MATCH HISTORY took place in Brisbane, Australia, when Australia tied the First Test Match with the Westindies. The first tied Test in history. Meckiff was dramatically run out when there were only two balls to go. Here the Westindies leapt jubilanty in the air as Meckiff's wicket was broken.

"...but Hall contrived a spell of fast bowling such as he had never before given any sign of achieving. Doubts that may have existed about his wayward direction simply vanished as he kept his aim unerringly on target, and in a torrid spell, removed Simpson (0), Harvey (5) and O'Neill (26), and reduced Australia in no time at all to 49 for three."

WEST INDIES TOURING TEAM, APRIL 1963. Left to Right. Back Row: Solomon, Butcher, Rodriquez, Allan and Murray. Middle Row: Nurse, Gibbs, Griffith, King, Carew and McMorris. Front Row: Valentine, Hunte, Worrell, Sobers, Hall and Kanhai.

LANCE GIBBS, 1975. Such feats of sustained, penetrating and triumphant bowling confirmed Gibbs's calibre as one of the great off-spinners in Test cricket. Most of all, he brought to his game an uncompromising spirit of fierce competitiveness that made him a formidable foe on good wickets and an unyielding one on any that gave him the slightest help.

Left to Right: Colin Cowdrey, England's cricket skipper and Gary Sobers, his Westindies counterpart, flank Dr Eric Williams, Prime Minister of Trinidad and Tobago during a cocktail party given by the government at Port of Spain, Trinidad. Geoff Boycott second from right.

Garfield Sobers - the rarest and brightest jewel in the glittering and glorious crown of international cricket.

WEST INDIES CRICKET TEAM, 1966. Left to Right, Back Row: Butcher, Hendriks, Carew, Brancker, Lashley, Nurse, Solomon. Front Row: Kanhai, Hall, Sobers, Hunte, Gibbs

ROHAN KANHAI falls after hooking against England in the Test Match at the
Oval, **1963.** The stroke that delighted the crowd the most was his flamboyant
falling hook which left him lying flat on his back across the crease, while the ball
careered to the boundary.

KANHAI (Left) and **SOBERS** leaving the Bourda pavillion, Georgetown, to resume their overnight innings. Kanhai went on to make 150 and Sobers made 152. Kanhai had established a reputation for charismatic stroke-play and dazzling aggression. On Sobers: "It seemed contradictory, almost irresponsible to observe the familiar, nonchalant, loping jauntiness of his walk to the wicket, the characteristic stoop forward, collar sticking up starch stiff under his chin. These were the unique trademarks of genius, and in that bleak atmosphere of Westindian misfortune, it required nothing less than genius to assert authority, and in partnership with his cousin Holford, to compile 274 runs, and pull off one of the most stunning transformations ever beheld on a cricket field.

Gerry Gomez

Gerry Gomez was the perfect all-purpose cricketer, not at the rarefied level of Sobers, but at the more attainable level of a reliable, modest (not mediocre) middle-order batsman, who could open the bowling, and fill in gaps especially when his side was in danger. Gomez was born in 1919. He attended Queen's Royal College, and was first picked for Westindies on the tour to England in 1939. In his first Test innings at Old Trafford in the second Test, Gomez made 0. He got 11 in the second innings of the same match, but finished with a grand total of 22 runs in his three Test innings of the tour (average 7.33). From this dismal beginning in Tests, Gomez bolstered his confidence with several huge scores in intercolonial matches before his next Test series during England's tour of Westindies in 1947/48. In the first innings of the first Test of this series, at Kensington Oval, Barbados, Gomez revealed his true mettle - a knock of 86, fortified by pluck, defiance, courage - qualities that later became second nature to him. Coming in with the total at 81 for two, Gomez and his comrade Stollmeyer put on 104 runs that set the innings on a sure footing. In the second Test, when Stollmeyer fell ill, Gomez took over the captaincy from him and scored 62 in the first innings; he might have won the match (which was drawn) if there was not a two-hour delay because of rain during the English second innings. In the four Tests of the tour, Gomez totalled 232 runs for an average of 46.40. His aggregate was second only to that of Weekes (293), and his average was third, after Carew (50.00) and Weekes (48.83).

Gomez next showed his stalwart qualities during the Westindian tour of India in 1948/49. Although this tour is remembered for enormous totals, it is interesting that at an early stage in the first innings of the first Test at Feroz Shah Kotla, Delhi, the Westindian score stood precariously at 27 for three when Walcott and Gomez came together and added 267 runs before end of play on the first day when Gomez was 99 not out. The next morning Gomez reached 101, his only Test century, before he was stumped. He made another 50 in the fourth Test, which helped him to a tour batting aggregate of 256 and an average of 36.57. Meanwhile, he excelled with the ball, claiming 16 Test wickets for 454 runs (average 28.37). Only Prior Jones (17) claimed more wickets. In England on the historic tour of 1950, his figures were similar: an aggregate of 207 in four Tests (average 41.40). These figures include a score of 70 by Gomez when he and Walcott (168 not out) added 211 for the sixth wicket in the second innings of the second Test match at Lord's.

The Westindian tour of Australia in 1951/52 provided exactly the atmosphere of disaster and distress in which Gomez flourished. In the first Test at Brisbane, he came in with the score at 184 for seven in the second innings. He added 45 runs with Marshall, and finished with 55 runs - the second highest score in a total of 245. In the event, Australia had to get 236 runs to win and got them, but only after a very tense struggle. Gomez came up with a contribution of at least 40 in each of the four remaining Tests, except the fifth. In the third Test match which Westindies won, victory was clinched in the second innings by a fifth wicket stand of 92 between Christiani (42 not out) and Gomez (46 not out). Gomez topped his team's Test batting averages on the tour by making 324 runs at an average of 36.00. He also opened the bowling, and collected 18 wickets at 14.22 apiece. In the fifth Test alone he got 10 wickets, and it is significant that with Stollmeyer as captain in this Test, he bowled 36 overs whereas his total overs in the previous four Tests under Goddard were: 12.5; 23; 12.3; 22.3.

Throughout the rest of his career Gomez never regained the form he exhibited in Australia. His four Tests against India in 1952/53 produced 62 runs (average 12.40). To some extent, he compensated for such meagre results by returning bowling figures of 11 wickets at 31.90 each. He did a little better against England in 1953/54, producing 127 runs (average 21), and claiming 7 wickets at 37.57 runs each. These statistics confirm that the great days of 1947 to 1952 were gone for good, and Gomez retired after 1954. In a career of 29 Tests he produced 1243 runs for an average of 30.31; he also collected 58 wickets at 27.41 runs each. His first class record is better: 6764 runs (average 43.63), and 200 wickets at 25.26 runs each. After retirement, Gomez served as a member of the Westindian Cricket Board of Control, and managed the Westindian team during their tour of Australia in 1960/61.

Jeffrey Stollmeyer

Jeffrey Stollmeyer first played Test cricket for the Westindies in 1939 when he was nineteen years old. He opened the batting in all three Test matches against England that summer. It was a beginning that augured well; for he made 59 twice: in the first innings of the first Test at Lord's, and again in the third Test at Kennington Oval. Between 1939 and 1945 when the world turned its attention to Hitler and World War Two, Westindian intercolonial cricket gave Stollmeyer an opportunity to mature; and in the English tour of Westindies in 1947/48, he played in two Test matches, his highest score being 78 in the first Test. On the Westindian tour of India in 1948/49, Stollmeyer registered his first Test century in the fourth Test at Madras - 160 - his highest Test score.

With Allan Rae, he formed what may still be regarded as the best opening pair in Westindian cricket; in twenty-one such partnerships in the late 1940s and early 50s, these two averaged 71 runs per innings. This partnership laid the foundation for Westindian success in England in 1950. Although Stollmeyer himself did not score heavily in the four Test matches in England, his 78 in the second innings of the first Test at Old Trafford, the only one that Westindies lost, was an innings of the highest class played on a treacherous wicket. Westindies were severely trounced on their Australian tour in 1951/52, when many of their players did not live up to expectation. In the second innings of the fifth Test, after Australia had already won the series 3:1, Stollmeyer produced his greatest Test innings - 104 - nearly half the Westindian total of 213; the next highest score was Rae's 25. He made another century in New Zealand on the same tour - 152 - in the second Test at

Auckland. Thereafter, he became Westindian captain in three home series: against India in 1952/53; England in 1953/54; and for two matches against Australia in 1955. While he played a more than competent role as a batsman in most of these matches, it was probably the combined effect of the captaincy, increasing age, frequent injuries, business commitments and changing political attitudes that encouraged him to retire after the Australian tour of 1955.

Stollmeyer's batsmanship was distinguished by its strength on the leg side. His leg glide, in particular, was a thing of beauty that, combined precision timing with supple wristiness and rhythmic grace. His career figures are 2,159 Test runs for an average of 42.33 in 32 Tests and 56 innings; he scored four Test centuries and took 13 Test wickets. After his retirement, he became selector, manager and administrator in Westindian cricket. He served four terms as President of the Westindian Cricket Board of Control. As a white Westindian who came from the land-owning class, Stollmeyer followed the Grants and Goddard in a line of white Westindian captains. But his retirement, five years before Independence, heralded the end of an era in which whites had formed the dominant racial, social and economic class in the Westindies. This means that in his administrative duties during the 1960s, 70s and 80s, he encountered some of the most troubling crises ever faced by Westindian cricket, for example, the Packer crisis and the controversy over playing in apartheid South Africa. But his instinct for natural diplomacy helped to bring Westindies through with the least possible damage. Such yeoman service intensified the enormity of the crime when he was shot during a robbery at his home in Port-of-Spain in 1989, and died shortly afterwards from his wounds.

Robert Christiani

Robert Christiani was born in Guyana in 1920. His Test career began in the four match series which England played against Westindies in 1947/48. In the first innings of the first Test, Christiani made one run. In the second innings, when Westindies were floundering at 87 for four, he contributed a dashing 99, the top score, which enabled his team to reach 351 for nine declared. A similar feat was almost repeated in the first innings of the third Test when Westindies were again struggling at 48 for three, and he and Worrell put on 79 magnificent runs before he was caught on the square leg boundary off a hit that looked a certain six. Like too many of his innings, this one was abruptly cut off when he was in full flow on 51. In this whole 1947/48 series against England, Christiani accumulated 175 runs for an average of 29.1. If figures can be deceptive, this is more true for Christiani than for most other cricketers: the number of runs he scored was less important than how he scored them. What Neville Cardus has said of Victor Trumper is true of Christiani: he was an artist-cricketer. He combined instinctive improvisation and acrobatic skill with the precision, and delicacy of a ballet dancer.

Christiani appeared in all five of the Test matches that Westindies played in

India in 1948/49. In the first innings of the first Test, he and Weekes put on 118 for the seventh wicket, and he went on to 107, his only Test century. In the next Test, he and Weekes once more teamed up to plunder 170 runs from the Indian bowlers. But he was out for 74 (lbw to Mankad), again when he was going strong. Although he did not make another fifty in the remaining Tests, he completed this Indian tour with an aggregate of 294 runs for an average of 42, figures which he never again equalled. The Westindian tour of England that followed in 1950 was a huge success for the team, but not for Christiani. In four Test matches he totalled 82 runs for an average of 16.4 He revived somewhat on the tour to Australia in 1951/52, scoring 261 runs for an average of 29. The contrast between these two tours is revealing. When Westindies dominated England 3:1 in 1950, Christiani did badly; but when Australia humiliated Westindies 4:1 in 1951/52, Christiani did a good deal better. In the second Test in Australia, he played an heroic innings, hoisting the top score of 76 when the fortunes of his side were low.

After the Australian tour, Christiani made occasional appearances against New Zealand, India, and England, but his Test career was in decline. His Test figures are 896 runs in 22 Tests for an average of 26.35 He also kept wicket a few times in the early part of his career, and as a slow bowler took three Test wickets for 108 runs. In addition, he was a dashing close fielder. But it has to be repeated that figures fail utterly to reflect the thrill, excitement, joy, exhilaration and splendour which Christiani's batting provided. He was all feet, wrists and reflexes, a dancing, darting, galloping figure who treated his crease like a springboard from which he would take off or jump back to perpetrate outrageous acts of acrobatic inventiveness that literally took one's breath away. Christiani's method was to crouch and wait, ready to pounce on the ball with lightning agility: once the bowler's arm came over, there would be a slight pause of anticipation, then a dazzling flurry in which feet would dance, arms would swing, and wrists would roll before the gleaming blade flashed, and the ball was peremptorily dispatched to some remote corner of the field.

For all that, one cannot escape the feeling that too many of Christiani's innings were cut short before their prime. One reason is that his most productive years happened to fall mostly in the early 1940s when there was no Test cricket being played. Then, by the late 1940s and early 50s, when Test cricket resumed after World War II, it just so happened that Westindies were blessed with the extraordinary talents of three batsmen - Weekes, Worrell, and Walcott - who permanently occupied the top batting order in the team. If all or one of these batsmen succeeded, there was less opportunity for Christiani to shine. It was generally on the rare occasions when all the Ws failed, that Christiani's talents were most fully stimulated. For these reasons, his best performances are not those which he played alongside the Ws in Test matches, but in the intercolonial tournaments when he represented Guyana, and in county and state matches when he was touring abroad. Against Middlesex at Lord's, in 1950, he hit a century in each innings of the match. Only Headley had previously achieved this feat at Lord's. Performances like this explain why Christiani's record in first class matches - 5,103 runs for an average of 40.50 - completely outdistances his Test match figures.

Frank Worrell

No star or other celestial body hovered suggestively over St. Michael, Barbados, when Frank Worrell was born there on August 1, 1924. Failure to provide a galactic marker of such a momentous event smacks either of divine neglect or discontent. For Worrell was destined to make a unique contribution to his native island, to the whole region of the anglophone Caribbean, and to the world of international cricket. After playing for his school - Combermere - Worrell was picked as a spin bowler for the Barbados team when he was only eighteen. Later, he found himself more and more inclined to batting, and at the age of 20, while playing for Barbados against Trinidad, he made 308 not out and shared in a partnership of 502 with John Goddard (218 not out). Two years later, once more against Trinidad, he made 255 not out while sharing in a partnership of 574 with Clyde Walcott (314 not out). Not since the young George Headley had such happy prognostications of batsmanship been entertained for any Westindian!

Worrell's chance at Test cricket came in 1948 shortly after he had moved to Jamaica. England were making their first post-war tour of the Westindies, and in his début in the second Test in Trinidad, Worrell made 97 and 28 not out. He followed this up with a superb 131 not out in the third Test in Guyana. By the end of the tour he had topped his team's batting aggregate (294 runs) as well as averages (147), and was recognized as the leading Westindian batsman of the time. Worrell then became a professional cricketer with Radcliffe Cricket Club in the Central Lancashire League in England. In 1949/50 he also made the first of three tours to India as a member of Commonwealth teams. When Westindies arrived in England in 1950, Worrell, Weekes and Walcott formed the backbone of their team's batting. Such were their accomplishments on the 1950 tour of England that their collective name - the three Ws - struck awe in the hearts of bowlers and opposing teams all over the world. Of the three Ws, Walcott was the mightiest hitter, Weekes the most dynamic run-getter, and Worrell the most graceful stroke player. With his slender build, lissome movement and restrained manner, Worrell's batsmanship combined elegance and dignity into strokes of exquisite beauty. In the four Tests in England in 1950, he emerged with the highest aggregate - 539 runs, and the highest average - 89.83. At Trent Bridge he hit 261, his highest Test score. He also made 138 in the Oval Test.

Following their success in England in 1950, Westindies were humiliated by Australia in 1951/52. In the dark moments of this Australian disaster, Worrell was one of two Westindian batsmen to lighten the gloom by making a Test century: 108 in the fourth Test at Melbourne. (Stollmeyer was the other centurion.) Throughout the 1950s Worrell represented Westindies regularly except when his studies or illness intervened. He hoisted 237 against India in the fifth Test in Jamaica in 1953, and 197 in the first innings of the first Test against England in 1960. Even in the sunset of his career, on the Westindian tour of England in 1963, his batting exuded enough grace and artistry for *Wisden* to comment that Worrell's 74 in the first Test at Old Trafford was "the most graceful exhibition of late cutting in the last fifty years." (*Wisden*, 1964, p. 271) One of his feats was against England in the third Test at Trent Bridge in 1957, when he opened the first innings, made 191 not out, and carried his bat; he opened the bowling as well. In addition to being a star batsman, Worrell served regularly as a fast medium bowler. His best bowling performance was in the fourth Test against England at Leeds, in 1957, when he took seven wickets for 70 runs in 38 overs. His career batting figures are 51 Tests and 87 innings for a total of 3,860 runs, an average of 49.48, and nine Test centuries. He also bowled 7,141 balls in Tests, and took 69 wickets for 2,672 runs: an average of 38.73 runs per wicket.

When Worrell was appointed captain of Westindies for their tour of Australia in 1960/61, it was the first time in thirty-two years of Test cricket that Westindies had a black captain for an entire series. This appointment coincides with an anti-colonial mood and agitation for independence in the Caribbean in the 1950s and 60s. The significance of the appointment is that when Worrell retired in 1963, after only three tours and fifteen Test matches as captain, the collective performance of his men had improved so vastly as to make Westindies, quite simply, unbeatable. It was only left for Worrell's successor - Sobers - to administer the "coup de grâce" to Australia in 1964, and make Westindies undisputed cricket champions of the world for the first time in their history. Of his fifteen Test matches as captain, Worrell won nine, lost three and drew two. The grandeur of his achievement is heightened by the fact that he led Westindies in two of the most remarkable Test matches ever played: the tied Test against Australia in Brisbane in 1960, and the drawn Test against England at Lord's in 1963. It cannot be accidental that Westindies, under Worrell, were the common factor in two instances of international sport whose dramatic intensity is universally acknowledged to be almost without parallel.

Worrell was intelligent and disciplined enough to sometimes neglect cricket in the 1950s in order to complete an economics degree at Manchester. It took patriotism, after he retired, in 1963, to serve both the university of the Westindies and the senate of Jamaica. His patience is acknowledged by his team-mates; and his shrewdness on the field seems increasingly legendary to those who saw him play. In 1964 Worrell was knighted for his services to cricket. Three years later, he was dead from leukaemia. The tragic impact of his death was acknowledged internationally when, in 1967, a memorial service was held for him in Westminster Abbey, the first time that this honour was accorded to a sportsman. Rare honour befits rare achievement! Worrell's achievement may be summed up in his own words: "to see Westindies moulded from a rabble of brilliant individualists into a real team." (Quoted in Cozier, *Fifty Years*, p. 45) This modestly understated assessment of the most valuable individual service ever rendered to Westindian cricket is typical of the calm, unassuming dignity of the man. If only someone had done for Westindian politics what Sir Frank Mortimore Maglinne Worrell did for Westindian cricket!

Clyde Walcott

Clyde Walcott is chiefly remembered for his batting exploits alongside Frank Worrell and Everton Weekes, during the first half of the 1950s. Walcott was born in Barbados in 1926, and attended Combermere school and Harrison College where his performance as a cricketer attracted attention and gained him selection, in 1946, to represent Barbados in Trinidad. In this match he and Worrell put on 574 runs together, a partnership that still remains the highest for any wicket in Westindian cricket. Walcott's contribution was 314 not out, and Worrell's 255 not out. This colossal partnership set the stage for Walcott's entry into Test cricket, in 1948, during England's tour of Westindies. Walcott was picked as wicket-keeper/batsman, and asked to open the batting in the first Test. His scores were 8 and 16, and he was moved down the batting order in later Tests. He finished with a paltry aggregate of 133 and an average of 22.16 in the series. Despite this disappointing Test entry, Walcott was picked to tour India at the end of 1948. This time he chalked up a total of 452 Test runs, including two centuries, for an average of 64.57. Walcott's reputation now became established as one of the mightiest hitters of the ball. Perhaps he played off the back foot with special relish, but he played off the front foot too, and could drive, hook and use his feet with surprising nimbleness for a heavily-built man who stood over six feet.

On the English tour of 1950, Walcott's contribution was 229 runs in four Tests for an average of 44.58. His highest score was 168 not out in the second innings of the second Test at Lord's when his 211 run partnership with Gomez set Westindies on the way to their first ever Test victory in England. In the winter of 1951, Walcott toured Australia with Westindies. His team's grim fate of losing 1:4 is reflected in his own batting figures of 87 runs for an average of 14.5. He did better on the brief New Zealand tour that followed Australia, but the Australian tour was an unhappy experience in which Walcott sustained a back injury that eventually forced him to give up wicket-keeping. For his next three series - all at home - against India in 1952/53, England 1953/54, and Australia 1954/55, Walcott achieved averages of 76.16, 87.25 and 82.70 respectively. Afterwards, although he distinguished himself with an average of 96.25 against Pakistan in 1957/58, Walcott's career had turned downward in flight, until it ended with a brief appearance against England in 1960.

In his Test career from 1947 to 1960, Walcott made 3,798 runs altogether for an average of 56.68. He held 53 catches, and claimed 11 wickets at 37.09 apiece. He also executed 11 stumpings. His first class figures are 11,820 runs for an average of 56.55, including 40 centuries. He took 35 wickets as well. Except against England in 1947/48, Australia in 1951/52, and England again in 1957, he was remarkably consistent, often coming to the rescue in a crisis, for example, in the first innings of the second Test against England in 1954, when he came up with 220 runs out of a total of 383. It is the highest and best innings of his Test career. But Walcott's best collective achievement was against Australia in 1955, when he totalled 827 runs in 10 innings with a highest score of 155. Westindies were thrashed

3:0, and time and again Walcott came to their rescue, mostly in vain. In the process, he became one of only five batsmen who have twice made separate hundreds in a Test match; and he is the only man ever to have achieved this feat in the same series. For four seasons, beginning in 1951, Walcott served as a professional for Enfield in the Lancashire league. Immediately afterwards, he became Cricket Organizer and Coach with the British Guiana Sugar Producers Association. He was also manager on various Westindian tours, and later President of the Westindian Board. Recently, he was named President of the International Cricket Council (ICC), and in 1993 he was knighted.

Everton Weekes

Born in 1925, Weekes was first picked for Tests during England's 1947/48 tour of Westindies. He made the following scores in the first three matches: 35; 25; 36; 20. These lacklustre figures caused him to be dropped from the fourth Test; but George Headley's illness created a space that brought Weekes back into the team. It was a God-sent reprieve which he grabbed with both hands. Not only did he score a century - 141 runs: he made it the first of five consecutive centuries, of which the succeeding four were compiled on the Westindian tour of India in 1948/49. His Test figures of 779 runs (average 111.28) made it look as if he had a mission to punish bowlers. If he did not exactly fulfil this mission on the next Westindian tour - to England in 1950 - he distinguished himself with 338 runs in four Tests for an average of 56.33. He came closer to his Indian form in the county matches which helped him to amass the leading tour aggregate of 2,310 runs - five hundred more than Worrell, his nearest rival.

Weekes exhibited a startling capacity for invention matched only by Kanhai and Headley among Westindian batsmen of the highest rank. On his first tour of England in 1950 *Wisden* commented on Weekes's exceptional quickness of eye and foot, and he was compared to Headley in build. Yet he failed in 1951/52, in Australia where ten Test innings yielded him no more than 245 runs and an average of 24.5. To a batsman with a reputation for Bradmanesque doings, this Australian contretemps must have been galling. At home, against India in 1952/53, Weekes bounced back with 716 runs and an average of 102.28 in five Test matches. Against England too, in their tour of Westindies in 1953/54, his batting reflected no loss of effectiveness: 487 runs, including a double century, and an average of 69.57. Even in 1954/55, when Australia again thrashed Westindies, Weekes managed 469 runs and an average of 58.62, thus giving valuable support to Walcott who led Westindian resistance against the Australian juggernaut. It says something about Weekes's batting that he made 139 and 87 not out in the second Test against opposition that included both Lindwall and Miller.

Weekes's first class career began in his native Barbados in 1944. Altogether he played in 48 Test matches and scored 4,455 runs, for an average of 58.61 which is still the second highest yet achieved by a Westindian batsman. By

Players

1964 when he retired, he had scored 12,010 runs in first class cricket for an average of 52.90. He also distinguished himself in league cricket in Lancashire where he played for Bacup beginning in 1949. He holds the record of being the first player in the league to achieve 1,000 runs in six separate seasons, but eventually he returned home where he served as national cricket coach for Barbados for many years and was awarded an O.B.E. for his services to cricket.

In ten Tests against India Weekes made a total of 1,495 runs, including seven centuries for an average of 106.78; his ten Tests against Australia yielded 714 runs, (less than half) including one century, and an average of 41.56; and his 17 Tests against England 1,313 runs with three centuries and an average of 48.56. If these statistics are considered along with his 418 Test runs, three centuries and average of 83.60, against New Zealand in 1955/56, they might suggest that Weekes excelled most against weaker teams; for neither India nor New Zealand could boast of very hostile bowling at this time. But all Westindian batsmen, with the notable exception of Walcott, tended to do better against India and New Zealand than against Australia and England during the period from 1948 to 1956. That Weekes did more than twice as well against India must be attributed mainly to his pugnacious style of batting rather than to any deficiency in his technique or temperament against Australia and England.

There can be no doubt about Weekes's status as a great Westindian batsman. In comparing him to Headley, *Wisden* states that he was not as resourceful or gifted with the same range of strokes. (*Wisden*, 1951, p. 207) And John Arlott writes: "I admired Frank Worrell immensely, but Everton Weekes was the most explosive cricketer of all. He had incredible speed of footwork and strokemaking. He was like Bradman but more extravagant". (Henry Blofield, "The Voice of Cricket", *Radio Times*, in Roy Peskett, *The Best of Cricket*, Hamlyn, London, 1982 p.76) Perhaps of the three Ws, Weekes took the most risks. This might explain why, when his luck held, he tended to amass larger scores. It might also explain why his batting exuded a special excitement. He contributed greatly to the collective achievement of the Ws who put Westindian batsmanship on the map of international cricket in a more general way, during the 1950s, than Headley's individual genius had done in the 1930s. His contribution to this collective achievement is what confirms a secure place of honour for Everton de Courcy Weekes in Westindian cricket, and in 1995, this was finally formally recognised with a knighthood, the last of the three Ws to receive this honour.

Sonny Ramadhin

Sonny Ramadhin should be remembered for at least two reasons: as the first Indo-Caribbean cricketer to reach Test level, and as the first great bowler to emerge from the Westindies. He was born in Trinidad in 1929 and his career in cricket was the product of raw, natural ability and sheer force of character. Growing up in the Trinidadian countryside, Ramadhin was first spotted by

Barbadian ex-inter-colonial cricketer Clarence Skinner who was working in Trinidad in the 1940s. Following Skinner's help, he was called up for two trial matches for Trinidad against Jamaica in which he took twelve wickets at 19.25 runs apiece. On this slender basis he was catapulted into the Westindies team that toured England in 1950, and on this tour, almost overnight, Ramadhin found himself with a reputation as one of the most remarkable right arm spin bowlers the world had ever seen.

The role of Ramadhin and his comrade-in-arms Valentine in helping Westindies to win the 1950 rubber - 3:1 - will be relished for generations to come, as will the story of the second Test match at Lord's which constituted the Unilateral Declaration of Independence by Westindies from half a century of English colonial rule over them in cricket. In this second Test, Ram's first innings figures were: 43-27-66-5, and in the second innings when England were bowled out for 274 to give Westindies victory by 326 runs, he sent down 72 overs for 86 runs and six wickets. It was a gargantuan effort, mesmerising in effect, and had he never bowled another delivery in his life, this match effort of 11 wickets for 152 runs would have been enough to earn him immortality in cricket. This triumph was followed by five wickets for 135 in the second innings of the succeeding Test at Trent Bridge which ensured another Westindian win. Although he took only four wickets in the fourth and final Test, Ramadhin gave enough support for Valentine to run through England by claiming ten wickets and clinching the rubber.

In the four Tests in 1950, Ramadhin took 26 wickets for an average of 23.23, while he topped the tour averages as a whole with 135 wickets at 14.88 apiece. Leading English batsmen who found difficulty in "reading" Ramadhin, were baffled by his ability to bowl both leg and off breaks using the same apparent action. This, plus the fact that he always kept his sleeves buttoned at the wrist encouraged speculation of mystery and magic, or guile of some inexplicable kind. But Ramadhin's success was not mysterious. Jeffrey Stollmeyer puts it well: "It was Ramadhin's amazing control of length and direction in addition to his naturally deceptive action that made him a great bowler." (*Everything Under the Sun* p.38) As Worrell also points out in *Cricket Punch*, (p.124) Ramadhin's secret had less to do with mystery than with his single-minded concentration on attacking the stumps.

Ramadhin's next tour was to Australia in 1951/52, but apart from his five for 90 in the second innings of the first Test at Brisbane, he could not reproduce the form he exhibited in England, and ended up with a tally of 14 wickets for 695 runs in five Tests. For one thing, Goddard - the Westindian captain - over-bowled Ramadhin and Valentine, and for another, hard Australian wickets were less responsive to the spin of Ramadhin and Valentine than those is England. But on the New Zealand leg of the same Australian tour, Ramadhin took nine wickets for 125 runs in the first Test and ensured another Westindian victory. In the second innings of the Barbados Test on the Indian tour of Westindies in 1952/53, he took five wickets for 26 runs, and handed Westindies a decisive victory.

Against England too, in 1953/54, he was the leading wicket-taker with 23 wickets at an average of 24.30 in the five match Test series. And in the first Test against New Zealand in 1956, he took six for 23 and confirmed another Westindian victory. In the first innings of the first Test against England at Edgbaston in 1957, Ramadhin returned his best figures ever - seven wickets for 49 runs. But in the second innings May and Cowdrey put on a crushing partnership of 411 runs that drew the match. Ramadhin sent down altogether 774 deliveries - still the record for a Test match - but he was disappointed, since he felt that May and Cowdrey could kick his deliveries away with impunity so long as they did so while playing a stroke well forward of the wicket as then required by the Laws of cricket. Despite this disappointment, Ramadhin continued to bowl effectively, for example, against Pakistan in 1958/59. But his career was almost over, and although he was picked for the Westindian tour of Australia in 1960/61, he played in only two Test matches.

Hutton, who faced Ramadhin in his earliest and best years between 1950 and 1954, calls him "the prince of slow bowlers." (*Just My Story*. p.58) Hutton continues: "To me Ramadhin was still as interesting and fascinating to bat against as Australia's Bill O'Reilly, the greatest of all slow bowlers against whom I played." (p.58) In the same book Hutton admits he could not pick Ramadhin's off spinner and leg cutter in England, and even when he could do so in the better Westindian light, he still found Ramadhin "a most puzzling bowler." (p.59) Over the years, in between Test series, Ramadhin played league cricket in England where he had settled after his first tour in 1950. He also represented Lancashire in 1964 and 1965, and after retirement enjoyed taking part in festival cricket until the 1980s. In the end, he served for some years as landlord of a pub in Oldham, Lancashire. In a Test career lasting from 1950 to 1960, Ramadhin appeared in 43 Test matches and claimed 158 wickets for an average of 28.98. Never before had a Westindian bowler achieved such distinction!

Alf Valentine

There are many well known pairs of cricketers - Hobbs/Sutcliffe, Lindwall/Miller, Compton/Edrich - but none more touched by romance than Ramadhin and Valentine, whose appearance in England, in 1950, as if out of nowhere, gave them an aura of mystery or magic all through that enchanted summer. When they went to Australia in 1951/52, their magic faded somewhat, although for almost a decade afterwards, it lingered fitfully in occasional series or matches without ever totally dying out. Valentine was born in Jamaica in 1930, and like Ramadhin, was picked for the Westindian tour to England in 1950. In the match against Lancashire, at Old Trafford, a few days before the first Test was due to start on the same ground, he laid thirteen Lancastrians low for the paltry cost of 67 runs. It convinced his captain, John Goddard, to include him in the team for the first Test. Thus was born the legend of those "two little pals of mine" celebrated in Lord Beginner's "Victory Calypso, Lord's, 1950."

Such was Goddard's faith in them that the "spin twins" accounted for 89.3 out of 128 overs, that is to say, almost 75 per cent of the overs bowled by their team in the first innings of the first Test. More to the point, they accounted for all ten wickets, Valentine claiming eight for 104, and Ramadhin two for 90. For Valentine it was pure romance: he had a match analysis of eleven wickets for 204 runs, and he claimed the first eight wickets, five of which fell before lunch. Valentine's eight wickets on his Test début is a record shared by A.E. Trott (England) and R.A.L. Massie (Australia), but neither Trott nor Massie took the *first* eight wickets. In the historic second Test at Lord's, he emerged with seven wickets for 127 runs; in the third, five wickets for 183; and in the fourth, ten wickets for 160 runs. This gave him a total of 33 Test wickets in the series for an average of 20.42.

The Westindian tour of Australia in 1951/52 proved a sterner test. Valentine collected ten wickets in the first two Tests at somewhat high cost, but in the third, the only one that Westindies won, he took six wickets for 102 runs in the only innings that he bowled. He had another six wickets in the fourth Test, and finished the tour with 24 Test wickets at 28.79 each. If the quality of his performance had dropped from what it was in England, it recovered in New Zealand on the same tour when he claimed 8 wickets at 19.12 apiece. While his three wickets in the first Test against India in 1952/53 may not look impressive, he sent down 84 overs that yielded barely one and a half runs each. In other words, he commanded great respect from batsmen in a series in which four out of five Tests were drawn. His best performances were in the last two Tests, with eight wickets in the fourth and nine in the fifth. On the tour as a whole he collected 28 Test wickets (average 29.57). Although this average was second to Frank King's (28.83), Valentine took twice as many wickets as any of his team-mates except King (17). Unfortunately, his form appeared to waver during the series against England in 1953/54 when the first three Tests yielded 7 wickets altogether. Again, in 1954/55, Valentine had to be content with 5 wickets (average 69.80) in three Tests against Australia. Despite these apparent lapses in form, he was picked for the tour to New Zealand in 1955/56, and took 15 Test wickets (average 18.86). He played a decisive role in the second Test at Christchurch when his figures in the second innings were: 22.4-11-32-5, and his match analysis - seven wickets for 80 runs. It was like old times. Illness prevented him from playing in any of the Tests on the Westindian tour of England in 1957, but he was picked for the tour to Australia, under Worrell, in 1960/61; and in 1961/62, played his final two Tests - against India - in the Westindies. His career record in Tests is 139 wickets (average 30.32), while in first class matches, he accumulated 475 wickets for an average of 26.21.

That Valentine was workmanlike could be seen in the intense concentration of his run up. He swung his arms and high-stepped to the crease as if on military parade. It was all part of a strategy to impart an amazing degree of spin to each delivery. In *Everything Under the Sun*, Stollmeyer quotes from *The Cricketer*'s description of Valentine in the early part of his career:

> This left arm spinner, with his left thumb cocked like a pistol-hammer
> at the moment of delivery, showed on the unresponsive jute matting in
> Trinidad that, in addition to being able to bowl a length, he could really
> spin the ball and get it to turn more than the average left-hander's. (p.110)

This confirms what we were to see later: Valentine's ability to control consistent line and length, over long periods, and to achieve the sort of accuracy that would keep the runs down even if it did not always gain wickets. His was an illustrious career, suitably taken over, in the end, by Garfield Sobers, as Ramadhin's was taken over by Gibbs.

Roy Marshall

Roy Edwin Marshall, was born in Barbados on April 25, 1930, and played as an opening batsman both for his home island and Westindies before he settled in England. He was also an occasional off-spin bowler, and always an alert fielder. Making his début for Barbados in 1945, Marshall was a prolific run-getter in intercolonial cricket, a reputation that earned him selection as one of the youngest players on the Westindian team that toured England in 1950. Because the team already had a reliable opening pair in Rae and Stollmeyer, Marshall was not picked for any of the four Tests on the tour. He showed his mettle on the county circuit, however, in his first English season: 1117 runs, including scores of 188, 143, and 135.

On the opening day of their match against Leicestershire in 1950, Westindies scored 651 for two, almost double the runs that most teams manage in one day. Worrell made 225 not out, and Weekes 190 not out. This day's play alone illustrates the stunning impact that the Westindian team of 1950 had on English spectators. Not even Bradman's 1948 Australians were as prolific, exciting and as carefree. Marshall opened the innings against Leicestershire, and by lunch had 93 to his credit. He was finally out for 188, made in 210 minutes. When people speak of the power, audacity, aggression, and excitement of Marshall's batting, it is innings such as this that they have in mind: on a good day, he could plunder and pulverise an attack as only the most gifted and greatest batsmen could.

Marshall was picked for the Westindian tour of Australia and New Zealand in 1951/52, and played in two Tests against Australia and two against New Zealand. His Test aggregate on the tour was 143 and his average 20.42. This cannot be easily explained away except by noting that few Westindian batsmen lived up to their reputation on that particular tour. Having begun to play league cricket, since 1950, Marshall settled in England in 1953 and began a career with Hampshire that was to last until 1972. This meant that he was lost to Westindian cricket. In his autobiography *Test Outcast*, Marshall justifies his decision to join Hampshire by pointing out that he had little chance of disturbing the regular openers, Rae and Stollmeyer. The fact is that in the early 1950s, apart from Rae and Stollmeyer, there were Bruce Pairaudeau, Ken Rickards, Andy Ganteaume, and J.K. Holt - all potential openers. No wonder Pairaudeau also emigrated, and settled in New Zealand.

Marshall's career with Hampshire comprises 504 first class matches in which he scored 30,303 runs and 60 centuries in nineteen years, during five of which he served as captain of the county. In one season alone - 1961 - he scored 2,455 runs and played no small part in helping Hampshire to win the English county championship that year. Until quite recently, Marshall's first class career aggregate of 35,725 runs (for an average of 35.94, and a total of 68 centuries) remained the highest by a Westindian. It has now been superseded by his fellow Barbadian Gordon Greenidge who also used to open for Hampshire. Marshall's batting had vigour, invention, zeal and zest; and he could mix a seemingly carefree, natural style with strokes of explosive, annihilating power. After retirement he settled in Taunton, Somerset, as landlord of a pub, just as Sonny Ramadhin did in Oldham, not far from Manchester. He died in England in 1992.

Ramadhin had pictures and other cricket memorabilia decorating his pub. Perhaps Marshall's pub was similarly appointed. Perhaps too stories were shared in both pubs; memories, recollections and evocations of heroic deeds on the field of play, and of mighty heroes from bygone days. What would we not give, over a pint of beer, to listen to such stories, and savour again their sweet dreams of past glory! But how sad for Marshall, Ramadhin and many others, that they could not share their stories and dreams with the people to whom, finally, they belonged! For, look as we might, we will not see in Marshall the excellence and grace of great English batsmen like Hobbs, Hammond and Hutton. Instead, we shall see the fiery power, daring, and razor-sharp dexterity of Headley, Worrell, Sobers and Kanhai. Is it any wonder, therefore, when we sit over a bottle of rum to bask in sweet memories of the glorious deeds of these heroes, is it really any wonder that deeds by Roy Edwin Marshall should float effortlessly into our happily rum-sodden minds!

Garfield Sobers

Although he was baptised in international cricket when playing for his native Barbados against India in 1953, Garfield Sobers's Test career began more than one year later at Sabina Park in the fifth Test against England in 1954, which England won by nine wickets. As a lad of seventeen, he then batted at number nine. He made 14 not out and 26, and took four wickets for 75 runs in 28 overs. He next appeared in four matches during Australia's tour of Westindies in 1954/55, by which time he was promoted to number six in the batting order. These early efforts revealed certain signs: in the third Australian Test at Bourda, for instance, Keith Miller reacted with disdain when he was beaten by the left arm spin of the stripling Barbadian youth - a mere upstart. The sign was that the upstart later had Miller caught by the wicket-keeper for 33. There was another sign when Sobers opened the batting in the fourth Test of the same series at Kensington Oval and hit Miller for seven successive fours. But in four Tests against New Zealand during 1955/56, this batting talent still lay dormant, unfulfilled. However, in the third Test of Pakistan's Westindian tour in 1957/58, it blossomed with an historic innings of 365 not out that eclipsed Len Hutton's twenty-year-old record of 364 to become the highest individual score in Test cricket, a record that lasted until Brian Lara's 375 against England in Antigua, in April 1994. After 1958, except for brief, out-of-form interludes, Sobers batted with prodigal fruitfulness. In 1966 alone, on the Westindian tour of England, he amassed 722 Test runs, including three centuries, for an average of 103.14.

Out of his prodigal offerings one may pick his 163 not out at Lord's in the second Test against England in 1966, an innings which Sobers himself declares as his best. He came in when the Westindian second innings total was 95 for five (in reality 9 runs for 5 wickets, since England had a lead of 86). It seemed contradictory, almost irresponsible to observe the familiar, nonchalant, loping jauntiness of his walk to the wicket, the characteristic stoop forward, collar sticking up starch stiff under his chin. These were the unique trademarks of genius, and in that bleak atmosphere of Westindian misfortune, it required nothing less than genius to assert authority, and in partnership with his cousin Holford, to compile 274 runs, and pull off one of the most stunning transformations ever beheld on a cricket field.

Other feats of genius were his 132 at Brisbane in 1960, and 168 at Sydney in the same series against Australia. There was also his 226 at Kensington Oval (Barbados) in 1960, 102 at Leeds in 1963, and 174 again at Leeds in 1966, all against England. In addition, there were equally inspired assaults on New Zealand, India and Pakistan. In all, Sobers played in 93 Test matches and scored 8,032 runs, including 26 centuries, for an average of 57.78. Only Vivian Richards, among Westindians, has scored more runs, and only Headley and Weekes can claim higher averages. Sobers's batting, essentially Barbadian, was warm-blooded, adventurous, swashbuckling, bedecked with gaiety and glamour, always the purest joy to behold. Whether through instinct or habit, what he had done was to mix Worrell's grace, Walcott's power, and Weekes's dynamism with his unique gifts of loose jointed, supple athleticism to produce a style of batting with his own majestic left-hander's stamp on it. This mongrel variety is probably why Cardus concludes that his "grammar of batsmanship" (*Wisden*, 1967, p.38) was not classical but lyrical.

Sobers's batting alone fulfils the wildest dreams of the most ambitious cricketer, but he also has a bowling record - 235 Test wickets at an average of 34.03 - grand enough to satisfy any bowler's claim to distinction. The greatest proof of his genius is his ability to combine these two separate vocations in cricket into a single career; for this ability is matched by none of the other great all-rounders, for example, Wilfred Rhodes, Walter Hammond, Frank Woolley, Keith Miller, Trevor Bailey, or Richie Benaud. If batting and bowling were all, Sobers would remain a unique all-rounder rather than a rare genius who, in addition to his skills already mentioned, could bowl in three different styles - fast medium, orthodox left arm spin, and wrist spin that begets the chinaman and googly.

Sobers was also a superb fieldsman who held 109 catches in his Test career, and served as Westindian captain from 1964 to 1972. Captaincy, perhaps, was his Achilles heel. To be sure, he won several series between 1964 and 1967, often, due to his own multi-faceted talents. But by 1973, Westindies had not won a Test in fifteen consecutive matches, and Sobers was replaced as captain, although he remained in the team, and was still capable of magnificent performances such as his 150 not out, and six catches against England at Lord's in 1973.

Sobers played league cricket in England in the 1960s, and later captained Nottinghamshire for several seasons. One of his most memorable feats in county cricket, apart from his aggregate of 7,000 runs and more than 250 wickets, was hitting six sixes off one over by Malcolm Nash of Glamorgan. He also served as captain of South Australia for a few seasons. In the end, after twenty years of first class cricket in which he scored 28,315 runs for an average of 54.87 (including 86 centuries), and took 1,043 wickets at 27.74 apiece, Sobers retired in 1974. He was knighted in 1975. He also wrote a novel (see Appendix iv) Let Cardus give the imprimatur to his all round genius:

> "Garfield St. Aubrun Sobers, thirty years old in July, 1966 - the most renowned name of any cricketer since Bradman's high noon. He is, in fact, even more famous than Bradman ever was; for he was accomplished in every department of the game, and has exhibited his genius in all climes and conditions... We can safely agree that no player has proven versatility of skill as convincingly as Sobers has done, effortlessly, and after the manner born." (*Wisden*, 1967, p.38)

Others may surpass Sobers in certain areas of the game; but as a complete cricketer - one who can bat, bowl, field, and possibly turn in a match-winning performance in any or all of these areas - he remains unrivalled, super-eminently alone, in a class of his very own. This, at any rate, is what Westindians believe. For a more considered view again let the sage Cardus speak:

> "It is, of course, vain to measure ability in one age with ability in another. Material circumstances, the environment which moulds technique, are different. Only providence, timeless and all-seeing, is qualified to weigh in the balance the arts and personality of a Hammond or a Sobers." (*Wisden*, 1967, p.38)

Cardus, himself an illustrious knight, is no doubt right, but there is not a Westindian who saw the master in the flesh who will not dauntlessly don the timeless garb, reserved solely for almighty providence and pronounce Sir Garfield St. Aubrun Sobers peerless, the rarest and brightest jewel in the glittering and glorious crown of international cricket.

Collie Smith

The death of O'Neil 'Collie' Gordon Smith in September 1959 is probably the most tragic blow ever sustained by Westindian cricket. For one thing, Smith who played his first Test match in March, 1955, and his last in March, 1959, was only twenty-six years old when he died. For another, it was while he was travelling, along with Tom Dewdney, in a car driven by his best friend Garfield Sobers, that Smith sustained injuries from which he later died, their car having collided with another vehicle at a corner. Neither Sobers nor Dewdney was seriously hurt. Perhaps, on the surface, statistics do not suggest a loss that can properly be regarded as tragic: 26 Tests for a total of 1,331 runs (average 31.69); and as a bowler of off-spin: 48 wickets at an average of 33.85. But these lacklustre figures tell a somewhat different story when examined against their actual circumstances. Smith's career slots neatly into a period of rebuilding in the second half of the 1950s when Westindies were shedding distinguished, ageing players in favour of new blood. Cognoscenti of the day fully expected that the great batting triumvirate of Weekes, Worrell and Walcott would be replaced by three promising stars - Sobers, Kanhai and Smith. Since we know the glorious heights later reached by Sobers and Kanhai, there is every reason to believe that Smith was destined for similar glory. This expectation was not based only on runs and wickets: it also had to do with Smith's warmth, generosity, and the overall exuberance of his personality, whether on or off the field.

In his first Test match at his home ground of Sabina Park, Australia had made 515 for nine declared, and in reply Westindies had mustered 101 for five wickets when Smith entered to partner Walcott. Consider the circumstances: the five top order Westindian batsmen, including Worrell and Weekes, had already gone, and an inexperienced twenty-two-year-old, last of the accredited batsmen, alone stood between Australia and almost certain victory. Nothing daunted, he stood his ground steadfastly, while Walcott pushed the score at the other end. The partnership realized 128 runs of which Smith contributed 44. It was a magnificent start. But Smith's baptism did not end with this tough-minded first innings' performance. Since only Atkinson and the bowlers were left, once Smith was out, Westindies collapsed for 259 in their first innings. Facing a deficit of 256, they had reached the slender total of 22 runs for two wickets in their second innings when, in a move that seemed to border on panic, skipper Denis Atkinson plucked Smith out from his relaxed position at number seven, and thrust him in at number four, straight into the limelight to face the full fury of Lindwall, Miller and Johnston. Admittedly, Worrell was hurt and Atkinson's options were limited. But consider again what might be expected from a youth in his first Test against the likes of Lindwall and Miller! Whatever his hopes Atkinson could never have expected the raw youngster to lash the Australian bowlers for 104 dazzling runs, and achieve the distinction of a Test century on début.

Smith did not maintain this high level of performance during the rest of the Australian tour: he ended with a batting average of 25.75 in eight innings, while he took five wickets at 68 apiece. In his next series, against New Zealand, he fared worse; but in the ill-fated Westindian tour of England in 1957, he topped the Test aggregate and averages with 396 runs and an average of 39.60. In the third Test in 1957, Westindies followed on, 256 behind England. Greater disaster loomed as they sank to 56 for four wickets in their second innings. But Smith entered and once again asserted stalwart, fighting qualities by scoring 168, including three sixes, one of which was straight driven with such power and daring that the bowler, Statham, had to applaud as the ball sailed backward high over his head. After 1957 Smith did not excel, although he scored well enough. His fourth and last Test hundred (exactly 100 runs) was against India at Delhi in February, 1959. In the end, the tragedy of Smith's loss lies in the combined impact on the game of his unfulfilled promise, his exuberant personality, useful bowling, enthusiastic fielding and sterling character.

Perhaps George Headley had a hand in the making of Collie Smith, batsman and cricketer. That six over the head of a fast bowler of Statham's reputation, and the many rearguard battles which Smith fought for Westindies are reminiscent of numerous innings that the greatest of all Westindian batsmen played in the 1930s. Such a connection illustrates a distinct batting tradition in a region notorious for either the absence of traditions, or their fragmentation. But even if something of George Headley was reincarnated in Collie Smith, the reincarnation was short-lived, flashing like a shooting star that, for a mere instant in celestial time, brilliantly lit up the firmament, both heaven and earth, before suddenly, tragically, fading away from our view.

Rohan Kanhai

Kanhai's Test career began with his selection for the Westindian team to tour England in 1957. It was a disappointing tour: in ten innings, he scraped together 206 runs (average 22.88). He did better against Pakistan in Westindies in 1957/58, when his 96 in the second Test at Queen's Park Oval showed distinct promise. This promise was fulfilled on the Westindian tour of India in 1958/59, when he totalled 538 runs in eight innings (average 67.25), including a devastating 256 at Calcutta - his highest Test score. On the Pakistan leg of the same tour, he made 217 in the third Test at Lahore and finished with an average of 54.80 in five innings. Against England, on the 1959/60 English tour of Westindies, Kanhai deployed a magnificent, face-saving 110 in the second innings of the second Test. His aggregate of 325 runs for an average of 40.62 in eight innings on this tour was at least respectable. By this time, as if by royal consent, Kanhai occupied the number three position on the Westindian team, leading storm troopers who formed the vanguard of the Westindian batting armoury. After 23 Tests, he had established a reputation for charismatic strokeplay and dazzling aggression.

The peak of Kanhai's career came between 1960 and 1965 when, in four series - against Australia in 1960/61; India in 1961/62; England in 1963; and Australia once more in 1964/65 - he clocked up the following aggregates: 503; 495; 497; 462: a total of 1957 runs out of 20 Tests. Previously, he had accumulated 1642 runs out of 23 Tests. Such was his consistency between 1960 and 1965 that he was considered by many to be the greatest batsman in the world, at that time. In 1960/61 Richie Benaud, who bowled against both Kanhai and Sobers, felt that Kanhai just "shaded" Sobers. (*Willow Patterns*, p.112) If runs were all, this view might be supported by the fact that, in the identical four series between 1960 and 1965, Sobers totalled 1528 runs - 429 less than Kanhai, although he (Sobers) had four fewer innings. Still, one has to remember that Sobers was also a bowler, and in one series, captain as well. Some of Kanhai's feats in this period were a century in each innings of the Adelaide Test in February 1961, and an exhilarating 77 against England at Kennington Oval in 1963. This 77, an innings of outrageous dare-devilry, is a perfect illustration of Kanhai's style of knife-edge riskiness, mercurial daring, and fertile inventiveness. These qualities are encapsulated in his falling hook, a stroke more properly described as a cross between a pull and a sweep, which, after its execution, left him flat on his back across the wicket, while the ball soared to the leg boundary somewhere between square and fine.

Although he never again attained his consistency of form during 1960 to 1965, Kanhai had reasonably good series in England in 1966, and in India in 1966/67. On the English tour of Westindies in 1967/68, he produced 535 runs for an average of 59.44; while against India in 1970/71, he came up with 433 runs (average 54.12), and against Australia in 1972/73: 357 runs (average 51.00). Persistent knee trouble affected some performances, but as late as 1973 he uncorked a vintage 157 against England - his first and only Test century at Lord's - ironically in the twilight of his career. Another landmark was his appointment as Westindian captain in 1972, a position he held for 13 Tests. Kanhai's period of captaincy was significant in reviving Westindian fortunes after long years of decline under Sobers. This was evident on their tour of England in 1973, when Westindies gained their first Test victory in four years, and their first rubber in six years.

Kanhai represented Warwickshire in English county cricket from 1968 to 1977. He came close to 2000 runs in his first season, and never missed a thousand runs in each of his first five seasons. He played in English League cricket, in Sheffield Shield matches for western Australia and Tasmania, and for the Rest of the World XI. After his retirement, Kanhai coached for many years in the Westindies before becoming manager of the Westindian team. Altogether, he appeared in 79 Test matches for a career aggregate of 6227 runs, an average of 47,53, and 15 centuries. His first class figures are 28,774 runs, an average of 49.01, and 83 centuries.

Kanhai was a ravaging, rampaging hero, whom L.T. Deakin, general secretary of Warwickshire County Cricket Club describes as a batsman who "can have few equals in the history of the game" (*Kanhai and Gibbs*, p.11). According to C.L.R. James, he is: "one of the greatest batsmen in living memory" (*Cricket*, p.282). Cardus comments on other Westindian batsmen and concludes that none: "has excited and delighted me, sent me eagerly on the tip toe of expectation as Kanhai, upright or flat on his back." (A *Fourth Innings with Cardus*, pp. 116-117). His front foot play was distinctive and his relentless pursuit of novel ways to get runs gave his batting a special edge which is what James recognized in deeming Kanhai "a creative batsman" (*Cricket*, p.282). It is also what the Barbadian novelist George Lamming recognized when, in an unpublished lecture, he referred to Kanhai as "the most original batsman of his time". For it is originality, after all - his instinct for inventiveness/ improvisation/ creativity - that makes Kanhai one of the most quintessential of Westindian batsmen, and so far as style is concerned, the equal of Headley himself. Unfortunately, he did not accumulate as large scores as consistently as Headley, or Sobers, which is why Kanhai must take third place, after Headley and Sobers, in the pantheon of Westindian batting heroes.

Like the archetypal Westindian trickster Anansi, Kanhai lived by his wits. When he came off there was nothing like him; when he did not, he and his admirers could be badly bruised, as Anansi often was. But never would he settle for the ordinary or mundane, safety or correctness, as he struck lustily out, heading boldly, precariously, for the high road of manful risk and threatening danger. The wonder was that despite risk and danger, it was a road that took Rohan Babulal Kanhai, the plantation coolie boy from Port Mourant, to what James calls: "regions Bradman never knew." (*Cricket*, p.210). Some plantation! Some coolie boy!

Gerry Alexander

As a wicket-keeper/batsman, Franz Copeland 'Gerry' Murray Alexander appeared in twenty-five Test matches in eighteen of which he was the Westindian captain. Altogether he scored 961 Test runs for an average of 30.03; he also took 85 catches and made five stumpings. Alexander's Test career began in 1957 when Westindies were beaten 3:0 by England. In four Test innings he scored 11 runs for an average of 3.66, all his runs coming in one innings, which meant that he made 0 three times, although, mercifully, he was once not out. With this doubtful record behind him, it is strange that Alexander was selected to captain Westindies in their next series, at home against Pakistan, in 1957/58. Under Alexander, Westindies gained a convincing 3:1 victory over Pakistan, one that did much to restore Westindian morale and inspire confidence in younger players such as Sobers, Kanhai, Smith and Gibbs. It was, after all, in this series against Pakistan that Sobers made his record-breaking 365, and Gibbs had his first haul of 5 wickets in an innings.

In their next series, against India, in 1958/59, Alexander led Westindies to victory by an even larger margin - 3:0. Indian batsmen simply had no answer to the fiery pace of Hall and Gilchrist, although their bowlers, Gupte in particular, often had the reverse effect on Westindies. Alexander's own performances as a player seemed undistinguished. His six innings against Pakistan yielded 133 runs, while five innings in India brought him 156 runs, not more than moderate success for a middle order wicket-keeper/ batsman. Yet such figures fail to reflect the real value of Alexander's contribution. For instance, in the first innings of the second Test at Kanpur in December, 1958, Westindies were completely seduced by Gupte's guile until Alexander rescued them from 88 for six, and with Solomon's help, brought them to 188 for seven. Together, Alexander (70) and Solomon (45) accounted for more than half of the Westindian total of 222. Immediately following this tour, Westindies lost 2:1 to Pakistan, partly because their irresistible fast bowling combination was broken by the disappearance of Gilchrist who was sent home for disciplinary reasons. The matter involved a dispute between Alexander and Gilchrist about bowling beamers to Indian batsmen; and the sad result of it is that Gilchrist never played Test cricket again.

When England toured Westindies in the winter of 1959, they encountered a very different team from the one they had demolished in 1957. England's slender 1:0 victory hinted at the narrow margin separating the two teams, and illustrated how far Westindies had come under Alexander. During this tour, Alexander equalled the world record at that time of 23 dismissals by a wicket-keeper in a series. A team which relied so much on pace might have lost this advantage without adequate support behind the stumps. Alexander's courage, skill and determination were evident in his wicket keeping and in the short innings (between 40 and 70) with which he sometimes rescued his team. When Worrell was appointed captain for the next Westindian series - against Australia, Alexander not only readily agreed to play under Worrell, but demonstrated the integrity of his support by producing the most impressive performance of his career: in five Test matches against Australia in 1960/61 he hoisted an aggregate of 484 runs (average 60.50), more than he had made in twenty preceding matches. In the process, he topped the Test batting averages of a team with Hunte, Kanhai, Sobers and Worrell in it. He also made his only Test century - 108 in the third Test at Sydney - and scored 150 runs in both innings of the fourth Test at Adelaide without once getting out. He took sixteen catches.

Then, as strangely as his Test career had begun, so it ended: Alexander retired after the Australian tour. His statistics do not match those of the great wicket-keeper/batsmen of our time - Marsh, Dujon (Alexander's countryman), Knott, or Wasim Bari; but none of these men was also captain. In 1957, Alexander had inherited a Westindian team in almost total disarray, and in less than two years supervised its transition to a mighty fighting force. In Australia in 1960/61, he played a major role in probably the most exciting Test series in which Westindies were involved. His magnificent accomplishments in Australia suggest that the cares of captaincy restricted his performance in preceding series, which implies a noble neglect of self for the sake of his team.

Joe Solomon

Among Indo-Caribbean cricketers, Joe Solomon occupies a rank below to Ramadhin, Kanhai and Kallicharan. He was born in 1930, and grew up in plantation Port Mourant in Berbice, Guyana, along with Kanhai, Butcher, Madray and Trim. Solomon entered Test cricket in the second Test of the Westindian tour of India in 1958/59: he made 45 in the first innings and 86 run out in the second. In the third Test he batted once for 69 not out, and in the fourth his scores were 43 and 8 not out. In the single Westindian innings of the fifth and final Test, Solomon scored 100 not out which enabled him to top his team's Test averages with a figure of 117. Predictably, he did not come near this figure again. In Pakistan on the same tour, his average plummeted by more than 75 per cent to 28.80, although he did bring off one score of 66 in the first Test and another of 56 in the third.

In due course, Solomon acquired the reputation of a solid, reliable middle order batsman, who wore opponents down with patient, unflagging, dour resistance. This was not as evident in 1959/60, in two Tests against England; but it was clear in Australia, in 1960/61, when his quiet reliability became almost legendary, and when he performed feats that are likely to live longer than those of many cricketers more flamboyant and prolific than himself. His aggregate of 250 runs in ten innings for an average of 27.77 in 1960/61 is scarcely better than mediocre. But these figures do not reflect the sturdy character of his batting and the uncanny accuracy of his fielding. In the first innings of the Brisbane Test in 1960, for instance, Solomon came in when the score was 243 for five, and the best Westindian batsmen already out: failure of the middle order at that point could have meant a total of about 300 which would have been risky to set before Australia. With perfect aplomb, Solomon participated in two crucial partnerships, one of 40 with Peter Lashley for the sixth wicket, and one of 64 with Alexander for the seventh wicket. Then he was unlucky to tread on his wicket and get out; but not before his own score reached 65 and the Westindian total 347 for seven. His 65 far outweighed its numerical value in so far as it helped Westindies to add many more runs through Lashley (19) and Alexander (60) and reach a "safe" total of 453.

Similarly, in the second innings, Solomon entered with the total at 127 for four (55 for four, since Westindies had a deficit of 52). Not only did he add 83 runs with Worrell, but when he was once more joined by Alexander, with the fate of his team still very much in the balance at 210 for six (158 for six), the two of them exhausted all of sixty-seven minutes and 12 overs in scoring 12 runs. This exhaustive exercise wore Australia down, as Westindies inched to 250 for eight at the fall of Solomon's wicket, and eventually to a total of 284. Again his score - 47 - was not large; but it helped to transform Westindian fortunes from certain defeat and give them at least a fighting chance. Australia was set 233 to win and the result was the first tie in the history of Test cricket. This unique result could not have been achieved without Solomon's resilient batting and extraordinary fielding in running out two Australians (Davidson and Meckiff) in their second innings although, in each case, he stood sideways, and had only one stump to aim at.

Apart from Test cricket, Solomon represented his county, Berbice, in local matches, and Guyana in the regional Shell Shield competition. His Test record is a total of 1326 runs in 27 Tests (46 innings), for an average of 34. This record also includes one century and four wickets. His first class figures are 5,318 runs in 156 innings for an average of 41.54. Solomon's combination of modesty with steadiness is caught by J.S. Barker who writes: "Solomon is the best maker of 60 in the business" (*Summer Spectacular*, p.84). Yet his fielding suggests that Solomon was not all grit and granite, and when the situation demanded it, he found the inspiration to spark two historic run outs at Brisbane in 1960.

Lance Gibbs

Gibbs was born of a Barbadian mother in Georgetown, Guyana, where he grew up. He joined the Demerara Cricket Club in Georgetown from which he launched himself, first into intercolonial cricket, then into Pakistan's tour of Westindies in 1957/58. He was picked in four Tests against Pakistan because Ramadhin was unavailable; and he finished the tour with 17 wickets for 392 runs (average 23.05). This got him a place on the tour to India in 1958/59 when he was little used, but against Pakistan on the same tour, Gibbs gathered 8 wickets for 180 runs (average 22.25). On the tour to Australia, in 1960/61, Ramadhin was unfit for the third Test, and Gibbs was brought in. He seized his chance with both hands by sending down 49 overs in the match for slightly over 2 runs per over, and taking eight wickets at less than 14 runs apiece. In the second innings alone, his figures were: 26-5-66-5, in the course of which he claimed three wickets in four balls. He followed up this feat with a more astonishing one - a hat-trick in the fourth Test.

In seven series in the 1960s, Gibbs led the Westindian spin attack with stunning success. Against India in 1961/62, he collected 24 wickets for 490 runs (average 20.41), and on his first tour of England in 1963, 26 wickets for 554 runs (average 21.30). He was less successful in Australia in 1964/65 - 18 wickets for 556 runs (average 30.88), but he bounced back against England in 1966 and India in 1966/67, when his figures were respectively: 21 wickets for 520 runs (average 24.76); and 18 wickets for 397 runs (average 22.05). In the course of these tours, there were many instances of Gibbs's outstanding prowess in varying conditions, and on all types of wickets. At Kensington Oval, Barbados, in the third Test, in 1962, by lunch-time on the final day India had virtually succeeded in drawing the match. Then Gibbs captured all the remaining wickets to come out with figures which at one stage read: 15.3-14-6-8. Westindies won by an innings and 30 runs. Gibbs's figures in the innings were eight wickets for 38 runs in 53.3 overs of which 37 were maidens.

Such feats of sustained, penetrating and triumphant bowling confirmed

Gibbs's calibre as one of the great off-spinners in Test cricket. He used natural gifts of a tall, lanky figure and long, bony fingers to achieve prodigious turn and dangerous bounce on the hardest wickets. In addition, he deployed the whole panoply of an off-spinner's weapons, varying flight, pace, direction and length with crafty discrimination. He was very much a thinking cricketer, who kept on his toes all the time. Most of all, he brought to his game an uncompromising spirit of fierce competitiveness that made him a formidable foe on good wickets and an unyielding one on any that gave him the slightest help. Yet, after 1968, Gibbs's skills and success seemed to diminish mysteriously. The mystery was an illusion: batsmen had discovered (as Cowdrey and May had done with Ramadhin at Edgbaston in 1957) that they could pad balls outside the off stump without playing a stroke or getting out lbw. Fortunately for Gibbs (but too late for Ramadhin) the law was changed in 1970 and breathed new life into Gibbs's career. In 1972/73 he captured 26 Australian wickets for 696 runs (average 26.76). He followed this up with 9 for 227 against England in 1973 (average 25.22) and other similar successes that confirm his unflagging accuracy and consistency.

Gibbs appeared in Lancashire and Durham League cricket in England, and in Sheffield Shield cricket for South Australia. He represented Warwickshire in English county cricket from 1968 to 1973 during which time he registered a total of 338 wickets for an average of 24.50. He also represented Guyana in Shell Shield competitions in the Westindies, and appeared for the Rest of the World XI. His Test career record is 309 wickets for 8989 runs in 79 matches (average 29.09). Eighteen times he claimed five or more wickets in a Test innings, and twice he accomplished the feat of ten wickets in a Test match: once at Old Trafford in 1963 and at the same venue again in 1966 - both times against England. If all this is hard to believe, his first class record of 1024 wickets for 27,878 runs (average 27.22) is just as incredible.

CHAPTER EIGHT

Writers

Learie Constantine, *Cricket in the Sun*
Stanley Paul & Co. Ltd., 1946

The opening lines of *Cricket in the Sun* sum up the book's subject, point of view, and tone:

> Trinidad was discovered by Columbus in 1496, and by M.C.C. in 1895.
> I came on the scene as a pickaninny in 1902 and discovered England in
> 1923, when I came over with a Westindian cricket team. Improving on
> Columbus, I settled down to make the most of my discovery. (p.11)

The subject is Westindian cricket, the point of view that of a black Westindian, and the tone unambiguously combative, zestful and outspoken. *Cricket in the Sun* is the author's second book. The first, *Cricket and I* (1933), written in collaboration with C.L.R. James, has useful perceptions and insights which do not reflect quite the same sunny or contented outlook that makes *Cricket in the Sun* such an aptly named book. The first quarter of *Cricket in the Sun* resembles *Cricket and I* in depicting the author's early years in Trinidad. As Constantine says, he grew up in a family that: "ate, drank and slept cricket" (p.15). He played with his parents, sister, and two brothers; and, like so many Westindian boys at the time, he often used oranges for balls. As a black Westindian of the lower middle class, Constantine did not have social or economic advantages. For economic reasons, he had to leave school in 1917 (aged 15). Since he fancied a career in law, he found work in a solicitor's office, while in his spare time, he continued to develop as a cricketer under the watchful eyes of his father and his uncle Victor Pascall. In 1922, he was selected for the Trinidad team to take part in the intercolonial cricket tournament that year, and from this springboard, he made it into the Westindian team to tour England in 1923. Selection for the English tour gave him an indescribable boost: "To go to England to play cricket was at that time my idea of heaven on earth." (p.17)

Constantine's visit to England in 1923 was an eye-opener. He is struck by the fact that the colour bar is less noticeable in England than in the Westindies:

> At home there is little social contact between whites and blacks. A famous Westindian captain once said: "we play and worship and eat together, but of course we don't mix socially". Therein lies the greatest cause of failure in Westindian Test cricket. (p.18)

This theme of the effect of social relations on Westindian cricket, so prominent in *Cricket in the Sun*, was to become a crusade in Constantine's life. No doubt the theme may now seem to be mainly of historical interest, but it is crucial to the development of Westindian cricket. Constantine argues that the "failure" of Westindian cricket during his playing career was due to many factors including a general lack of organization. Another factor was the policy of appointing only whites as captains. In his view, this policy did not promote cohesion in the team, and, as an example, he cites their tour to Australia in 1930/31, when Westindies were defeated 1:4. Constantine argues that one reason for this crushing defeat was the appointment of a white captain - Jack Grant - who was not fully acquainted with members of his team:

> We [the team] lacked cohesion. We lacked assurance and strategy. Our batting order was not always right, and some batsmen who might have given us many victories were left out of the team until the end. The reason, as usual, was that we had not worked together enough beforehand, and the captain did not know his men. (p.49)

When Westindies, led again by Grant, were beaten by England in 1933, Constantine repeats his criticism: "Once more, however, inexperience in captaincy and incoherence as a team were sad drawbacks to us." (p.61) The spotlight is turned on perhaps the most endemic problem in Westindian cricket before 1960 - the team's lack of cohesion or staying power.

One may suspect Constantine's objectivity in dealing with this problem partly because of an implied feeling that he might have done a better job solving it than Grant. Repeated emphasis on his tactical acumen suggests that he wants us to believe he possessed what Grant lacked. His description of catching Hendren in the second innings of the fourth Test against England at Sabina Park in 1935 is a case in point: "I crept very close - I suppose about five feet from the bat - for I knew what he would do; and he did it." (p.79) It is possible that Constantine was better qualified than Grant to be captain of Westindies; and although there is no written evidence for it - except Jack Grant's own high-minded admission of his relative inexperience for the job as captain (in *Jack Grant's Story* p.31) - there is reason to believe that Constantine could have been appointed captain if he was white. Still, there is no definite evidence of vindictiveness in *Cricket in the Sun*; nor does Constantine explicitly advance his own claims to the captaincy. After the 1933 defeat by England he writes: "Grant did his best, but he did not know us [the team] well enough. How could he? He might not even have known the game well enough; but that is a personal opinion." (p.62) This tone reveals frustration, sadness, disagreement certainly, but neither bitterness nor animosity; for the aim is principled - to expose flaws in Westindian social relations which produce flaws in Westindian cricket. Constantine's exposure is aimed less at Jack Grant than against the racially based ethics of the colonial society from which they both came.

Cricket in the Sun considers the merits and demerits of coaching, and the financial problems of cricketers; it shows particular relish for the author's experience in league cricket, and provides an interesting variety of anecdotes, observations and statistics drawn from the leagues as well as from Test and county cricket. There are many colourful portraits of players, and vivid sketches of matches, incidents and conversations. Constantine's comments on the English countryside strike a similar note of conviction. It was: "as if someone planted it [the English countryside] all by hand a long, long while ago, and generations of loving gardeners had kept it so ever since." (p.19) How accurately this matches the reaction of Westindians when they first visit England! Constantine's literary achievement is to have incorporated all these anecdotes, observations, and statistics in *Cricket in the Sun*, and to have organised and analysed them with the craft and cogency of a born writer.

Clyde Walcott, *Island Cricketers*
Hodder & Stoughton, London, 1958

As its name implies, *Island Cricketers* is a general account of Westindian cricketers. Walcott was born in Barbados and first played intercolonial cricket, for Barbados against Trinidad, in 1942. He began his Test career for Westindies in 1947, and played in his last series against England in 1959/60. *Island Cricketers* provides detailed accounts, in chronological sequence, of each of the Test series with which Walcott (and/or Westindies) were involved from 1947 to 1957. Walcott's approach to his subject is disarmingly candid. In the account of his first Test series during England's tour of Westindies in 1947/48, he frankly states that the tour was a great disappointment, and that England had "seriously underestimated the strength of Westindian cricket" (p.31) by not sending their best team because: "they [the best English players] couldn't be bothered to play cricket against lowly Westindies." (p.31) He is equally blunt in explaining the Westindian Cricket Board's decision, at the start of the series, to announce different captains for each Test match. By his account, this was an ill-concealed ploy to continue the Board's traditional policy of appointing white captains; it was because they realized that public opinion favoured George Headley (black) as captain, and that appointment of a white captain might provoke widespread uproar, especially in Headley's native Jamaica, that the Board appointed Headley as captain for the Test matches in Barbados and Jamaica, and Stollmeyer (white) and Goddard (white) for Trinidad and Guyana respectively.

Walcott's account of the next Westindian series - their tour of India in 1948/ 49 - illustrates his disarming use of the objective anecdote. Like most commentators, he doubts the fairness of the Indian umpire who gave Weekes run out for 90 in the fourth Test, a decision that deprived Weekes of his sixth consecutive hundred in Tests. But Walcott claims that Indian wicket-keeper Sen had dropped Weekes at least once in each of his four preceding hundreds on the tour, which implies that his "unfair" run out in the fourth Test might constitute poetic justice. Whether he is serious or not, Walcott's claim considers the feelings of the Indians who had been bludgeoned mercilessly by Weekes in almost every innings he played against them. This is one of many anecdotes that greatly enrich *Island Cricketers* and help to make it a priceless storehouse of information. How interesting to recall, for instance, that the term 'Ws' - now universally accepted as a collective description of Weekes, Worrell and Walcott - was first coined by English journalists in April, 1950, soon after Westindies arrived in England! And which of us would remember that Hutton's 202 not out, made in England's first innings of the fourth Test at the Oval in 1950, was not as unblemished as the record books imply! Walcott claims that Hutton was caught by Christiani at leg slip soon after he came in, and that he was later very lucky to survive an lbw appeal by Valentine.

Sound reasons are given for the Westindian defeat in Australia in 1951/52: over-confidence following their enormous success in England in 1950; heavy injuries, including the author's own strained back that eventually made him give up wicket-keeping; and an ill-planned itinerary that did not allow the tourists time to settle in. It is especially interesting to learn that Goddard might not have received the full support of his vice-captain Stollmeyer because of a long-standing rivalry between the two men. This is interesting because Goddard and Stollmeyer played a central role in Westindian cricket in the late 1940s and early 1950s when their personal relations deeply influenced the fortunes of Westindies. Unless Walcott is mistaken, his claim of rivalry between the two men might help to explain why Goddard disappeared from the scene of Westindian Test cricket after 1952, when Stollmeyer became captain, then re-appeared as captain in 1957 after Stollmeyer had retired.

Walcott's candour and objectivity combine with a chatty, conversational style and anecdotal skill to produce a narrative that is richly informative, often controversial, and always lively. A good example is his account of the bottle-throwing incident in the Bourda Test of England's 1953/54 tour to the Westindies. While he admits that the incident was "decidedly nasty" (p.91), he suggests it was probably started by someone who had lost a bet. In other words, it was not an attack on the English players. If anything, it was an attack on umpire Menzies, a fellow Guyanese. But Walcott also hints that the incident might not have occurred at all had not the general atmosphere been poisoned by examples of what he calls "doubtful sportsmanship" (p.91) from some English players.

In the final Test of the same series Walcott tells the astonishing story of Hutton, the English captain, snubbing the Jamaican Chief Minister, Alexander Bustamante, who was waiting to congratulate him after his magnificent innings of 205 runs. Although Walcott sympathizes with Hutton for the *faux pas* as described in Hutton's book, *Just My Story*, he takes exception when Hutton argues that: "the gradual exclusion of white folk is a bad thing for the future of Westindian cricket." (pp. 95-96) It is significant that racial implications come up again and again in *Island Cricketers*, whereas they are almost totally absent from Stollmeyer's *Everything Under the Sun*, especially in those parts of the book which deal with the same events as *Island Cricketers*. The possibility that Walcott emphasizes these implications while Stollmeyer silences them is an example of the complexity of the socio-political kaleidoscope of Westindian cricket. This is why both books are valuable; for truth is many-sided, and lived life is only one of its sides. Even if *Island Cricketers* does not yield the whole truth, either about Walcott or about Westindian cricket in the 1950s, it accurately describes the rise and fall of Westindian fortunes between 1947 and 1957, and evokes players and the period with candour, objectivity, liveliness, and more than a dash of truth.

Frank Worrell, *Cricket Punch*
Stanley Paul, London, 1960

Cricket Punch is Worrell's account of his cricket career from when he was at Combermere School, to the 1957 Westindian tour of England. Although he began as a bowler in his native Barbados, by 1947, when he moved to Jamaica, Worrell was a star batsman, a reputation that was handsomely confirmed by his Test match deeds during England's tour of Westindies in 1947/48. After this tour, Worrell left home for a career in English league cricket. From his new home in England, he went on the 1949/50 Commonwealth tour of India which involved cricketers from all parts of the Commonwealth. Their team played four unofficial "Test" matches against India, and Worrell considers his 223 in the fourth of these "Tests", at Kanpur, as the best innings he ever played. He admits it is difficult to compare one innings with another: "mere figures tell you nothing about the strength of the opposition or the state of the wicket or the state of the game," (p.59) but he considers that two of his most famous innings, both at Trent Bridge - 261 in the third Test in 1950, and 191 in the third Test in 1957 - are inferior to his 223 at Kanpur because Trent Bridge is a "feather bed".

Cricket Punch leaves the reader with a sense of no losers and no winners: the book "simply" shows how everything happened and why it did. Worrell shows, for example, that the 4:1 thrashing that Australia dealt to Westindies in 1951/52 was not as bad as it looks: Westindies let themselves down by bad fielding. More importantly, he suggests that the hardness of Australian wickets: "nullified the spin of Ramadhin and Valentine" (p.54), and since Goddard gambled everything on the spin twins, it was no wonder he lost everything. So far as the landmark 1950 Westindian tour of England is concerned, while he does not diminish the glory of Westindian success, Worrell observes that England were in a state of post-war doldrums at the time, as reflected by the fact that they didn't have a stable team: not one of their players appeared in all four Tests of the rubber.

Worrell calls the 1954 English tour of Westindies a "colossal failure," (p.75) and suggests that Trueman was made a scapegoat for mistakes shared by many of his colleagues. He also makes Westindian humiliation - defeat by 0:3 in England in 1957 - look almost respectable. For example, in the second Test at Lord's, when Westindies were skittled out for 127 and England were 192 for six in reply, both sides were about even, except that there then followed a seventh-wicket partnership of 174 runs between Cowdrey and Evans that put the game unquestionably into English hands. This was not entirely due to fantastic English batting: there were ten dropped catches! Still, bad fielding alone does not fully explain England's smashing success of three victories, each by an innings. Most commentators attribute Westindian humiliation in 1957 to the fact that Ramadhin and Valentine failed to repeat their runaway success of 1950. By 1957, these commentators claim, English batsmen (notably May and Cowdrey) had mastered Ramadhin who no longer held any mystery for them. In Worrell's view, Ramadhin never held any mystery in 1950, and consequently no one mastered him in 1957. The "truth" was that seven years of playing league cricket had changed Ramadhin's approach from one of constantly attacking the stumps, to one of bowling defensively to his field in order to save runs, as league professionals were accustomed to do.

Cricket Punch confirms Worrell's acute insight and intelligence as a writer on cricket. At the same time, his indiscriminating adulation of English culture is noticeable, as in Chapter One where he chides English people for modesty and self-depreciation in not relishing their well deserved success over Westindies in 1957. When British prestige is let down by the poor behaviour of some English tourists on England's Westindian visit in 1954, he confesses that the loss of prestige: "hurt we [us] lovers of Britain and all that is British." (p.88) Then, on the last page of *Cricket Punch* he recalls his ten happy years in English league cricket, and argues that because: "England has been kind to me," (p.137) he cannot agree with those who: "are sharply critical of the Mother country or her people." (p.137) To all this one must add Worrell's explanation of the bottle throwing incident at Bourda in 1954. By his account, the incident was caused by spectators innocently lobbing mineral water bottles just over the boundary line as part of a "local custom," but the custom was misunderstood by an English player who threw a bottle back at the crowd and provoked retaliation.

To ignore the crowd's sense of provocation, however misguided or ill-judged, and the tense political situation caused by suspension of the country's constitution, the previous year, creates an unmistakable impression of strong anglophile sentiment inducing defensiveness in Worrell. Similar defensiveness is found in Walcott's *Island Cricketers* when the author attributes the Bourda bottle throwing to the probable loss of a bet by someone in the crowd. Nor are Worrell and Walcott unique in this respect. Ambivalent loyalty to British culture and Westindian nationalism was shared by most Westindians of their generation, including political leaders, intellectuals, writers, and cricketers, although it did not induce defensive attitudes in every case. Worrell's attitudes towards Britain are complemented by an equally "rosy" attitude toward his homeland as expressed in his chapter "Life in the Westindies" where he paints a glowing portrait of multi-racial harmony in the Westindies:

> Nobody cares two hoots about a man's colour, and there is no obvious colour bar to advancement in any trade or profession ... It is not easy for a Westindian to write about 'the colour problem' because there is ostensibly no such thing on our islands. (p.73)

These are unusual statements from a man who was himself perhaps the most celebrated victim of an alleged "whites only" policy of captaincy practised by the West Indian Cricket Board of Control between 1928 and 1957. Worrell is evidently a less reliable commentator on society than on cricket in the Westindies. On cricket he is acute, profound, magisterial, as we can see especially in his chapters on the Westindian tour to England in 1950, and Australia in 1951/52. In his chapter "The Three Ws" he also gives portraits of Walcott and Weekes that are incomparable for their insight and selfless admiration. Such chapters prove that Worrell's cricket commentary is flawless and confirms *Cricket Punch* as one of the most illuminating commentaries that we have of Westindian cricket during the 1950s.

Christopher Nicole, *West Indian Cricket*
The Sportman's Club, London, 1960

Christopher Nicole is a white Guyanese and a prolific novelist who, under his own name and the pen name of Peter Grange, has produced more than a dozen novels, not a few of which are romantic pot boilers advertised as containing "scandalous secrets" (*Lord of Sin*), or "fiery forbidden pleasures" and "reckless sexuality" (*Sunset*). It need hardly be said that such descriptions do not apply, even remotely, to *West Indian Cricket*, which is a work of exquisite scholarship inspired by the purest, most unworldly devotion to cricket. Pot boilers notwithstanding, Nicole's experience as a professional writer, enables him to bring enviable skills of organisation, description and expression to his cricket book, which opens with the earliest occurrence of a first class match in the Westindies (1882), and systematically discusses each subsequent development of the game in strict, chronological sequence, until the end of the Westindian tour of New Zealand in 1956. This chronological, historical approach is something *West Indian Cricket* shares with a good many other books of its kind: where it differs is that it also includes a systematic survey of regional or intercolonial matches as well as Test matches, and so gives a fuller portrait of pre-1956 Westindian cricket than almost any other book on the subject.

The opening chapters of *West Indian Cricket* give a rare portrait both of early contests between the major cricketing territories in the region and of pre-Test encounters between English and Westindian teams. The first Triangular (Trinidad,

Guyana, Barbados) intercolonial tournament occurred in 1891, and the first visit by an English team (captained by Slade Lucas) took place in 1895. Two other English teams toured in 1896, and Sir Pelham Warner who was a member of one of these teams, wrote an article in the 1898 *Wisden* praising Westindian bowling and fielding, and lending support to the idea of a Westindian tour of England which had been in the air for some time. This support was something of a breakthrough, and in 1900 a Westindian cricket team toured England for the first time. On this historic tour, the team played seventeen matches, some against first class counties, although, in no case, did they meet English teams that were at full strength. At any rate, the Westindians won five matches and lost eight. When another Westindian team toured England for the second time six years later, the results were similar: seven games won, and ten lost out of a total of nineteen.

After 1906, there were visits by two M.C.C. teams to the Westindies before Westindians ventured on a third tour of England in 1923. This time, their results were quite different: out of twenty six matches, they won twelve, lost seven and drew seven. Their batting star was George Challenor who accumulated an aggregate of 1556 runs (average 51.86), and came third, behind " Patsy" Hendren and Phil Mead, in the English averages of the season. This was impressive indeed, and the team as a whole made such a good impression that, after they encountered visiting English teams at home in 1926 and 1927, they acquired Test status in 1928. But their performance in their first Test series, in England, in 1928, did not live up to their promise of 1923. Not only did they lose all three Tests, each by an innings; they recorded twelve losses and five wins out of thirty first class matches. For all that, England visited Westindies for another Test series in 1929/30, when the home team succeeded in drawing the four-match series by winning one Test and losing another. This astonishing Westindian success owed much to the appearance of George Headley who scored 703 runs in four Tests (average 87.87).

Throughout his book Nicole relies on objective analysis and succinct, lucid exposition, combined with rigorous and diligent research. Besides giving records, results, commentary and analysis, his accounts reveal little known facts and sharp insights, for example, that Headley was named by *Wisden* as "cricketer of the year" in 1933, and Constantine in 1939; and that the intercolonial series of 1942 produced a stunning result when Barbados were dismissed on a "Kensington gluepot" (p.131) for 16 runs, and Derek Sealy inveigled eight wickets for 8 runs. As the author concludes:

> This [result] was quite the most remarkable occurrence in Westindian cricket history, and Trinidad's score is by a long way the lowest recorded in Westindian big cricket. (p.131)

Nicole does his best to explain the Westindian failure in Australia in 1951/52, by arguing that Rae was intimidated, Stollmeyer and Weekes out of form, and Walcott injured "just as he was running into form," (p.171) Above all, he writes with rare sympathy of Goddard:

for some unexplained reason this splendid cricketer's captaincy suffered a marked decline almost parallel to the experience of Percy Chapman in 1930. (p.171)

Towards the end of *West Indian Cricket*, Nicole includes two chapters of "Comparisons" which consider the relative merits of Westindian batsmen and fieldsmen. Not surprisingly, Headley comes at the top of the author's list of batsmen, and Constantine or "Electric Heels" (p.218) as he was nicknamed, at the top of the most outstanding fieldsmen. Nicole's description of Constantine is incomparable:

> We have seen many great and active fieldsmen, and many men whose hands seemed coated with glue, but we have never seen a man at once so agile, whose anticipation over large distances was so remarkable, whose throw was so deadly, and whose hands were so sticky. (p.218)

Surprisingly, Nicole's praise of the Grant brothers as fieldsmen is almost as fulsome:

> "They [the Grants] were afraid of nothing, would stand as close as possible, and could hold on to the hottest hit." (p.218)

West Indian Cricket also contains two Appendices. Appendix B is more run of the mill: it is short (just over one page) and furnishes a list of important dates in the history of Westindian cricket. Appendix A, on the other hand, is twenty-three pages long, and like *Wisden*, serves up a rich pot-pourri of records, results, lists and statistics. There is, for instance, a summary of the results of all Westindian Test matches between 1928 and 1956; and a list of all cricketers who represented Westindies during the same period, including mention of the series in which they appeared. There are statistics of "Highest Totals," "Lowest Totals," a list of Westindian Test centurions, first class career statistics for all Westindians, and much else.

Ernest Eytle, *Frank Worrell*
The Sportsmans Book Club, London, 1965

Strange as it may seem, Ernest Eytle's *Frank Worrell* is the first and only full-length biography of the greatest of all Westindian cricket captains. In discussing Worrell's development as batsman, bowler and leader, Eytle takes his cue from the brief foreword to his book in which Sir Learie Constantine describes Worrell as a: "great cricketer and a great man." In the spirit of this remark, Eytle's aim is to celebrate Worrell. No wonder that the opening chapter of his book is entitled "Australia's Tribute to a Great Captain" for the chapter shows Worrell in all his glory on the occasion of his greatest triumph: his moral victory against Australia in 1961 when an estimated half a million people thronged the streets of Melbourne and snarled the city's traffic in order to bid affectionate farewell to Worrell and his men at the end of their series of five Test matches. That Worrell should be the object of such spontaneous outpouring of public gratitude in Australia when his very leadership had been subject to doubt and controversy in his homeland merely months before, is a telling commentary on the history and administration of Westindian cricket! But Eytle has no time to indict Westindian cricket administration; he simply makes the case that Worrell was: "the main cementing agent of the successful teamwork of his side." (p.182)

The early chapters of *Frank Worrell* describe Worrell's beginnings in Barbados, then Jamaica until his Test début in the home series against England in 1947/48. Worrell emerged from this series not simply as the best Westindian batsman, but as the purveyor of a batting style distinguished by grace, elegance and a glow of high culture. Today, his grand exploits in leadership tend to obscure the fact that he is also one of the greatest and probably the most graceful of all Westindian batsmen. His batting average in his first Test series was 147; and his 261 against England at Trent Bridge in 1950 was the highest Test score of the series. Although Eytle focuses mainly on Worrell's performance as captain, he does well not to neglect other aspects of his career. He provides brief summaries of all Test series in which Worrell took part during the 1950s, and gives detailed comments on the most notorious Westindian defeats - against Australia in 1951/52 and 1955, and England in 1957. He notes, for instance, that Worrell's use as new ball bowler in Australia in 1951/52 probably impaired his batting, and since he was the best Westindian batsman, this impairment seriously damaged the entire team effort.

Guyanese by birth, and a barrister by profession, Eytle knows Westindian culture from the inside, and writes about it with authority. Here, for example, are his comments on the effect of beach cricket on the peculiar style of Westindian cricketers:

> "These novel forms of cricket [such as beach cricket] sharpen the eye in a way no professional coaching can. What they lack in orthodoxy is compensated for by a passion for hitting the ball hard, getting it away from the fielders, and above all, getting on with the game." (p.19)

Is this the source of that fabled zest and verve for which Westindian cricketers are almost universally envied? If not, it is a plausible explanation, lucidly expressed, with knowing sympathy. Nor is there any vehemence or ugliness in Eytle's writing. Notice his poise when Sobers's confident appeal for a catch off Mackay is disallowed in the fourth Test against Australia in 1961. He reports the incident without protest, although the umpire's decision enabled Mackay and Kline to achieve a draw which Eytle magnanimously describes as "richly deserved." (p.171) Eytle includes commentaries by Worrell himself at the end of each chapter of his book. This is a stroke of inspiration; for these commentaries are pure gold. By their succinctness they convey more wisdom than is found in much longer works. Who else would have the authority to claim that card playing was the cause of poor performances by Westindian cricketers in the 1950s? So convinced is Worrell by this claim that when he became captain in 1960 he banned card playing by the team. The result, according to him, was entirely positive: "I attribute our impressive fielding in Australia to the enforcement of the card playing rule." (p.33) Worrell gives informed reasons for Westindian failures in the 1950s. One of the chief reasons is serious factionalism within the team during most of the decade. On the other hand, he attributes the team's success in Australia in 1960/61 to: "no suggestions of factions and no show of insularity." (p.152) No doubt these comments might appear old hat today. Not so. For factionalism and insularity are ever present dangers in a region as marked by racial and cultural diversity and a history of colonial divisiveness as the Westindies. They were almost certainly present, for instance, in helping to exclude Indo-Caribbean players from the Westindian team throughout most of the 1980s and early 90s. This is why current Westindian players and administrators have much to gain from *Frank Worrell*.

Roy Gilchrist, *Hit me for Six*
Stanley Paul, London, 1963

Hit me For Six gives the author's side of a story that explains why he was sent home from the Westindian tour of India and Pakistan in 1958/59 when Gerry Alexander, also a Jamaican, was the Westindian captain. Gilchrist was black and of working class, rural, plantation origin, whereas Alexander was a brown, Cambridge-educated veterinary surgeon of urban, upper middle class origin. While the respective social origins of these two men may not completely explain the implied conflict between them - the possibility of personal antagonism cannot be ignored - Gilchrist's story does reveal an interaction between social class and cricket in the Westindies in the first half of this century; it also hints at the difficulty faced by socially less privileged cricketers of this period, not only Gilchrist, but Ramadhin, Kanhai, and many others.

The story begins in the rural parish of St. Thomas in Jamaica where Gilchrist lived and where, in true, story book fashion, he was spotted by Mr. William Stewart, "a [Jamaican white] fairy godfather" (p.11) who helped him to get a job and settle in Kingston, the capital city, where he could develop his talent in cricket. (Stewart was a brown-skinned man, like Alexander, and like him belonged to an upper middle class social bracket that defined them both as "Jamaican white.") Gilchrist's talent quickly got him in the Jamaica side, and in the 1956 Quadrangular Tournament involving Jamaica, Barbados, Trinidad, and Guyana. Then, just as quickly, his performances in these matches got him a place as a fast bowler in the Westindian team that was picked to tour England in 1957. He appeared in four Tests in England in 1957. In the second Test at Lord's, when Trevor Bailey took seven wickets for 44 runs in the Westindian first innings, Gilchrist took four wickets in England's only innings for 115 runs. His comments on this performance are revealing: "If I had had Bailey's cricketing sense then those four wickets of mine might have been eight." (p.27) These appear to be the words of a man who is willing to learn, and they suggest, even faintly, that later events might have turned out differently if they were handled differently. Gilchrist realizes that he was not using English conditions well: his deliveries were seaming behind the wicket, turning his speed, which was superior to Bailey's, into a hindrance rather than a help.

Gilchrist has nothing but praise for John Goddard, the Westindian captain in 1957. Goddard was white and upper class, although it may have been significant that he was Barbadian. Gilchrist's bitter reference later on to the "Jamaican bosses" of cricket tend to strengthen this significance. At any rate, there were no complaints during the 1957/58 Pakistan tour of Westindies when Gilchrist played in all five Tests with Alexander as captain. The trouble erupted in India and the account of it given here is based only on *Hit me for Six*, that is to say, on Gilchrist's side of the story, not Alexander's. In the first Test against India, at Bombay, in 1958, Gilchrist frankly admits: "I sprinkled a lot of bouncers in my bowling and a beamer or two for good luck." (p.49) A beamer is a fast, high full toss aimed at the batsman's head; it constitutes "unfair play" according to Rule 42 of the Laws of cricket. Whether Gilchrist knew the Laws of cricket or not, his aggressive or combative approach to bowling is evident from his own words. His bowling in the Bombay Test which was drawn raised concerns, and after the match, Alexander told all three of his fast bowlers - Wes Hall, Jaswick Taylor and Gilchrist - that they must cut beamers out because they were dangerous.

The next incident involving Gilchrist occurred during fielding practice: Gilchrist hit Butcher on the knee, as he claims, accidentally. When Butcher remonstrated with him, he walked off. He was ordered back by Alexander and ignored the order by going into the pavilion instead. As a disciplinary gesture, the Westindian selection committee omitted Gilchrist from the second Test. The Butcher incident was followed by another in which Alexander reprimanded Gilchrist for making too much noise in the pavilion. Gilchrist describes his reactions as follows: "I did not want any more trouble, so I just dried up inside and let things ride. But deep down I was wild. Alexander, I felt, had treated me like a schoolma'am treats a first-term boy." (p.66) Despite deteriorating relations between Gilchrist and Alexander, Gilchrist played in the remaining three Tests against India, taking 26 wickets altogether and helping Westindies to win the series 3:0, with 2 matches drawn.

In the last match of the tour against North Zone at Amritsar, Gilchrist was upset by the North Zone captain Swaranjit Singh who hit him for a four and walked down the pitch to taunt him. He let Singh have a beamer, then a fast ball which Singh snicked and Alexander, as wicket-keeper, dropped. Gilchrist makes much of the fact that Singh was a friend of Alexander's at Cambridge. Anyhow Gilchrist admits to being "fighting mad" and let go two more beamers at Singh. At the end of the session, Alexander told Gilchrist he could no longer play in the match. Then the Westindian selection committee comprising John Holt, Sonny Ramadhin, Berkeley Gaskin (manager) and Alexander decided that Gilchrist should be sent home, although the Pakistan leg of the tour was still to come. Gilchrist played league cricket afterwards in England where he ran into more trouble with cricket authority, and was banned by the North Staffordshire League. This put paid to any chance he might have had of being selected for Westindies again.

In the end, Gilchrist appears contrite: "I lost my temper. I broke the 'rules' when I bowled beamers. I take the blame." (p.60) But he also admits to being "a fighting fast bowler." (p.98) In other words, conflict was inevitable between him and Alexander, and the seeds of conflict were planted in their national soil where they germinated in a hothouse of symbiotic reaction between race/colour and the hierarchical social values of the Westindian plantation. For this reason, neither Gilchrist nor Alexander is fully responsible for what happened. Each was true to his historic role, and their respective roles were set on a collision course long before either of them was born.

R. Kanhai, *Blasting for Runs*
Souvenir Press, London, 1966

Blasting for Runs covers the author's career from his earliest days in first class cricket, in the mid 1950s, to the Australian tour of Westindies in 1965. Kanhai takes pride in the fact that he was born in Port Mourant, a Guyanese sugar plantation that produced four other Test cricketers - John Trim, Ivan Madray, Joe Solomon, and Basil Butcher. Like Ramadhin in Trinidad, Gilchrist in Jamaica, and several other Westindian cricketers, Kanhai's entry into first class cricket was not helped by his social origins. At the time, few cricketers from the plantations or rural districts of Guyana had a chance to appear in Georgetown, the capital city where first class cricket was played. Kanhai expresses his situation well: "I had never seen a first-class match before let alone played in one. Names like Walcott and Pairaudeau belonged to the newspapers and radio, not real everyday life on the sugar plantation." (p.20) Through sheer luck, he got his chance to play in a first-class match when "Cobra" Ramdat, a left arm spinner, who was selected for a match in Georgetown was injured: Kanhai was chosen to replace him. In the match Kanhai served as wicket-keeper/batsman, and although he made 0, he took five catches, which led to his selection for further trial matches, until he was picked for Guyana against Barbados in February 1955. Later the same year, he represented Guyana against the visiting Australians and made a plucky 51. By 1956 his place in the Guyanese side was more or less assured, and during the Quadrangular Tournament between Barbados, Trinidad, Jamaica and Guyana, he scored three centuries including 195 run out against Jamaica. These were the performances that earned him a place in the Westindies team to tour England in 1957.

It is interesting to learn from *Blasting for Runs* that Kanhai was picked as wicket-keeper/batsman for the first Test against England at Edgbaston in 1957 mainly because Gerry Alexander, the specialist wicket-keeper, could not pick up Ramadhin behind the stumps. There is also much information of more general interest, for example, when Kanhai claims: "Pakistan, like India, are relatively easy meat for any reasonable side when they are on tour - but in their own backyard it's easier to get blood out of a stone than win." (p.39) He is unlikely to make such claims today, but he may have had a point more than thirty years ago.

It is particularly interesting to hear Kanhai's own version of the incident during the third Test of England's Westindian tour in 1960, when the English captain Peter May denied him the use of a runner after he developed cramp in his left leg. It was on the final day of the match at Sabina Park, when Westindies were chasing a target of 230 to win. With five wickets intact and only 80 runs needed in 90 minutes, Kanhai was batting with his captain Gerry Alexander, and both were intent on a Westindian victory. This is when a runner was requested for Kanhai and May refused. A short while later, because he could not move quickly enough to the pitch of a ball from Trueman, Kanhai was bowled for 57, and the match dwindled into a draw. May's apparently unsportsmanlike action has to be seen in the perspective of the five-match series, in which England had won the second Test after the first was drawn. From there on, according to Kanhai, England adopted a "no lose" or defensive strategy that brought them ultimate victory by 1:0 and four drawn matches. At any rate, after the match, when May discovered that his objection to a runner was not authorised by the rules, he apologised to Alexander. In his defence, as Kanhai admits, May was ill and later had to return to England for medical attention, leaving his vice- captain Cowdrey to complete the tour.

On the 1960/61 tour of Australia, Kanhai achieved a record aggregate of 1093 runs, and won the R.K. Nunes trophy for "the outstanding Westindian of the tour." (p.70) The general success of this tour is well known since it included the extraordinary tied Test at Brisbane, and the final motorcade in the streets of Melbourne to wish farewell to the Westindian tourists. But there were disagreements as in the fourth Test when umpire Egar refused to give Mackay out to a catch by Sobers which Sobers and all the Westindians thought was genuine. Kanhai is in no doubt about the catch: "Now this was never a bump ball and everyone knew it except Egar and Mackay." (p.75) At the same time, Kanhai admits that Egar and Mackay may have acted sincerely although they were wrong.

Kanhai's positive appraisal of his colleagues, not only of Sobers, Hunte, Gibbs and Butcher, but more controversial ones such as Griffith (who was suspected of throwing) and Gilchrist (who was sent home from India because of indiscipline) implies an admirable sense of loyalty and solidarity. But one can't help noticing too the popular, colloquial English working class idiom in *Blasting for Runs*. This no doubt comes from the influence of John Gibson who collaborated with Kanhai in writing the book. Expressions such as: "mighty proud; fair old; right old; fair old slog; I ask you;" are alien to Westindian ears. Yet *Blasting for Runs* remains a most valuable addition to Westindian cricket literature for two main reasons: it illustrates the interaction of race, class and cricket in the Westindies; and it captures a flavour of excitement that correctly matches the invigorating style of one of the bravest, most forceful and adventurous of all Westindian batsmen.

Tony Cozier, *The West Indies: Fifty Years of Test Cricket*
Angus & Robertson, Brighton, 1978.

Fifty Years is one of several books by Cozier. It is a commentary on the first fifty years of Westindian Test cricket from 1928 to 1978, and it succeeds in giving: "a Westindian interpretation on our 50 years in Test cricket", as Sir Garfield Sobers suggests in his Foreword. The volume is divided into five major sections each concerned with one of the five nations against which Westindies regularly played: England; Australia; New Zealand; India; Pakistan. These five sections are further divided into numerous sub-sections, each of which considers one rubber of usually four or five Test matches between Westindies and a single country. This has the advantage of observing Westindian performance continuously against one particular country, without interruption from accounts of intervening matches played against other countries. As a rule, the four or five Tests in each sub-section are described in two or three pages which, in the hands of a lesser writer, would probably consist only of sketchy details about scores, results or statistics. Yet it is marvellous how Cozier is able to present such details along with commentaries of astonishing fullness and fluency. His opening piece in the sub-section on the Westindian tour of England in 1963 reads as follows:

> The magnificent series in Australia in 1960-61 had elevated the prestige of Westindian cricket to new heights and the sweeping victory in all five Tests over India in the Caribbean in 1962 was proof that a great side was in the making. Worrell's leadership had been the major factor in moulding the team into a happy and effective unit and his success, after the concerted campaign on behalf of him being appointed in the first place, must have given him immense satisfaction. (p.40)

Such leisured writing belies constraints of space, and what we get in each sub-section is not only scores, statistics and details, but commentary and analysis, highlights of individual performances, brief biographies of outstanding players, comparisons with other matches, and a variety of information on history and politics. Only writing of superb economy could include so much information in so little space.

Apart from his economical writing, Cozier reveals objectivity and tact in dealing with issues that may be considered controversial, contentious or delicate. Such an issue was the appointment of the white Barbadian, Denis Atkinson, as Westindian cricket captain in 1955, when many people believed that Frank Worrell, a more deserving candidate, was passed over because he was black. The issue provoked vociferous and widespread public protest, and Cozier writes:

> Public meetings were held, resolutions passed, cables despatched. This
> was a time of political and social transition in the Caribbean and the
> furore was part and parcel of that transition. Yet it did nothing for the
> unity of the Westindies cricket team nor, it might be added, the West
> Indies as a whole. (p.92)

The explosiveness of the issue is effectively defused by an acknowledgement,
even if a somewhat grudging one, of the righteousness of Westindian nationalism.
As a white Barbadian himself, Cozier is tactful enough to go on to show judicious
sympathy for Atkinson without explicitly saying whether his appointment was
or was not justified.

Similar tact is shown when Cozier discusses the captaincy of John Goddard,
another white Barbadian, in Australia, in 1951/52. His criticism of Goddard's
alleged over-use of his spin bowlers, Ramadhin and Valentine, is couched in
language worthy of a diplomat: "Perhaps if Goddard had put less faith in his
spinners and more in his fast and medium-pace bowlers his returns might have
been richer." (p.86) This is a mark of the professionalism that may allow an
author to be accurate or candid without causing ill-feeling. Another example is
when Cozier implies that Sobers's record 365 was made against a weakened
Pakistan bowling attack in 1958. He lists the injuries to three of Pakistan's
main bowlers - Mahmood Hussain, Nasim-ul-Ghani and Abdul Hafeez Kardar,
and concludes: "the team was down to two fit bowlers - Fazal and Khan
Mohammad. So Sobers had things pretty much his own way, a fact which he
undoubtedly appreciated." (p.191) Although what he says is true, without his
touch of professional expertise, he might have appeared to disparage one of the
most famous exploits of a legendary Westindian cricketer.

Cozier's Introduction illustrates his economical writing best by giving a five-
page survey of Westindian cricket. Here is a typical comment: "It [Westindian
cricket] is the one Westindian endeavour which has endured without fragmentation
although, because of its very nature, it had to overcome its share of trials and
tribulations." (p.xiii) One would be hard put to find a more crisp or succinct
description of the role of cricket in the Westindies. As for the levelling influence of
cricket on historic divisions in Westindian society, Cozier writes:

> Nor does the addiction to the game know any class divisions. The rich
> and the poor, the employer and the worker, the tinker, the tailor, the
> candle-stick-maker, all follow Westindian fortunes on the field and off it
> with equal keenness.

It is surprising that he leaves out race and colour which go hand in hand with
class; nor was the levelling process quite as immediate or automatic as he implies;
but in the end, after a long struggle, cricket did help to level out historic social
divisions. Ironically, it is on the troubled subject of captaincy that Cozier finally
confirms his profound understanding of Westindian cricket:

> As significant as anything else was the administration's [Westindian

Cricket Board of Control] reluctance to appoint a black Westindian to the captaincy. It was historically understandable at a time when it was generally considered by the ruling classes that the black man was not ready for leadership, political, social, sporting or otherwise. Yet it generally meant that several fitting candidates for the position were eliminated and this could have done nothing for team spirit. (p.xi)

This hits the nail on the head. It is forthright and accurate, and expressed with the magisterial tact, succinct compression and brevity that make *Fifty Years* probably the handiest, most condensed history of Westindian Test cricket yet available.

Jack Grant, *Jack Grant's Story*
Lutterworth Press, Guildford and London, 1980

For someone who was not only Westindian cricket captain (v. Australia, 1930/31; vs. England, 1933; vs. England 1934/35), but the first such captain of stature, Jack (G.C.) Grant puts remarkably little about cricket into his autobiography: *Jack Grant's Story*. Cricket appears in two or three of the book's eighteen chapters, and is properly the subject only in Chapter 15. That cricket played a secondary role in Grant's life is confirmed by the fact that he retired from the international game at the end of England's 1934/35 tour of Westindies when he was twenty-eight years old and at the peak of his playing career. Not that he entirely stopped playing cricket afterwards; but never again at Test match level. As his motive for retirement, he writes: "to me cricket was a game, not my life... I was seeing that cricket was becoming the right hand that offended and that I would have to cut it off." (p.51) Grant's compulsive calling to become a missionary and teacher overpowered his love of cricket. Nor were there any regrets. Shortly before his death in 1978, he describes his decision to give up Test cricket as one: "which I have always been glad that I made." (p.52) Unlike David Sheppard, for instance, Grant could not combine his religious vocation with a career in Test cricket: the times and society in which he lived made such a combination impossible. This is why *Jack Grant's Story* is at least as interesting for what it says about the author's times and society, as for what it says about the author.

Strangely enough, the story begins in Canada which Grant's paternal grandfather Kenneth Grant left as a Presbyterian minister, in 1870, to work among indentured Indians in Trinidad. In 1907, the year of Jack's birth, Grant and his wife returned to Canada, but their son Thomas Geddes Grant remained behind and brought up a family of ten children of whom Jack is the second to last, while the last is Rolph who succeeded Jack as Westindian captain in 1939. As a successful businessman Thomas Geddes Grant provided his family with social and economic advantages enjoyed by most white Westindians up to the middle decades of this century. Grant's description of Queen's Royal College (Q.R.C.) the government, boy's secondary school (like Queen's College in Guyana) that he attended, hints at some of the advantages to be enjoyed in a society dominated by linked values of race, colour and class:

> In 1917 Q.R.C. had an enrolment of about 260 students. They came from all walks of life and from all races - black, white, coloured, Indian, and Chinese. But as it was in the main a fee-paying school the majority of its students came from the better-off homes. Race- as later I experienced it in other lands - was not a major or ever-pressing issue. Without effort we accepted each other and took it for granted that we were fellow students. As a colloquial saying put it, 'All a we is one.' As far as I am aware, this was the prevailing attitude of members of staff. But possibly I speak from a privileged position, as in those days a white skin was privileged. (pp.7-8)

The candour and self-examination of this passage are exceptional; for seldom are members of privileged groups moved to admit even the possibility of their privilege. At the same time, Grant distinguishes white Westindian privilege from the same phenomenon in Africa where he spent much of his later life. The difference is that race and colour were never institutionalised in the Westindies as they were in southern Africa. If identical race, colour and class distinctions prevailed in both places, they were more flexible in the Westindies where they could sometimes be transcended by exceptional talent or luck.

After Q.R.C. Grant attended Christ's College, Cambridge university, from 1926 to 1930. His entry was facilitated by the master of Christ's College, Sir Arthur Shipley, who was visiting Trinidad at the time. While there is not the least hint of impropriety in Grant's indirect social contact with Sir Arthur, it was nevertheless a privilege unavailable to most Trinidadians. When Stollmeyer, another white Trinidadian like Grant, was selected for the Westindian tour of England in 1939, and his time of departure conflicted with exams at the Imperial College of Tropical Agriculture where he was a student, the college set a separate exam for him alone, outside of its regular schedule, to enable Stollmeyer to go on the tour. Here again, it is unlikely that the college would have offered the same facility to a Trinidadian who lacked Stollmeyer's social contacts or, in other words, who was not white.

At Cambridge, Grant gained a blue in both soccer and cricket. His batting average in 1929 was 44.75, and in 1930 it was 34,57. On this basis, he was requested to lead Westindies against Australia in 1930/31. It was an extraordinary request to make of a young man of twenty three who had never been captain in a first class cricket match. Yet again, it is unlikely that this request would have been made by the West Indian Cricket Board of Control to a Westindian unlike Grant in race or colour or class. Grant himself comments on this when he is later accused of treating one of his black players as a "black boy":

> I affirm that I was aware that I was a white man. Unmistakably, therefore, I was colour conscious. Also I was aware that in the prevailing circumstances of the day I, as a white man, had advantages which a black man was unable to have. Take the captaincy of the team. I was younger than all of the sixteen players, save three; and most of these

> sixteen had already played for the Westindies, while I had not. Yet I was
> the captain. It could not be disputed that my white colour was a major
> factor in my being given this post. Also, consciously or unconsciously,
> I was heir to certain assumptions on race that were sociological rather
> than theological, and passing rather than permanent. (p.31)

This passage constitutes an illuminating commentary on Westindian social history. It does not blame anyone; it faces facts, acknowledges reality, and seeks to understand. Above all, it has the triumphant ring of truth.

But the plain fact is that *Jack Grant's Story* is less about cricket than about the author's career as a missionary and teacher. It is also a great love story, for at Cambridge, Grant met Ida Russell from Rhodesia (today Zimbabwe) and they became partners for life: in Grenada in the 1930s, Zanzibar in the 1940s, South Africa in the 1950s and Rhodesia in the 1960s. With Ida at his side, Grant demonstrated principled and unbending opposition to apartheid and white minority rule in southern Africa. His book has a "Foreword" by Alan Paton and "Epilogue" by Garfield Todd, both well known for similar opposition based on Christian conviction. Such opposition had its limitations: for it would never have changed apartheid without the imposition of economic sanctions on South Africa by western nations. After all, South African apologists of apartheid had been exposed, since 1948, to Alan Paton's splendid novel *Cry The Beloved Country* and its beautiful, timeless message of Christian loving-kindness; but it left them utterly unmoved. At the same time, the spiritual solidarity of men like Grant, Paton and Todd helped to sustain hope in hundreds of thousands of victims of apartheid during their long, frustrating and despairing years of racial oppression.

So far as cricket is concerned, Grant is best remembered for two distinguished achievements: leading Westindies to their first Test victory on foreign soil - in the fifth Test against Australia at Sydney in 1931; and leading Westindies to their first victory rubber - 2:1 against England in 1934/35. But his greatest distinction was in the realm of spiritual activity, not cricket. Sixteen years before he died he divided his inherited wealth into four equal parts, and gave one part each to his wife, son, daughter, and Mission Board; and when it came to the subject of sport and politics on which the best of his cricketing contemporaries were given to endless temporising, vacillation, and entanglement in an unsightly web of egregious cant and hypocrisy, he was as straight as an arrow: "Sad it is that politics should disrupt relationships. But sadder still if we set more store on cricket than on politics which is basically concerned with human relations and justice." (p.180) Let no one doubt why Jack Grant did not combine cricket with his religious vocation like David Sheppard: he realized that for most people in the third world societies in which he lived, the division between sport and politics was too sharp, too urgent, and too much a matter of life and death. Other people, including some cricketers, realized this too; but with the possible exception of C.T. Studd who also rejected cricket for missionary work, it is doubtful whether this realization led any other cricketer - white or black - to a life of equally self-less service as Jack Copeland Grant.

Jeff Stollmeyer, *Everything Under the Sun*
Stanley Paul, London, 1983

As its subtitle 'My Life in Westindies Cricket' suggests, *Everything Under the Sun* is mainly about its author's involvement in Westindian cricket from the 1940s to the 1970s. The book carries a superb foreword by E.W. Swanton. Of German stock on his father's side, and English on his mother's, Jeffrey Stollmeyer was born in 1921 after his father had established himself as a cocoa planter in the Santa Cruz Valley district of Trinidad. This means that in Westindian terms, Stollmeyer's social origins were in the so-called plantocracy or landowning, white, privileged upper class. *Everything* sketches this family history together with Jeffrey's schooling at Queen's Royal College, participation in football and cricket, interest in horse racing; and after school, a career in agriculture, in pursuit of which Stollmeyer attended the Imperial College of Tropical Agriculture between 1938 and 1941. Years later he retired from agriculture and moved to business. He also served as a senator in the Parliament of Trinidad and Tobago from 1966 to 1971.

Everything follows a clear and coherent structure that describes chronological stages in the development of Westindian cricket beginning with the 1939 Westindian tour of England, the English series against Westindies in 1947/48, and the Westindian tour of India in 1948/49. Stollmeyer's comments on these and later events carry a special authority that derives from first hand knowledge of the events themselves and from intimate relationships with the cricketers involved. He comments not only on famous names such as the Ws, Ramadhin and Valentine, Constantine and Headley (Stollmeyer's choice as the greatest Westindian batsman), but on forgotten figures such as Cyril Merry "the best batsman in Trinidad" (p. 34) during the 1930s, Rupert Tang Choon the brilliant Chinese-Trinidadian batsman, and S.M. Ali an Indo-Trinidadian spinner, as promising as Ramadhin, but whose career was cut short because of his controversial action.

In addition to such biographical sketches, *Everything* provides interesting analysis of familiar issues in Westindian cricket. Seldom before has anyone explained why the Westindies tour of England in 1950 was such a landmark event. Stollmeyer makes it clear that before 1950, England had not taken Westindies seriously as a cricketing force. This is partly why, in 1947/48, their team to the Westindies did not include some of their best players - Hutton (who went out later), Compton, Edrich, Bailey, Bedser: these players were being reserved for the real enemy - Australia. At the start of the 1950 tour, Stollmeyer reports that there was little press coverage of the Westindian team, "and what there was concerned the amount of rum we had brought with us." (pp.76-77) But the Ws and Ram and Val wrought such ravage on English soil in 1950, that never again did England dare to treat Westindies with condescension. History was made. Westindies came of age. And when England visited Westindies again in

1953/54, they sent not only Hutton, Compton and Bailey, but the pride of their youth - May, Graveney, Trueman and Statham.

Stollmeyer gives a plausible explanation of the Westindian defeat in Australia in 1951/52: it was not simply captain Goddard's overuse of Ramadhin and Valentine: it was his apparently deep-seated and nonchalant disregard for tactical forethought and strategic planning. Stollmeyer states that, by his own admission, Goddard "never read a cricket book." (p.68) For a man who served as captain of Westindies on three overseas tours - to England in 1950, and 1957, and Australia in 1951/52 - (Goddard was also player/manager against New Zealand in 1955/56), this admission is remarkable to say the least. At the same time, Goddard's strained relations with Stollmeyer as reported in autobiographies by Clyde Walcott and Roy Marshall, probably suggest that we should look askance at Stollmeyer's comments on Goddard.

Stollmeyer's account of the three series in which he served as captain, against India in 1952/53, England in 1953/54, and Australia in 1955, is especially interesting for its comprehensive evocation of the atmosphere of Westindian cricket in the first half of the 1950s. His account blends knowledge of cricket with shrewdness, discretion, and tact, and is presented in a style whose clarity, poise and grace vividly recall the author's classic leg glide. *Everything* also appears to exhibit a lofty, patrician disdain for tawdry feeling or intemperate expression. For example, in his treatment of England's 1953/54 tour, when Hutton's men had a less than happy time off the field, and when there were rumours of racial comments and incidents, Stollmeyer is the soul of discretion, and simply says that Hutton had apparently asked his men "not to mix with their Westindian counterparts." (p.143) Goddard's failings mentioned above are not accompanied by any explicit indictment or condemnation. Similarly, when Denis Atkinson, instead of Worrell, was selected as Westindian vice captain in 1955, Stollmeyer calls the decision "preposterous" but blames no one. Even if such reticence stems from patrician disdain of unpleasantness, it ignores or conceals the seriousness of an issue of radical importance to Westindian cricket. For the decision about Worrell derives from racial, social and political factors that assigned a dominant or managerial role in Westindian cricket to white, upper class Westindians, until the 1960s when Independence came to most Westindian territories and reversed the dominant role of whites in politics and society and therefore in cricket. This is especially important in the final chapters of *Everything* which consider such crucial topics as the Packer crisis and the controversy about playing in South Africa that threatened the very survival of Westindian cricket in the 1970s and 1980s.

There is an inescapable irony running through Stollmeyer's commentary in *Everything*: that the health and progress of the game he so deeply loved were interdependent with the political and social decline of the race and class to which he belonged. If he was dismayed by such political change, he does not explicitly say so. On the contrary, he says that he welcomes the social improvements which this change produced. Stollmeyer describes *Everything* as follows: "This is one man's story. It is one man's experience. It tells one side of the picture." (p.222) This is true in a political sense. Yet, so far as purely cricketing events and issues in the post-war era of Westindian cricket are concerned, the book provides a vivid picture of rare insight and authority and immense historical value - a fitting tribute to the last of the great, amateur Westindian cricketers.

Michael Manley, *A History of West Indies Cricket*
André Deutsch, London, 1988

Michael Manley's previous books - *The Politics of Change: A Jamaican Testament*; *A Voice at the Workplace: Reflections on Colonialism and the Jamaican Worker*; and *Up the Down Escalator: Development and the International Economy* - give little indication of his interest in cricket. Nor would one expect the Prime Minister of the most populous anglophone Caribbean territory (Jamaica) to have either the inclination or time to write a solid (575 pages) volume on sport. Yet, by analysing the development of Westindian cricket from its origins to 1987, and by including a complete scorecard of all Test matches played by Westindies up to 1987, plus a directory (Appendix E) giving the batting, bowling, and fielding averages of all Westindian Test cricketers, *A History of West Indies Cricket* offers the most comprehensive survey of its subject to date. That is not to say that Manley's *History* matches either the theoretical rigour or philosophical amplitude of James's *Beyond the Boundary*; for it is not that sort of book; it is what it claims to be: an historical survey of facts, figures, players, matches, dates, records, results and other similar information about Westindian cricket, although, as we shall see, it is not entirely bereft of Jamesian or Constantinian resonances.

Each chapter of the volume opens with brief comments on one stage in the first Test of England's tour of Westindies in 1985/86, before flashing back to reflections on an earlier period of Westindian cricket history. In this way, since the stages of the 1986 Test match and Westindian cricket history are presented in sequence, the chapters of Manley's *History* collectively provide a consecutive, chronological survey of both the 1986 Test match and Westindian cricket. This type of survey may owe something to Constantine's *Cricketers Carnival* (1950), which also intersperses its author's comments on the cricket of his own time (the 1930s) between sequential snippets describing progressive stages of an imaginary match, involving an Old Timers' Eleven composed of players like Grace and Ranjitshinji, and a team of cricketers from Constantine's own generation. One virtue of this structure is to unveil the entire panorama of Westindian cricket and create the illusion of it all happening before the eyes of the reader, as it were, in the time taken to complete a single match.

Although the author does not exactly advertise the fact that he is a socialist politician, a former Prime Minister of Jamaica, a trade union leader of long standing, and the son of Norman Manley - the first Prime Minister of independent Jamaica, his credentials emerge when he employs a narrative strategy establishing significant correspondence between a process of historical evolution in Westindian cricket, and a similar process in the growth of Westindian cultural and political nationality. The principal argument of his book is to demonstrate an intimate interdependence between these two processes. In Chapter 3, for instance, strikingly entitled "A Genius Emerges - 1929-30", Manley observes that George Headley (the genius) began his career in 1929, the same year that the People's Political Party was founded by Marcus Garvey, one of the first Westindians to emphasize the African origins of most Westindian people. Garvey attempts to restore in Westindians a sense of their dignity as black people after centuries of slavery and colonial indoctrination in feelings of humiliation and self hatred. According to Manley, this attempt and Headley's emergence in cricket should be seen as twin products of parallel processes that germinated in a social ferment of the 1920s, that was produced partly by new ideas brought back by soldiers of the West India Regiment who had returned from the First World War, and partly by Jamaicans who had returned home after fulfilling labour contracts in Panama and Cuba. These ideas had to do with regeneration through a new sense of black self-awareness or identity; they also went hand in hand with a rejection of colonialism and a call for social and political change. Inevitably, such ideas led to anti-colonial strikes, demonstrations and disturbances which must be seen as incipient nationalism in the Westindies in the 1930s.

In Manley's view, Headley's scores of: 21; 176: 8; 39:114;112:10;223 in his first Test series (against England) during the first three months of 1930: "ignited the Caribbean imagination" (p.37) and: "demonstrated black capacity" (p.37), so that: "The aspiring middle class found in him [Headley] the reassurance which they needed" (p.37) and: "Even the white upper classes were willing to be proud" (p.37). "But it was to the black masses that Headley had the deepest significance" (p.37) since: "he [Headley] became the focus for the longing of an entire people for proof: proof of their own self-worth, their own capacity." (p.37) In Manley's words, Headley was: "one of the first answers to the challenge of Marcus Garvey. He [Headley] was black excellence personified in a white world and in a white sport." (p.37). Since Garvey had called for: "the awakening of the black man everywhere to a sense of his destiny and his capacity to mould it for himself" (p.36) Headley's prowess in cricket was the first widely popular Caribbean example of this awakening.

To clarify the joint impact of Headley and Garvey in the 1930s, Manley includes another superbly titled chapter (5): "Captaincy - A Special Preserve" which portrays Westindian social structure as a pyramid, the peak of which was occupied by: "the small, white and near-white upper classes, consisting of the owners of sugar estates and the great merchant houses" (p.54). The middle of the pyramid was occupied by "the mainly brown professional classes" (p.54). In the lower middle class were a mixture of brown and black skilled artisans, junior civil servants, nurses and small shopkeepers, while at the base were the majority of the Westindian population - predominantly black workers and peasants. Although forces of social change such as the demonstrations and disturbances mentioned earlier were at work during the 1930s and 40s, the traditional colonial structure of Westindian society remained intact up to the 1950s. As Manley says: "No island had even so much as a minor form of representative government on a basis of universal adult suffrage." (p.60) and "The Westindies Cricket Board of Control (WICBC) was in every respect the creature of the social structure of the region." (p.61) In other words, it was a body dominated by: "the upper echelons of Caribbean society" (p.61).

Since the WICBC, formed in 1927, reflected existing Caribbean social structure in the first half of this century, it was inevitable that it would only appoint Westindian captains who were white: R.K. Nunes (1928); G.C. Grant (1930/31; 1933; 1934/35); R. Grant (1939); J. Goddard (1948/49; 1950; 1951/ 52; 1957); J. Stollmeyer (1952/53; 1953/54; 1955); D. Atkinson (1955; 1955/ 56). Perhaps Constantine and Headley might have made better captains than the Grants in the 1930s; but the social imperatives of the time dictated that they should not even be considered. And while it is true that Headley was eventually appointed captain for two matches against England in 1947/48, Manley points out that: "he [Headley] was still not the automatic choice," (p.71) and that his case had to be championed by Noel Newton "Crab" Nethersole, a member of the WICBC with unusually "progressive views." (p.71) Still, despite Nethersole's advocacy, Headley had to share the captaincy for the 1947/48 series with Goddard and Stollmeyer. It sounds like trying to get blood out of stone; for as Manley rightly implies, Headley's partial appointment was another devious, tendentious compromise designed to delay the appointment of a black Westindian captain until, finally, Worrell became captain for a full series against Australia in 1960/61.

Manley makes no secret of his approval of Worrell's appointment. He is simply ecstatic, and sees the appointment as an historic vindication of a long struggle against racial injustice in Westindian society and cricket. Nor is his point lost that Worrell's appointment coincided with a period of decolonization in the Westindies, in the 1960s, when the colonial structures that had sustained white supremacy in Westindian society and cricket for centuries were at last beginning to crumble. Although his *History* contains much information about specific matches, series, incidents, issues, and players, along with sophisticated analysis of tactics and strategy, and commentary on all aspects of Westindian cricket, its main value remains its consistent demonstration of the regenerative function of cricket in promoting social and political change in the Westindies, especially during the first half of this century. Everything Manley says is imbued with his conviction in this unique connection between politics and cricket in the region. For this reason, and because of its wealth of cricketing information, including scorecards, pictures, statistics and full career records of players, *A History of West Indies Cricket* remains the most comprehensive, one-volume survey of its subject to date. That such a book is written by a former Prime Minister of a Westindian territory serves to justify the book's argument, and confirm the unique role of cricket in Westindian history and society.

W. Hall, *Pace Like Fire*
Pelham Books, London, 1965

Pace Like Fire considers Halls's career from his earliest days in Barbados to his high maturity during the Westindian tour of England in 1963. Hall began as a wicket-keeper/ batsman at his school, Combermere, and discovered his talent for fast bowling when he was later asked to substitute for a missing fast bowler in a club match: he was surprised to find himself the proud destroyer of six wickets. In this inauspicious fashion began the career of a man who, by the early 1960s, was considered the fastest bowler in the world. Hall was first picked by Westindies for their tour to England in 1957, but he did not play in any of the Tests partly because he had trouble adapting to English conditions, and partly because the position of leading Westindian fast bowler then belonged to Roy Gilchrist. On the tour to India/Pakistan in 1958/59, Hall's chance came after Gilchrist was sent home following a dispute with his captain (Alexander). This is Hall's version of the dispute:

> Gilly, a person with definite views on everyone and everything, felt that the Cambridge University man [Alexander] was speaking down to him rather than at him. We all tried to convince him differently, but he would not budge an inch. (p.45)

Gilchrist's misfortune thrust Hall into the role of spearheading the Westindian fast attack, and he took the responsibility seriously by capturing 30 Indian wickets at 17.66 each, and 16 Pakistani wickets at 17.93 each. Not only that: in the second Test at Kanpur, he had the magnificent reward of eleven wickets for 126 runs. Even more magnificent: he contrived a hat-trick in the third Pakistan Test at Lahore, when he dismissed Mushtaq Mohammed, Fazal Mahmood and Nasim-ul-Ghani in successive balls.

Pace Like Fire recounts these early events as well as Hall's subsequent tours and matches in chronological sequence. The tone is consistently direct and outspoken, sometimes light-hearted and often self-deprecatory. His account of the tumultuous last over in the tied Test at Brisbane in 1960 captures the heat and frenzy of the last four balls of the match when four runs were needed for an Australian victory, or two wickets for a Westindian win. Hall bowled a good length ball to Grout who hit it to square leg where Kanhai stood ready to take the catch. Hall continues:

> Suddenly I realised I had to get there and, although following through on the off, twisted sharply and hared after the ball. I was under it when Kanhai's head struck my elbow, the ball spilled out of my hands and on to the turf. (p.67)

If this is the most celebrated over in the history of cricket, one must expect different versions of it. Ernest Eytle omits the collision of Hall and Kanhai altogether in *Frank Worrell*. In *With the West Indies in Australia* A. G. Moyes saw four fielders converging for the catch, and in *A Tale of Two Tests* Richie Benaud states that Kanhai set himself under the ball before: "the ball was whisked away from Kanhai's steady hands" (p.37) by Hall. In *Blasting for Runs* Kanhai says that his hands were: "scooped like a bucket" to welcome the ball, when: "I felt his [Hall's] elbow crash against the side of my head." (p.68) In the tumult of expectation, tension and desperation, it is understandable that different people saw different things. This is verisimilitude, not falsehood: it demonstrates the complexity of truth.

Two other incidents in the same 1960/61 series against Australia illustrate persistent Westindian scepticism about Australian umpiring which was a feature of Westindian tours to Australia in 1930/31; 1951/52 and 1960/61. In *Cricket in the Sun*, Constantine writes: "We suffered badly from umpiring during that tour" (p.47) and he cites many examples. There were similar reports of Goddard's tour in 1951/52. In Hall's case, the first incident came in the fourth Test at Adelaide, when Mackay stood his ground despite a confident appeal for a catch by Sobers. Hall says: "I was fielding at silly mid-on and was convinced that it was not a bump ball" (p.75). The second incident came in the fifth Test when Grout attempted to cut a ball from Valentine and a bail fell. The umpires conferred and gave Grout not out because they did not see him hit the wicket. The alternative explanation was that Alexander's glove dislodged the bail, but the umpires rejected Alexander's denial. Hall comments:

> We all felt down in the dumps at getting the wrong end of two doubtful decisions. After the Mackay bump ball incident at Adelaide we thought the umpires may have accepted Alexander's word in much the same way as 'Slasher' [Mackay] was given the benefit" (p.80).

Despite frustration over this incident, Hall describes meeting Mackay one year afterwards and teasing him to admit he was out, since it no longer mattered. Mackay replied that he really believed he was not out. This was all taken in good part and illustrates the light-hearted tone that runs through *Pace Like Fire*.

Hall modestly omits dwelling on his more triumphant moments such as his five wickets in the second innings of the tied Test at Brisbane, or his marathon spell in the second innings of the second Test at Lord's in 1963. Instead, he reports sympathetically on several of his colleagues, and sings Worrell's praises as captain. But he does not conceal the fact that he required only 20 Tests, fewer than any other bowler, to gain 100 wickets. Like Kanhai, he too appears to have received literary advice from the English journalist John Gibson whose colloquial English idioms are evident in *Pace Like Fire*, although they do not obtrude or rob the book of its Westindian flavour. Consequently, *Pace Like Fire* remains a modestly genial autobiography of the greatest fast bowler produced by Westindies before 1966.

CHAPTER NINE

"Test", "Rites" and
Beyond a Boundary

V.S. Naipaul's "Test"

I t is neither strange nor scandalous to claim that V.S. Naipaul's *A House for Mr. Biswas* is one of the chief glories of Westindian and world literature, or that Kanhai's 110 at Port of Spain in February, 1960, Sobers's 132 in Brisbane in December, 1960, and Gibbs's six for 29 at Georgetown in April 1965, are lasting glories of Westindian and international cricket; for Naipaul, Kanhai, Sobers and Gibbs came from similar social origins, and established careers in the same English-speaking, postcolonial cultural context, during the 1950s and 60s, when Westindian achievements in literature and sport combined with advances in politics to generate a new sense of social, cultural and political self-awakening in a region, until then, disparagingly dismissed as a convenient source of rum, sugar, and negroes.

Naipaul is one of several writers including Edgar Mittelholzer, Samuel Selvon, George Lamming, Roger Mais, Vic Reid, John Hearne, and Jan Carew, whose careers began in this golden age of Westindian self-awakening. Since then, with four decades of continuous writing behind him, and seventeen volumes concerned mostly with fiction and travel, Naipaul has won universal literary acclaim, based partly on a luminously graceful style, and partly on sharp, clinical insights into worldwide afflictions of exile and homelessness. Were it not for the historical connections already cited, it might indeed appear strange or scandalous for someone of such literary distinction to be regarded as a writer on cricket; but Naipaul has written at least one piece "Test" on cricket - an account of the second Test match, played at Lord's between Westindies and England, from 20th to 25th June, 1963.

Aficionados of cricket do not need to be reminded that the Lord's Test match of 1963 is a classic in the history of the game, as bejewelled as Jessop's match in 1902 at the conclusion of which one commentator says: "Delirium prevailed. Strong men wiped tears from their eyes. Perfect strangers embraced." (Gerald

Moore, "G. Moore Run Out 3" in M. Meyer, *Summer Days*, pp. 171-172); or
the 1960 Brisbane tied Test, of which Jack Fingleton writes:

> Let agnostics scoff if they wish, but do not disbelieve that Divine
> providence, with Dr. Grace the likely chairman of the advisory committee
> did ordain and control those tumultuous last minutes of play at Brisbane
> last Wednesday. No earthly cricket mind could have thought up such a
> fantastic finish. If presented in fiction, publishers would have spurned it
> [as] beyond human credibility.

In the same way, agnostics and atheists will almost certainly scoff at the suggestion
that the Lord's Test of 1963 - and particularly events in its last over - are of
heavenly origin. Whether V.S. Naipaul is an agnostic or atheist, or neither, he
too appears to scoff at this suggestion in "Test". The Lord's Test match in 1963
was not merely an exciting contest between two teams of acknowledged cricketing
prowess: it was a battle between contrasting cultures, like the struggle between
the disciplined, coldly cerebral, dominating values of the English hero Rochester
and the freer, warmer, more natural, relaxed and instinctive attitudes of the
Westindian heroine Antoinette in Jean Rhys's novel *Wide Sargasso Sea*. The
novel is set in the colourful, tropical surroundings of Antoinette's Westindian
homeland, whereas, the Lord's Test unfolded in Rochester's England, in grey,
grim, rather stark, unpromising and unsporting conditions of cloud, rain, cold,
and occasional, niggardly outbreaks of fitful sunshine. Nature herself seemed in
distress, or in the process of waging some elemental, losing battle for the forces
of light against those of darkness. On this stage was enacted a five-day drama
unique in the annals and lore of cricket for divinely inspired feats of courage,
heroism, sacrifice, honour and glory.

As one might expect, Naipaul's reputation for unflinching integrity, unblinkered
candour, and self-lacerating fidelity to truth, inhibit him from dwelling on either
the drama and heroism of the match, or on its capacity for sacrifice, honour and
glory. Not that he fails to perceive these virtues in the match: he has no stomach
for them. If he had simply failed to acknowledge the glittering resplendence of
heroism or of golden deeds on the field of play, his account could be dismissed as
blind, ignorant, trivial, not worth further attention: it was rather that his pitiless
gaze, reversing the touch of Midas, turned gold into dross.

Naipaul's account is divided into five sections, "First Day", "Second Day"
and so on, each dealing with one day's play in the match. "First Day" announces
a familiar pattern of fictional skills being used to describe people, places, and
events, as Naipaul does in his travel books. He begins with a detached,
unappetizing sketch of the arrival of mixed trainloads of people at Lord's on
the morning of the match, after which "First Day" is mainly devoted to the
dialogue of anonymous Westindian spectators commenting, in desultory fashion,
on social, political, economic, and other subjects, as well as on events of the
match itself. Conversation is disconnected and elastic, though not incoherent,
held together by a stream of consciousness technique that captures the
indiscriminate welling up of subconscious thoughts and preoccupations mixed

almost involuntarily with more cerebral judgements on cricket:

> 'I hear the economic situation not too good in Trinidad these days.'
> 'All those damn strikes. You know our Westindian labour. Money,
> Money. And if you say "work", they strike.' But the cricket ever returns.
> 'I don't know why they pick McMorris in place of Carew. You can't
> have two sheet-anchors as opening batsmen. Carew would have made
> 16. Sixteen and out. But he wouldn't have let the bowling get on top as
> it is now. I feel it have a lil politics in McMorris pick, you know.'
> (p.178)

Such aimless, disconnected conversation contributes an eerie sense of weary victimisation and helplessness combined with an air of futile routine reminiscent of dialogue in the plays of Samuel Beckett and Harold Pinter.

Although scattered, the comments on cricket catch the tense, combative flavour of events during the first day of the match when, in wretchedly inhospitable batting conditions, Westindies exhibited uncharacteristic restraint in scoring 245 for six. Kanhai's top score of 73 was an innings of unusual control and responsibility punctuated by more characteristic flashes of naturalness, inventiveness and instinct. (Like Naipaul, I attended every day of the match, and still remember the effect of Kanhai's dismissal like a dagger in my chest when Trueman's outswinger moved rather faster than expected off the pitch, took the edge of Kanhai's bat, and flew to gully where Edrich caught it.) It is interesting that Naipaul dwells neither on Kanhai's distinguished innings, nor on Trueman's formidable skill in exploiting unsettled conditions of wind and weather to take five wickets for 64 runs in 32 overs on the first day. While it is understandable that Naipaul does not wish to reproduce the lifeless statistics of a forgotten scorecard, he also appears not to be interested in evaluating the cricket. His interest is focused more on the interaction of the Westindian spectators both with themselves and, from time to time, with the game.

"Second Day" opens with observations on a practice session of Westindian players at the nets, while their tailend colleagues add another 56 runs and take their first innings total to a final score of 301. As on the previous day, we hear little about this score itself, or about Solomon's resilient 56, Hall's defiant 25 not out, or about Trueman's magnificent final figures - six wickets for 100 runs in 44 overs. Trueman, after all, was the linchpin of England's attack: with rigorous accuracy and unflagging stamina, he sustained an extremely hostile assault on the Westindian batsmen that kept them on their toes every minute of the time. Similarly, when England batted and made 235 for seven by the end of the second day, few details of their innings are given. Instead, at the fall of a wicket to the Westindian fast bowler Griffith, Naipaul notices that: "A Jamaican, drunk on more than the bitter he is holding, talks of divine justice. Griffith's previous ball had been no-balled." (p.180) He also reports an incident in which a Westindian insurance salesman contrasts thrifty Barbadians with his more demanding Jamaican clients, and casts slurs on the latter: "They pay three weeks' premiums, and they want to borrow three hundred pounds." (p.181)

The satiric edge of this statement is sharp though not wounding; it compares well with much of the humour in Naipaul's fiction, and reflects perception into Westindian personality as expressed through the diction, stress, intonation, cadence and rhythm of Westindian speech. Such humorous or satirical comments and statements are as typical of Naipaul's writing in "Test" as in his fiction.

To his credit, Naipaul does notice the batting of the English captain Ted Dexter who came in when the score was 20 for two, and in a grand if abbreviated exhibition of blazing aggression, took it to 102 before he was out. Dexter scored 70 runs off 75 balls in one of the bravest, most brilliant and fearless counter attacks ever seen in a short innings of cricket. Yet here is Naipaul:

> But then Dexter. Tall, commanding, incapable of error or gracelessness. Every shot, whatever its result, finished, decisive. Dexter hooking: the ball seeming momentarily arrested by the bat before being redirected. Dexter simplifying: an illusion of time, even against these very fast bowlers. (p.181)

If this is faint praise or a subtle attempt to undermine the grandeur of human achievement in sport, it will not please lovers of cricket. Even partisan Westindian supporters cheered deliriously as Dexter pummelled Hall and Griffith who were bowling at their fastest and most dangerous. Perhaps it was the "Westindian quality" of Dexter's performance that appealed to them, that is to say, his flamboyant aggression, zest and energy. Dexter showed such power and command that journalists spoke of his majestic, regal presence at the wicket where, like a lion among lesser creatures, he was held back only by the bars of an imaginary cage from tearing the Westindian bowlers to pieces. But Naipaul is less interested in Dexter's royal, command performance than in the worries, fears, inconsistencies, excesses and ready jocularity of his fellow Westindians. Nor is it only Dexter who suffers from this neglect: Naipaul almost totally ignores Barrington's sturdy, yeoman-like innings of 80 which provided conviction and credibility to England's response. True enough, Barrington's performance was more solid and earth-bound than Dexter's in its soaring, heaven-ward flight. At the same time, through the runs he made, and the length of time he took, Barrington gave England plausible hope of recovery and even victory.

"Third Day", the longest section, records a day's play in which England progress steadily from their overnight 235 for seven to a first innings total of 297. On the same day Westindies score 214 for five in their second innings. It was a Saturday, and the ground had filled up early so the gates had to be closed, shutting out thousands. Like the previous days, this was also one of densely packed eventfulness and shifting fortunes. At the conclusion of England's first innings, the match had lasted for two days and eighty minutes, and neither side had gained the advantage, separated as they were by a margin of merely four runs. But for the quixotic Dexter, the English batsmen - Barrington (80) and Titmus (52) in particular - had clawed and clutched for every run against a varied Westindian attack which contained distinguished fast bowling (Hall and Griffith) and expert spin (Sobers and Gibbs). Griffith dominated by taking five wickets for 91 runs, and like a Greek classical tragedy, the match reached its peak soon after the Westindian second innings had started, and both openers were lost for 15 runs. Kanhai and Butcher stabilized the situation briefly, but in vain, for Kanhai was soon out, and was tragically followed by Sobers and Solomon to bring Westindies to the brink of defeat at 104 for five. At this low point in Westindian fortunes the drama reached its climax.

Rather than describe them directly, Naipaul indirectly refracts these soul-shattering events through the responses of the Westindian crowd. Betting is a favourite response:

> Titmus won't get 50; England won't make 300, won't make 301. These are the bets being made in the free seats, Westindian against Westindian. Lord's has restrained them: in the West Indies they will gamble on who will field the next ball, how many runs will be scored in the over. For them a cricket match is an unceasing drama. (p.182)

Accurate, but detached. Perhaps trivial betting is a means of controlling anxiety - Naipaul does not say. His aim, as always, is humorous revelation of Westindian culture and conduct. When Kanhai is dismissed though, at 64 for three, we get an example of Naipaul's best descriptive writing without humour or satire:

> Just as no one runs down the pavilion steps more jauntily, no one walks back more sadly. His [Kanhai's] bat is a useless implement; he peels off his gloves as though stripping himself of an undeserved badge. Gloves flapping, he walks back, head bowed. (p.183)

Here, where the subject is defeat, failure or retreat, Naipaul is in his element. This is his forte: usually through mordant humour to express an instinctive, deeply inbred rapport with human fragility, inadequacy, and mortality, and to deny consolation by undermining the comforting illusions and strategies that we all invent to cope with these limitations. He shuns the fact that Kanhai's dismissal is a grave blow to the Westindian cause; he is attracted purely by Kanhai's personal reaction.

Whether it is the Westindian plight of being in mortal danger at 104 for five, or their subsequent heaven-sent recovery from that score to 214 for five by the end of the third day, Naipaul shows little appreciation of feelings of initial sorrow and subsequent joy that are involved. The recovery was achieved by a glorious stand between Worrell and Butcher and an innings from Butcher that may now be seen as heavenly, although it looked at the time as if it was being forged in the very fires of hell. But Naipaul keeps a careful distance from all such tension and heart-stopping excitement, although he does report one spectator's reaction: "boy, I nearly faint when Solomon out," (p.185) that is, at 104 for five. True to his fashion, he reports that middle class Westindians who earlier tended to hold themselves aloof, were driven by the danger of defeat to join: "the plebeian Westindians, to draw comfort from their shouting." (p.185) As always, it is the social foibles and cultural frailties of Westindians that attract Naipaul.

When the match resumes on the Monday, still in threatening weather, the grand partnership of Butcher and Worrell which had saved Westindies from certain defeat on Saturday, is quickly broken, and they decline from the hard won safety of their overnight score of 214 for five to 229 all out. Jeopardy again. This has been the pattern of the match: no sooner has the advantage gone one way than it is quickly swung back to the other. But the grief of this tragic dénouement that has brought Westindies from the joyful, overnight possibility of victory to the present dismal prospect of defeat seems lost on Naipaul who opens "The Fourth Day" as follows: "After the weekend tension, farce. We are scarcely settled when the five remaining Westindian wickets fall, for 15 runs. England, as if infected, quickly lose their two opening batsmen." (p.185) To consider this sudden, grievous, heart-rending reversal as "farce" seems perverse; for surely such changes and reversals of human planning, effort and expectation raise a serious question about the malignity or benignity of Providence, unless they are to be attributed entirely to the neutral agency of blind fate.

At any rate, although Westindies begin the fourth day disastrously, they quickly take three English wickets, including Dexter's, and restore some balance to the moral and dramatic equation of the contest. Now, with the instinct of a born artist, Naipaul introduces an element of comic relief to assuage the grief and tension of events in which human beings (the cricketers), despite their best efforts, appear like helpless pawns at the mercy of more powerful forces. Nothing farcical in that. But, ever driven by his instinct for humour and satire, Naipaul reveals conspiratorial whispers among the Westindian spectators suggesting that certain Westindian cricketers have sent confidential, inside information that a Westindian victory is imminent. When these "confidential" revelations are contradicted by the stout resistance of a fourth wicket partnership between Cowdrey and Barrington, the reader realizes that they are another example of the Westindian penchant for good humoured, fun loving story telling, exhibition and display, like betting on trivial expectations, or making firm predictions based on no reliable or visible evidence. Naipaul can scarcely resist quoting another spectator: "Rohan Kanhai did send a message, too, remember? He was going to get a century on Saturday." (p.186) Kanhai, in fact, made 21. There is also some irrelevant discussion on the impressive names of Westindian cricketers and a brief mention of the queen's traditional visit to meet the players in the Lord's test match each year. Then after comic relief, comes the "deus ex machina": Cowdrey is hit on his right arm by Hall and sustains a fracture. This injury could be critical to the outcome of the whole match as, soon afterwards, play is curtailed by bad weather with England on 116 for three at the end of the fourth day. This effectively means 116 for four, since it is announced that Cowdrey would bat only "if absolutely necessary".

"The Fifth Day" is the shortest, most potent section of "Test". It consists entirely of commentary on the cricket, whereas the four preceding sections consist mostly of dialogue on assorted topics including cricket. It is as if Naipaul himself finally responds to the drama he has resisted for four days. The situation at the start of the fifth and final day is that England need 118 more runs to win with seven (in reality six) wickets left. Since the injured Cowdrey and Barrington (55 not out) are the only remaining top order English batsmen, the odds have shifted slightly to Westindies once more. But rain prevents a start until 2.20pm which means that only three hours and twenty minutes of play are possible, allowing for the tea break. With telling economy, Naipaul notes the fall, firstly of Barrington (60), then of Parks (17) when the score is 158. With Close and Titmus together, 75 runs are needed. Now Naipaul is seen at his magisterial best producing writing of great tensile strength - taut, condensed, implicit with suggestion and meaning:

> Titmus is caught off Hall by - McMorris. And, next ball, Trueman goes. Only Close now remains for England, with 31 runs   to get, and the clock advancing to six. Every ball holds drama. Every run narrows the gap. Hall bowls untiringly from the pavilion end. Will his strength never give out? (p.187)

The fact is that, except for the tea break, Hall bowled continuously from 2.20pm to 6.00pm an herculean effort, and one of the great exhibitions of fast bowling in modern cricket. It is wonderful to see Naipaul's appreciation of it, and his acknowledgment, at last, of the drama he has witnessed for five days. As he succinctly says, in the battle between Close and Westindies: "it is Close who cracks." Close's immense courage and daring had earned him 70 runs and a good many blows about the body from Hall. His was a lofty enterprise of honour and noble self-sacrifice; but fearful that he might run out of time, he took a swing at Griffith and was caught by wicket-keeper Murray. He had brought England to the verge of victory, and when he departed, 15 more runs were needed and twenty minutes left.

Thus, by the time Hall began bowling the last, fateful over, England were 226 for eight - 8 runs short of victory. Although Allen and Shackleton - the last English pair - are sent instructions from the English balcony to do or die, their best efforts yield only two runs from the first three balls of the over. On the fourth ball, Shackleton is run out as a result of a desperate scramble. In his book *Blasting for Runs*, Kanhai claims that this run out is achieved by some premeditation from Worrell, Murray and himself. Kanhai's claim, and Worrell's consequent caution in running out Shackleton by sprinting to the wicket with the ball in his hand, rather than throwing down the wicket, confirms the thrilling excitement and potency of every ball of the final over. The fall of the ninth English wicket - Shackleton's - means that Cowdrey's entrance, beyond all reasonable expectation, has indeed become "absolutely necessary", even though his injured right arm is encased in plaster. The one merciful thing is that he will not be exposed to Hall's final two thunderbolts because he will remain at the non-striker's end. At that stage, six runs are needed for an English victory, while Westindies require one wicket to win. What are the options of Allen, the English batsman facing Hall? A mighty six, or a four and a two would do it. Or undo it if he gets out. But Allen is not to be tempted either by true glory or vainglory: he plays both balls quietly down and brings the match to a draw, the final scores being Westindies - 301 and 229; England - 297 and 228 for nine.

In an elemental drama of such mounting conflict, unbearable tension, and unexpected changes, it was perhaps the best of all possible resolutions; for neither side had won nor lost, and moral justice or equilibrium seemed achieved. In the midst of all that, Cowdrey's courageous resistance with Barrington, his painful injury, and final entry for two balls at the non-striker's end certainly stands out as a rare example of heroism and patriotism. Most people would think so. Not Naipaul:

> And this is the ridiculous public-school heroism of cricket: a man with a bandaged arm saving his side, yet without having to face a ball. It is the peculiar style of cricket, and its improbable appreciation links these dissimilar people - English and Westindian. (p.188)

The passage casts a baneful eye a little too readily on an act of at least genuine devotion to duty. After all, if Cowdrey had not come in, the English innings would have automatically come to an end and England would have lost by five runs. Cowdrey's act was inspired by necessity, if nothing else. Naipaul makes it sound as if there was something fraudulent in the rules of cricket which allowed Cowdrey to appear for two balls and face neither. It was due to sheer luck, as agnostics or atheists might think, or divine Providence as all true believers know, that Cowdrey did not have to face Hall, although he was prepared to do so. Had Allen been run out instead of Shackleton, Cowdrey would have had to face Hall. That a one-armed batsman should take strike from the fastest, most fearsome bowler in the world is a prospect too cruel to imagine even at this safe distance in time! And when we learn from Kanhai's book that, fifteen minutes before he came in, Cowdrey had practised batting left handed against Trueman and Titmus in the English dressing room, and that: "If he had been forced to face the bowling he'd made up his mind to do it the wrong way round to save his injured arm." (p.98) we know there was nothing remotely fraudulent about Cowdrey's heroism and magnanimity that day, nor indeed about the entire dramatic spectacle of cricket in the second Test at Lord's in 1963.

Naipaul takes his allegedly incorruptible candour too far in "Test". Hall was not simply tireless in bowling continuously for three and a half hours at top speed, in the most challenging conditions, against a brazenly defiant opponent like Close who, in one instance, thought nothing of walking out of his crease toward the bowler, who then felt constrained to hold back the ball almost at the point of delivery, and risk injury to his back. Trueman's eleven wickets in the match are unforgettable, as are Barrington's two stout-hearted, rock-like innings (80 and 60), the second of which included two remarkable sixes off Gibbs during England's darkest moments on the fourth day. As for the transcendent glory of Butcher's nation-saving 133 in the second innings: it inspired in the faces of many Westindian spectators the beatific ecstasy that is evident in paintings of Christian saints (for example, St. Theresa of Avila) at the moment when they think they see God. Butcher hit two sixes as well, both off Allen, one of which sailed high and free, right over the bowler's head to the long on boundary. This stroke alone confirmed the existence of a divine spark in the boy from Port Mourant. (Kanhai and Solomon are also from Port Mourant, but their performances in this match do not measure up to Butcher's.) Worrell's 33 in the second innings is another performance worth more than its weight in gold in so far as it reflected maturity and grace, and gave just the tempered support that Butcher needed at the right psychological moment. Even if these and other incidents in the match are noticed, they are generally underplayed by Naipaul in "Test"; some, like Butcher's divine afflatus are neglected; and others, like Cowdrey's heroism are denigrated. Throughout, Naipaul's tone is so sternly distanced, that when he speaks of the peculiar "style" of cricket and its improbable appreciation by people from contrasting cultures in England and the Westindies, he might as well be standing on the moon, so completely does he isolate himself from his subject and from all human hope of warmth, comfort, satisfaction or consolation.

At the same time, such is his integrity, that Naipaul's instincts are seldom completely wrong, either in "Test" or in his writing generally. Despite its flaws of exaggeration, petulance and inadequate historical research, the Trinidad section of his much maligned *The Middle Passage* is the finest, most truthful piece of documentary non-fiction writing ever done about the Westindies, and its reputation will change as its insights are seen, more and more, to explain much of the chaos, corruption, and misgovernment that have affected Guyana and Trinidad and Tobago especially since Independence. Similarly, in "Test", in the same breath as he wrongly indicts Cowdrey's "ridiculous public-school heroism," Naipaul recognizes the "improbable" allegiance to cricket of two contrasting cultures- English and Westindian. The contrast is not explored; but it acknowledges the essential conflict that sustains the whole drama of the match. For this drama derives from a conflict between one culture that prizes tradition, discipline, and the rules and regulations of coaching manuals, and another which celebrates innovation and individualism, and frowns on the rules and regulations of coaching manuals. The difference between these two approaches is evident in the difference between Barrington's sterling batting - solid, reliable, responsible, even dour, and Butcher's 133 - adventuresome, resilient, combative, even flashy. Barrington and Butcher each made crucial contributions to their respective teams; but their styles contrasted sharply, and this contrast nourished the drama of the match inspiring change from day to day, often from hour to hour, and in its final stages from ball to ball. This type of drama purges and entertains as Greek classical drama does. No wonder C.L.R. James sees similarities between Greek drama and cricket in *Beyond a Boundary*.

Curiously, in his last paragraph, Naipaul admits that he is "emotionally drained" by the match, that he is equally exhausted" as the other spectators, and that "this has been a match of heroes on both sides." This is an astonishing "volte face" since, up to his last paragraph, Naipaul studiously deflates the dramatic and heroic content of the match. If all through the match he really did respond to its drama and heroism, then his gentle mockery of Westindian spectators and his tone of detachment are best regarded as artistic devices to insulate himself from the shocks, disappointments and fleeting joys of the cricket, just as humour and satire in his fiction insulate him from the harshness and pain of Westindian or human failure and inadequacy. This, no doubt, is why he does not acknowledge the joys and glory of golden deeds throughout five days of cricket; he is quite right: gold so often, so quickly, and without adequate explanation, turns to dross in human hands. If this is true - that his instinctive, unceasing denial of human comfort or consolation will not permit him to fully expose himself to the drama of the match until the last day when the tension is finally resolved - then, ironically, his persistent denigration or neglect of cricketing heroism, courage, honour and glory re-affirms the presence of these qualities in the Lord's Test of 1963.

"Test" is included in *Summer Days* an anthology of writing on cricket by well known authors such as Kingsley Amis, Beryl Bainbridge, Ted Hughes, and Harold Pinter, most of whom give personal, often informal reminiscences about their contact with cricket either at school or in their local community. Almost alone, Naipaul chooses to present a single Test match in a rather formal, analytical way. In the process, however, apparently in spite of himself, he captures the joys and sorrows if not the glories of cricket, as most of his fellow contributors do. David Wright's piece "A Deaf Man Looks at Cricket" is especially interesting because it describes Wright's own reaction to the Lord's Test in 1963 as one who cannot hear the so called "music" of willow on leather. This is his reaction when Dexter was bowled by Gibbs for 2 in the English second innings:

> While the bails were still flying, coats, hats cushions, umbrellas, sandwiches, for all I know babies even, were hurled into the air by some nine or ten thousand Westindians in the free seats where I was watching. Up went a simultaneous roar of delight. Hearing that sound, for me not very loud but like a croaking bark, was a queer spooky experience. I have never forgotten it." (p.244)

In old age, after he had lost his sight, a former captain of England R.E.S. Wyatt was known to attend Test matches and make perceptive comments on the cricket being played purely on the basis of the "music" of willow on leather. If cricket can make the deaf hear and the blind see, as well as cause distinguished authors to lose their scepticism, who can deny its heavenly origin? Strange as it seems, Naipaul virtually acknowledges the divinity of cricket when he asks rhetorically in his last paragraph: "And what other game can leave such little sense of triumph and defeat?" (p.188) The Lord's Test of 1963 did, in truth, seem to be managed by a benevolent, impartial Providence which ensured that neither side won or lost. As such, the Test achieves the moral equilibrium of the best works of art.

Like art, sport is a simulation of reality governed by agreed rules or conventions. While it is perfectly true that the Lord's Test of 1963 does not equal the range of feeling, depth of insight and richness of meaning in a novel like *Wide Sargasso Sea*, it is strange how it captures much of the alternating tumult and calm inspired by the conflict between Rochester's stiff, unnatural, calculating and dominating culture, and Antoinette's sprightly, spontaneous, victimised naturalness. In the re-enactment of the scene from Charlotte Bronte's *Jane Eyre* that ends *Wide Sargasso Sea*, when Antoinette sets fire to Rochester's house, she becomes an archetypal Westindian heroine who liberates herself from English confinement and imprisonment by causing her own death, and her action must be seen as God's validation of freedom for all humankind, just as Butcher's 133 validates the best in Westindian culture. That is why, when Hall bowls those final two balls, all human passion is spent, and there is no longer any sense of loser or winner, victim or victimizer. "All in compassion ends" as Derek Walcott writes in his poem, "A Far Cry From Africa" (From *In a Green Night*). This is exactly the effect at the end of the match as Naipaul describes it. All that remains in the memory, he says, is "he who has purged the emotions by delight and fear." (p.188). This is also the feeling at the end of *Wide Sargasso Sea*.

Edward Brathwaite's "Rites"

In "Limbo", the second section of *Islands* (1969), which is itself the final volume of Edward Brathwaite's celebrated poetic trilogy *The Arrivants* (1973), there is a poem "Rites" that captures an interesting moment in the development of Westindian cricket. The moment is the mid-1950s, a period highlighted in *The Rise of Westindian Cricket* by the idea of "Rise and Fall", inconsistency or fickleness. This idea is repeated three times in "Rites". In one instance, the narrator says:

> when things goin' good, you cahn touch we; but leh murder start an' you
> cahn fine a man to hole up de side" (p.201)

Expressed in pungent creole idiom that informs the text of the entire poem, this idea is a pithy comment on alleged Westindian notoriety for brittle cricket performances during the 1950s, when the team flourished in favourable conditions, but were liable to collapse when faced with difficulties such as illness, injury, or an unexpected or concerted challenge. This unflattering view of Westindian cricket is supported, among other examples, by the sharp contrast between their performances in England in 1950 and in 1957. On the earlier tour, when they had powerful batting resources (the three Ws), and the magical inspiration of two brilliant, young spin bowlers (Ramadhin and Valentine), they marched right through England, from one end to the other, laying everything low before them. Not even Bradman's "all conquering Australians" had blazed such trails of incandescent glory during their own triumphant march through England two years before. But in 1957, when Westindies had to put up with illness, injury and other difficulties, they collapsed like a pack of cards: in 1950 they had demolished England three:one; in 1957, almost the exact opposite happened, when they were crushed nil:three.

The scene of "Rites" is laid in a tailor's shop in Brathwaite's native Barbados during England's 1954 tour of Westindies. The shop proprietor, an unnamed tailor, is speaking to a visitor about cricket while he continues with his work, sewing. It is a familiar Westindian scene during this period when people generally congregated in tailor's shops, barber's shops, shoemaker's shops, rum shops, bridges, street corners, and other public places to discuss anything from local gossip (especially sexual scandal) to cricket, politics, and religion. The scene is important in illustrating the educational, democratizing and nation-building function of Westindian cricket through its promotion of discussion in which everyone, from the illiterate labourer to the exalted school teacher or civil servant, was free to take part. This democratic forum played a unique role by maintaining channels of communication between different racial groups and social classes, and encouraging a sense of solidarity in people from different districts and even island territories. For when a Guyanese extolled the virtues of Barbadian Everton Weekes, for example, he expressed solidarity with people from an island he would likely never visit, and whose history, politics, economics, even accent he could scarcely recognise. Whatever role cricket may have played in other countries, in the Westindies, it has served as a prime instigator of national sentiment.

It goes without saying that discussions held in barber's shops and similar establishments increased in frequency and intensity during cricket tours. Well known 1950s' world issues like the Korean war, Cold War tension, and the Mau Mau war of liberation (or "rebellion" as Anglo-centric opinion then designated it) took a distant second place to the fate of Westindies in a Test match. The tailor in "Rites" has no time for such mundane political matters: his concern is with a local cricket match at Brown's beach in which the batting side collapsed. The collapse leads him to reflect on a Test match played the previous week against England at Kensington Oval, the Test cricket ground in Bridgetown, Barbados. The tailor's Test match is not the actual Test match played by Westindies against England at Kensington Oval from 6th to 12th February, 1954. Westindies were never 197 for three in this match; nor did Everton Weekes and Johnny Wardle appear in it, as they do in the tailor's match. The point again, as in his choice of a typical tailor's shop, is that Brathwaite has chosen a representative (if imagined) Test match rather than an actual match whose facts and figures can be verified. This suggests that his poem is less concerned with literal accuracy than with general concerns, interests, attitudes, and reactions inspired by Westindian Test matches in the 1950s. There may be something too in the fact that the enemy is England, which raises implications of historic conflict between slave and master, colonial outpost and imperial centre.

In the Brown's beach match with which the tailor opens his narrative in "Rites", a batsman named Lambert is caught in the slips off Hop-a-long Cass, a fast bowler with the romantic nickname of a Hollywood cowboy. Lambert is replaced by Gullstone who starts off shakily, playing and missing. According to the tailor, Gullstone's playing and missing is predictable, because he (Gullstone) did not take the tailor's advice to: "watch what you doin." (p.198) At once the tailor is revealed, if only by his own words, as an authority on cricket. His confident tone suggests that his expert advice was freely given to Gullstone who richly deserves to suffer for ignoring it. Now that Lambert is out and Gullstone unlikely to survive for long, their team seems to be heading for calamity. The tailor is exasperated since the calamity could have been easily avoided if his advice was followed, but his exasperation derives from sympathetic concern as we can also tell from his tone of regret:

> Is all very well when it rosy an sweet
> but leh murder start an' brungalungdung
> you cahn fine a man to hole up de side. (p.198)

This sounds like rare wisdom from a self-made expert who speaks with aphoristic authority and dogmatic certainty. It is bad enough that fickleness has afflicted Gullstone's team: what is worse - and it becomes the main subject of the poem - is that it has also afflicted the Westindian (national) team which betrayed fickleness in their (imagined) Test match against England the previous week.

   As the subject of a narrative poem, mainly in the form of a dramatic monologue, Westindian cricketing fickleness looks unpromising or trivial, hardly serious enough to hold interest for long. Yet it is no exaggeration to claim that "Rites" is probably the best poem ever written about cricket: its text is layered, packed with information and replete with suggestions that greatly enrich the narrative with implication, irony, ambiguity and allusiveness that transport the poem far beyond the realms of cricket. Take the narrator's advice to Gullstone: "watch de ball, man" or: "watch what you doin." (p.198) The dogmatism that leads the tailor to repeat this admonition over and over again is ostentatious. The advice itself is commonplace, normally given to any incoming batsman: start off cautiously until you get accustomed to the light, pitch, bowling and general conditions of play. That the tailor wishes us to regard such advice as unusual or unique, as his dogmatism might imply, raises doubts about his alleged expertise in cricket. Again, he warns Gullstone that starting an innings:

> isn't no time for playin
> the fool nor makin' no sport; this is cricket (p.198)

   The tailor's claim is that cricket is not just sport as it may seem to the uninitiated: sport is one thing; cricket quite another; which makes a collapse of the Westindian team not a sporting matter at all. This is a serious view of cricket as something other than sport, but since it comes from a narrator of doubtful credibility, one is led to sift through examples of irony, ambiguity or doubt in order to discover the poet's true meaning.

   The tailor speaks throughout "Rites" except for two brief instances: one in which his unnamed listener, the interlocutor, intervenes to say that he knows that the Brown's beach bowler Hop-a-Long Cass had a deformed foot caused by a cow kicking his pregnant mother shortly before he was born; and another instance, in which the interlocutor's actual words are not reported, but when we can guess that he confesses ignorance/unawareness of the Test match at

Kensington Oval. The tailor eagerly seizes the opportunity of this confession to expound more learned opinions, and expatiate on his general vision of cricket. With the skilled artifice of a born raconteur, he begins by upbraiding his listener for entering his shop so casually:

> "you sprawl you ass
> all over my chair widdout ask-
> in' me please leave nor licence" (p.199)

His invective is later combined with disparaging comments on his visitor's informal dress "like a touriss." (p.199) The tailor is flabbergasted that his visitor didn't know about the Test match, a momentous event of national significance. So disconcerted is he by what he regards as his visitor's casual attitude and gross irresponsibility that he accidentally pricks his finger with a needle.

The tailor might be unlettered and unschooled, but he is an expert rhetorician who reveals a repertoire of narrative techniques and strategies sophisticated enough to satisfy the most skilful story teller. This means that we cannot take him directly at his word. In the Westindies, visits to tailor's shops, barber's shops etcetera are generally casual and informal. The tailor's objection on this point is a rhetorical ploy: he wants to give the impression that his visitor's ignorance/ unawareness has put him to inconvenience bordering on provocation, and that it takes forbearance and magnanimity for him to divulge events at the Oval the previous week. But the relish with which he recounts details of this match belies any forbearance or magnanimity. His excitement in re-enacting particular details of the match confirm that, far from being an inconvenience, his visitor's presence is really a godsent opportunity for him to indulge his abiding passion for cricket. His rhetorical flourishes must be taken as clues which might help to discover whether the tailor's definition of Westindian cricket as something other than sport is really genuine, or whether it is merely uncritical indulgence in a typical but bizarre example of Westindian tailor-shop-wisdom.

As a practised and resourceful raconteur, the tailor knows that if he can make his visitor feel guilty about being uninformed, especially on a matter of national importance, he might persuade him more effectively. His instinctive story-telling strategies derive mainly out of an African oral tradition that has been indigenised in the Caribbean over four centuries. It is a tradition that thrives on impromptu situations, casualness and informality which require formidable powers of improvisation and inventiveness. The tailor is familiar with his audience from long experience, and he knows the techniques he must use - allegory, proverbs or commonly accepted sayings, aphorism, banter, ribaldry, invective, wit, and constant repetition. These techniques help him to secure his visitor's attention before he launches into his main narrative by saying:

> "We was only playin' de MCC, man." (p.199)

His "we" at once establishes solidarity with his listener, as a fellow Barbadian or Westindian. It is interesting that the tailor says "M.C.C." rather than "Inglan".

The letters carry more weight by virtue of their official, technical look, which will best be appreciated by knowledgable insiders like himself.

In the Test match he is describing, Westindies have reached 197 for three; Walcott is facing Wardle whose "sweet, sweet, slow-medium syrup" bowling appears all the more innocent, innocuous and vulnerable because of the alliteration and assonance used to describe it - the combination of sibilants and open vowel sounds reinforce an effect of guileless, inviting, slow bowling that begs for punishment - and Walcott obliges with a cover drive of massive power off the back foot for four runs:

> Clyde back pun he back
> foot an' prax!
> is through extra cover an' four red runs all de way. (p.200)

This description illustrates unbounded admiration and delight in Walcott's exploit: it has both aural and visual appeal. The onomatopoeia of "prax" marvellously simulates the sound of Walcott's bat when it makes contact with the ball; and alliteration and assonance are again effective in almost making us see the colour of the ball as it speeds on its way to the boundary. The repeated "r"s in "four red runs" help to visualise the bright colour of the ball in its continuous rolling movement, and the metonymic attachment of the ball's redness to runs somehow makes the runs seem more highly prized. One can imagine the gestures of the narrator in physically demonstrating Walcott's stroke while speaking so eloquently in celebration of it. To confirm his celebration, he reports the crowd's spontaneous reaction in appropriating Walcott's success as their own: Walcott's boundary aroused such appreciative comments, shouts and gestures from the spectators that it was:

> as if *they* wheelin' the willow
> as if *them* had the power: (p.200)

Happiness is universal, and one spectator is so overcome by pure, unbridled joy that he rushes on to the field carrying a rooster to present to Walcott; it takes the full force of the law in the form of a policeman to stop him from interrupting the match in order to make his presentation. Another spectator who has worked as a passive, inoffensive functionary in the post office for twenty-five years, is suddenly stung into action by Walcott's stroke and: "like a sun-shatter daisy" yells "B...L...O...O...D". (p.201) It takes the irresistible stimulus of cricket to pierce his shield of innate torpor and reveal a depth of passion that has lain, so far as we know, concealed and untouched for twenty-five years. His behaviour is eloquent proof that, at that stage of the game, there are no bounds to Westindian joy and exultation.

In his article "Cricket, Carnival and Street Culture in the Caribbean" Richard Burton considers similarities between Westindian carnival, street culture and cricket as a means of explaining the pure, unalloyed commitment of Westindian spectators to cricket. He suggests that just as carnival may be regarded as a: "symbolic subversion of the structures of [order and authority in] everyday life." (pp.185-186) so far as most (black) Westindians are concerned, cricket may play an equally revolutionary role in their lives:

> Often springing shaman-like from the lowest strata of black society, the
> Constantines, the Headleys, the Walcotts, the Soberses, the Richardses,
> are the carnival kings and princes of the people, symbolic subverters and
> destroyers of a world where white is might and, as such, embodiments of
> a dream-world in which, by identification and projection, every black
> Westindian, be he never so poor, is monarch for the day." (p.186)

This is a plausible explanation of the unique urgency and intensity of Westindian
spectator participation in cricket, as if their very lives depended on it. It may
also explain why the exploit of a Headley or Walcott may be taken personally
as a vindication of the spectator's own talent, ability, indeed right to exist.

But in the middle of savouring Walcott's glory and the crowd's euphoria, the
tailor repeats his dark warning about Westindian brittleness, which comes as an
abrupt, albeit sober foreshadowing of misfortune, and arouses suspicion that
Walcott's glory will prove short-lived. Yet, the tailor feeds this suspicion by
delaying his dénouement and building up further suspense. Just as he had earlier
described his visitor's casual arrival in mock critical terms that set the scene of
the story, so he now describes the new bowler, Jim Laker, and his mannerisms,
as a way of preparing his audience for Walcott's imminent comeuppance. He
further dallies, with pregnant and tantalizing suggestiveness, as he explains
technical or strategic aspects of the contest: that Laker's off-breaks are pitched
on the off stump turning toward leg, with a leg trap of fieldsmen "shinin' like
shark" waiting for a catch. Then, gradually, almost without the reader realizing
it, he unleashes the dénouement through a dramatic change as Walcott, exultant
scorer of four red runs, and invincible punisher of syrupy slow bowling, is
suddenly, inexplicably, transformed into a fidgety, fearful, confused, and defensive
plodder, intent upon mere survival, never mind about scoring runs. It is a shattering
transformation that takes no more than a few lines to turn Laker into the
aggressor and Walcott into prey that is cornered and taunted like a mouse
suffering the perverse pleasure of a cat before being dispatched.

Suspense builds further as Walcott plays forward confidently to Laker's
first ball and is hit on the pad - an ominous portent. The second ball has Walcott:
"stretchin' right out like a man in de dark", although he somehow succeeds in
smothering the ball. Meanwhile, after each delivery, the tailor repeats the line:
"Boy, dis is cricket" changing the emphasis from "dis" in the first instance, to
"cricket" in the second. In other words, the tailor would like to remind his listener,
if not the whole world, that two deliveries without runs or wickets might appear
boring to non-cricketers, but to cricket aficionados like himself, they represent
an infinitely thrilling and absorbing contest. In the tailor's words, Laker wraps
the third ball in his hand "like a package" with deadly contents: "AN' MAKE
CLYDE WALCOTT LOOK FOOLISH." (p.202) The capitals signify the colossal
scale of destruction wrought by Laker. Not only that: all through "Rites", Walcott
is called "Clyde" in the friendly, chatty, informal style of the poem; that he now
becomes "CLYDE WALCOTT", in capital letters, ironically reflects his reduction

from the dignified and powerful status as invincible punisher of syrupy bowling and glorious scorer of "four red runs" to a humbled, fumbling fool.

Walcott's capitulation could not be more abject. And the crowd which was formerly bubbling and overflowing with comments of approval, shouts of approbation, and exclamations of joy, is simply stunned. Total silence descends on the packed cricket ground that, only moments before, was bristling with activity and resounding with a clattering cacophony of exclamations, ejaculations, cachinnations and what passes for animated conversation, but is in reality a babble of discordant oratory in which no one is listening and everyone is speechifying. Now, all that can be heard are flies buzzing around the bread carts. As Brathwaite puts it: "could' a hear if de empire fart." (p.202) Ignoring the political implication of a farting British empire, the more literal idea of a farting umpire confirms that this is no time for politeness, manners or decorum. Not that there was much of that to begin with; but as the tailor has said: "this is cricket", not sport; and calamity in cricket invokes inconsolable distress in Westindian hearts. Hence the lamentable sight of Kensington Oval in Bridgetown, Barbados, fabled scene of numberless, proud, vociferously proclaimed feats of glory and exaltation, now meekly enshrouded in a stifling, funereal pall of stupefied, dumbfounded silence!

At this stage of the narrative, Walcott has reached a peak of worldly glory from which he is evidently about to tumble into a pit of disaster that will provide the resolution required by the dénouement. But the narrator who has so far recorded every human reaction in "Rites" with flawless verisimilitude, now transforms the stunned spectators into a screaming mob intent on self-defensively retaliating against English tormentors of their hero Clyde. Hence shouts of aggression threatening murder and mayhem: "Kill one o' dem Clyde ... knock he skull off". (p.202) At a time when Walcott is deeply perplexed by Laker, and struggling for very survival, such advice is unhelpful to say the least, although, psychologically, it is intended to bolster his spirits by offering solidarity. The tailor sees through all this and comments sardonically: "Every blabber mout' talkin." Unseduced by the nervous bravado of the crowd, he lets us have the grim, unsparing truth phrased in his own unspoken terms:

> we so frighten now at what happening there
> we could piss we pants if we doan have a care (p.202)

It is only left for the tragic hero to be dispatched, and predictably, Walcott swings blindly at Laker and is out lbw. In a wonderfully expressive line that captures the complex mixture of surprise, shock and grief of the crowd, the tailor succinctly concludes: "Ev'ry mout' loss". (p.203) Then soberly, and for the last time, he repeats his sage asseveration whose aphoristic, axiomatic truth is now utterly beyond dispute:

> when things goin' good, you cahn touch
> we; but leh murder start
> an' ol man, you cahn fine a man to hole up de side. (p.203)

227

Evidently, "Rites" reveals much more about its narrator, Westindians and Westindian cricket than meets the eye. At a literal level, the narrator's revelations, based on a local as well as international match, confirm his belief: that the Westindian team in the 1950s wilted too easily under pressure or, to be blunt, lacked backbone. As a home-grown expert on cricket, the tailor would have relished the Westindian triumph over England in 1950 just as he would have been devastated by their shameful surrender to Australia in 1951/52. He would also have been little comforted by the fact that in five matches against India in 1952/53, despite distinct advantages in both batting and bowling, Westindies achieved one solitary win, and even that through something of a freak: it was achieved on a turning Kensington Oval wicket on which Ramadhin proved virtually unplayable, and on which he bowled 24 overs for 26 runs and took five wickets in India's second innings. The English tour of 1953/54 reflected similar lack of resolution: it opened with Westindian victories in the first two Tests, and ended in an inconclusive rubber, which was really a moral victory for England in so far as they had found the will to come back and win the third and fifth Tests.

In all these matches there were many incidents to support the tailor's claim of brittleness, for example, in the first innings of the fifth Test against England in 1954 when Westindies could only muster 139 runs, and Trevor Bailey garnered seven wickets for 44. Only four Westindian batsmen reached double figures, while the remaining seven, including Holt, Stollmeyer, Weekes, Worrell and Gomez, made 32 runs between them! In the 1950s, perhaps the most notorious instances of lack of resolution occurred during the Australian tour of 1955 and the 1957 Westindian tour of England both of which Westindies lost nil:three. What was lacking was concentration, discipline, solidarity, in short, teamwork. Although Westindies had many talented and brilliant players who gave their team a strong appearance on paper, quite often, their talent and brilliance did not materialise, or did so inconsistently during actual matches. A criticism that was frequently made at the time was that Westindies were less of a team than a collection of talented individuals. Frank Worrell called them "a rabble of brilliant individualists". This implies that leadership was a crucial problem. Nor is it difficult to imagine how continuing controversy and public disagreement over the selection of successive Westindian captains, who were all white, could adversely affect the morale of a team that was predominantly black.

If the distinction of "Rites" is mainly to illustrate or justify a thesis about cricket, it would be no better than the poems of cricket writers like John Arlott and R.C. Robertson Glasgow - which are more notable in their affection for cricket than their imagery or style - or poems by well known literary figures such as Sir Arthur Conan Doyle ("A Reminiscence of Cricket"), Francis Thompson ("At Lord's"), or Edmund Blunden ("Pride of the Village") all of whom affectionately celebrate what Blunden calls "worship in the summer sun". Yet no other poem equals "Rites" in density of texture, range of social and cultural reference, richness of meaning, wit, gaiety and humour. This must appear an extraordinary claim considering the long tradition of cricket writing in England; but it is no more extraordinary than the superiority established by the Westindian team over all others, despite their youthful Test cricket history. No doubt it will be argued that a long history of cricket (or a large population) are directly related neither to excellence in cricket nor to artistic quality. Besides, all teams have good and lean times, and artistic genius often flourishes in the most unlikely conditions. Certainly India, with almost the same Test history as Westindies (they started Test cricket in 1932), and an infinitely vaster population, has produced nothing like the results of Westindian cricket; nor poems like "Rites".

Even if it is hazardous to relate cricket or art to history and society, the difference between Westindian cricket and the rest, or between Brathwaite's poem and the rest calls for some explanation. English poets celebrate cricket as lovingly as Brathwaite. Who can fail to be moved by the haunting, nostalgic refrain of Thompson's well known lines?:

> As the run-stealers flicker to and fro,
> To and fro:
> O my Hornby and Barlow of long ago! ("At Lord's")

The appreciation of ordered symmetry and rhythmic grace conveyed by these lines is in sharp contrast to the raucous, explosive reactions of crowds on Westindian grounds. Numerous other poets evoke the beauty of the English countryside or celebrate village cricket with lively wit and humour. But the quality and tone of the celebration are again altogether different from the tone in "Rites". For there is a cultural divide between the playing and appreciation of English cricket on one hand, and Westindian on the other: hence the difference between Westindian and English poetry on cricket.

The sedately ordered, organised, tailored and controlled activities and reactions on an English cricket field are a world apart from the wilder, bubblier, gutsier, more boisterous and rumbustious carryings on of Westindian players and spectators. There is a world of difference between a quiet, picnic lunch of dainty cucumber sandwiches and tea on the manicured lawn of an English Test ground, and the spicy patties and hot-flavoured delicacies loudly advertised, and openly peddled by a host of competing vendors on Westindian cricket grounds. This is not to mention bottles of rum and beer to wash down the food, nor the gay rowdiness of a contradictory and improbable atmosphere heightened by fits of outlandish laughter, scurrilous banter, outbursts of ribaldry, violent arguments and heated debates about everything and nothing. In his essay mentioned earlier, Richard Burton suggests that Westindian cricket grounds reflect behaviour patterns "of Westindian male street culture in general: expansiveness, camaraderie, unruliness, jesting, joking, verbal and bodily bravado, clowning - in a word 'playing'." (pp.187-188) This is the atmosphere reproduced in "Rites"; it is eloquently proclaimed in the coarseness of an umpire farting, or the outrageous jocularity of a spectator holding up play in order to present a rooster to a batsman.

It is significant, by the way, that Brathwaite uses the colloquial term "fowl cock" instead of "rooster". "Rooster" and "fowl cock" imply a spiritual difference between English and Westindian cricket, the one polite, guarded, correctly descriptive, the other common or vulgar, uninhibited, raw, ribald and slightly roguish. No wonder Brathwaite's poem is written in a demotic, gutsy, deliberately indecorous style with fresh metaphors and on-the-spot coinages that brilliantly catch the instantaneous, extraverted exuberance and light-hearted, individualistic surface exhibitionism that are intricately woven into Caribbean cricket and society. For all its haunting beauty, Thompson's "O my Hornby and Barlow of long ago" could never match the condensed expressiveness of: "Ev'ry mout' loss". Thompson's language is, by comparison with Brathwaite's, almost anaemic, bloodless. It would tax Shakespeare (see Appendix iii) himself to find linguistic resources in standard English to match the succinct vigour, idiomatic piquancy, rhythmic versatility, accuracy and colourfulness of Brathwaite's creole in "Rites".

"Rites" portrays a Westindian style of cricket that is part and parcel of a larger culture or lifestyle regarded as rootless because it belongs to a motley group of people exiled in the new world, away from their original homelands in the old continents of Africa, Asia and Europe. That exile, in its early stages, produced uncertainty, confusion, wavering and unpredictability is not to be wondered at. The flashiness, brittleness or inconsistency of Westindian cricket emanates from a society which itself, historically, resorted to arbitrariness, improvisation, eccentricity and individualism as strategies of survival to cope with the stark consequences of cultural deracination, displacement and discontinuity under the uncertain aegis of colonial rule. As a professional historian and author of such seminal texts as *The Development of Creole Society in Jamaica 1770-1820*, (London, O.U.P 1970), and *Folk Culture of the Slaves in Jamaica* (London, New Beacon, 1970), Brathwaite is not unmindful of the consequences of a fractured Caribbean past. His poetry in *The Arrivants* and later works, illustrates and analyses this fracture; it also identifies elements of continuity that have survived it. Earlier Westindian writers such as George Lamming had invoked the fracture of the African past mainly in dreams. But Brathwaite lived in Africa and his writing benefits from both historical scholarship and personal experience of Africa. His African-derived Westindian oral tradition in "Rites" is informed and heightened by historical insight, practical experience and the special sympathy of his poetic imagination. Hence the antiphonal, almost choral structure in "Rites", in which the tailor's speaking voice continuously anticipates possible interruption from his listener. This structure owes much to a call and response pattern that comes from an African oral tradition which Brathwaite has inherited in adapted form, and which has also survived in other African diasporic cultures, for example, in congregational responses of sound and movement to preachers in black churches of the American South.

"Limbo" in which "Rites" appears, is one of five sections of *Islands*, each of which represents a stage in Westindian history. The first section "New World" evokes the uprooting of Africans and their transplantation in the Caribbean and the Americas; "Limbo", the second section, deals with the initial consequences of uprooting and transplantation: rootlessness, and unstable, inconsistent or fickle behaviour patterns; remaining sections of *Islands* speak of "Rebellion" - political protest bred out of mounting dissatisfaction with rootlessness; "Possession" which implies effort to accommodate to a new, unstable reality, and "possess" the new world in a spiritual sense; and "Beginning", ironically the final section, in which the consequences of fracture and displacement are left behind, and a fresh start is made in a new world that has become home. If "Arrivants" connotes the ghostly or unreal identity of uprooted and displaced people upon their arrival in the Caribbean, "Beginning" suggests that the arrivants have finally arrived. According to Brathwaite, it has taken these "unreal" (rootless) arrivants a centuries-long process of settlement, adaptation and indigenisation within the context of slavery and colonialism, to become "real" (rooted) arrivals. "Rites" illustrates the early, "Limbo" stage of this long process when the arrivants were most deeply troubled by uncertainty, instability and fickleness.

In "Rites", through an inspired blend of historical scholarship with the poetic imagination, Brathwaite evokes a moment in Westindian history with compelling vigour and vibrancy. It is a moment of rootlessness reflecting rites that form an essential stage in the rise of Westindian nationality. That the moment is evoked in terms of cricket illustrates the central importance of the game to the history of the Westindies; for nothing catches the Westindian national imagination more comprehensively than cricket, and nothing reflects national weaknesses more accurately. It is neither uncritical nor bizarre for the tailor in "Rites' to claim that cricket is something other than sport; and once we see through his self-advertising rhetorical flourishes, we realize that he is making a serious claim both for cricket as a barometer of national sentiment, and for the consequences of cultural displacement and exile in the Westindies. This is why "Rites" surpasses all other poems on cricket. Cricket in the Westindies is not what it is elsewhere - a game, however dramatic, intense, honourable or ennobling. English, Australian or Indian poets who celebrate the joys or virtues of the game as a pastime are unlikely to match the historical scope, psychological depth, and linguistic prodigality of a poem like "Rites" which gathers fundamental aspects of Westindian history, culture and nationality into an illuminating statement on the past, present and future of the Westindian people. In this sense, "Rites" should not be regarded as a poem about cricket, but simply as a poem. As the tailor says:

> this isn't no time for playin.
> the fool nor makin' no sport; this is cricket (p.198)

Quite so. When cricket is no longer sport, poems about cricket become just poems.

C.L.R. James's *Beyond a Boundary*

C.L.R. James has produced the most and by far the best writing about Westindian cricket. He began as cricket correspondent for the *Manchester Guardian* in 1933; and apart from mainly political endeavours, notably between

1938 and 1953 when he lived in the US, wrote regularly on cricket until his death in London, in 1989. Although his cricket writings are spread over more than fifty years, and scattered in newspapers, periodicals and books in different countries, they consist of fairly standard features - descriptions of cricket matches, portraits of cricketers, together with commentaries mixing political and cultural analysis, and broad, general comparisons expressed through a fluent, loose-jointed style touched by a hint of benign intellectual paternalism. Not that James is ever guilty of condescension; for that would run counter to his general purpose of social and political upliftment for (particularly black) victims of worldwide discrimination and exploitation; but his role as an inveterate lecturer and public speaker has invested his writing with a taste for declamation, oracular pronouncements, and a schoolmasterish tone that sometimes betrays a note of didacticism.

Since the bulk of James's writing is on ostensibly more "serious" subjects, it is surprising to claim that *Beyond a Boundary* - the purest distillation of his thoughts on cricket - almost rivals *The Black Jacobins*, his historical masterpiece about the career of Toussaint l'Ouverture, a former African slave who led a successful revolution against French colonial rulers in Haiti at the end of the eighteenth century. James states in his preface to *Beyond a Boundary* that the volume: "is neither cricket reminiscence nor autobiography. It poses the question what do they know of cricket who only cricket know?" This also is surprising since much of the volume is about James himself and his interests, or about people whom he knew. But it is correct to claim that *Beyond a Boundary* is not only about cricket; for it includes history, sociology, philosophy, literature, aesthetics, and much else, in addition to cricket reminiscences and autobiography. It is a multifaceted, interdisciplinary volume, global in scope, the work of a true polymath; and like most of James's writings, it illuminates its subject through comparisons drawn from an enormous storehouse of encyclopaedic knowledge. If literary parallels are needed, *Beyond a Boundary* belongs to a species of writing, like Izak Walton's *Compleat Angler*, which takes fishing as its subject but ranges much further afield, or Hemingway's *Death in the Afternoon* which encompasses rather more than bull fighting.

The first section of *Beyond a Boundary* consists of reminiscences, autobiographical memoirs and sketches of early Westindian cricketers, and describes the author's early years in his homeland, Trinidad, up to 1932 when he left for England. At the time Trinidad had an old, feudalistic crown colony government and social manners traditionally regulated by criteria of race, class and colour, as James's portrait of Wilton St. Hill illustrates:

> W. St. Hill was a very curious man of strongly marked character of which the defects belonged more to his time than to himself. He was born in 1893, of the lower middle class. The family was brownish, but Wilton was the lightest of them. By 1912 he was a great batsman and a universal favourite. He got a job selling in a department store, and I believe he worked there for the rest of his life. (p.93)

Such perceptive, finely detailed and condensed portraiture would elude the combined skills of a social historian and novelist. No wonder that, in addition to his reputation as historian, biographer, literary critic, political and social theorist and commentator on cricket, James also wrote a novel *Minty Alley* (1936) and a number of short stories. His few lines on St. Hill comprehensively evoke the mixed social background of colonial Trinidad with its intertwined, racial and social hierarchies, and a seemingly improbable hint that cricket somehow provided a means of transcending these hierarchies.

Like St. Hill, James belonged to the black, lower middle class and hoped to excel through intellectual talent, as St. Hill attempted to do through his talent in cricket. We learn a good deal about the opportunities, obstacles, and general circumstances facing people like James and St. Hill in colonial Trinidad during the first half of this century. In James's case, a scholarship to the government boys' school, Queen's Royal College, (QRC) allowed him to indulge his voracious appetite for reading, and confirmed that education offered his most likely opportunity of advancement. It also confirmed the type of education he would get, as we can see from the reading material that was available to him at school and at home: Thackeray, Dickens, George Eliot, Matthew Arnold, Shelley, Keats, Byron, Hazlitt, Lamb, Coleridge, not to mention the *Review of Reviews, Tit-Bits, Comic Cats,* The *Strand* Magazine and *Pearson's* Magazine. This solidly British reading material is a crucial element in James's intellectual development; for in *Beyond a Boundary* and in much of his other writing, he acknowledges a deep British or western influence both on himself and his fellow Trinidadians. He emphasizes this influence in a lecture "The Making of the Caribbean People" delivered in 1966:

> I denounce European colonialist scholarship. But I respect the learning and the profound discoveries of Western civilisation. It is by means of the work of the great men of ancient Greece; of Michelet, the French historian; of Hegel, Marx and Lenin; of DuBois; of contemporary Europeans and Englishmen like Pares and E.P. Thompson; of an African like the late Chisiza, that my eyes and ears have been opened and I can today see and hear what we were, what we are, and what we can be, in other words - the making of the Caribbean people." (*Spheres of Influence*, p.38)

In *Beyond a Boundary*, James argues with equal force that British public school ideals were imprinted on Westindian culture through cricket. This imprint is illustrated in six chapters (12-16) of *Beyond a Boundary*, which include two on W.G. Grace alone. These chapters range back and forth in history from the first Olympic Games in ancient Greece, to cricket in nineteenth century England. If Westindians excel at cricket, James claims, it is partly because of the imprint of western (British values) on their culture; and when he writes: "cricket is first and foremost a dramatic spectacle. It belongs with the theatre, ballet, opera and the dance." (p.206) He is suggesting that the westernized culture of Westindians gives them direct access to cricket as a western art form which they can readily adopt and master.

Perhaps James stretches himself too thinly in elucidating features of cricket as a western art form; for this section of his narrative fails to elicit the visceral sense of conviction of the rest. It may be that the range of ideas in this section -

from aesthetic values in ancient Greece to public school ideals in Victorian England - is too vast, or its method too theoretical:

> "It [cricket] cannot express the emotions of an age on the nature of the last judgment or the wiping out of a population by bombing. It must repeat. But what it repeats is the original stuff out of which everything visually or otherwise artistic is quarried. The popular democracy of Greece, sitting for days in the sun watching "The Oresteia"; the popular democracy of our day, sitting similarly, watching Miller and Lindwall bowl to Hutton and Compton - each in its own way grasps at a more complete human existence." (p.206)

This will tax the conviction of the most ardent lover of cricket. Nevertheless, James makes a coherent case, and his conclusion is unerring, namely that Westindian society and cricket are imprinted with Victorian values, an idea crystallized in the last sentence of his book: "Thomas Arnold, Thomas Hughes and the Old Master [W.G. Grace] himself would have recognised Frank Worrell as their boy." (p.252) This conclusion gains credence from an article "The Elite schools and Cricket in Barbados: A Study in Colonial Continuity" by Keith Sandiford and Brian Stoddart who claim there was an "élite school" system in Barbados from the 1870s onwards:

> a system based quite consciously on the public and grammar school ideology of Victorian Britain...The old boys of Eton, Harrow, Cambridge and Oxford arrived in the colonies with cricket, classics and Christianity as the principal components in their intellectual, ideological and cultural baggage...Nowhere was this more clear than in the British Westindies. (*The International Journal of the History of Sport*, IV, iii, 1987, pp. 333-334)

At the same time, the fact that the mind and attitudes of Frank Worrell should be imprinted with the cultural, moral and aesthetic values of three English exemplars of Victorian culture appears controversial or contentious, to say the least. After all, Worrell's exploits between 1960 and 1963 came at the height of the movement for Independence in the Westindies, when all the nationalist agitation of previous decades was at last beginning to pay off. It seems contradictory to attribute British - derived ideals to someone whose talents as cricketer and captain led to the overthrow of British supremacy over Westindies in cricket. Perhaps there is an implied paradox here. At any rate, James makes a parallel case in *Beyond a Boundary* for the grandeur of cricket as: "a game which, in lands far from that which gave it birth, could encompass so much of social reality and still remain a game." (p.97) If this means that Westindian cricket encompasses and reflects the peculiarities of a distinct social reality, it again seems unlikely that an authentic Westindian social reality would include Victorian ideals. Yet this is precisely the conclusion to which Sandiford and Stoddart come in their article mentioned above: "In Barbados...cricket became even more a national obsession than it had ever been in Victorian Britain, the best single testament to the creation of a British mentality in a constructed colonial social order." (pp. 347-348)

The argument about cricket encompassing a Westindian social reality is evident in sketches of four cricketers in *Beyond a Boundary* - George John, Wilton St. Hill, Learie Constantine and George Headley. Of these, St. Hill was scarcely the most distinguished, his Test record being 6 innings for 117 runs, an average of 19.50, and an highest score of 38 made in the second innings of the second Test against England at Old Trafford in July 1928. Yet, in his chapter "The Most Unkindest Cut", James transforms this unpromising subject into what John Arlott has called: "the finest portrait of a cricketer ever created." (Quoted by David Frith in *Wisden Cricket Monthly*, May 1994, p.61) Such success is primarily due to skills - as biographer, historian and critic - which James perfected in *The Black Jacobins* and which he deploys in *Beyond a Boundary* with the deftness of long experience, and a degree of intellectual sophistication rare in cricket literature. Here, for instance, is a comment on George John's fast bowling: "Other bowlers can be qualified as hostile. John was not hostile, he was hostility itself. If he had been an Italian of the Middle Ages he would have been called Furioso." (p.81) As nothing more than a passing remark thrown away half in jest, this comment has penetration, sympathy and a quality of erudition that leaves most other cricket commentaries miles behind.

James's erudition and writing skills combine with a profound knowledge both of cricket technique and of Trinidad's social background to produce an unforgettable portrait of St. Hill:

> "No one I have seen, neither Bradman nor Sobers, saw the ball more quickly, nor made up his mind earlier. Time; he always had plenty of time... With most of his strokes the only sign of tension or effort was the head very slightly bent forward on the shoulders so as to assist the concentration of his eyes riveted on the ball... His right toe was always towards point, left elbow high and left wrist as a fulcrum. (p.88)

Precise technical detail is an essential aspect of the sense of authority that emanates from this portrait of St. Hill; and authority is a feature in all of James's best writing which analyses his subject down to the minutest technical detail. What he says about St. Hill's abilities, circumstances, and performance also implies a personal interest and excitement in the fortunes of the man himself; so that one feels that the author's own fortunes are somehow mixed up in St. Hill's. This feeling is reinforced by observations of James's own bowling to St. Hill, along with results of research, reports from different matches in which St. Hill has appeared, and reactions of other bowlers and fielders. James also makes comparisons with players from different generations and countries, and what comes out is a thoroughly exhaustive and authoritative account that leaves the impression there is nothing more left to find out about St. Hill.

The facts about St. Hill are that he distinguished himself in intercolonial matches in the 1920s, but failed in the trial matches from which players were picked for the 1923 Westindian tour to England. When he was finally picked for the 1928 tour, he failed in England. Yet, as James says:

> He [St. Hill] made his centuries in intercolonial matches, against the M.C.C. team in 1926 and again in 1930. Lord Harris, who knew of George Challenor's form in England in 1923 and saw him at his best in the Westindies in 1926, said of Wilton St. Hill that year that he was the finest batsman in the Westindies and certain to be a great success in England in 1928. In England he was a terrible, disastrous failure, so that even now it hurts to think of it, the solitary painful memory of those crowded cricket years. (p.93)

The agony of St. Hill's failure is wrenching. By James's account, he is a tragic example of sublime, ethereal promise mysteriously withering into sordid decline and humiliation. A sense of tragedy and mystery is admirably caught in James's concluding lines:

> For myself, I stick to the technical. He [St. Hill] saw the ball as early as anyone. He played it as late as anyone. His spirit was untameable, perhaps too much so. There we must leave it." (p.103)

This captures the mystery of genius whose origin and function may be recognized but never fully fathomed by ordinary mortals like ourselves. All an author can do is stick to what he has seen and understood; the rest is left to heaven; for who can explain why St. Hill arrived, as it were, unheralded and unasked for, to display such sublime talents in colonial Trinidad, then neither to develop them nor satisfy the expectations that his talents stimulated!

Despite its ethereal quality, St. Hill's batting was not all art for art's sake: it aroused less abstract, more concrete feelings which bear out James's view that: "cricket is an art, a means of national expression." (*Cricket*, p.38) Since these feelings were broadly enough based to constitute national sentiment, St. Hill's tragedy was not simply in failing to develop his artistic gifts as a batsman, but in letting down feelings of national pride among people who were his supporters and admirers:

> I know that to tens of thousands of coloured Trinidadians the unquestioned glory of St. Hill's batting conveyed the sensation that here was one of us, performing in excelsis in a sphere where competition was open. It was a demonstration that atoned for a pervading humiliation, and nourished pride and hope. (p.99)

Whether he knew it or not, by failing as batsman, St. Hill failed admirers and supporters who thought that his batting could atone for their humiliation as historic victims of a plantation society disfigured by slavery and exploitation. They saw his batting as a symbol of achievement that gave them hope of regeneration from this humiliation, and a corollary of this hope was the promise of political advancement as a racial, social or national group.

Regeneration through a desire for freedom from injustice is a basic theme running through all of James's writing. Following many slave revolts in Westindian history, and some political advances after emancipation, cricket emerged as the most widely shared idiom through which, symbolically,

Westindians could articulate their desire for social justice, political freedom, and economic progress. In his article "Cricket, Carnival and Street Culture in the Caribbean," Richard Burton suggests that cricket, carnival and street culture merge together in the Westindies to express underlying social, cultural, and psychological feeling. This suggests how St. Hill's batting could serve as a means of national expression. It also reveals how St. Hill "betrayed" his supporters and admirers - the ordinary people of Trinidad. James confirms all this through an anecdote in which he was visited by one of St. Hill's admirers who: "came to the match on Saturday to see Wilton bat, as nationalist crowds go to hear their political leaders." (p.95) This was in 1912 when St. Hill, nineteen years old, had made a century in an intercolonial tournament in which Victor Pascall's bowling had wrought devastation. James had written a poem in praise of Pascall which is what provoked the visit by St. Hill's admirer:

> He [the anonymous admirer] didn't beat about the bush. The article on
> Pascall, he called it the article, was fine. But what about Wilton? Couldn't
> I do something on Wilton? The man was in dead earnest." (p.95)

James describes the quandary in which he was placed, and how, in the end, he "sweated out a sonnet to W. St. Hill" (p.96) that appeared in the same paper as his poem on Pascall. Then "the watchful guardian of St. Hill's interests who had commissioned it [the sonnet] sought me out and told me it was 'good." (p.96) A link between St. Hill's batting and the national aspirations of his countrymen gives this anecdote a significance that deepens the tragedy of his failure and transports it from an insignificant, if interesting, incident in Westindian sport to a poignant episode in a simultaneous Westindian process of national development and struggle for freedom.

Bound up in the argument about cricket symbolically advancing the national aspirations of Westindians is the issue of the special identity of Westindian cricket. James quotes from a London *Times* correspondent on St. Hill's batting in a two-day game during the 1928 Westindian tour of England:

> W. St. Hill...performs amazing apparently double-jointed tricks with
> his wrists and arms. Some of those contortions are graceful and
> remunerative, such as his gliding to leg, but some are unsound and
> dangerous, such as an exaggerated turn of the wrist in cutting. He will
> certainly play some big and attractive innings, but some others may be
> easily curtailed by his exotic fancy in dealing with balls on the off-side.
> (pp.102-103)

"Double-jointed tricks", "contortions", "unsound and dangerous", and "exotic fancy" indicate that although he admires St. Hill, the correspondent has some reservations about elements of his batting. That these elements are unsound, dangerous or exotic does not matter. What matters is that the anonymous correspondent notices them, and considers them as different from the norm in England. To what extent these different elements in St. Hill's batting constitute a distinct Westindian style is not certain, but his wristy cutting, "exotic fancy", tricks and contortions strike a familiar note in commentaries by English writers on the batting of Constantine, Headley, the Ws, Sobers and Kanhai, who were later acknowledged as purveyors of an unmistakable style of Westindian batting. Despite his failure in Tests, St. Hill, like Challenor, must be seen as the precursor of a peculiar Westindian batting style that would later become more universally recognized in exploits by Headley, the Ws, Sobers and Kanhai.

In *Beyond a Boundary*, James alludes to frequent occasions in the 1930s when, in addition to strategies in cricket, he and Constantine discussed political strategies that could lead to Westindian self-government. These discussions formed part of a general strategy to prove to English people that the Westindies were politically mature, no longer in need of colonial tutelage. Just as Westindians were politically mature and independent enough to deserve self-government, so in cricket they were demonstrating a mature and independent style of playing that was as cerebral in conception and execution as English cricket itself. This is why James and Constantine took such pains to convince their English hosts that Constantine's ebullient, charismatic style of batting, bowling and fielding was not instinctive but the product of deep cogitation and patient practice. There is a note of defensiveness when James writes: "Constantine the magician, is the product of tradition and training." (p.148) Both men wrote at length on this point, making perhaps too elaborate a case for deliberation and technical planning in Westindian cricket in order to counter what they saw as an English tendency to dismiss Westindian cricketers as natural, spontaneous and instinctive athletes who never gave a thought to what they were doing.

Stollmeyer complains about Constantine's incessant theorizing in *Everything Under the Sun*:

> As young players we used, at first, we used to hang on to Learie's every word, but as time went on we found many of his theories foreign to our thinking. When in later years we were discussing Learie with Don Bradman, the latter made a rather caustic assessment: "It was a difficult game when he talked about it." Fair comment. It was. Of course, Learie played it differently and that was why he was such a great attraction despite his complicated theories of events. (p.35)

Constantine theorized mainly about cricket, whereas James's theories linked cricket to fundamental social and cultural processes in Caribbean history. James states that: "an investigation of Worrell, Walcott and Weekes would tell us as much about the past and future of the people of the Westindies as about cricket." (p.148) Thereby linking the evolution of Westindian national identity, in cultural and political terms, with the emergence of a distinctive style in cricket:

> Westindians crowding to Tests bring with them the whole past history and future hopes of the islands. English people, for example, have a conception of themselves breathed from birth. Drake, and mighty Nelson, Shakespeare, Waterloo, the *Charge of the Light Brigade,* the few who

did so much for so many, the success of parliamentary democracy, those and such as those constitute a national tradition. Underdeveloped countries have to go back centuries to rebuild one. We in the Westindies have none at all, none that we know of. To such people the three Ws, Ram and Val wrecking English batting, help to fill a huge gap in their consciousness and in their needs. In one of the sheds in the Port of Spain wharf is a painted sign: 365 Garfield Sobers. (p.225)

According to James, if cricket means to Westindians what Shakespeare and Waterloo mean to the English nation (and English cricket), then cricket reflects Westindian nationality, and the style of the Ws, Ram, Val, Sobers and Kanhai represents a collective type of behaviour or expression that gives Westindians a sense of themselves as a nation.

When we get down to it, there is no basic contradiction between an assertion of strong English influence on Westindian cricket or culture, and acceptance of cricket's role in advancing Westindian national aspirations; for Westindian national identity is the product of a gradual process of social and cultural evolution which began when the Westindian territories, as British colonies for centuries, naturally absorbed strong English or Western influence in law, education, politics and culture as in sport. It was equally natural for this influence to decline as the Westindies acquired their own identity over time. As we have seen, English or Western influence was very marked in the early 1900s when James was a young man, although it had weakened when Independence came in the 1960s. The trouble is that by asserting a formative British or Western influence on himself and the Westindies in the early decades of this century, James admits to a degree of cultural ambivalence during this period; and mere admission of ambivalence provokes resentment in critics who accuse Westindians like James of lack of patriotism or of being Uncle Toms or Afro-Saxons.

It is undeniable that up to the middle decades of this century, strong Western influence was deeply woven into the intellectual fabric of all Westindians whether they were university graduates or not. Influence tended to be stronger in graduates or those who had gone furthest in education, and it can be seen in well known political leaders of the time such as Grantley Adams of Barbados, Norman Manley of Jamaica, and Eric Williams of Trinidad, all of whom studied in Britain and became Prime Ministers of their respective countries. But the influence also existed in those who did not take a university degree like James, and his Trinidadian contemporary Albert Gomes, an author, editor and politician who frankly admits to similar influence in his autobiography *In a Maze of Colour*. In reflecting similar English influence, cricket also became an instrument of ambivalence that, paradoxically, both asserted and resisted English colonial values. Kenneth Surin, in his essay "C.L.R. James's materialist ethics of cricket", makes roughly the same point:

> *Beyond a Boundary* itself testifies that cricket was imbricated in 'the old Colonial System' (and thus the 'new' neo-colonial system?) just as much as any other area of Westindian life cited by James, and this inevitably had, and maybe even still has, the effect of transmuting and blunting,

while still expressing and embodying, some of the radical social and political
passions associated by James with his beloved game. (in A. Kennery, ed.
Intellectuals in the Twentieth Century Caribbean, Vol 1, p. 136)

Surin admits to the need for more work to be done on what he calls: "the
ambivalent functions served by Westindian cricket in the colonial and neo-
colonial dispensations." (p.136)

The truth is that James's general proposition of strong British or Western
influence in the Westindies during the colonial period does admit the risk of
shallow or perverted cultural attitudes, not just ambivalent or harmless anglophile
sentiments such as those expressed in Frank Worrell's *Cricket Punch* or Clyde
Walcott's *Island Cricketers*, but more self-destructive symptoms of slavish
imitation or mimicry that are probed in V.S. Naipaul's classic novel *The Mimic
Men*. James's own essay "The Westindian Middle Classes" denounces exactly
the kind of soul-destroying imitation of foreign and imperfectly understood
models that Naipaul identifies as sapping Westindian initiative, creativity and
self-respect. But, though alive to the danger of mimicry, James relentlessly
reminds us of the importance of cricket in helping to transmit the influence of
British culture and manners to the Westindies:

> "Cricket was one of the means whereby the general population of the
> Westindies incorporated into their ways of life and thinking much of the
> style and manners inherent in the English way of life." (*David Frost
> Introduces Trinidad*, p.38)

It is as if he wants to make quite sure that his point is taken, and so overdoes the
English influence in Westindian culture and cricket. Perhaps. But his claim of
English influence during the colonial era and its decline during the period of
Independence is incontestable, even if one disagrees with his estimate of the
strength of this influence or his timing of its decline.

In terms of cricket itself, James has written in "The Artist in the Caribbean"
that: "Sobers was born into a tradition, into a medium which though transported
was so well established that it has created a Caribbean tradition of its own." (*Future
in the Present*, p.38) This clarifies what has been said before: that Sobers is the
product of a cricketing tradition that came to acquire an identity of its own although
it originated in a tradition that was borrowed from England. There is no
disagreement about the historical fact that cricket came to the Westindies from
England along with considerable Victorian cultural baggage. Nor will many
disagree that Westindian cricket, as it is played today, is poles apart from English
cricket. But there will be different views about exactly when or how Westindian cricket
deviated from its English sources. In a speech, "The 1963 Westindians" given to the
Cricket Society in the Tavern at Lord's, on September 5, 1963, James said:

> "The Westindies have reached where they are because certain of them
> have had the opportunity to absorb to a large degree, and to adapt to
> their own uses, a certain definite [English] tradition. But they have to
> bring something of their own now to the life that they have to live, and I

believe in the cricket they have been playing over the last two or three years they have found something of their own. (*Cricket*, p.38)

James perceives a different identity in Westindian cricket during the early 1960s, when the team came under the captaincy of Frank Worrell. This makes sense. It is not that elements of a separate identity did not exist before, for example, in the batting of Wilton St. Hill in the 1920s, and in the bowling of Constantine and the batting of George Headley in the 1930s. The Ws and Ram and Val also made a definite impact on English players in the 1950s. But throughout all this time Westindian cricket was carried largely by individuals rather than by a collective team. It was under Frank Worrell that Westindies first functioned coherently and effectively as a team and registered their full impact, to universal acclaim, as members of a national entity.

Nevertheless, *Beyond a Boundary* appears animated by powerful, anglophile feelings. Although from his earliest portraits of George John, Wilton St. Hill, and those of Constantine and Headley, James constantly stresses departures from English influence, the primary premise of his book is an umbilical cultural and cricketing connection of the Westindies to England up to the 1950s. In a letter to V.S. Naipaul, James wrote:

> But the book [*Beyond a Boundary*] is very British. Not only the language but on page after page the (often unconscious) literary references, the turn of phrase, the mental and moral outlook. That is what we are, and we shall never know ourselves until we recognize that fully and freely and without strain.
>
> But that does not end it, not at all. That is only the beginning. I believe that, originating as we are within the British structure, but living under such different social conditions, we have a lot to say about the British civilization itself which we see more sharply than they themselves. (*Cricket*, p.117)

James is not afraid to lay his cards on the table. He has nothing to hide. Over and over again he has asserted his British cultural connection as a Westindian, while steadfastly supporting efforts to remove British colonial rule worldwide. From his first published work, *The Life of Captain Cipriani: An account of British Government in the West Indies*, which appeared in 1932, in the heyday of colonial rule when the very thought of colonial liberation seemed a pipe-dream, James was a redoubtable fighter against colonialism. There is a prophetic note in his writing during the 1930s, as he implies in his Preface to the Vintage edition of *The Black Jacobins* in 1962: "In 1938 only the writer [James] and a handful of close associates thought, wrote and spoke as if the African events of the last quarter of a century were imminent." These credentials plus his later association with left wing political groups and his prolific writings on Marxism and radical politics confirm James's unwavering dedication to colonial liberation.

If his anti-colonialism seems at odds with his assertion of English or Western influence in the Westindies, it is neither because of insincerity or self-contradiction: James sees history moving in stages. In his portrait of the calypsonian The Mighty Sparrow, James notes similarities and differences between the Westindies and other places with a colonial inheritance:

> Here I tread very cautiously but I think I see that our own historical existence and the kind of world in which we live, are forcing upon us a rapid combination of historical stages which took centuries in the older nations. Ghana, Ceylon, India do not have the same premises. They have a native language, native religion, native way of life. We haven't. We are Western, yet have to separate what is ours from what is Western, a very difficult task. (*Future in the Present*, p.38)

The outsider status of the Westindies within the framework of Western history and culture is crucial to an appreciation of *Beyond a Boundary*, and explains why there is no self-contradiction in James's views, for as he writes in another context:

> We [Westindians] have the same language as the British and the outline of our civilization is based on theirs, we are in the same situation that has created the great writers of the twentieth century. We are members of this civilization and take part in it, but we come from outside. (*Savacou*, p.60)

The English-speaking Westindies are not exactly like former British colonies in Asia and Africa because they were "created" by Britain in the sense that the populations were trans-shipped to the Caribbean from elsewhere. On the contrary, former colonies in Asia and Africa retain their ancient and continuous history with their own languages and cultures, despite the impact, however grievous, of British colonialism. Although they retain cultural survivals from their original homelands, Westindians lost much of their original languages and cultures: hence their being shaped or, as James says, *imprinted* by Britain. Their destiny is inextricably linked with the West. Even former colonies in Asia and Africa which retained their cultures and were never displaced, find it difficult nowadays to resist domination by global Eurocentric power. James's point is that, like it or not, the Westindies have inherited an ambivalent insider/outsider cultural status in the Western world. This is what he articulates in *Beyond a Boundary*. But the ambivalence is not static; it becomes less and less as the Westindies grow in cultural and political maturity.

The core of the argument in *Beyond a Boundary* is that partly and perhaps paradoxically because of its English cultural antecedents cricket acted as a catalyst to the process of evolution by which the Westindies evolved to cultural and political maturity. Just as there is an element of ambivalence in the anglophile Worrell orchestrating the removal of English sovereignty over Westindies in cricket, so it is paradoxical that a game, deeply imprinted with British influence, should, in the end, promote the removal of British influence in the Westindies. Nor is this paradox unusual in former British colonies most of which gained independence from Britain through the agitation of British-educated leaders - Nehru, Gandhi, Kenyatta and Nyerere, not to mention Norman Manley, Grantley Adams and Eric Williams. In his letter to V.S.

Naipaul already quoted James writes: "Curiously enough, I have little doubt that in England it [*Beyond a Boundary*] will be understood. It is the Westindies that I am concerned about." (p.117) This shows that James was aware of the sensitivity of some of his countrymen to his ambivalent views on Westindian history, culture and cricket, for they would regard ambivalence as contradictory, unpatriotic or worse. As James predicted, *Beyond a Boundary* was well received in England. John Arlott thought it contained: "fire and contemplation, facts and imagination, breadth and depth." (Quoted by David Frith, *Wisden Cricket Monthly*, May, 1994, p.61) These qualities are visible in the fire of James's fiercely combative writing, the contemplation of his perceptive portraits and analytical studies; facts that are of encyclopaedic scope and variety, and the imaginative boldness in his very conception of the whole work itself. As for breadth and depth, there is not another book on cricket with similar largeness of vision.

Beyond a Boundary encompasses a critical half-century (1910 to 1960) in the social and cultural evolution of the Westindies. It provides historical, cultural, political and social analysis together with an illuminating explanation of the process by which Westindian cricket rose from Cinderella status to become the star of the international ball. The book goes further to include philosophical speculation and reflections on art. This is why it ranks with those few books whose ostensible subject is sport, but whose range is far wider. This species of writing is splendidly described by John Arlott in his comments on an early classic of cricket literature, John Nyren's *The Cricketers of my Time* (1833) in the preparation of which he was assisted by Charles Cowden Clarke, teacher and friend of the poet John Keats:

> Nyren's is one of the very few books ever written on any game which can stand squarely upon its merits outside the literature of sport. *The Cricketers of my Time* is such a book because it comes out of a deep enthusiasm which had become a faith, a nostalgia which was as searching as intense, and a certainty which comes of knowing a game as a craft and one's fellow-practitioners as human beings. (*From Hambledon to Lord's*, p.10)

It is impossible to miss James's enthusiasm for his subject in *Beyond a Boundary*, and it is evident from his career that this enthusiasm did grow into political if not religious faith. Nostalgia springs naturally out of his reminiscence and autobiography, and nothing else in Westindian cricket literature matches the analytical rigour and factual richness of *Beyond a Boundary*. As for James's certainty which comes out of a profound knowledge of the craft of cricket, there is the technical detail and absolute authority, for example, in his portrait of St. Hill; Arlott cannot be more right: it is James's awareness of Westindian cricketers as human beings, and his commitment to their collective, national well being that transforms *Beyond a Boundary* from a superb work on cricket into a classic of Westindian literature.

Conclusion

I f colonialism justified a Westindian cricketer saying: "We come to learn sah" during the Westindian tour of England in 1900, it also justified the deference of R.K. Nunes who, as President of the WICBC, acknowledged that Westindies (the pupil) had a "responsibility" to prove they deserved the "honour" of playing four Test matches against England (the mentor) in 1950. Deferential Westindian attitudes toward England survived through the first half of this century, because they were nurtured by deeply rooted relationships within an Anglo-centric colonial structure that was itself sustained by a Eurocentric world order. These relationships fostered attitudes of deference, servility, mimicry and ambivalence not only in the Westindies, but in English-speaking countries the world over. Here, for example, is part of a speech given in 1930 by K.S. Ranjitshinji, the Jam Sahib of Nawanagar:

> The countries which together compose the British Empire constitute the greatest cricket team which the world has ever seen. Just as the members of a cricket team differ from each other in stature, in personal characteristics, in ability of one kind or another, so the various components of the British Empire differ widely among themselves. But, in the one case and in the other, it is not with a series of individual units with which we are concerned, but with a great team working for common good by bringing out the best from each component member. (Marcus Williams Ed., *Double Century*, p.261).

Ranji took it for granted that England was the centre of his world, and that everything of value, including cricket, emanated from England. (See Appendix i) So for him, and not him alone, Lord's represented the Mecca of cricket, a holy shrine to which all cricketers, from Port of Spain, Calcutta or Perth owed rightful homage. This belief facilitated the organisation and administration of the game, and until recently, promoted the role of Marylebone Cricket Club (M.C.C.), with its headquarters at Lord's, as the chief authority and law giver in international cricket. Today, although M.C.C. remains responsible for revisions of the Laws of cricket, its imperial, authoritarian role has changed, and many of its administrative functions

245

have been taken over by more "democratic" bodies: the International Cricket Council (ICC) and the Test and County Cricket Board (TCCB).

As a Victorian like Sir Pelham Warner, Ranji accepted the imperial assumptions of his time and showed little awareness either of the synthetic nature of the Anglo-centric structure on which these assumptions were based, or of their illusory ideals. As far as he was concerned, *Heart of Darkness* (1900) may never have exposed darkness in the hearts of those whom Conrad called self-proclaimed European emissaries of "light, pity, science, progress and the devil knows what else". (p.235) The illusion of an imperial ideal like "working for the common good" so filled Ranji with the conviction that he was an English cricketer that it blinded him to any patriotic or moral duty he might owe toward his homeland, India. That his neglect of India, an "individual unit" contradicted a true realization of "the greater cricket team" that he so eloquently championed totally escaped him.

Although it was smaller than India and less important in world affairs, Westindies also formed an individual unit within Ranji's greater cricket team. If the imperial ideal of working for the common good really existed, Westindies would have faced England on more equal terms during the time when Ranji spoke. The terms were far from equal, and Westindies lost their first Test series in England in 1928 by the overwhelming margin of three innings defeats in three Tests, which, in the social Darwinist, evolutionary thinking of the time, raised doubts about Westindian readiness for Test cricket. Comments in the 1929 *Wisden* bear this out:

> Considering what the Westindies team of 1923 had accomplished the performance of the side which visited England last summer proved extremely disappointing. The earlier combination, engaging in 26 matches, of which 20 were first class, gained 12 victories, played seven draws, and met with seven defeats. Tours of English cricketers in the Westindies since that time suggested such progress at the game in that part of the world that the programme arranged for the men led by R.K. Nunes [the Westindian captain in 1928] included three encounters with the full strength of England. Unhappily expectations were rudely shattered. So far from improving on the form of their predecessors, the team of 1928 fell so much below it that everybody was compelled to realise that the playing of Test matches between England and the Westindies was a mistake. (p.12)

Wisden's tone does not suggest equality: it carries a hint of the pained forbearance of a benevolent patron whose trust in his/her protegé has been rudely shattered, and who must reluctantly confess disappointment and administer reprimand. Even if this exaggerates *Wisden's* paternalism, it underlines the low esteem in which Westindian cricket was held in 1929, and tends to contradict the ideal of benevolent imperialism in which Ranji believed.

The main reason for low Westindian esteem in the 1920s and much later on is not that the team lacked "stature" or "ability": Westindies had individual cricketers of great ability: the trouble was that they did not function as a coherent unit. Two of the most outstanding individuals of this period - George Headley and Leariè Constantine - accomplished deeds that still evoke delight and wonder. Yet, between 1928 and 1939, their team won four Tests and lost twelve - results that are best explained by James's remark that: "Cricket expresses the social relations of the [Westindian] islands," (*Cricket*, p.119) for it was their client/colonial status (not membership of a great team working for the common good) and the spectrum of inherited social relations that it spawned - fragmentation, insularity, factionalism, petty jealousies, rivalries, racial, ethnic or class considerations affecting Westindian captaincy and team selection - that was responsible for the Westindian failure in realizing collective solidarity and being able to function coherently as a team. This failure in cricket solidarity matches the political failure of Federation which was another imperial ideal that ignored idiosyncratic needs of the individual units or territories that were to federate. Federation was as illusory an aim for Westindian politicians as cricket solidarity was for Westindian cricketers before 1960.

At the same time, while social relations adversely affected team spirit, they fostered an archetype of Westindian cricket as consisting of inspired but inconsistent performances on the field, and uncontrolled emotional reactions both on and off the field. In his Preface to Constantine's *Cricket and I*, Cardus comments:

> His [Constantine's] movements in the field are almost primitive in their pouncing voracity and unconscious beauty. There are no bones in his body, only great charges and flows of energy. A genius, and, as I say, a representative man! ... At Lord's last year while Constantine played a wonderful innings a number of his compatriots wept for joy and shook hands in brotherly union. Constantine was their prophet; they saw in his vivid activity some power belonging to their own blood, a power ageless, never to be put down, free and splendid. (p.xi-xii)

Cardus does not patronize anyone: presumably without inside knowledge of Westindian history or society, he seems to put his finger both on Constantine's individual genius and on Westindian reactions to cricket that seemed out of all proportion to the game itself. More importantly, by linking Constantine's ebullience with his compatriots' uninhibited emotionalism, Cardus confirms that Constantine's style of cricket and his compatriots' reactions are products of a particular type of society.

Alan Gibson hints at the similar effect of social relations on George Headley:

> He [Headley] was probably the best Westindian batsman there had ever been, despite the magnificence of Worrell, Weekes, Walcott, Sobers and Richards. None of the others was so unsupported as Headley.
> When he began shortly after Westindies Test cricket began, it was usually a case of "Headley out, all out". He had no comparatively easy Tests to boost his figures: his opponents were England and Australia. (In Marcus Williams, ed. *Double Century,* p.606)

Gibson is less explicit about social relations than Cardus, but his comments imply that Westindian social peculiarities involving leadership and team selection forced Headley to stand virtually alone as a black batsman during his playing career. Since his greatness grows out of his magnificent response to standing alone, it is a product of these peculiarities.

Through Constantine, an image emerged of the Westindian cricketer as a gifted individual capable of brief, virtuoso performances, and through Headley the image of a lonely genius gleaming in bright sunlight with lesser lights dimly glimmering around him. By the 1930s, these two images had fused into a single archetype, or if viewed negatively, a stereotype of the Westindian cricketer as an individual noted for brief, blistering bouts of outlandish extravagance, deployed more out of fun or personal exhibitionism than as a considered contribution to his team's collective interest. This is what James and Constantine tried so hard to counter in England in the 1930s: a Westindian penchant for impromptu, instinctive performances geared mainly to satisfy narrow, personal motives or limiting, temporary, often eccentric objectives.

An excerpt from Sir Pelham Warner - despite his Eurocentricity, the earliest reliable commentator on Westindian cricket - suggests that black Westindian cricketers were capable of quite bizarre behaviour:

> When the Westindians played Gloucestershire at Bristol in 1900 Mr. Jessop scored a "century", hitting six fours in one over, when all the black members of the team sat down on the ground and shrieked with laughter at their own discomfiture." (*Double Century,* p.196)

If that was in 1900, things had not changed much in 1933 when Constantine reports that during the Westindies match against M.C.C, at Lord's, "a famous cricket writer" was moved to comment:

> These Westindians are lovably sensitive to the course of events. When they take a wicket, they shake hands and smile and show their white teeth; when a catch is missed they indulge in gestures of intensest dismay, and they seem always about to drop a catch not because they are not clever fieldsmen but because they expect their hands to be in a dozen different places at the same time." (*Cricket in the Sun*, p.57)

Whether this stereotype of Westindian cricketers is the product of social relations alone, or of unsympathetic accounts by English commentators, or of both is less important than the fact that it existed and adversely affected Westindian cricket at least until the 1950s. It is interesting that while Cardus shows some willingness to understand or appreciate the archetype, both Sir Pelham and Constantine's "famous cricket writer" tend to be supercilious and condescending.

The social circumstances which gave rise to the stereotype of individualistic, temperamental but talented Westindian cricketers also influenced the policy by which Westindian cricket captains were selected. Whether Constantine or

Headley would have made better captains than the Grant brothers we shall never know. Perhaps Constantine and/or Headley might have been able to weld their fellow players into a real team as Worrell was to do in 1960. At any rate, they were not considered. Since the captain's role is crucial to team spirit and solidarity, the question is whether and to what extent the policy of white captains restricted the development of team spirit and solidarity in Westindian teams up to the 1950s. For all their considerable merits as individuals and players, evidence exists of less than cordial relations between the Grants and their men on account of race. Jack Grant, thanks to his near saintliness, reports at least one instance of racial resentment from a member of his team; and Constantine records an undercurrent of dissatisfaction with the captaincy of both Grants throughout his Test career.

Although no specific racial incidents are reported in teams under Goddard and Stollmeyer, disunity is mentioned by Roy Marshall in the Westindian team both to England in 1950, and to Australia in 1951/52. When Atkinson was chosen as captain in 1955, and led the team to defeat in the first Test against Australia, it brought this comment from Stollmeyer:

> To say that he [Atkinson] was in any way responsible for us losing the test match [the first Test] would be grossly unfair to him. Yet it would be equally true to say that it was well nigh impossible for him to command the respect of the players and get their full support." (*Everything*, p.152)

Considering what Stollmeyer has already said about Atkinson's choice as captain over Worrell - that it was "preposterous" - it is possible to see a link between Atkinson's lack of support from the team and his choice for the captaincy in place of Worrell, a more qualified black player. If Atkinson could not command respect or get the support of his team who were mostly black, it was partly because he was less experienced than some of the men he was leading, and partly because he was white. The same thing must have occurred in 1930 when Jack Grant was selected as captain over a team of mainly black men who were mostly older and more experienced cricketers than him. It was the same again when the relatively inexperienced Rolph Grant was chosen captain in 1939 along with the totally inexperienced Stollmeyer as vice-captain, and they were expected to lead stalwarts of long experience like Constantine and Headley. The potential for tension, resentment and disunity was strong in all these cases and could not help but work against team spirit. Nor is it unreasonable to perceive race as a prime factor in each case, for black players under a less experienced white captain could hardly be expected to separate his whiteness from what they would have perceived as the unfairness of his appointment.

When Rolph Grant was injured on the 1939 tour to England, Constantine temporarily took over captaincy of the team against Lancashire. He felt he should have been captain in the next match as well - the first Test at Lord's, but, by his account, he was passed over in favour of Cameron, a coloured (brown) Jamaican. Although *Wisden* lists Grant as captain in the first Test, Constantine's response is relevant:

had I been a white player, no doubt I should have led the game at Lord's also. To be brown skinned, that is to say to have any trace of white blood in one, always gives a man an advantage in the Westindies, not only in cricket but in business...

The fact is, Westindian captains, and as far as possible Westindian players, have always been selected from among the same coterie. This coterie, fifty years ago, included all the good cricketers we had. Today, of course, the majority of good cricketers are outside it. (*Cricket in the Sun*, p.64)

This suggests that, in 1939, the policy of selecting both captain and team was not in the best interest of Westindian cricket: whereas at one stage (before 1920), selecting a team on race or class criteria would likely have caught the best captain and players, the situation had changed by the 1930s and certainly by the 1950s when, because of democratic and economic changes, blacks and "the lower classes" were producing the best cricketers, and when it was sheer folly to persist with outmoded (not to say immoral) race, class and colour criteria of selection. As early as 1898 Sir Pelham Warner had recognised the necessity of picking black players when he wrote in *Wisden*:

The visit of a Westindian team to England is by no means improbable and there can be little doubt that a capital side could be got together from the different islands and British Guiana if the black men were included. Without them it would be absurd to attempt to play the first-class countries. (Quoted in B. Green ed. *Wisden: Anthology 1963-1982*, p. 125)

The last notorious example of tension, resentment and disunity caused by the enforced selection of a white/brown captain was the fiasco between Alexander and Gilchrist. That Gilchrist's resentment was probably based, partly or wholly, on imaginary examples of condescension from Alexander emphasizes the deep-rootedness of the plantation values which dictated the policy of selecting white captains in the first place.

The furore over the choice firstly of Denis Atkinson and secondly of Alexander rather than Worrell as captain in the mid-1950s could have been avoided if the WICBC had realized they were flogging a dying horse; but their wilful efforts to perpetuate the feudalistic criteria of an outmoded plantation social model were not to be denied. According to James, up to the 1950s a black captain in the Westindies or in India would have been bad enough for the WICBC, but a black Westindian captain in England or Australia would have been unthinkable:

Their [the WICBC's] whole point was to continue to send to populations of white people, black or brown men under a white captain. The more brilliantly the black men played, the more it would emphasize to millions of English people: 'Yes, they are fine players, but, funny, isn't it, they cannot be responsible for themselves - they must always have a white man to lead them.' (*Beyond a Boundary*, p. 225)

Conclusion

Up to the 1950s such Kiplingesque notions of racial propensities and political irresponsibility were popular everywhere. Constantine was one of the first Westindians to expose the adverse effect of such notions on Westindian cricket. He came close to prophecy when he wrote:

> Until players and captains are considered on their merits by a justice blind to the colour of their skins, the Westindies will never take a place in Test match cricket commensurate with the skill of individual Westindian exponents. (*Cricket in the Sun*, p.65)

Happily this prophecy was fulfilled in the 1960s when Kiplingesque notions had begun to weaken and Dr. Eric Williams, Premier of Trinidad, triumphantly announced: "Massa day Done!"

Strangely enough, the progressive evolution of the Westindian team of the 1950s was helped by the course of World War Two which had permitted intercolonial cricket tournaments to go on in the Caribbean, away from the main theatres of conflict. These tournaments produced many of the players who made up the team in the 1950s, and who helped Westindies to beat England two:nil in 1947/48, and India one:nil in 1948/49. These victories created a sense of euphoria that seemed wholly fulfilled by the three:one triumph that then followed against England in 1950. Yet these victories are not nearly as impressive as they seemed. In 1947/48 England were decidedly under-manned, and the 1950 English team, ravaged by war, were nothing like what they were before the war. Even India, a moderate cricketing power at the time, held Westindies to a draw in four matches and revealed a fatal lack of penetration in Westindian bowling. Up to 1952, Prior Jones, John Trim and Hines Johnson never produced a pair of match-winning fast bowlers between them, and often had to be supported by all-rounders Gomez and Worrell. Nor were Goddard and Ferguson spinners of craft and guile like Ram and Val who provided a welcome balance to the top heavy batting skills of the Westindian team in 1950. Ironically, Ram and Val also exposed a major weakness of the post-1950 team: that without them (Ram and Val) Westindies were just as unbalanced as they were during 1947 to 1949. Some of the team's inconsistency in the early 1950s stems from this weakness.

There were other compounding reasons for inconsistency in the 1950s: Rolph Grant, captain in 1939, had to give up cricket because he contracted tuberculosis, and his vice-captain Stollmeyer, as heir apparent, should have succeeded to the crown in 1947/48; but his illness in the second Test and Headley's withdrawal from the fourth Test gave Goddard a chance to establish himself as captain. Ensuing rivalry between Stollmeyer and Goddard has been reported by more than one player. In *Test Outcast* Marshall says: "Stollmeyer, I believe, always thought he should have been the captain of the side [in 1950]" (p.38). And in *Island Cricketers*, Walcott writes:

251

I did feel that Jeff Stollmeyer, our vice-captain, could have given John Goddard more help and advice than he did: but his slight aloofness was understandable, for Goddard and Stollmeyer have always been - in the best sense - rivals in their cricket careers, both for the Westindian captaincy and also because they have led opposing colony teams back in the Westindies. (p.67)

Walcott is here trying to explain Westindian failure in Australia in 1951/52. Less than cordial relations between captain and vice-captain would certainly have contributed to this failure.

Marshall points to: "occasional disruptions caused by inter-island disputes" (*Test Outcast*, p. 39) on the 1950 tour, and claims that these disruptions became more open on the Australian tour when Goddard's leadership was probably undermined by the fact that Cyril Merry (manager), Stollmeyer (vice-captain), and Gerry Gomez (the most senior player), were all Trinidadians, whereas Goddard was a Barbadian like Marshall himself. According to Marshall, Goddard's captaincy suffered more from these rivalries on the Australian tour than in 1950 when Ram and Val were in spate in England. From all this, it seems that the extraordinary success of Ram and Val papered over disunity or division in the 1950 team. Worrell also speaks of "divisions" in the team in the 1950s:

> The Westindies team never really recovered from the splinter groups of this tour [to Australia in 1951/52] until Gerry Alexander began to mould the team in 1958. As late as 1960 some of the individuals who were members of the divided Westindian teams of the fifties tried to impress Alexander that there was a division in his side that played against England in the Westindies [in 1959/60]. (Eytle, *Frank Worrell*, p.119)

In the same book Worrell also speaks of "disgruntled players" and "factions in the 1957 [Westindian] team to England." (p.135)

There can be no greater contrast than between the performance of Westindies in England in 1950 and in Australia in 1951/52. Here is the verdict of *The Times* on the second Test in England in 1950:

> Playing on their own sunny ground Westindian cricketers have beaten English teams before. Once, at Sydney nineteen years ago, they beat Australia, with Bradman playing. But yesterday was their finest hour. They have handsomely laid an All England XI low at Lord's. JOHN GODDARD and his men have made a new mark in cricket history. To win by 326 runs at the headquarters of cricket, in spite of the brave English recovery led by WASHBROOK on Wednesday, puts these Westindians for good among the great ones. There have been giants before in Westindian cricket - GEORGE CHALLENOR, LEARIE CONSTANTINE AND GEORGE HEADLEY, each of them among *Wisden's* best through the ages. This is the first Westindian team to bring the promise of so many fine cricketers to full fruition. (*Double Century*, p.367)

The historic nature of this match and the indispensable role of Ram and Val in it are indisputable. In *Everything* Stollmeyer genuflects to the success of the 1950 tour but does not fully explain why it was reversed in Australia in 1951/52:

> Never, since this tour [in 1950] has the Westindies cricket team been other than world class. True there have been brief lapses and cyclical failures, but seldom have we been other than rated among the top teams of the world. If we are now undisputed world champions, it may truthfully be said that it all started in 1950. (p.106)

Stollmeyer slides a little too easily over the disaster in Australia in 1951/52. "Brief lapses and cyclical failures" does not match this disaster, nor the ones against Australia in 1954/55, and England in 1957; it also does not explain the fight back by England in 1953/54.

Stollmeyer does not acknowledge the essentially brittle structure of the Westindian team that underlay the glittering surface of their success in England in 1950. The poet Brathwaite expresses this brittleness best in his line: "an' ol man, you cahn fine a man to hole up de side." It is clear from Marshall's observations that Goddard's leadership was seriously affected in Australia in 1951/52. Goddard had a wretched tour which made him lose weight and become ill by the last Test from which he withdrew. Not only did he withdraw from this Test, but he played no Test cricket again until four years later during which time Westindies, under Stollmeyer, had three full series with India, England and Australia. There is more to Goddard's withdrawal than meets the eye, and it probably had an important bearing on the general performance of the Westindian team in the 1950s. But written accounts of Westindian cricket reflect a dearth of information, for example, on the behind-the-scene events which influenced the decline of Westindies in Australia in 1951/52. The truth is that Westindies came very close to winning the first and fourth Test matches in Australia, in addition to the third which they did win. In each case, their process of disintegration had more to do with psychology, strategy, and internal divisions than with playing ability.

In his account of the fourth Test, the Australian commentator and former opening batsman Jack Fingleton states that on the last day, Australia began with 68 for one, having been set 260 to win. Despite Valentine dropping an easy caught and bowled chance off Moroney, and Guillen missing a chance to stump Hassett off Ramadhin, Westindies were able to reduce Australia to 147 for five, at which point Goddard took off Gomez who had bowled four overs for one run. Nevertheless, when the Australian score had reached 222 for nine with only tailenders Ring and Johnston at the wicket, the odds were clearly on a Westindian victory. Ring and Johnston then resorted to playing tip and run, and Goddard failed to place close-in fielders to stop them. When Weekes fumbled a run out chance, it looked as if Westindies were seized by panic. Fingleton's summary in *Masters of Cricket from Trumper to May* is sharp but sympathetic:

> It was this tip-and-run strategy that demoralised the Westindians and snatched victory from them.

> I have seen no more blatant bluffing on a cricket field. To watch
> it in operation, and mark its effects, was to realise why it is that
> Westindian cricketers on Australian fields have yet to do full justice
> to their ability." (p.166)

Fingleton's comments in 1958 show insight into the brittleness of the Westindian team, and confirm the stereotype of brilliant, temperamental cricketers lacking in discipline and team spirit.

In one incident during the last Australian partnership, Ring hit Valentine for 13 runs in one over, and Goddard directed Atkinson to field further out, but the bowler asked Atkinson to come back in, whereupon Ring hit the next ball over Atkinson's head to the spot that Goddard had placed him. Whatever other factors contributed to the Westindian débacle in Australia in 1951/52 - the hardness of Australian wickets, a poorly planned itinerary, over-confidence from the success in England, over-use of Ram and Val - a major factor was the stereotype of Westindian flashiness, emotionalism and indiscipline which combined with administrative and other rivalries to produce fragmentation and disunity. There is strong similarity between the behaviour of Westindies on the last day of the fourth Australian Test in 1952 and the last day of the fifth Australian Test in 1931: in both cases near panic induced repeated fielding errors that cost Westindies the game in 1952 and nearly cost them the game in 1931. What a contrast between these two performances and the last day of the Brisbane tied Test in 1960 when Westindies were again in a situation of tension and anxiety, but under the generalship of Worrell, maintained such discipline that they brought the match to a rare and spectacular conclusion! The excitability and disunity that threatened Westindies in 1931 were somehow submerged in England in 1950, but surfaced again and dogged the team in Australia in 1951/52 and during most of the 1950s.

Harold Dale, another Australian journalist catches the flavour of volatile, spendthrift talent, squandered through indiscipline and lack of control in Australia in 1951/52. Dale describes the Westindian performance as "cricket lunacy":

> Throughout the whole tour we had repeated evidence of it [cricket lunacy].
> If the Islanders [Westindies] could have been inoculated against it, they
> could have beaten Australia handsomely and easily, fielding errors and
> all. But nearly every innings they played was part brilliance and part
> chaos. In this one [the second innings of the fourth Test] they had Guillen
> 0, Goddard 0, Weekes 2, Trim 0, Ramadhin 0, but still they were pressing
> their opponents. Imagine what their position might have been without
> their susceptibility to folly. (p.170)

This prodigal squandering of natural riches is the hallmark of Westindian cricket up to the 1950s. Whether it is due to "folly" or "lunacy", up to the 1950s, far too many Westindian performances were "part brilliance and part chaos". The argument in *The Rise of Westindian Cricket* is that the folly or lunacy of these performances is related to divisions and difficulties which the Westindian team inherited from their social history.

Despite its reputation for inconsistency and unreliability, the decade of the 1950s is pivotal in the rise of Westindian cricket, for it was also a period of social and political agitation and ground-breaking advances in literature. In all this flux and change, the fate of cricket went up and down many times. It reached its apogee in 1950 in England, and fell disastrously in 1957 also in England. During these seven years the Ws and Ram and Val faded out as a combined force. In 1950, the Ws alone accounted for 1106 (nearly 50 per cent of the team's total) Test runs between them, while their remaining eight team mates managed 1133 runs together. In 1957 the Ws managed 792 runs (less than 40 per cent of the team's total) and the remaining batsmen 1255. Similarly, in 1950 Ram and Val accounted for 59 (more than 75 per cent of the total) Test wickets, while the remaining bowlers took 18 wickets between them; in 1957 Valentine did not bowl, but Ramadhin took 14 wickets - just over half of the 26 he took in 1950. While the decline of the Ws and Ram and Val is disappointing, it made room for younger players. In any case, despite its reputation for fickle and inconstant cricket, the 1950s suggest improvement to the extent that the fate of the team rested with five men - the Ws and Ram and Val - rather than with one - Headley - as in the 1930s. Intrinsically, the same brittle structure persisted in the team, but responsibility was more widely shared, although still not shared by the team as a whole.

Alexander's accession to the Westindian captaincy in 1957, marked a break with the old policy of appointing white captains, and was an important step in the rise of Westindian cricket. As someone of mixed blood, Alexander was an ideal "bridging" figure. But it was not an easy role to play. He was vulnerable to both sides: whites who regretted that blacks were encroaching on a white preserve, and blacks like James who took the view that Alexander was not black enough, and represented the old order. James's strident advocacy of Worrell's captaincy aroused annoyance from Alan Ross in his book *Through the Caribbean*:

> Who but a malicious xenophobe could write, during a Test match, 'that the idea of Alexander captaining a side on which Frank Worrell is playing is to me quite revolting'? 'Revolting' is the parlance of the irresponsible agitator. Worrell's great gifts as a player, his intelligence and charm, and no doubt his capacity for leadership, cannot benefit from such advocacy. (p.89)

No doubt James was too strident. There is not the slightest doubt about Alexander's integrity, unselfishness and professionalism: he offered to stand down in favour of Worrell in 1959/60, and played brilliantly under Worrell in 1960/61. But Ross's annoyance ignores the historical validity of James's over heated advocacy of Worrell.

While the comments of English writers such as Cardus, Arlott, Swanton, and numerous others have generally helped to promote the rise of Westindian cricket, (see Appendix x) others have been less helpful. The first such writer Sir Pelham Warner helped to introduce Westindian cricket to English audiences, and his Eurocentricity should not be held against him considering the time when he was writing. Constantine also quotes Home Gordon as writing in the 1930s that Jack Grant: "undertook captaincy adequately, though to some English eyes the familiarity he permitted from some of his coal-black professionals appeared rather strange." (*Cricket in the Sun*, p.63) As late as 1954, in his book *Just my Story*, Len Hutton recalls his disappointment on the unhappy English tour of Westindies in 1953/54:

> There were many reasons for my disappointment. One was the decreasing activity of white people in the Westindies.
>   Still, while deploring that so few white people play cricket in the Westindies, and even fewer take active part in the administration of the game - my view is that the gradual exclusion of white folk is a bad thing for the future of Westindies cricket. (p.68)

Just my Story is full of perceptive and sympathetic comments on Westindian cricket. Yet the persistence of Eurocentric views in someone like Hutton, captain of England, illustrates the seriousness of the obstacles that Westindian cricket had to struggle against both from forces within the region and those from outside.

Another obstacle that Westindies had to struggle against was the absorption of Westindian cricketers by English leagues and counties. Since there was no professional cricket in the Westindies, cricketers engaged in week-end competitions between members of different clubs. The best known clubs were Kingston Cricket Club at Sabina Park, Jamaica; Queen's Park Cricket Club at Queen's Park Oval, Trinidad; Georgetown Cricket Club, at Bourda, Guyana: and Empire Sports Club at Kensington Oval, Barbados. Only a few individuals could be accommodated in the Test team and get remuneration from Test cricket. This meant that many Westindian cricketers were drawn to the English leagues like a magnet. The first to be drawn was C.A.Ollivierre of St. Vincent who was a member of the Westindian touring team to England in 1900. Ollivierre proved to be the best batsman scoring 883 runs on the tour, but he remained in England and later played for Derbyshire. Another casualty was S.G. (Sydney) Smith of Trinidad who toured England with Westindies in 1906; he made the most runs (1107 runs, average 33,54), and took the most wickets (116 wickets, average 19.31). Smith remained in England and later represented Northamptonshire. Later still, he immigrated to New Zealand where he continued as an active cricketer. Constantine became, as James said, the league cricketer "par excellence", and his commitments to his club, Nelson, restricted him to playing in only one of the three Tests (at Old Trafford) on the Westindian tour of England in 1933.

By the 1950s, the English leagues had claimed many Westindians including Clairmonte Depeiza and Roy Gilchrist. Roy Marshall, who first played league cricket, later had a long career with Hampshire which was the prelude to many other Westindian cricketers including Sobers, Kanhai and Gibbs, joining English counties in the 1960s. The effect of this "brain drain" on Westindian cricket is incalculable. It could be regarded as another example of exploitation of the natural resources of a colony. This is a good example of the post-colonial predicament of places like the Westindies: Independence has not changed, and perhaps cannot change the structure of their dependent relationship to their former rulers; hence continuing exploitation now, as it were, with the consent and collaboration of the former colonies.

A persistent obstacle to the rise of Westindian cricket was the sharp division between the city and countryside, the effect of which was either to exclude rural cricketers from possible selection, or make it more difficult for them to be selected because they had less opportunity to watch or play first class cricket. Gilchrist, Kanhai and Ramadhin were lucky to evade this division. Many talented cricketers from the countryside were less lucky. While many Afro-Caribbean cricketers were "lost" in this way, especially in Jamaica, more Indo-Caribbean cricketers were probably "lost" in Guyana and Trinidad where Indians formed the bulk of the rural population up to the 1950s. Ramadhin, the first Indo-Caribbean Test cricketer, did not appear until 1950 although Indian indenture began in 1838. And since 1950 Indo-Caribbean representation on the Test team does not match the fact that Indians form about twenty percent of the five million population of the English-speaking Caribbean. This disparity is more noticeable in Guyana and Trinidad where Indians now form a majority of the population. The problem is that to the outside world the Caribbean is black or African, and within the region itself historical factors have favoured the notion of a creole or Afro-centric culture that is pan-Caribbean. In his essay "Cricket and Carnival in the Caribbean", Richard Burton argues that cricket in the Westindies has become reassuringly "African" in character, "reflecting 'black' values and mores and giving rise to unforgettable displays of black triumphalism". (p.180) By "black" Burton means "African." Michael Manley who shows such a lively appreciation of white/black issues, also adopts an Afro-centric view of the Caribbean that ignores or marginalises the ethnic identity of Indo-Caribbean cricketers such as Ramadhin and Kanhai, whose achievement cannot be properly estimated without considering ethnic aspects of their careers. Manley's view is probably influenced by his experience in Jamaica where Indians are few, and do occupy a marginalised position.

In his article "Ethnicity Not Out", Kevin Yelvington discusses the implications of cricket on the voting patterns of Indo-Trinidadians in 1976 when local elections coincided with a cricket tour by India. During the tour "feelings were expressed that East Indians were traitorous" (p.19) in supporting India rather than Westindies. The issue was publicly discussed by politicians and journalists. Here is part of Yelvington's conclusion:

> Cricket is not divorced from the social structure, so it cannot be analysed as if it were. It is reductionist to suggest that cricket and the cockfight can tell us all about the society: Cricket in Trinidad is a 'site' of inter-societal conflict and the convergence of social relations, with their attendant symbolic, structural, and cultural aspects. (p.11)

The issue is serious, not at all to be ignored. The views of an Indian journalist

Mihir Bose reinforce this point:

> It is a reflection on modern Westindian society that none of its writers,
> not even C.L.R. James or Michael Manley, has looked at this interaction
> between India and the Westindies or examined the feelings of their own
> Indian-origin population towards cricket. The story they tell of Westindian
> cricket is in conventional terms: the story of black and white. The Indian
> element is not seen to be significant, almost as if Indians do not belong
> to the history of the Westindies. (*A History of Indian Cricket*, p.197)

This is interesting coming from an Indian outsider - no one else would dare to
perceive Afro-centricity in James's writing - and it confirms the divisive potential
of ethnic issues in Guyana and Trinidad which are strong enough to alter the
fate of Indo-Guyanese and Indo-Trinidadian cricketers. These issues are another
aspect of the colonial legacy that bedevils social relations in the Caribbean. But
the wonder is that despite all these obstacles and restrictions which cricket
inherited from a peculiar Westindian social history, it produced a balanced
team by 1960, led by a captain who was poised to take them to the top of world
cricket.

Before 1960, no other Westindian captain came remotely close to Worrell's
success as captain. In *Blasting for Runs* Kanhai says: "Under Frank Worrell
our cricket had become hard and disciplined ... it was harnessed into a controlled
and deadly weapon." (p.94) In *Hit me for Six*, Gilchrist is more outspoken:

> here for once was a man among boys; a man who could really put spice
> in Westindian cricket and give you something to fight for; a thing that
> Westindian cricket needed...I saw boys who were as tough as leather
> break down and cry because they felt that, by being out, they had let
> their hero down. (105-106)

Kanhai and Gilchrist give an insider's view of Worrell's captaincy. After his
brilliant campaign in England, in 1963, the English journalist Michael Parkinson
comments:

> For during this tour Westindian cricket arrived finally and indisputably at
> maturity. It has taken three generations to achieve their present state, where
> they are not only a fine team but good enough to shape the destiny of the
> game. It is worth repeating, just to hammer the fact home to the blimps in
> the Long Room, that they beat England not because they scored faster or
> bowled quicker but because strategically and technically their game was
> superior to ours. They won , not with the improvised flair which has always
> been their natural and sometimes only ally, but with a toughness and hardness
> which made even Yorkshire look like a gang of cream puffs. Their cricket
> has steel in it. It is hardened and disciplined. They are no longer the black
> and white minstrels of the cricket field but a team capable of beating
> anyone in the world at any level of this difficult and complex game. ("West
> Indian Summer" in R. Peskett, *The Best of Cricket*, p.127)

Parkinson identifies the main quality lacking in previous Westindian teams - professionalism, which implies discipline, solidarity and team spirit. His comments also show how far Westindies had risen from 1929 when *Wisden* condescendingly thought it was a mistake to stage Test matches between Westindies and "the full strength of England".

Under Worrell, Westindies did ascend to the top. Under Sobers, between 1964 and 1966, they confirmed their international supremacy which they have not relaxed for thirty years, except for "brief failures and cyclical lapses" to use Stollmeyer's phrase. As already mentioned, this phrase did not fit the period of the 1950s when Stollmeyer first applied it to Westindian cricket; for the Westindian team had not yet attained the professionalism that they first exhibited under Worrell. Only after their victories over Australia and England between 1964 and 1966 did they confirm that they had finally overcome the flashy exhibitionism, personal pyrotechnics, lack of team spirit and all the other disabilities that were part of their Westindian legacy of plantation ethics and social relations.

At the same time, Westindian professionalism should not be confused with Australian, English or any other type of professionalism. No doubt to be "hardened and disciplined" in Parkinson's words, Westindian cricketers had to show control and restraint like other teams. But this does not mean that they lost Constantine's ebullience or Headley's inventiveness: it means that these qualities were exhibited in the interest of the team instead of individual satisfaction. Worrell's 1963 Westindians were as professional as Dexter's English team, yet the two teams played different styles of cricket. An early post-colonial visitor to England, Washington Irving, observed English sport in the early nineteenth century:

> As the English are methodical even in their recreations, and are the most scientific of sportsmen, it [angling] has been reduced among them to perfect rule and system. (*The Sketch Book*, p. 322)

Although he writes about fishing, Irving's comments apply to cricket as well. The scientific nature of English cricket is alien to Westindian reflexes and temperaments. *The Times'* journalist who found St. Hill's batting unsound and dangerous, could say that because St. Hill was not truly professional. If he was professional, the journalist might have said what Michael Parkinson said of Kanhai in 1963: that he played: "the kind of a shot you would never find described in any English cricket coaching manual." (R. Peskett, *The Best of Cricket*, p. 129).

It is no accident that the rise of Westindian cricket was finally achieved in the 1960s along with the establishment of freedom from colonial rule and a literature that is internationally acclaimed. Politics and literature evolved side by side with cricket, each interacting with the other in a complex, interdependent process through which each influenced and was influenced by the other in awakening the Westindian people to full self-expression. Something of this process had been recognised as early as in 1933 by Neville Cardus:

> Constantine is a representative man: he is Westindian cricket, just as
> W.G. Grace was English cricket. When we see Constantine bat or bowl
> or field, we know he is not an English player, not an Australian player,
> not a South African player. We know that his cuts and drives, his whirling
> fast balls, his leapings and clutchings and dartings - we know they are
> the consequence of impulses born in the blood, a blood heated by the
> sun and influenced by an environment and a way of life much more
> natural than ours; impulses not common to the psychology of the
> overcivilised places of the earth. His cricket is racial. (*Good Days*, p.38)

By "racial" Cardus means the regional character and style that cricket acquired
in its adaptation from the English game that was brought to the Westindies in
the eighteenth century. It needed the greatest of all cricket writers to perceive
the makings of nationality in Constantine's cricket before there was a full blown
Westindian nation.

Nothing expresses Westindian nationality more accurately than cricket, for
the game as played by Westindians, is not identical to the game played by
Englishmen, Australians, Indians, Pakistanis, New Zealanders or others who
do not reproduce quite the same improbable combination of vigour, spontaneity,
quickness, and naturalness. Others do express their own nationality through cricket
as the Australian novelist Thomas Keneally reveals in his essay "The Cyclical
Supremacy of Australia in World Cricket":

> When we [Australians] spoke of literary figures, we spoke of Englishmen.
> But when we spoke of cricket, we spoke of our own. We couldn't make it
> in literature because we had none of the right seasons, the plants laughed at
> European botany, the absurd animals had no mythology behind them. But
> cricket was possible! We knew why it was. We had more sunshine, we ate
> more protein, we washed more regularly than the Poms! In the manner in
> which soccer is the great way up for children from the economic sumps of
> Brazil, so cricket was the great way out of Australian cultural ignominy.
> No Australian had written *Paradise Lost*, but Bradman had made 100
> before lunch at Lord's. (Michael Meyer ed. *Summer Days*, p.115)

If Trumper, Bradman and Harvey gave Australians a sense of identity so did
Headley, Worrell and Sobers give Westindians a clearer sense of who they were.

The Australian journalist Pat Landsberg expressed disbelief at the Westindian
public's reaction when it was announced that Ramadhin and Valentine would
be dropped from the Westindian team to meet Australia in the third Test against
Australia at Bourda in 1955:

> News of the omission of Valentine and Ramadhin was received in
> responsible cricket circles in the same way as the House of Commons
> listened Winston Churchill tell of the fall of Singapore. (*The Kangaroo
> Conquers*, pp.94-95).

Quite so. Without underplaying the suffering and loss of life entailed by the Japanese capture of Singapore, the omission of Ramadhin and Valentine in 1955 might be considered as grievous in the sense that it could affect the success of the Westindian team in restoring self-respect and self-esteem to their countrymen, victims of four equally destructive centuries of slavery, indenture and colonialism.

If foreigners are puzzled by Westindian reactions to cricket, it is because they do not understand the unique role of cricket in Westindian social relations. Jack Grant tells a story of his ship stopping in Panama City on the way to Australia in 1930. His team was supposed to play a one-day game against local Westindian residents, but rain prevented play on the day of the match:

> once the rain stopped they [the residents] did something I had not seen before and have not seen since. The poured kerosene on the pitch and set it alight in the hopes of drying it. (*Jack Grant's Story*, p. 28)

People who equate the fall of Singapore with the selection of their cricket team, or who will dry a cricket pitch by setting it alight are not guilty of unsound or dangerous practices, or of cricket or any other type of lunacy: they are expressing an original pattern of behaviour, as James has said, one that is "sui generis", with no parallel anywhere else.

Where else will one find a Prime Minister or political leader who has written the fullest account of his nation's cricket history, as Michael Manley, former Prime Minister of Jamaica has done in *A History of West Indian Cricket*? And where else has cricket proved the most popular way of gaining an international reputation? While a few Westindians have been awarded knighthoods as a mark of international recognition for their distinguished achievement in fields such as scholarship, politics, and business, an unusually high percentage of knighthoods have been awarded to Westindian cricketers, for example, to Sir Learie Constantine, Sir Frank Worrell, Sir Garfield Sobers, and Sir Clyde Walcott.

The uniqueness of Westindian cricket is expressed in his Introduction to Manley's *History of Westindian Cricket* by Clive Lloyd, the greatest of the post-Worrell Westindian captains:

> As captain of the Westindies for ten years I can honestly say that cricket is the ethos around which Westindian society revolves. All our experiments in Caribbean integration either failed or have maintained a dubious survivability; but cricket remains the instrument of Caribbean cohesion the remover of arid insularity and nationalistic prejudice. It is through cricket and its many spin-offs that we owe our Caribbean consideration and dignity abroad. (p.v)

Despite political tensions and ethnic divisions in the Westindies, cricket has remained an enduring beacon of Westindian nationality. This is curious when one considers the strong English influence on cricket that James has emphasized. But James recognized the paradoxical influence of cricket, as does the radical

Antiguan journalist Tim Hector who writes in the *Guardian Weekend* of April 23, 1994: "If cricket was part of the colonising process, it also emancipates." (p.16) In helping to emancipate the Westindian people from centuries of colonialism, cricket played a dual role as a generator of national feeling and as a barometer of national well being. Nowhere else has cricket played such a role.

In the beginning was the British empire; but Independence ended empire in the Westindies in the 1960s. Yet if the brief evidence of post-Independence Westindian history is anything to go by, Independence has made little difference to the consequences of empire, for example, poverty and under-development, and an ingrained structure of dependence no longer on England alone, but on the wider Euro-American metropolis. The claim in *The Rise of Westindian Cricket* is that of all anti-colonial efforts and strategies, Westindian cricket has transcended the legacy of colonialism with greatest success. This is confirmed by the rise of Westindian cricket between 1928 and 1966; for Westindians believe deeply in what Dickens calls in *The Pickwick Papers*: "the art and mystery of the noble game of cricket;" (p.119) except that the Westindian version of cricket is better expressed by the tailor in Edward Brathwaite's poem "Rites", where cricket is an unnameable antidote to unnameable ills:

> isn't no time for playin
> the fool nor makin' no sport; this is cricket (p.198)

Like the game Dickens knew, Westindian cricket was profoundly influenced by Victorian illusions - the art and mystery of Dickens, Ranji and many others. Historically, the illusions were useful, as James shows in *Beyond a Boundary*. But they had to be transcended, just as today, the illusion of Westindian Independence needs to be transcended.

Appendices

(i) Ranji

K.S. Ranjitsinhji was born of Rajput stock in India, in 1872. As a prince when India was the reputed "jewel" in the British crown, it was natural for Ranji to complete his education at Cambridge University. After distinguishing himself as a member of his university cricket team, Ranji went on to play for Sussex and England. His cricket career lasted from 1893 to 1920, and he was captain of Sussex from 1899 to 1903. His first class figures are 24,692 runs for an average of 56.37, and a total of 72 hundreds. Between 1896 and 1902, Ranji played in 15 Tests, all against Australia; he made two hundreds: 154 not out in his début at Manchester in 1896, and 175 at Sydney in 1897. He also twice scored over 3000 runs in an English season - 3159 for an average of 63.18 in 1899, and 3065 for an average of 87.57 in 1900. These are impressive statistics, but they do not convey the stunning impact that Ranji had on cricket in the game's Golden Age - the period lasting from the 1890s to World War One. It was a period when cricket was conditioned mainly by Victorian English values, and hierarchical, essentially Darwinist notions of social order and moral conduct. These values encouraged Rudyard Kipling, then at the height of his fame, to speak confidently of "lesser breeds" from Africa and Asia, while claiming with smug certainty, that "East is East and West is West/And never the twain shall meet." Ranji's achievement was to shake this smug world of English cricket and culture to its very foundations.

His achievement may be illustrated by comparison with his Sussex partner C.B. Fry, an athlete, scholar and cricketer who typified English culture, sportsmanship and cricket at its best. According to Cardus, in "Ranji, Fry and Sussex," Fry was superb: "but of comprehensible earth. When you looked upon Ranji at the other end, you turned from the known world of law and order to the world of the occult; you turned from the West to the East." (*Play Resumed with Cardus,* p.79) The stroke that mesmerised English spectators was Ranji's leg glance which has been called "the most elegant stroke in cricket," and about which more has probably been written than any other single exploit in sport; for it was no ordinary flick, tickle or deflection, but an authentic, full-blooded stroke, played with the full face of the bat, at the last conceivable moment, when the ball had virtually passed the batsman's pads. One can scarcely imagine the acuteness of concentration, split second timing, keenness of eyesight, and general preciseness of execution required. As one commentator said, it was as if Ranji struck a match to the ball as it went by on its way to the fine leg boundary; and indeed there are stories of the ball singeing the grass when it descended to earth again after being despatched by the maestro's bat. So dazzling was Ranji's batsmanship that , according to Cardus, Ted Wainright - the Yorkshire bowler - confessed Ranji "never made a Christian stroke in his life" (*Good Days*, p. 71) while, again according to Cardus, George Giffen was known to exclaim: "Call him [Ranji] a batsman? Why he's a blooming conjurer!" (*Play Resumed with Cardus*, p.80).

Apart from his prowess as a player, Ranji wrote the *Jubilee Book of Cricket* in 1897, and dedicated it to Queen Victoria. In 1906, he became maharajah of the small Indian state of Nawanagar, and in 1920 he represented the Indian states at the League of Nations. In 1930 he attended the first Round Table Conference to consider the Constitution of India. The political aspects of Ranji's career reveal a paradox that he shares with two other Indian princes - Duleepshinhji, Ranji's nephew, and the Nawab of Pataudi (Snr.). The paradox is that the distinction achieved by these princes in playing cricket for England which held their own nation (India) in colonial subjection, reflects a reactionary political stance suggesting that they supported British imperial interests. But one may argue that as the first Indian to touch the imagination of the broad British public, Ranji stimulated a more sympathetic understanding of India in Britain. In other words, far from supporting British racial, social, and cultural exclusiveness, one may conclude that Ranji's cricket rejected Darwinist and Kiplingesque notions of society by demonstrating that East and West could meet.

Today, after the British empire has disappeared, the worst that can be reasonably held against these Indian princes is that they accepted the "de facto" Eurocentric structure of the world that they were born into. They were not reformers. But through their cricketing exploits, they improved race relations in England and invoked a greater measure of social justice for themselves and others like them. No doubt this will be considered too insignificant a benefit compared with what they might have attempted in India itself. In a way, Ranji's role in Edwardian England was similar to that of Othello in Shakespeare's play: through extraordinary prowess, he overcame the prejudice of the white, host society in which he lived. Like Othello, he did the state some service, and his reward was public admiration and gratitude. But in the process, like another Shakespearean hero - Coriolanus - he neglected (some would say betrayed) his own people. He thought of himself as an English, not Indian cricketer, and as Mihir Bose reports in *A History of Indian Cricket* (p.40), he did little to help Indian cricket when implored to do so. Perhaps his neglect of India was an inevitable price he had to pay for bringing East and West together. This is probably the central paradox of Ranji's career: that his political contribution to race relations in England contradicted his moral obligation to the liberation and development of India. In such a case, he is not the first great man who failed to reconcile an inherent conflict between politics and morality. His greatness is that his fame as a cricketer survived this failure.

Besides, Ranji's Englishness is not all it has been cracked up to be. It is doubtful that he was as fully assimilated into upper class English circles as we are led to believe. His extravagant generosity, for instance, sounds like a continuing effort to gain fuller acceptance; and his reported grief when people associated him with Edward the Black Prince surely confirms some unhappiness with his reception in England. Glowing accounts of his cricketing prowess must also have unsettled Ranji inwardly. Here, for instance, is an account written after his death, but typical of many that appeared during his lifetime:

> the slim, incredibly supple figure with the dark, smiling face; fluttering silken sleeves ...the faint suggestion that the whole thing was fantasy and that this bizarre prestidigitator would suddenly vanish in smoke on a magic matting" (A. A. Thomson, *Cricket my Happiness*, p.84)

Although the author genuinely admires Ranji, he adopts a British (Eurocentric) point of view which sees Ranji's Indian characteristics - "silken sleeves", and "bizarre prestidigitator" - as alien, exotic, somehow improper or at least abnormal even if admirable.

In *Beyond a Boundary*, Ranji is praised by C.L.R. James as dedicated a fighter against colonialism as one could wish for. James realized that Ranji's reputation should be based on his cricket rather than on his politics. Consequently, the man we should remember is not Colonel His Highness Shri Sir Ranjitsinhji Vibhaji, the Jam Sahib of Nawanagar, but the Indian prince who battered Australia for 154 not out on his Test début, who could hit a century off the fastest bowlers with merely a rolled umbrella in his hands, or who was just about the only man in the world agile enough to catch a darting sparrow while fielding in the slips. Thus are the facts of history supplemented by the fiction of memory to create the truth of legend. Yet in this truth lies the best hope of all true believers in cricket: the vision of a cricket field, perpetually bathed in celestial light, wherein, with a rolled umbrella firmly in his supple wrists, an illustrious Indian prince still stands despatching the fastest possible deliveries to all parts of the field, to nowhere more often than the remotest recesses of the fine leg boundary.

(ii) Westindies vs. Middlesex
Lord's, London, 9,10,12 June 1928

Sir Learie Constantine is remembered for achievements in several fields including politics, broadcasting and race relations; but he is remembered best for his exploits in cricket. When he died in 1971 at the age of sixty-nine, he was described in *The Times* of London as: "the finest all-round fieldsman the game of cricket has ever known." Such was the dynamic quality of his fielding that spectators attended matches merely to see Constantine field. Fielding, however, was only one aspect of cricket at which Constantine excelled: he was also a very forceful batsman, and a bowler capable of ripping through an innings in one sudden, unstoppable spell. Constantine's achievement as a cricketer may be judged from his performance in perhaps his most memorable match, when he played for Westindies against Middlesex, at Lord's, in June, 1928. The Middlesex team consisted of Test players like J.W. Hearne, "Patsy" Hendren, G.O. Allen, and F.T. Mann. The chief Westindian batsmen were George Challenor and C.A. Roach backed up by M.P. Fernandes and W.H. St. Hill. The main Westindian bowlers were G.N. Francis, J.A. Small and Constantine.

At the end of the first day's play, Middlesex had reached 313 for 6 wickets, with Hendren 62 not out. The next morning Middlesex declared after Hendren got his century and their total had reached 352. Westindies made a disastrous start and were struggling with a total of 79 and their five best batsmen gone: Challenor, Roach, Fernandes, St. Hill, and Bartlett were all out when Constantine joined F.R. Martin for the sixth wicket. Constantine's entry was like the transfusion of fresh blood into a dying patient. In eighteen minutes he scored 50 runs. In the process he hit the fast bowler G.O. Allen for 9, 10 and 17 in consecutive overs. This was typical of Constantine - to respond fearlessly and aggressively when his side was in danger. On this occasion it worked, for he stayed altogether 55 minutes with Martin and scored 86 runs which enabled Westindies to reach a total of 230 and save the follow-on. A measure of Westindian self-respect had been regained. By the end of the second day, Middlesex had scored 40 runs for two wickets in their second innings, and were 166 runs ahead with eight wickets remaining.

When play resumed on the third and final day, Middlesex clearly held the upper hand. It was reasonable to think that they could not lose; at worst they might have to accept a draw. From 40 for two, however, Middlesex could only manage a total of 136 runs. Their second innings was completely devastated by Constantine who, in one spell of 35 balls, took 6 wickets for 11 runs. Facing Constantine that day, the Middlesex batsmen may well have thought they were up against the raw force of a Westindian hurricane. His analysis in that innings was 7 wickets for 57 runs in 14.3 overs. Five of his victims were clean bowled, including both Middlesex opening batsmen. Scarcely any runs were scored off him except from the edge of the bat. Hendren who made a century in the first innings was caught in the slips playing a defensive stroke to Constantine. The fury of the bowling may be gauged from the fact that only three Middlesex batsmen reached double figures in their second innings. The main effect of such furious bowling was that it gave Westindies an outside chance of victory: in their second innings, they were set 259 runs for victory in about four hours.

Challenor and Roach recognized their chance and played sensibly to put on 63 runs before the first wicket fell. They had also scored at almost a run a minute which was about the rate required if Westindies were to win. But their good work was undone by the fall of four quick wickets for another 58 runs. With their total at 121 for 5, Westindian prospect of victory had sharply diminished. When Constantine came in to partner M.P. Fernandes, Westindies needed another 138 runs to win. More to the point, Middlesex needed five more -

mainly tailend - wickets to win. It was a daunting situation that faced Fernandes and Constantine. But Constantine's response was typical. With incredible daring he set about the bowlers, hitting with controlled aggression that brought runs in a flood, and made victory again possible for the batsmen. In one hour Constantine raced to his century. He hit two sixes and twelve fours and drove with such power that one of the fielders - Hearne - injured his hand trying to stop the flow of runs, and could not play cricket for the rest of that summer. Meanwhile, Fernandes gave stalwart support, holding his end, and watching the slaughter at the other. Eventually, Constantine was caught when he had scored 103 and the total was 254. Victory duly came, and Westindies won by 3 wickets. Seldom can it have been said with more justice that a player had single-handedly won a match. Constantine's feat is surely one of the most memorable performances by a Westindian in first class cricket: he scored 86 runs out of a first innings total of 230, and 103 out of a second innings total of 259. On top of that, he took 8 wickets for 134 runs in the match. He had snatched victory from defeat, and twice on the final day, the pavilion at Lord's rose to acknowledge the achievement of the most remarkable Westindian cricketer of his generation, with the sole exception of George Headley.

(iii) Shakespeare on Cricket
by Professor E. Kerr Borthwick (Edinburgh)

Shakespearian scholarship has recently been stirred by claims of new discoveries, but generally not recognized are the extensive references to cricket in his plays. For - very properly and naturally - 'the Bard' is well-informed about England's national game, and has many shrewd comments to make about recent and forthcoming events.

'Where go you with bats and clubs?', asks Agrippa (*Cor.* 1.1.57), and the answer is clearly given in *3Hen.* vi5.1.113, 'Lords, to the field.' Basic terminology of the game is commonplace - 'Let me be umpire' (*1Hen.vi* 4.1.151), 'Fetch my bail' (*All's Well* 5.3.296), 'Thy stumps will let thee play' (*T.Andron.* 2.4.4), 'Play, sirs!' (*2Hen.iv* 2.4.246), 'I will open' (*M for M* 3.1.198), 'Give me a bowl' (*J. Caes.* 4.3.158). Many of the standard field placings are mentioned - 'one slip' (*W. Tale* 4.4.100), 'short leg' (*2Hen iv* 5.1.28), 'third man' (*Temp* 1.2.445), 'long on' (*L.L.L.* 5.1.41), 'you are at point' (*Cor.* 3.1.194), 'they have a god cover' (*Much Ado* 1.2.8). Now the innings commences: 'How's that?' (*Lear* 1.5.48), 'Not out' (*2Hen iv* 5.3.71), 'Play on' (*12th Night* 1.1.1), 'O! I am out' (*W. Tale* 2.1.72), 'Wide I'll ope my arms' (*Ham.* 4.5.145), 'I see you stand like greyhounds in the slips' (*Hen* V 3.1.31), 'It is a chance' (*Lear* 5.3.266), 'I saw him put down' (*12th Night* 1.5.90), 'When he caught it, he let it go again' (*Cor.* 1.3.66), 'Cry out and run' (*J. Caes.* 3.1.97), 'Throw in' (*Tro* 2.2.71), 'Well run!' (*L.L.L.* 5.2.233), 'All run' (*R&J* 5.3.192), 'Sudden push gives them the overthrow' (*J.

Caes 5.2.5), 'Throw him out with wondrous potency' (*Ham*. 3.4.169), 'A maiden never bold' (*Oth* 1.3.94), 'Change now at my end' (*Ant*. 4.15.51), 'Ah hah! You're caught' (*Ant*. 2.5.15), 'A hit, a very palpable hit' (*Ham*. 5.2.292), 'O let me see thee walk' (*Taming of S*. 2.1.258), 'A touch, a touch I do confess' (*Ham* 5.2.297), 'And, as I am a gentleman, betook myself to walk' (*L.L.L*. 1.1.237), 'Last man in' (*M. of Venice* 1.3.61). 'He'll strike, and quickly too' (*Lear* 5.3.285), 'Bait the hook well this fish will bite' (*M.Ado* 2.3.114), 'Hector shall have a great catch' (*Tro* 2.1.109), 'Well held!' (*12th Night* 4.1.5), 'Ah! Sweet ducks...What a pair of spectacles is here!' (*Tro*. 4.4.12-14), 'All out' (*Macbeth* 2.1.5), 'And now declare' (*1Hen iv* 2.5.41).

Shakespeare is even aware of the current concerns about the over-rate (or o'er-rate, as he quaintly calls it, *Cymbeline* 1.4.41), and about the danger to batsmen of intimidatory bowling ('Give him a box', *2Hen vi* 4.7.91), especially with too many bouncers - 'Batter his skull (*Temp*. 3.2.98), 'You have broke his pate with your bowl' (*Cymb*. 2.1.8), 'Look you, what hacks are on his helmet' (*Tro*. 1.2.222). He sees the dangers of getting out through over-cautious batting ('He is bold in his defence', *Lear* 5.3.114), but sounds a disapproving note about contemporary histrionics in the field - 'Whenever yet was your appeal denied?' (*2Hen iv* 4.1.88), 'There was casting up of eyes, holding up of hands' (*W.Tale* 5.2.51), 'When they are out, they will spit' (*As You Like It* 4.1.76).

He is concerned about recent events in the County Championship, with little joy in his home team's record (God help Warwick', *2Hen vi* 1.1.205), some sympathy for Gloucester ('Woe is me for Gloucester', *1 Hen vi* 3.2.72) and Yorkshire (Alas, poor York, I should lament thy miserable state', *3Hen vi* 1.4.84), and has mixed feelings about Kent ('The filth and scum of Kent', *2Hen vi* 4.2.130, 'Noble and true-hearted Kent', *Lear* 1.2.126). Somerset's poor showing is a little unfairly attributed to loss of form by a distinguished batsman ('Hath not thy Rose a canker, Somerset?, (*1Hen vi* 2.4.68, but, in one recent controversy, he takes their part ('I more incline to Somerset than York', *1Hen vi* 4.1.154), and recommends conciliation ('Good cousins, both of York and Somerset, quiet yourselves', ib. 4.1.114), 'No more, good York, sweet Somerset be still', ib. 3.1.304).

As regards the current Caribbean tour, there is some nostalgia for the past, both distant ('Grace go with you', *M. for M.* 2.3.39), and more recent ('Keep Close, I thee command', *Hen.V* 2.3.65, 'England was Geoffrey's right', *K. John* 2.1.105), an, as a Warwick man, he regrets the selectors' 'judgement that did never choose Amiss' (*M. of Venice* 2.9.65). But he thinks that 'Gower is a good captain' (*Hen V* 4.7.156), and, after his Australian triumph, even a positive veteran (*Pericles, Prologue* 2 'From ashes ancient Gower is come'), and he expresses high hopes about the going on tour of Messrs Edmonds and Emburey ('Hence, you long-legged spinners, hence', *M.S.N.D.* 2.2.21). But, finally, while he expects that our 'eleven die nobly for their country' (*Cor*. 1.3.26), he expresses what one might call a singular fear of the new Westindian captain whom, in an evocative phrase, he calls 'Hell's black intelligencer', *Rich III* 4.4.71) - 'Oh bloody Richard(s) 'Miserable England' 'I prophesy the fearfull'st time to thee' (ib. 3.4.105), 'I'll give my voice on Richard's side' (ib 3.2.53).

I conclude with one final curious point: for long, ingenious Shakespearean scholars have sought oblique autobiographical references in the sonnets and dramas, and practically any occurrence of 'Will' has been declared to signal the poet's own concealed signature. Note therefore the following, among a dozen or so examples of the succession of letters WILLIS in the extant corpus: - ' My *Will is* strong, past reason's Weak removing' (*Lucrece* 243), 'My *will is* back'd with resolution (L. 352), 'Good *will is*' (*Ant.* 2.5.8), 'God's *will is*' (*Hen.* v, 5.1.34). Can it be that there is some mysterious *rapport* between the poet, and the former captain, of Warwickshire and England? (Reprinted with permission from *The Cricketer.*)

(iv) Garfield Sobers,
Bonaventure and the Flashing Blade
Pelham Books Ltd., London, 1967

Improbable as it sounds, in 1967, when he was at the height of his fame as captain of Westindies, Sir Garfield Sobers published a novel - *Bonaventure and the Flashing Blade* although, between 1963 and 1967, he played regular Test cricket in one series after the other against England (twice), Australia, and India. The action of *Bonaventure and the Flashing Blade* takes place presumably in the 1960s. Its hero, Clyde St. Joseph Bonaventure, is the son of a Westindian family living in South London. Clyde is a brilliant student who decides to pursue further training in computer technology, despite encouragement to become a cricketer from his uncle and from Garfield Sobers who is an allegedly neutral character in the novel. The plot of the novel involves Clyde's association with a group of superintelligent scientists at the Star Computer Company in Tunsted, England. These young men create a computer programme which enables their company's cricket team, entirely by mechanical means, to know the strengths and weaknesses of opposing teams and instantly prepare measures to deal with them. There is also a subplot involving rival companies which try to kidnap Clyde or use deception and bribery to obtain his or his team's technological expertise. The rivals are eclipsed and the novel ends with a climactic cricket match between Clyde's team and one captained by Gary Sobers (the character). The match ends in a tie, reminiscent of the Brisbane tied Test of 1960 in which Sobers played such a vital role. More importantly, the match elicits the realization that the use of computers in cricket to "build a team of supermen" (p.73) would introduce a degree of mechanization that would cancel out the human factors that are the life and soul of the game.

Although the author introduces some differences in speech and behaviour between Clyde's colleagues and other characters, these differences are too generalized to confirm their individual identities and sustain conviction in the characters or their doings. Similarly, although incidents are clearly described, they too lack sufficient definition and sharpness. The narrative acquires a nondescript taste despite such ostensibly exciting elements as commercial rivalry, treachery, suspense, and even espionage. It is hard to decide whether lack of strong definition in the narrative is a product of the writing itself, or of the story alone, or of the author's basic conception of the novel. Perhaps it is the joint effect of all three. The story stretches credibility: Clyde is a genius associated with other geniuses in an institution whose standard is "the highest in the world". (p.24) His success looks so easy and even when evil and skulduggery enter to frustrate his plans, they are quickly overcome, and everything set right again. The basic idea of the plot - the transformation of cricket by computers - is preposterous and is expected to fail. That it takes attempted kidnapping, bribery, and other sinister dealings to convince Clyde that the human factor in cricket is more valuable is a little like using a sledge hammer on a nut. It produces a sense of anti-climax that is compounded at the end of the novel by the cliché of Clyde's revelation that the human factor in cricket consists of "interest, discipline, enthusiasm, loyalty and physical fitness." (p.160)

There are other curious features of *Bonaventure and the Flying Blade*. After the opening scene we do not see Clyde's mother or his uncle Bengo again, although they represent strong influences in his life. Sobers (the character) also disappears after the opening scene and doesn't reappear until the end. More curious still is the fact that Clyde's family is evidently Westindian, like the cricket coach Frank Wayne, yet there is no mention of skin colour throughout the novel. Most curious of all is an observation by Sobers (the character) who states that Clyde's whole experience with computers and cricket "sounds like a science fiction story." (p.141) This is true, and it leads one to wonder why Sobers (the author) decided to write a novel about cricket that sounds like science fiction.

One should look in *Bonaventure and the Flashing Blade* for those special insights into the technique or history of cricket that can come only from the pen of one of the game's most illustrious exponents. Here is one example:

> Very few bowlers can change their style of bowling a great deal in one over of six or eight balls. They can vary the flight, the speed, the length and the spin. The batsman then can use the stroke which will score off any of these balls. But a good batsman has a larger number of strokes he can use than a bowler has types of bowling he can use in one over. (p.95)

This is what one should expect from a man who had the unique gift of bowling in three different styles, and of batting like God in human form. But there are alas, too few comments like this in the novel, and those which exist tend to be obscured by unconvincing elements of so-called "science fiction".

Still, one cannot be ungrateful for anything from the hand and mind of Sir Garfield Sobers. Player-writers abound in cricket, for example Sir Learie Constantine whose daredevil exploits as a cricketer so overwhelmed an English school boy that once in his history class, he confused Sir Learie with Constantine the Great who, as the first Roman Emperor to officially accept Christianity, changed the course of world history. Sir Garfield Sobers will not confuse anyone with his achievement in *Bonaventure and the Flashing blade*; but through his magnificent performances on the playing field, in a career lasting from the mid-1950s to the mid-1970s, he has already changed the course of world cricket if not world history.

(v) John Arlott: An Appreciation

John Arlott was born in Basingstoke, England, in 1914, and died in Alderney, the Channel islands, on December 14, 1991. Apart from his numerous books, mostly on cricket, he wrote regularly for *The Guardian*, first as cricket correspondent, and later as wine correspondent as well. No doubt Arlott's writing made him well known; but it was his role as cricket commentator on B.B.C. radio for more than thirty years that made his name a household word wherever the game was played. Certainly, it was as a cricket commentator that we came to know him in the Westindies; and it was wholly fitting that *The Guardian's* final accolade should include the claim for him as the "greatest broadcast commentator of the twentieth century." Arlott's countrymen have noted, with due admiration, his skill in painting vivid word pictures of cricketing incidents and events in the very moment of their unfolding on the field of play. They have also correctly lauded his enthusiasm for cricket, his comprehensive knowledge of the game, and his incomparable gift for picturesque phrase-making, spectacularly original metaphors, and natural descriptions based on everyday experience. His accent, too, Hampshire in origin, has been praised for its warm, comforting forthrightness. Thus the conclusion, universally acknowledged, that Arlott was the voice itself of cricket.

It was not that we Westindians did not appreciate Arlott's virtues: we did; but not in the same way as English people who were our political overlords and our superior in the practical, cricketing sense that they had a long and illustrious tradition of talking and writing about cricket. Living, as we did, in British Caribbean colonies, we could not hope for anything so grand. Even the few writers we did have - C.L.R. James and Learie Constantine - because of the colonial system, wrote for our overlords rather than for us. So when we first heard Arlott and other English commentators during the Westindian tour of England in 1950, their commentary affected us in a way that it would not have affected English schoolboys. We were both enthralled and confounded when Arlott spoke of the ball's movement through the air and off the seam, or of its following something called a trajectory. Elementary notions of swing, turn and bounce we understood, in some sort of fashion, but moisture in the pitch, and early morning heaviness of atmosphere had us completely baffled. As for the host of tactical intricacies that the English commentators discussed, they seemed less due to craft, resourcefulness, or desperation - seeing that England were the weaker team - than the mysterious machinations of a white civilization and culture that dominated the world in which we lived: we admired Arlott, but could not hope to understand him.

If Arlott's knowledge of the game appeared somewhat dismaying, so also did the fluency and richness of his descriptions, especially when they included such references to the English landscape as the gasometers at Kensington Oval, or the houses of Parliament in the distance. These were nice, natural touches that no doubt brought the commentary vividly alive to an English audience; but to us they constituted part of the romance that England held for all her colonial subjects. It was this touch of romance that we Westindians found most exhilarating in Arlott's commentary, precisely because it remained fundamentally remote and mysterious. In the 1980s, when a Westindian in Canada joyfully recalled Arlott's description of the weather before a cricket match, it was clear that it was the sound of Arlott's words that entranced him, not their meaning.

In addition to his knowledge and fluency, there was another impressive feature of Arlott's commentary - his generosity. During the fourth and final Test in 1950, Westindies scored 503 in their first innings, and England replied with 344, almost entirely due to a glorious innings of 202 not out by Len Hutton. Hutton had batted throughout the innings. When England followed on, and Hutton opened their second innings, only he stood between Westindies and victory. But hardly had the second innings started, when Hutton was out for two, and England was doomed. Yet it was at this low point for England that Arlott praised Hutton fulsomely for his heroism and courage in opening the second innings although he was utterly exhausted, and could have chosen to bat lower in the order, thus giving himself a chance to recover. England duly lost the match and the series, and we were overjoyed, but wondered how Arlott could have found something nice to say about a man who had let England down when he alone could have saved them. There are numerous other examples of Arlott's generosity, not all restricted to English players. In his account of the 1946 Indian tour of England, for instance, he bends over backwards, citing Indian vegetarianism and the Indian difficulty of adjusting to English conditions as mitigating factors in the performance of some Indian players.

Our most powerful impression of Arlott was his principled opposition to apartheid in South Africa. He refused to do his usual B.B.C. commentaries on the proposed South African cricket tour of England in 1970. The B.B.C. punished him for it. But he was steadfast. It was Arlott, after all, who had given Basil D'Oliveira his chance of playing cricket in England and making a name for himself. This had surely brought him closer to us, English though he was. It was another curious example of how the British empire which we hated for controlling and dominating us, also introduced us to individuals such as John Arlott, who inspired in us admiration, solidarity and love. We must not allow the English alone to praise Arlott; for he touched us too, albeit differently from the way in which he touched them; and he taught us more than either he or they could ever know. In truth, through the ambivalent workings of our colonial love/hate, it is possible that we learnt more from him than, even now, we dare acknowledge.

Select Bibliography

Books

Anthony, Michael and Andrew Carr. *David Frost introduces Trinidad and Tobago*. London: Andre Deutsch. 1975.
Arlott, John. *Cricket the Great Ones: Studies of the Eight Finest Batsmen of Cricket History*. London: Sportsman's Book Club. 1968.
Bailey, Trevor. *Sir Gary*. London: Fontana/Collins. 1977.
Barker, J.S. *Summer Spectacular: The West Indies vs. England, 1963*. London: St. James's Place. 1963.
----------.*In the Main: West Indies vs. M.C.C. 1968*. London: Sportsman's Book Club. 1969
Bannister, Alex. *Cricket Cauldron: With Hutton in the Caribbean*. London: Stanley Paul. 1954.
Batchelor, Denzil. *The Match I Remember*. London: Werner Laurie. 1950.
----------. *Game of a Lifetime*. London: Werner Laurie. 1953.
Benaud, Richie. *A Tale of Two Tests*. London: Hodder & Stoughton. 1962.
----------. *The New Champions*. London: Sportman's Book Club. 1970.
----------. *Willow Patterns*. London: Sportsman's Book Club. 1970.
Blunden, Edmund. *Cricket Country*. London: Imprint Society. 1945.
Bose, Mihir. *A History of Indian Cricket*. London: Andre Deutsch. 1990.
Bradman, Don. *Farewell to Cricket*. London: Hodder & Stoughton. 1950.
Brathwaite, Edward K. *The Arrivants*. London: OUP. 1973.
Caple, S. Canynge. *England vs. the West Indies, 1895-1957*. Littleburg: Worcester Press. 1957
Cardus, Neville. *Good Day, London: Jonathon Cape. 1934.*
------------*Autobiography*. London: Collins. 1947.
----------. *Full Score*. London: Quality Book Club. 1970.
----------.*Play Resumed with Cardus*. London: Souvenir. 1979.
----------.*A Fourth Innings with Cardus*. London: Souvenir. 1981.
Clarke, John and Brian Scovell. *Everything That's Cricket: The West Indies Tour 1966*. London: Stanley Paul. 1966.
Conrad, Joseph. *Great Short Works*. New York: Harper and Row. 1966
Constantine, Learie. *Cricket and I*. London: Philip Allan. 1933.
----------. *Cricket in the Sun*. London: Stanley Paul. 1946.
----------. *Cricket Crackers*. London: Stanley Paul. 1949.
----------.*Cricketers' Carnival*. London: Stanley Paul. 1950.
Constantine, Learie and Denzil Batchelor. *The Changing Face of Cricket*. London: Eyre & Spottiswode. 1966.
Cowdrey, Colin. *The Incomparable Game*. Newton Abbott: Sportsman's Book Club. 1971.
Cozier, Tony. *The West Indies: Fifty Years of Test Cricket*. Brighton: Angus & Robertson. 1978.
Dale, Harold. *Cricket Crusaders*. London: Sportsman's Book Club. 1953.
Dalrymple, Henderson. *50 Great West Indian Cricketers*. London: Hansib. 1983.
Dickens, Charles. *The Pickwick Papers*. New York: New American Library. 1964.
Engel, Matthew. *The Guardian Book of Cricket*. London: Pavilion. 1986.
Eytle, Ernest. *Frank Worrell*. London: Sportsman's Book Club. 1965.
Figueroa, John. *West Indies in England: The Great Post-War Tours*. London: Kingswood. 1991.
Fingleton, J.H. *Masters of Cricket from Trumper to May*. London: Heinemann. 1958.
Frindall, Bill. *The Wisden Book of Test Cricket: 1876-77 to 1977-78*. London: Book Club Assoc. 1979.
Gilchrist, Roy. *Hit me for Six*. London: Stanley Paul. 1963.
Grant, Jack. *Jack Grant's Story*. London: Lutterworth. 1980.
Green, Benny, ed. *Wisden Anthology 1963-1982*. London: Guild. 1984.
Grubb, Norman P. *C.T. Studd: Cricketer and Pioneer*. London: Lutterworth. 1933, 1946.
Howat, Gerald. *Learie Constantine*. London: George Allen & Unwin. 1975.
Hutton, Len. *Just my Story*. London: Hutchinson. 1956.
Irving, Washington. *The Sketch Book*. London: Macmillan. 1911.
James, C.L.R. *The Black Jacobins*. New York: Alfred A Knopf. 1963.
----------. *Beyond a Boundary*. London: Hutchinson. 1969.
----------. *The Future in the Present*. London: Allison & Busby. 1977.

----------. *Shperes of Existence*. London: Allison & Busby. 1984.
----------. *At the Rendezvous of Victory*. London: Allison & Busby. 1984.
----------. *Cricket*. London: Allison & Busby. 1986.
Kanhai, Rohan. *Blasting for Runs*. London: Souvenir. 1966.
Landsberg, Pat. *The Kangaroo Conquers*. London: Museum. 1955.
Lawrence, Bridgette with Reg Scarlett. *100 Great West Indian Cricketers*. London: Hansib. 1988.
Lawrence, Bridgette and Ray Goble. *The Complete Record of West Indian Cricketers*. London: ACL & Polar. 1991.
Manley, Michael. *A History of West Indian Cricket*. London: Andre Deutsch. 1988.
Melford, Michael. *Pick of "The Cricketer"*. London: The Cricketer/Hutchinson. 1967.
Meyer, Michael, ed. *Summer Days: Writers on Cricket*. London: OUP. 1983.
Miller, Keith. *Cricket from the Grandstand*. London: Sportsman's Book Club. 1960.
Moyes, A.G. *With West Indies in Australia, 1960-61*. London: Sportsman's Book Club. 1963.
Naipaul, V.S. *The Middle Passage*. London: Penguin. 1962.
Nicole, Christopher. *West Indian Cricket* London: Sportsman's Book Club. 1960.
Plumptree, George, ed. *The Essential E.W. Swanton*. London: Willow Books. 1990.
Rhys, Jean. *Wide Sargasso Sea*. London: Penguin. 1966.
Roberts, E.L. *Test Cavalcade: 1877-1947*. London: Edward Arnold. 1948.
Robertson-Glasgow, R.C. *46 Not Out*. London: Hollis & Carter. 1948.
Robinson, Ray. *The Glad Season*. London: Sportsman's Book Club. 1956.
Ross, Alan. *Through the Caribbean*. London: Pavilion Library. 1960.
----------, ed. *The Cricketer's Companion*. London: Bibliographic Books. 1986.
Ross, Gordon. *A History of West Indies Cricket*. London: Arthur Barker. 1976.
Rundell, Michael. *The Dictionary of Cricket*. London: George Allen & Unwin. 1985.
Sanyal, Saradindu. *India-West Indies Test Cricket 1948-1971*. Delhi: Macmillan. 1974.
Selvon, Samuel. *Ways of Sunlight*. London: MacGibbon & Kee. 1957.
Shiwcharan, Clem and Frank Birbalsingh. *Indo-Westindian Cricket.* London: Hansib. 1988.
Sobers, Gary. *Bonaventure and the Flashing Blade*. Loondon: Pelham. 1967.
----------. *Gary Sobers's Most Memorable Matches*. London: Stanley Paul. 1984.
Stollmeyer, Jeffrey. *Everything Under the Sun*. London: Stanley Paul. 1983.
Swanton, E.W. *West Indian Adventure with Hutton's M.C.C. Team 1953-54*. London: Sportsman's Book Club. 1955.
----------. *West Indies Revisited*. London: Heinemann. 1960.
----------. *Sort of a Cricket Person*. London: Fontana. 1974.
Thomson, A.A. *Cricket: My Pleasure*. London: Sportsman's Book Club. 1954.
----------. *Cricket: My Happiness*. London: Sportsman's Book Club. 1956.
Walcott, Clyde. *Island Cricketers*. London: Hodder & Stoughton. 1958.
Warner, Pelham. *Cricket Between Two Wars*. London: Sporting Handbooks. 1946.
----------. *The Book of Cricket*. London: Sporting Handbooks. 1948.
----------. *Long Innings*. London: George G. Harrap. 1951.
Williams, Marcus, ed. *Double Century: Two Hundred Years of Cricket in The Times*. London: Willor/Collins. 1985.
Wooldridge, Ian. *Cricket Lovely Cricket*. London: Robert Hale. 1963.
Worrell, Frank. *Cricket Punch*. London: Stanley Paul. 1959.

Articles

1. Richard D.E. Burton, "Cricket, Carnival and Street Culture in the Caribbean", *The British Journal of Sports History*, II, ii, (1985). pp. 179-197.
2. Keith A.P. Sandiford and Brian Stoddart, "The Elite Schools and Cricket in Barbados: A Study in Colonial Continuity", *The International Journal of the History of Sport*, IV, iii, (1987), pp. 333-350.
3. Kevin A. Yelvington, "Ethnicity 'Not Out': The Indian Cricket tour of the West Indies and the 1976 Elections in Trinidad and Tobago", *Arena Review*, xic, I, (1990) pp. 1-12.
4. Kenneth Surin, "C. L. R James's materialist aesthetics of Cricket," in Alistair Hennessy, ed., *Intellectuals in the Twentieth Century Caribbean* Vol.1 London: Macmillan Caribbean. 1992, pp.131-162.

Index

200
Manjrekar, Vijay 75, 77, 78, 79, 80, 105, 106, 107, 126, 127, 128, 129
Mankad, Vinoo 59, 61, 62, 63, 75, 76, 77, 78, 79, 80, 107, 108, 164
Manley, Michael / Manley, Norman 8, 20, 21, 96, 98, 206, 207, 242, 257, 258, 261, 274
Marshall, Norman 8, 15, 16, 23, 70, 73, 91, 173, 205, 249, 256
Martin, F.R. 29, 30, 31, 32, 40, 41, 43, 266
Martindale, E.A. 16, 43, 44, 45, 46, 47, 48, 49, 50, 51
Marylebone Cricket Club, (M.C.C.) 17, 27, 65, 69, 155, 158, 185, 192, 224, 236, 245, 273, 274
May, P.B.H. 81, 82, 83, 84, 86, 87, 97, 98, 99, 111, 112, 113, 114, 115, 171, 184, 190, 198, 205
McCabe 20, 39, 40, 41, 42, 119
McMorris 113, 116, 128, 129, 137, 138, 213, 217
McWatt 81, 82, 86, 87, 91, 112
Melbourne Cricket Ground, (Melbourne) 73, 123
Merry, Cyril 44, 204, 252
Miller, Keith 70, 93, 94, 174, 175, 274
Modi, R.S. 59, 60, 61, 63
Morris, A.R. 69, 72, 89, 90, 91, 93
Moyes, A.G. 210, 274
Murray, Deryck 130
Mushtaq, Mohammed 209

Nadkarni, R.G. 128
Naipaul, V.S. 4, 8, 26, 211, 212, 213, 214, 215, 216, 217, 218, 219, 220, 221, 240, 241, 243, 274
Nasim-ul-Ghani 102, 200, 209
New Zealand 6, 22, 25, 32, 38, 95, 96, 162, 164, 167, 169, 170, 171, 172, 173, 174, 175, 178, 191, 199, 205, 256
Nicole, Christopher 8, 13, 48, 155, 157, 191, 274
Nunes, R.K. 18, 20, 29, 38, 198, 208, 245, 246
Nurse, Seymour 113, 122, 139, 141, 142, 143, 144, 146, 147, 148, 150, 151, 152
Nyren, John 243

Old Trafford (Manchester) 30, 31, 44, 65, 66, 115, 129, 131, 147, 149, 153, 161, 162, 166, 171, 184, 235, 256
Ollivierre, C.A. 256
OiNeill, Norman 120, 121, 122, 123, 124, 125, 142, 143, 144, 145, 146

Pairaudeau, Bruce 16, 76, 77, 78, 80, 83, 96, 99, 100, 174, 197
Pakistan 6, 23, 25, 38, 47, 95, 101, 102, 103, 104, 105, 109, 110, 111, 167, '171, 175, 178, 180, 181, 182, 183, 195, 196, 198, 199, 200, 209, 260
Parks, J.M. 115, 116, 117, 132, 133, 138, 139, 148, 150, 151, 152, 153, 217
Pascall, Victor 156, 185, 237
Pataudi, Nawab of (Snr.) 96, 264
Phadkar, Dattu 59, 61, 63, 64, 75, 76, 77, 78, 79, 107
Pierre, Lance 57

Rae, Allan 59, 61, 62, 65, 67, 69, 70, 76, 77, 103, 162, 173, 174, 192
Ramadhin, Sonny 8, 11, 25, 26, 42, 65, 66, 67, 68, 69, 70, 71, 72, 74, 75, 77, 78, 79, 81, 82, 83, 84, 85, 87, 89, 90, 91, 94, 95, 96, 97, 98, 99, 102, 104, 105, 109, 110, 112, 113, 115, 116, 119, 120, 151, 169, 170, 171, 172, 173, 174, 182, 183, 184, 189, 190, 195, 196, 197, 198, 200, 204, 205,

Other titles by Hansib

CORNERED TIGERS
A History of Pakistan's Test Cricket
Adam Licudi with Wasim Raja
The first comprehensive account of the history of Pakistani Test Cricket from its beginnings in 1952 up to the 1996 season. This unparalleled collection of profiles includes every Test player, including the first Test captain, Abdul Hafeez Kardar, in addition to the giants of the nineties, Wasim Akram and Waqar Younis. It pays tribute to other 'Tigers' such as Imran Khan and Javed Miandad, in a meticulous chronicle of one of the great cricketing nations. Includes full scorecards from every Pakistan Test Match up to August 1996, and all Test and One-Day Averages for every player.
£16.95 Paperback, 304pp
1 870518 31 4

100 GREAT WESTINDIAN TEST CRICKETERS
Bridgette Lawrence
with Reg Scarlett
Westindian Test cricket is traced from its 1928 debut at Lords to the unmatched triumphs of the 1980s. This unique publication is more than a record of cricket supremacy, it is also a human document, vividly recapturing some of the great moments both on and off the field. Illustrated with many rare and dramatic photographs, this superb book is a must for all cricket-lovers.
£14.95 Hardback, 232pp, illustrated
1 870518 65 9

INDO-WESTINDIAN CRICKET
Frank Birbalsingh and Clem Shiwcharan
Much is written about the massive achievements of Westindian cricketers of African background, but the availability of literature on some of the equally powerful cricketers of Indian origin is somewhat thin on the ground. This book serves to redress the balance by featuring the genius of such Titans as Kallicharan, Kanhai and Ramadhin, and places the Indo-Caribbean role in Westindian cricket in the political and cultural context.
£7.95 Hardback, 136pp
1 870518 20 9

ST LUCIA - Simply Beautiful
Voted 'Best Honeymoon Destination' in 1995 and 'Best Wedding Destination' in 1996, St Lucia has become a popular choice for newlyweds throughout the world. With its serene beaches, dramatic waterfalls and lush mountain rainforests, this beautiful Caribbean island is a sight to behold. Illustrated using more than 300 colour photographs, this is the first book to highlight the historic and contemporary aspects of this tropical paradise.
£25.00 Hardback, 320pp, colour
976 8163 07 0

BARBADOS - Just Beyond Your Imagination

As one of the world's leading tourist destinations, many visitors consider that Barbados is the Caribbean. Its natural beauty and stunning beaches, coupled with the warmth and friendliness of its people, make it a first class and popular choice throughout the year. Illustrated with more than 280 colour photographs, this book evokes the spirit of the country both past and present.
£25.00 Hardback, 320pp, colour
1 870518 54 3

INDIA - Wealth of Diversity

It is the same size as Europe and is the world's largest democracy. It is home to 960 million people and more than 1600 languages. It boasts the sixth largest economy in the world and produces more movies every year than any other nation. It experiences every conceivable climate, every type of landscape and is rich in most of the world's natural resources. India. It is rich, it is spectacular, it is diverse.
Using more than 230 colour photographs, this book unlocks the door to a magical nation. Experience the diversity for yourself.
£29.99 Hardback, 352pp, colour
1 870518 61 6

UGANDA
- Africa's Secret Paradise

From snow-capped mountains to lush rain forests; vast national parks to spectacular lakes and rivers - including the mystical source of the Nile - Uganda is, truly, one of Africa's best kept secrets. As well as uncovering the historic and cultural treasures of a relatively untapped nation, this book presents a vivid picture of modern Uganda as it moves into the 21st century. Commissioned by the President of the Republic of Uganda, this publication includes over 300 colour photographs which feature many aspects of daily life in addition to the natural splendours of this ancient civilisation.
£25.00 Hardback, 320pp, colour
1 870 518 66 7
Spring 1998

JAMAICA - Absolutely

As the third largest Caribbean island, Jamaica accounts for nearly half of the region's English-speaking population. This book takes a close look at a nation born out of 300 years of colonial rule and highlights its contribution to the rest of the world in areas such as music, religion, cuisine, literature and lifestyle. With the help of more than 300 colour photographs, every aspect of Jamaican life is featured. From the tranquil waters of Montego Bay to the hurly-burly of Spanish Town, this vibrant, island nation should not to be missed.
£25.00 Hardback, 320pp, colour
976 8163 06 02
Spring 1998

GRENADA - Spice Island of the Caribbean

For the first time ever, a comprehensive study of this three-island state (Grenada, Carriacou and Petit Martinique) from past to present. More than 260 colour

photographs depict today's Grenada - a flourishing, independent nation born out of French and British colonial rule. Appropriately nicknamed 'Spice Island of the Caribbean', Grenada produces one third of the world's nutmeg.
£25.00 Hardback, 304pp, colour
1 870518 29 2

ANTIGUA AND BARBUDA - A Little Bit of Paradise
A spectacular book - with more than 650 colour photographs - capturing the essence of this renowned twin-island nation. Highlighting the past and present of one of the world's most exclusive tourist destinations, this publication is a must for historian and hedonist alike.
£25.00 Hardback, 304pp, colour
1 870518 53 5

DOMINICA - Nature Island of the Caribbean
From rugged volcanic peaks to stunning rainforests, Dominica's natural beauty and wildlife is unrivalled anywhere in the Caribbean. With more than 350 colour photographs, this book reveals the unique splendour of this emerald isle.
£19.95 Hardback, 320pp, colour
1 870518 17 9

THE EMPTY SLEEVE
The Story of the West India Regiments of the British Army
Brian Dyde
The story of the West India regiments which came into existence 200 years ago in 1795. Formed to assist England in the war against France in the Caribbean, there were 12 of these little-known units at one stage, with a total strength of 10,000 men - mostly slaves - under British officers. Written with frankness, compassion and humour by an author with strong and possibly controversial views, The Empty Sleeve will appeal to anyone wishing to know more about military, Westindian, colonial or West African history.
£11.95 Paperback, 208 pp
976-8163-09-7

NAOROJI:
The First Asian MP
Omar Ralph
Known as the 'Grand Old Man of India', Dadabhai Naoroji became Britain's first non-European Member of Parliament. Berated by the then Prime Minister, Lord Salisbury, as unelectable on account of his being a 'black man', Naoroji proved his foremost critic wrong by being elected to the London seat of Central Finsbury in 1892.
£11.95 Paperback, 208pp
976 8163 05 4

THE GREAT MARCUS GARVEY
Liz Mackie
One of the towering figures of the 20th Century, Marcus Garvey devoted his entire life to the political and economic emancipation of Africans throughout the world. This colossal undertaking laid the foundations of black consciousness, black power and the evolution of Pan-Africanism on a global scale.
£5.95 Paperback, 160pp
1 870518 50 0

WOMEN OF SUBSTANCE
Profiles of Asian women
in the UK
Pushpinder Chowdhry
More than 200 entries are included
in this celebration of the
achievements of Asian women in the
UK. From trades union activists to
business women, the sciences to the
arts, this publication reveals the ever-
changing roles of Asian women.
£10.95 Paperback, 168pp
1 870518 56 X
Published with AWP

PRIDE OF BLACK
BRITISH WOMEN
Deborah King
A collection of individual profiles
featuring successful black women in
Britain. Entries include the famous
and the not-so-famous.
£5.95 Paperback, 80pp, illustrated
1 870518 34 9

A NEW SYSTEM OF
SLAVERY
The Export of Indian Labour
Overseas 1830-1920
Hugh Tinker
Originally published in 1974, this
book was the first comprehensive
study of a hitherto neglected
migration - the export of Indians to
supply labour needs on sugar, coffee,
tea and rubber plantations in
Mauritius, South and East Africa, the
Caribbean, Guyana, Sri Lanka,
Malaysia and Fiji. This practice
followed the legal ending of slavery,
but Professor Tinker shows how the
two systems had much in common.
£11.99 Paperback, 448pp
1 870518 18 7

THE OTHER MIDDLE
PASSAGE
Journal of a Voyage from
Calcutta to Trinidad, 1858
Extracts from the journal of Captain
and Mrs Swinton of the 'Salsette', a
ship bound for the Caribbean and
carrying Indian indentured
labourers. The diary of this horrific,
108-day journey, evokes the stark
terror that overshadowed the entire
voyage. Although not slavery by
name, the effect of the indentured
labour movement on the lives of
these migrants was the same.
£3.95 Paperback, 64pp, illustrated
1 870518 28 4

LEST WE FORGET
The Experiences of World War
II Westindian Ex-Service
Personnel
Robert N Murray
Few people know of the significant
participation of Westindian men and
women during the Second World
War. Their stories are told - largely
through oral histories and personal
recollections - from arrival during
the war effort, to subsequent
settlement of a substantial number
after the war.
£11.95 Paperback, 192pp, 8pp
photographs
1 870518 52 7

RASTA AND RESISTANCE
From Marcus Garvey
to Walter Rodney
Horace Campbell
Rastafarianism is not, as some of its
detractors say, a fad of intellectual
dilettantes, but a well thought out
and coherent philosophy of ideas

and actions to bring about fundamental changes in the condition of the oppressed. This book is both a record of the resistance to tyranny and a refreshing critique and analysis of the imperialist conspiracy to perpetuate its dominance by any and all means necessary.
£9.95 Paperback, 252pp
0 9506664 7 5

PROSPERO'S RETURN?
Historical Essays on Race, Culture and British Society
Paul B Rich
In this wide-ranging collection of essays, Rich explores the nature and meaning of race and racism in British society and the nature of British and English national identity. Using political, social and cultural sources, he shows that many of the contemporary issues surrounding the position of black minorities in British society have a long and complex history.
£8.95 Paperback, 216pp
1 870518 40 3

A READER'S GUIDE TO WESTINDIAN AND BLACK BRITISH LITERATURE
David Dabydeen and
Nana Wilson-Tagoe
Two experts in this specialist area, chart the highly productive and very rewarding literary terrain of the Westindies and black Britain. This title provides an excellent introduction to an important part of world literature, its history and development, and recommendations of suitable texts for further reading.

£8.95 Paperback, 192pp
1 870518 35 7
Published in association with the University of Warwick Centre for Caribbean Studies

INDIA IN THE CARIBBEAN
Edited by David Dabydeen and
Brinsley Samaroo
A collection of enlightening essays, poems and political and historical analysis celebrating the Indian presence in the Caribbean. Some of the leading Indo-Caribbean scholars and writers provide an insight into the cultural, social and economic impact since the Indian arrival in the early 19th century.
£8.95 Paperback, 328pp
1 870518 00 4
£11.95 Hardback, 328pp
1 870518 05 5

THE WEB OF TRADITION
Uses of Allusion in V S Naipaul's Fiction
John Thieme
Few will deny that V S Naipaul is one of the most stylish, elegant and thought-provoking essayists of the 20th century, and a novelist of world class. Thieme explores classics such as 'In a Free State' and 'A House for Mr Biswas' in the context of the Western literary canon, while at the same time revealing their 'essential Indianness'.
£6.95 Paperback, 224pp
1 870518 30 6

THE IDEOLOGY OF RACISM
Samuel Kennedy Yeboah
A masterly study of the peoples of the African Diaspora with a long overdue reminder of their gigantic, but unrecognised, contribution to art, science and technology. This is a searing analytical account of the ideology of Western racism and its horrific consequences for Africa and the Diaspora.
£9.95 Paperback, 320pp
1 870518 07 1

THE WEST ON TRIAL
My Fight for Guyana's Freedom
Cheddi Jagan
First published in 1966, this re-printed title is a moving, personal account of the struggle against imperialism by one of the leading political figures in the Caribbean. The late Dr Jagan passionately weaves together his own life-story with that of his people's battle for independence and freedom in an environment dictated by race and class factors, and colonial attitudes.
£9.95 Paperback, 496pp
976 8163 08 9

FORBIDDEN FREEDOM
The Story of British Guiana
Cheddi Jagan
The name of Cheddi Jagan was synonymous with anti-imperialist struggle. But his work did not end with the expulsion of the British Occupation, it was the beginning of another struggle against the most vicious neo-colonialism the Third World has ever seen. This noble statesman became his country's first ever genuinely patriotic President in a world asphyxiated by corruption, greed and sleaze.
£4.95 Paperback, 128pp (Second edition) 1 870518 23 3
£5.95 Paperback, 144pp (Third Edition) 1 870518 37 3

CHEDDI JAGAN Selected Speeches 1992-1994
One of the world's most outstanding leaders, the words of Guyana's President, Dr Cheddi Jagan, bears witness to his vision, integrity and concern for the potential as well as the plight of the Guyanese people.
£6.95 Paperback, 144pp
1 870518 49 7

PASSION AND EXILE
Frank Birbalsingh
The English-speaking Caribbean has produced a quantity and quality of literature that is renowned throughout the world. Birbalsingh gets to the heart of the literary Caribbean in an accomplished and riveting work.
£7.95 Paperback, 192pp
1 870518 16 0

INSEPARABLE HUMANITY
An Anthology of Reflections of Shridath S Ramphal
Former Commonwealth Secretary-General, Shridath Ramphal reflects on his own world view with eloquence and rationality. A man of action, his deeply moral approach to world politics made him an influential player in the field of human rights on the international stage.
£14.95 Hardback, 424pp
1 870518 14 4

BENEVOLENT NEUTRALITY
Indian Government Policy and Labour Migration to British Guiana 1854-1884
Basdeo Mangru
This ground-breaking study examines the issue of indentured labour from India and how the new arrivals adapted to life in a strange and sometimes hostile environment.
£12.95 Hardback, 272pp
1 870518 10 1

SPEECHES BY ERROL BARROW
Edited by Yussuff Haniff
The late Errol Barrow was one of the most revered statesman of the Caribbean. He was a remarkable Caribbean patriot, whose speeches not only gave an insight into the evolution of modern Barbados under his prime ministership, but also his vision of a united and politically and economically sovereign Caribbean.
£10.95 Hardback, 200pp
1 870518 70 5

THE NORMAN MANLEY MEMORIAL LECTURES 1984 - 1995
Caribbean and world issues are addressed in this collection of lectures presented by such noted world figures as Sir Shridath Ramphal, The Rt Hon Tony Benn MP and The Rt Hon Michael Manley.
£6.99 Paperback, 96pp
976 8163 00 3